EMPIRE AND THE SOCIAL SCIENCES

EMPIRE AND THE SOCIAL SCIENCES

Global Histories of Knowledge

Edited by
Jeremy Adelman

BLOOMSBURY ACADEMIC
LONDON • NEW YORK • OXFORD • NEW DELHI • SYDNEY

BLOOMSBURY ACADEMIC
Bloomsbury Publishing Plc
50 Bedford Square, London, WC1B 3DP, UK
1385 Broadway, New York, NY 10018, USA
29 Earlsfort Terrace, Dublin 2, Ireland

BLOOMSBURY, BLOOMSBURY ACADEMIC and the Diana logo are trademarks of
Bloomsbury Publishing Plc

First published in Great Britain 2019
Paperback edition published 2021

Copyright © Jeremy Adelman, 2019

Jeremy Adelman has asserted his right under the Copyright, Designs and Patents Act, 1988, to be identified as Editor of this work.

For legal purposes the Acknowledgements on p. vii constitute an extension of this copyright page.

Cover image: Alexander Humboldt and Aime Bonpland on the Orinoco River
(© Nastasic / Getty Images)

All rights reserved. No part of this publication may be reproduced or transmitted in any form or by any means, electronic or mechanical, including photocopying, recording, or any information storage or retrieval system, without prior permission in writing from the publishers.

Bloomsbury Publishing Plc does not have any control over, or responsibility for, any third-party websites referred to or in this book. All internet addresses given in this book were correct at the time of going to press. The author and publisher regret any inconvenience caused if addresses have changed or sites have ceased to exist, but can accept no responsibility for any such changes.

A catalogue record for this book is available from the British Library.

A catalog record for this book is available from the Library of Congress.

ISBN: HB: 978-1-3501-0251-4
PB: 978-1-3501-9623-0
ePDF: 978-1-3501-0252-1
eBook: 978-1-3501-0253-8

Typeset by Deanta Global Publishing Services, Chennai, India

To find out more about our authors and books visit www.bloomsbury.com and sign up for our newsletters.

CONTENTS

Acknowledgements	vii
List of contributors	viii

INTRODUCTION: SOCIAL SCIENCE AND EMPIRE –
A DURABLE TENSION
    Jeremy Adelman   1

A NEW SYSTEM OF IMPERIAL GOVERNMENT: POLITICAL ECONOMY
AND THE SPANISH THEORY OF COMMERCIAL EMPIRE, CA. 1740–50
    Fidel J. Tavárez   15

POOR MAO'S ALMANACK? EMPIRE, POLITICAL ECONOMY AND THE
TRANSFORMATION OF SOCIAL SCIENCE
    Sophus A. Reinert   31

UTILITARIANISM AND THE QUESTION OF FREE LABOUR IN RUSSIA
AND INDIA, EIGHTEENTH–NINETEENTH CENTURIES
    Alessandro Stanziani   51

GEOGRAPHY AND THE RESHAPING OF THE MODERN CHINESE EMPIRE
    Shellen Wu   63

THE PERIPHERY'S ORDER: OPIUM AND MORAL WRECKAGE IN
BRITISH BURMA
    Diana Kim   79

CUSTOM IN THE ARCHIVE: THE BIRTH OF MODERN CHINESE LAW AT
THE END OF EMPIRE
    Matthew S. Erie   93

NITOBE INAZO AND THE DIFFUSION OF A KNOWLEDGEABLE EMPIRE
    Alexis Dudden   111

MODERN IMPERIALISM AND INTERNATIONAL LAW: CARL SCHMITT
AND ERNST RUDOLF HUBER ON THE 'INTERNATIONAL LEGAL
ORDER OF GREAT SPACES'
    Joshua Derman   123

KNOWLEDGE AS POWER: INTERNATIONALISM, INFORMATION AND
US GLOBAL AMBITIONS
    David Ekbladh   141

KNOWLEDGE FOR EMPIRE: AMERICAN HEGEMONY, THE
ROCKEFELLER FOUNDATION AND THE RISE OF ACADEMIC
INTERNATIONAL RELATIONS IN THE UNITED STATES
  Inderjeet Parmar   153

CIRCUMVENTING IMPERIALISM: THE GLOBAL ECONOMY IN LATIN
AMERICAN SOCIAL SCIENCES
  Margarita Fajardo   177

WESTERN INTERNATIONAL THEORY, 1492–2010: PERFORMING
WESTERN SUPREMACY AND WESTERN IMPERIALISM
  John M. Hobson   191

EPILOGUE: EMPIRE AND THE GLOBAL KNOWLEDGE REGIME
  Jeremy Adelman   215

Index   219

ACKNOWLEDGEMENTS

This volume is the result of many years of interdisciplinary discussion about empire, resistance, collaboration and global order in the wake of the American war in Iraq. I am very grateful to the many colleagues at Princeton University who participated in these debates funded by the Princeton Institute for International and Regional Studies (PIIRS). Thanks to its former director Mark Beissinger for his wonderful support. The original team of colleagues included Molly Greene, John Ikenberry, Atul Kohli, Nick Nesbitt, Rachel Price and Michael Reynolds. Teresa Shawcross and Cyrus Schayegh also played important roles in our group. I am especially grateful to all of them for the years of companionship. *Empire and the Social Sciences* was the theme of a PIIRS conference which originally included comments and interventions from Sebastian Conrad, Paul Kramer, Daniel Rodgers and Emmanuel Szurek. Finally, none of this would have been possible without the support and warmth of Jayne Bialkowski.

LIST OF CONTRIBUTORS

Jeremy Adelman is the Henry Charles Lea Professor of History and director of the Global History Lab at Princeton University. He is the author and editor of ten books and is currently writing a history of interdependence.

Joshua Derman is an associate professor of humanities at the Hong Kong University of Science and Technology. His research focuses on the intellectual history of modern Germany. His book, *Max Weber in Politics and Social Thought: From Charisma to Canonization*, is the first comprehensive history of Weber's early impact in Germany and the United States. He is currently completing a project about the theory of 'great spaces' in twentieth-century Germany.

Alexis Dudden is a professor of history at the University of Connecticut. The author of two major books on empire, war and memory in northeast Asia, she is currently completing *The Opening and Closing of Japan, 1850–2020*, about Japan's territorial disputes and the changing meaning of islands in international law.

David Ekbladh is an associate professor of history, core faculty in international relations, and faculty associate with the Center for Strategic Studies of the Fletcher School at Tufts University. His books include, *Beyond 1917: The United States and the Global Legacies of the Great War* and *The Great American Mission: Modernization and the Construction of an American World Order*, which won the Stuart L. Bernath Prize of the Society of American Historians and the Phi Alpha Theta Best First Book Award. He is completing studies entitled *Look at the World: The Birth of an American Globalism in the 1930s* and *Knowledge as Power: Information and Internationalism in a World in Crisis*.

Matthew S. Erie is an associate professor of modern Chinese studies at the University of Oxford. His interdisciplinary work in law and anthropology examines the role of normative pluralism in international ordering, with a focus on China. He has written extensively on Chinese domestic law and China's impact on international law. His first book, *China and Islam: The Prophet, the Party, and Law* is the first ethnographic study of the relationship between sharia and state law in China. His current research examines China's approach to law and development in weak states.

Margarita Fajardo is an assistant professor at Sarah Lawrence College. She recently received a fellowship from the National Endowment of the Humanities to complete her book manuscript tentatively titled *The World that Latin America Created*. She is interested in intellectual history and the politics of science and expertise as well as in the history of Latin American and global capitalism.

John M. Hobson is a professor of politics and international relations at the University of Sheffield and is a Fellow of the British Academy. His primary research interest is to provide a critique of Eurocentrism within IR, IPE, world history and historical sociology. He is currently finishing a book that advances a non-Eurocentric account of the global economy.

Diana Kim is an assistant professor at Georgetown University in the Edmund A. Walsh School of Foreign Service. Her research interests include modern state formation, illicit economies and transnational histories of colonialism and Empire across Southeast and East Asia since the late nineteenth century.

Inderjeet Parmar is a professor of international politics at City, University of London, and head of the Department of International Politics. His most recent book is *Foundations of the American Century: Ford, Carnegie, and Rockefeller Foundations in the Rise of American Power*. He has held research fellowships at Oxford and Princeton universities. Parmar is past president of the British International Studies Association.

Sophus A. Reinert is the Marvin Bower Professor of Business Administration at Harvard Business School. He works on the histories of business, capitalism and political economy from the Italian Renaissance to today's emerging markets.

Alessandro Stanziani is directeur d'étude (professor) at the École des Hautes Études en Sciences Sociales in Paris and is a senior researcher at the CNRS. His research interests include global history, labour history especially in Russia, the Indian Ocean, and France in the eighteenth and nineteenth centuries.

Fidel J. Tavárez is an historian of the eighteenth-century Spanish Atlantic with a particular focus on issues of political economy and empire. At present, he holds a research fellowship from the Alexander von Humboldt Foundation at the Freie Universität Berlin's Center for Global History. He is completing a book about political economy and empire in the Spanish world.

Shellen X. Wu is an associate professor of history at the University of Tennessee, Knoxville, where she has research interests in the history of science in modern China, spatial history, imperialism and how changes in the uses and exploitation of natural resources affected the modern Chinese state and society. Her *Empires of Coal: Fueling China's Entry into the Modern World Order, 1860-1920* narrates the history about how Chinese views of natural resource management underwent a major change as a result of the late Qing engagement with imperialism and science.

INTRODUCTION: SOCIAL SCIENCE AND EMPIRE – A DURABLE TENSION

Jeremy Adelman

The study of modern societies, politics and economics has been intimately associated with life in the nation. The arc of the social sciences overlaps with and, to a large extent, conforms to the arc of modern nation states. It would be hard to separate how scholars have understood modern ideas of government or work from the pulse of national communities. From the political economists who pressed French or Spanish rulers in the eighteenth century to open trade in grains to the health policy gurus embroiled in America's interminable debate about how (or whether) to insure all its citizens, writers, pundits and growing ranks of university professors as well as cognoscenti in foundations and think tanks have been mobilized to – indeed they were created to – serve the nations of which they were a part.

The reasons for this alliance between social scientists and nation states are many. Most of all, the challenges of new forms of rule, especially with the emergence of mass democracy and the risks of living by market rules, summoned intellectuals to make sense of a world that was no longer subject to the traditions of estates, feudal structures and *ancien régime* privileges. The habits, identities and norms that arose as societies re-amalgamated into nation states yielded pressures to integrate, to shelter and to mobilize an emerging and evolving citizenry. The need to understand money, plan cities, resolve labour disputes and chart national histories for schools and universities meant that intellectuals got enlisted in the project to make their societies knowable, legible and even predictable and were called upon to advise rulers on policies for the co-members of their nations. Others, by contrast, felt called upon to challenge rulers – to speak truth to power, as the saying goes – as moral voices of the nation. The very word 'intellectual' sprang to life as an epithet during the French controversy over the trial of the Jewish officer, Alfred Dreyfus, in the 1890s. This courtroom and public square battle over the limits of tolerance and the legitimacy of the guardians of the French nation ripped through the country's intellectual and university life. By the late nineteenth century, the very idea of the intellectual as a critical observer was starting to take visible shape.[1]

Thereafter, a fundamental divide opened up. On one side, there were voices calling for intellectuals to serve a public, state-driven purpose. They argued for the importance of governing, modernizing, reforming and disciplining. They were the voices favouring engagement. On the other side were those who defended the need for the observer and the scholar to stay removed, to refuse to be, as Julien Benda famously put it in the late 1920s, 'clerks', 'playing the game of political passions'. We remember Benda now as a crank, as someone who was grumpy about the pressure on thinkers to be relevant and who was nostalgic for a time when philosophers in particular thought about the world from their sanctuaries of knowledge. But it is worth recalling that the source of his scepticism was in part fuelled by his concerns about nationalism; he believed that scholarship should be devoted to the betterment of 'humanity' and not the nation, 'with its appetites and its arrogance'.[2]

When it came to the social sciences per se, there was never much doubt about the purpose of scholarship – social science was born worldly. It would only be much later, under the pressures to become more theoretically rigorous and formally precise, emulating the scientific styles of what some social scientists imagined was happening on the other side of the scholarly street, in laboratories and in mathematicians' ateliers – where natural scientists were supposedly separate from the world – that we see other-worldly aspirations. This impulse would drive some branches of the social sciences, very controversially, to try to lob off the adjective 'social' from their self-identification and to pursue the discovery of timeless and placeless laws. But for most of the history of the social sciences, relevance, engagement and prescription were core features of the enterprise. The twentieth century saw the emergence of what has been called 'knowledge regimes' carefully calibrated to the contours of national institutions and national social problems. In short, the history of social science has been entangled from the start with national-level social demands, identities and economic pressures.[3]

However, the debate over whether or not to be committed to the betterment of the nation is not the only story to be told about the history of the social sciences. The rise of the modern social sciences has also been part of a wider and deeper process of global integration that long predated the emergence of the nation state as the modal form of political community after 1815. In fact, one might say that global integration is what marshalled social scientists to serve national purposes; it was global entanglement that compelled nation-builders to bulk up, to create nations capable of competing, cooperating and recognizing in a world of interdependent structures. As flows of people, capital and commodities knit societies across borders, national governments got created and summoned to make markets work. The marketplace was always, as Karl Polanyi famously noted, embedded in institutions to forge systems of the rule of law, to protect private property, to manage resources and to create or promote trading and settling nations. In short, global integration summoned practices, norms and institutions that would buoy societies through the opportunities, strains and risks of making the adjustment to transborder forces. Global integration mobilized knowledge producers to think across borders over the longue durée which concerns this volume, because the instrument of ordering and the source of disordering were the empires of Asia, Europe and the Americas – and their colonial progeny. Social sciences got enlisted in thinking about the world because their knowledge and service were so often asked to serve or to challenge the empires of which they were a part.

Why empire? It may be objected that there are good reasons why the history of the social sciences is usually tied to the history of nation-building. For starters, the modern social sciences were born contemporaneously with nations. Training in universities and the creation of professional associations of economists and demographers coincided with the professionalization of public administration. It was national governments that mobilized experts to service publics for at least one intrinsic reason: national governments were at least rhetorically committed to the principle of protecting their citizens equally. There may have been – and there continues to be – a quarrel over who gets to be a member of the national community and thus eligible to make claims as a citizen. Empires, and especially monarchical empires, did not presume that they ruled over equal citizens. Faced with this co-dependency of knowledge production and nation-building, empires would seem to be mere precursors or antecedents.

But this makes two kinds of assumptions which global historians have lately been challenging. The first concerns an assumption about the line between nations and empires, a line that was never so sharply etched in theory or practice. Indeed, nations were often born or reimagined as empires. This was true of Haiti and Brazil in the early nineteenth century; it was no less true of Germany, Japan and Italy by 1870. The reason for this was that empires dominated the global political stage until 1945. Some wonder, now that the Cold War is over, whether empire – and its informal or 'soft power' edges – is reclaiming a place on the global stage. By the same token, the switch to nations as modern political structures replacing archaic empires only makes any sense if one removes large parts of Latin America, Africa and Asia from the picture – because there it was a long and enduring experience of colonialism that summoned social science to help govern or 'civilize' others (often because they were seen to need the help of 'experts'), or eventually to resist empire and dream of a postcolonial alternative. To write a global history of knowledge requires transcending Eurocentric assumptions.

The second concerns the assumption that social scientists served domestic visions. In fact, they were equally mobilized for global purposes – and for many years it was empires that were the political, economic and social engines of global integration. It was empires that produced global interdependence and hierarchy at the same time. To a large extent, the haves and have-nots of our day have been shaped by the past. Even China, as Robert Bickers has recently argued, self-defines its historical experience and its national narrative as a redemption against Western empire, as having been the subject of a 'scramble' by predators in the same way that Africa had been in the late nineteenth century.[4] For better or for worse, empire has been the dominant mode and effect of global integration.

So, why empire? Our view is simple: until relatively recently, when observers and commentators reflected on entangled worlds, they did not refer to 'world' or 'global' processes; the former gained traction after 1918, and the latter only after 1980. For most of modern world history, it was empires that served as the carriers for connecting distant parts and making a more global whole. Not even the twentieth century buried the idea of empires as integrative agents. The idea that entanglements took an imperial mien persisted through the Cold War and continues to frame a sense of global military prowess and interventions, like the 'evil empire' metaphor of the Reaganite 1980s (and the Star Wars box-office hits which inspired the American president), or by contrast the portrait of the US invasion of Iraq in 2003 or the normative language to describe the International Monetary Fund's recipes for indebted countries. To many, Germany's insistence that Greece honour its financial obligations by belt-strapping citizens smacks as imperial.

In this book, we therefore take a global approach, which erases the national–imperial boundaries, embeds national yearnings and structures within deeper and wider imperial entanglements and looks at the circulation of ideas and thinkers across cultural borders – very often it was these social scientists who helped create cross-border systems of understanding and rule. By global, we do not mean that we provide coverage of the whole world. Indeed, there are many gaps in this anthology, and there are regions we do not cover. Global, rather, is the approach to the subject that seeks to overcome methodological nationalism and the open structures in which social agents operated. Indeed, a global history of social scientists can help readers appreciate the ways in which servicing and resisting empires also created visions of a wider, interdependent, order – which we now call global. In earlier days, such visions circulated under other banners, like international, worldly or for humanity.[5]

If empires were world-making political structures, this does not mean that imperial agents developed common world views or 'converged' in the same way that commodities, capital or prices became the indices of globalization. Indeed, paradoxically, we can see how entanglement and convergence of markets and networks often simultaneously produced divergences of perspective and tensions within global interdependence. Going global does not mean globalizing and homogenizing views of world order. In the global history of intellectual life, perspective and place matter. As you read the chapters in this book, consider one comparison: how social scientists interpreted global processes and derived lessons and recipes for national survival in China, Bourbon Spain and post-1945 Argentina. What these cases shared was the perceived need for nations to adjust to increasingly inescapable international pressures and threats. By contrast, another strand of social science represented world forces as an opportunity for empire-nations to mould the world in the mind's eye of the social scientist serving – and spurring – national ambitions on a global stage. We see this clearly among eighteenth- and nineteenth-century British thought and twentieth-century American ideas. More recently, social scientists have been at the forefront of debates about the plausibility and uncertainties of a post-American world. This meant that social scientists were also summoned to think globally as well as nationally; working for the nation, creating institutions and drafting narratives to unify citizens often implied thinking globally.

Considering the ways in which social scientists serviced nation-building purposes by grappling with the challenges and risks of global interdependence requires reframing the way global and national histories have been dichotomized and separated into two competing scales of narration. There was a time in which world or transnational history got rolled out as a 'post-national' framework, the source of stories to fit our age of globalization. But one might argue, and the chapters in this book illustrate, that global integration re-signifies the nation by giving it a place in a broader assembly of agents and recasts the role of social scientist as an agent of managing and imagining of nations seen as parts of a wider web of nations, sometimes cooperating, sometimes competing, sometimes allying and other times dominating each other.[6]

But there was more: the creation of an interdependent, global, order did not only mobilize thinkers to help envision and manage how states and societies would fit into, or leap across, the emerging hierarchies of entangled nations. By the end of the nineteenth century, increasing ranks of social scientists got enlisted for the task of managing the global order itself for the sake of the nations that comprised it. In other words, their positionality began as servants of the nation working on international peace and security for the nation, and with time we witness a cadre of social scientists engaged in the creation of an international tier of institutions, structures and commitments that Akira Iriye has labelled a 'global community' floating above nation states, and often drawing powers, responsibilities and capacities away from nation states. From the late nineteenth century, a growing number of conferences devoted to peace-making, treaties and scientific exchange and 'international' associations of social policymakers created and pooled their knowledge for the service of something called 'humanity'. These were the seedlings of something that would flourish, often led by social movements and civic federations we would later call 'non-governmental organizations' in the 1960s, involving writers, analysts and engagé scholars.[7]

Cutting both ways, serving the nation by engaging the world and making transnational structures to safeguard the world from unruly nations has been part of the social scientist's wheelhouse from the time that a self-imagined science of society and of the market took form in the eighteenth century. Yet, little attention has been paid to the global effects on the social sciences. There is a paradoxical gap, for the paradigms of realism, materialism, area studies and 'civilizations', indeed the very idea of modern humanity and the possibility of a universal history, all sprung to life in response to convergences and divergences across borders. Entire areas of study, from international trade to the analysis of democracy, from 'ethnic' identities to human geography, fuelled the expansion of higher education and its networks of exchange. The year 1916 had seen the creation of the School of Oriental and African Studies in London; 1923 saw the founding of the Social Science Research Council in New York, devoted to international social science research. Orientalism went from being a field devoted to understanding languages, cultures and archaeological processes to becoming a framework for studying contemporary affairs. Witness the transformation of the École des langues orientales vivantes in Paris, which cashed in philology for new epistemic foundations, strongly inflected by the global spread of the new sociology, scientific racism and geneticist models. It was, until 1935, when the Ministry of Foreign Affairs opened up a recruitment competition, the monopoly institution training French dragomans and interpreters for the empire and mandates. Around the world, the study of the 'Other' became a cornerstone of social science. If this book seeks to place the social scientist working across scales, from national to international tiers, it also explores the ways in which social scientists interpreted wider-world happenings to local and national audiences, creating knowledge from and of the world for readers, students and clients seeking to understand the forces beyond their borders but which affected life within them.

Where social scientists most clearly functioned as intermediators across historical scales, reconciling the parts of a wider global order and recommending policies and designing institutions for local purposes, was in moments of perceived crisis of the wider system. In economic or political upheavals, threats to national security or economic prosperity triggered reminders that even the most powerful states were dependent upon the whole. For instance, the sense of a fundamental rupture in the eighteenth century spurred new forms of knowledge about the world and its parts; the same happened after 1848. But it was only with the spread of literacy, the printing press and the modernization and diffusion of universities that international flows of knowledge truly occurred and with it the creation of a global knowledge regime that foreshadowed the emergence of national knowledge parts.[8]

If social scientists started as imperial servants, they also nurtured a global knowledge regime. With time, this regime redoubled the work of the global social scientist by creating like-minded concepts and debates that straddled empires and nations. In contrast to national knowledge regimes, the global one that this book explores was stitched together by observing the same international phenomena, sharing (or debating) ideas of modernization, confronting similar incentives to professionalize and moulding interlaced institutions of universities, foundations and international actors. In effect, twentieth-century national knowledge regimes were preceded by and then foreshadowed by one that criss-crossed them, one that this book seeks to bring to light. At the same time, on a global scale, this regime did more than straddle borders; it created contradictions and a plenitude of tensions and arguments about the risks and injustices of being part of an interdependent order.[9]

The catastrophe of the First World War was a major turning point in its making; it sparked for the first time a worldwide panic and proliferation of alternative models of interdependence, starting with the idea of a socialist, working-class internationalism. The contestation took many forms, from the scramble for supremacy within the international order to the creation of a communist counterpoint, to defiance from colonial voices searching for an alternative, post-European order. This mayhem kindled a new turn in the global social sciences. It created a sense that the internationalist order had failed, and the threats of new conflicts and economic upheavals compelled fledgling organizations like the Rockefeller Foundation and the Carnegie Corporation of New York and new institutions like the Council on Foreign Relations in New York, the Royal Institute of International Affairs in London and the League of Nations (and cousin institutions like the International Labour Organization and the Permanent Court of International Justice) in Geneva to create a latticework of think tanks and scholarly problem-solvers devoted to networks of research and advocacy on world affairs. Some of these organizations still loom large; they also spawned offspring and successors. And so it was that generations of social scientists served not just national masters but also a global order that secured national welfare. How much this executive training for world affairs would spread around the globe is a question at the heart of a coming agenda for the global history of intellectual life – one which this volume seeks to motivate.[10]

Of course, the appeal to a new kind of universalism left large swathes of humankind out; colonial peoples in particular seldom sat at the table where new international commitments and declarations of solidarity got hammered out. It is important to note, therefore, that all visions of 'the international' were always contested; the idea of liberal interdependence at the expense of national sovereignty made more than a few anxious about their nations. We now see this strain of global anxiety flourishing in doubts about global interdependence, with questions raised by left- and right-wing thinkers.[11]

Others saw the new brands of internationalism as simply the new guises of colonialism and as languages and systems aimed at erecting a new hierarchy. Efforts to create new international orders often met challengers who argued that the new was simply a mask for reinventing the old. For instance, no sooner had the ink dried on the Versailles Treaty than leaders and economists caucused to rebuild an economic order with worldwide horizons. In Brussels in 1920, a summit called for the creation of a multilateral free trade order – to stymie the drift to sauve qui peut policymaking. The fledgling treaty system was immediately put to the test in resolving crises in the Middle East and East Asia. Across the Middle East, the response to the mandate system was resignation, outrage and revolt. How new was it to swap Ottoman authorities for French or British officials? In Asia too, there was a sense of disenchantment. Sun Yat-sen returned to Guangzhou to pen a warning that the treaty left Eurasian conflicts unresolved, or worse. Sure enough, Japanese expansionists, upset that their yearnings went unrecognized in Paris, set their sights on mainland claims, especially in Shandong Province. What did this flawed world order look like from Chinese, Indian, Latin American and African perspectives, where nationalist currents argued that internationalism mostly served older imperial impulses and rarely allowed the concept of self-determination to go beyond its Eurocentric hearth?[12]

Between the architects and the challengers of world orders, something fundamental began to change after 1945. The lessons of the Great Depression and the horrors of the Second World War gave rise to visions of what some call 'globalism' – the idea that the world needed new ideas, structures and commitments to prevent backsliding into ruinous competition, for the old preconceptions and compromises had debased the world to the edge of pointlessness. Hannah Arendt would call this urge 'thinking without a bannister', letting go of previous crutches and certainties.[13] Of course, such a radical vision of civic-minded co-dependency did not quite materialize. But still, the post-1945 years, fuelled in part by Cold War rivalries, with each contestant waving their version of internationalism, sired an unprecedented mobilization of social scientists in the service of wider missions. One might argue that the heirs of that global knowledge regime got more institutionalized as the United Nations, interleaved think tanks and bulked up universities with their disciplinary departments and expanding study abroad programmes deepened the very idea of expertise. Increasingly, global forces were not shaping the social sciences as much as social sciences were shaping the global order – this began, just to take two Cambridge examples, with John Maynard Keynes's role in chartering the Bretton Woods financial architecture and Hersch Lauterpacht's role in drafting the precepts of the international law of crimes against humanity. That model of expertise took flight after 1945. Seventy years later, some worry, the cycle of global social science expertise has run afoul of a breed of populists who decry elitist, cosmopolitan, rootless – the stigmata hurled at the pointy-headed *penseurs* of the world is now quite elaborate – experts for worrying more about their global ties than local lives.

Empire and the Social Sciences seeks to explore that global history of social sciences. It examines the ways in which economists, legal scholars, anthropologists and geographers grappled with processes at a global scale for national and imperial purposes, before and through the long arc of expertise and disciplinary professionalization. Indeed, it accents the ways in which, seen from a global standpoint, the creation of disciplinary boundaries is a relatively recent phenomenon and less entrenched than it may seem from within the sausage-making machine of Anglo-American universities. It is important to appreciate the antecedents of modern, disciplinary social sciences nested in less academic vocations as well as the porous boundary between the social scientist and social institutions in which they were embedded – and in which some strains of social science still seek to trespass.

The aims of this book are three: first, to show how global integration mobilized intellectual life; second, to illuminate the ways in which social scientists made sense of an interdependent global order for their readers and clients; and third, to transcend the limits of methodological nationalism – that is, to explore the ways in which 'national' social scientists were in fact shaped by global knowledge currents because they served empires and their challengers. The sum is to contribute to a flourishing interest in global intellectual history by showing the ways in which cross-border forces shaped intellectual life and how social scientists interpreted them.[14]

Empire preceded the emergence of the social sciences and has foreshadowed their histories. For most of the history of the social sciences, empire was significant for three basic reasons. First, it has been the term to denote a scale beyond local or national lives; it was, in effect, the coinage to capture extensions and entanglements between peoples, neighbours and distant strangers. It was a subjective, or native, category for historical subjects. Second, it is a category of analysis that we use as historians to describe political formations that range from tributary regimes (like Ming China or Ottoman Turkey) to predatory (like the Mongol empire or Hitler's) and commercial regimes (the Spanish, British and, some would argue, the current structure of multinational firms that make earnings of long-distance supply chains). What is common to them all is the asymmetry of the geographic distribution of power and the need to govern social and cultural differences across the spatial range; empire is, therefore, fundamentally different from the legitimating principles of nationhood, which denote, in theory, uniformity and homogeneity of power to the regime's territorial limits and the equality of political subjects within them.[15]

Third, as the chapters in this volume show, empire – making it, reforming it, resisting it – is a heuristic device to illuminate the global processes that shaped the modern social sciences. Border-crossing social science did not turn intellectuals into rootless, cosmopolitan free-floaters. This was the label slapped on to them by sceptics, often nativists, from the Dreyfus Affair onwards, to represent a kind of social actor who criticized and claimed to observe society and stand outside it, often proud of his or her distance from the subjects and societies he or she studied.[16] But this confuses one of the claims of some social *science*, a claim of distanced impartiality, with its purpose to imagine, to engage and to create empires. The social scientist – unlike the idealized natural scientist or philosopher – imagined himself or herself as part of the human world, observing, reflecting and engaging in the study of distant people or remote processes; however, imperial purposes ensured that social scientists were never unmoored, placeless or footloose actors. Moreover, empires provided the mechanisms and subjects for looking beyond local or national boundaries; empires created the means and motives for bridging distances between worlds, and social scientists joined natural scientists, missionaries, traders, officials and migrants in crossing those bridges.

Most often social scientists were empire-makers. Matthew Erie shows the ways in which lawyers created ideas of customary law in China, partly to envision an empire of laws even as its sovereignty was under assault by other empires. Diana Kim illustrates how British ideas of commerce and free trade took shape at home while policies abroad accentuated coercion and violence in the wake of the Opium Wars. It was not just the free trade in commodities that spurred imperial entanglement. Alessandro Stanziani explains the ways in which political economy drew upon ideas of free labour to stigmatize (in the case of Russia) and apologize for (in the case of the British in India) rival empires. Chinese geographers helped create the idea of the Chinese empire as a spatial, and not just a juridical, unit. In part, they were emboldened because right beside China was a rising empire in Japan, which had to imagine itself as such – as Alexis Dudden shows in her study of Nitobe Inazō. And Sophus Reinert and Fidel Tavárez show how eighteenth-century political economists grappled with the sense of a rapidly shifting trade landscape in the Spanish and British realms – and in so doing laid the groundwork for the idea of a commercial society and the ideal of well-mannered men who should dominate it, a basic concept in the modern social sciences.

By the time we reach the twentieth century, however, being an empire-maker was tricky. Colonial peoples posed unsettling questions about the legitimacy of empires. Some scholars and writers at home echoed these concerns. The economist John A. Hobson, while reporting on the Boer War in South Africa for the *Manchester Guardian*, would return to London to write one of the most influential interpretations of the modern economics of empire in 1902, a tract that would have a lasting impact on how we understand global unfairness and dependency. Doubts only spread as the notion of self-determination took off after 1918. Empire ceased to be such a natural way to coil societies together and became increasingly challenged and pilloried. Indeed, many social scientists began to dream of an 'international' global order to replace the fractious imperial one that plunged the world into crisis in 1914. But which internationalism? This question plagued two important German legal thinkers, Carl Schmitt and Ernst Rudolf Huber (whose ideas are discussed in Joshua Derman's chapter), who argued that liberal internationalism and new technologies conspired to create a new mode of empire but did not eclipse the concept altogether. Meanwhile, a network of Latin American economists and sociologists were hard at work after 1945, as Margarita Fajardo describes, trying to create an international economic order that would put an end to the commercial unfairness marking transactions between industrial countries and primary product exporters, which, they insisted, had a deep taproot in old empires and which the United States inherited and was defending; their internationalism counterposed what many Third World people would begin to see as an American empire. And there was some justification for this. How different was 'international' from imperial? David Ekbladh shows how social scientists from the United States, while repudiating the idea that they were agents of empire, wielded a soft version of power – their ideas, their knowledge – to project a form of American hegemony that was deeply asymmetrical and in practice took on many imperial trappings. Inderjeet Parmar, likewise, describes the role that American foundations played in training social scientists in the Third World precisely to internalize the values and norms that would make US hegemony seem natural. And finally, John Hobson's sweeping retrospective on the tradition of Western international relations thinking argues that it has been, in ways that the tradition frequently obscures, a framework to make sense of and to legitimate Eurocentrality ever since the first European empires were created in 1492.

Social scientists therefore performed many roles in the service of empires and their alternatives. Indeed, the many kinds of engagements described in this book show just how rooted social scientists were in the service of empire. And they were more than just rooted; many social scientists sought to create places in the world and to attach them to each other through imperial fabrics. One underlying theme of this book is that we have to look not just at how social scientists think, but what they do in producing knowledge for and about peoples scattered across distant places. This is what is meant by the social scientist operating as an intermediator between scales (global and local) and as an intermediator between peoples (colonial and metropolitan). By making the world of empires and an imperial world intelligible, governable, reformable and imaginable, social scientists have been, in effect, important world-makers.[17]

The chapters in this book identify basic traits about the world-making impact of social science. For one, social scientists expanded the horizons of what was knowable and claimed to be known. This is why, as Reinert, Kim and Tavárez illustrate, imperial rulers and readers were so anxious to widen the radius of what could be fathomed about a world they increasingly recognized as a unit that they depended upon. Social scientists, in effect, played an important role in creating a spatial imagination for those who consumed their knowledge. For Wu and Erie, knowing something about the territorial edges and fringe peoples of Qing, and even Republican China, was a condition for modern empire. In so doing, they made the worlds connected by empires more intervisible.

Making the world intervisible did not mean – though they tried, and many claimed to have accomplished the task – creating a complete, untinted ability to view and understand strangers; far from it. Rather, an intervisible world was one in which knowledge flowed in many directions at the same time between places. It may have been asymmetrical and susceptible to the subjective framings that social scientists gave to what they learnt; plenty also got lost in translation as ideas moved across borders. But it did move across borders, thanks to the printing press, intellectual sociability, student exchanges and funding incentives – the components of the global knowledge regime. Increasingly, this regime that made the world intervisible got its basic anchor bolts which, by the modern age, were defined by their location as knowledge hubs for the world: universities. Indeed, increasingly, these fraught, freighted and overloaded institutions would become gauged by a global rankings game.[18]

One force that fuelled the intervisibility was competition and emulation between the imperial parts. The ways in which rivalry and mimesis affected understandings of interdependence and the study of others shot through the patchwork of institutions that sustained social science, whether it was the creation of Japanese universities and disciplines which borrowed from American and European models to do the work for Tokyo's wider ambitions, as Dudden shows, or Latin Americans' commitment to creating UN agencies in order to shore up alternative sources of knowledge to American models of social science, as Fajardo shows. And then, there's the way in which knowledge about other empires helped frame one's own. Creating images and representations of the Spanish empire gave substance and purpose to the promoters of the British empire, while Spanish imperial reformers looked at the newcomers as a reason to fix their own. As Stanziani shows, British utilitarian thinkers were fixated with the Russian empire. Ekbladh and Parmar show how Cold War America was also obsessed with its Slavic rival.

If social scientists expanded horizons and made societies more intervisible, they were also critics. They chastised imperial oppression when they saw it; they called for reform from within. For all the commitment to engage in empire, there is a more subdued strain throughout the chapters in this book: social scientists envisioned themselves as observers, as drawing upon or discovering certain laws of motion to create an objective form of knowledge separate from the practical reasons of state or power, even if they were often serving that power. This conception – seeing themselves as being part of an imperial order while being distanced from it – made for an uneasy compromise, and it often became the source of confused intentions if not rising tension. But we can see it at work in the ways in which the social scientists as distanced observers made room to criticize their own masters, or at least to urge them to reform, catch up or even – as Ekbladh shows – join an imperial order to be able to develop in the first place. And then there were the more out-and-out critics, such as those referred to in Fajardo's and

Derman's chapters. One might read Hobson's final chapter and his critique of the Eurocentric foundations of his own discipline as a continuation of this critical tradition in the global social sciences.

This observational turn, the urge to look, to categorize, to differentiate and to classify the world as empires, opened the world up and remade it through various stages – from the eighteenth-century commercial empires to the rise of a racially ordered world held together by civilizing missions and the developmental prospects of the twentieth century – made social scientists the effects of global convergences and divergences. They, too, require a global history to accompany what we know about the flows of capital, commodities and labour. They, too, have been the subjects of global integration and disintegration. But they were also the objects and makers of these processes; they reinforced and questioned the very structures that made interdependence possible and legible. This volume is a variant on global intellectual history. But it is more than that: its chapters are committed also to the notion that intellectuals contributed to making the world into the unstable, fragile but interdependent order of today.

Notes

1 Edward Said, *Representations of the Intellectual* (New York: Random House, 1994), 3–24.
2 Julien Benda, *The Treason of the Intellectuals* (New Brunswick: Rutgers University Press, 1990), 45, 202.
3 John L. Campbell and Ove K. Pedersen, *The National Origins of Policy Ideas: Knowledge Regimes in the United States, France, Germany, and Denmark* (Princeton: Princeton University Press, 2014); Mark Blyth, 'Same As It Never Was? Typology and Temporality in the Varieties of Capitalism', *Comparative European Politics* 1, no. 2 (2003): 215–25; Frank Dobbin, 'The Social Construction of the Great Depression: Industrial Policy during the 1930s in the United States, Britain, and France', *Theory and Society* 22, no. 1 (1993): 1–56.
4 Robert Bickers, *Out of China: How the Chinese Ended the Era of Western Domination* (Cambridge: Harvard University Press, 2017).
5 For a recent sampling, see Sven Beckert and Dominic Sachsenmeier, eds, *Global History Globally: Research and Practice around the World* (London: Bloomsbury, 2018).
6 Sebastian Conrad, *What is Global History?* (Princeton: Princeton University Press, 2016), 205–32; Jeremy Adelman, 'What is Global History Now?' *Aeon*, 10 March 2017, https://aeon.co/essays/is-global-history-still-possible-or-has-it-had-its-moment
7 Dan Rodgers, *Atlantic Crossings: Social Politics in a Progressive Age* (Cambridge: Harvard University Press, 2000); Or Rosenboim, *The Emergence of Globalism: Visions of World Order in Britain and the United States, 1939–1950* (Princeton: Princeton University Press, 2017); Akira Irye, *Global Community: The Role of International Organizations in the Making of the Contemporary World* (Berkeley: University of California Press, 2004).
8 Jürgen Osterhammel, *The Transformation of the World: A Global History of the Nineteenth Century* (Princeton: Princeton University Press, 2014), 779–823.
9 Campbell and Pedersen, *The National Origins of Policy Ideas*.

10 Michael Barnett, *Empire of Humanity: A History of Humanitarianism* (Ithaca: Cornell University Press, 2011), 97–106; Kiran Klaus Patel, *The New Deal: A Global History* (Princeton: Princeton University Press, 2016), 190–259; Ludovic Tournès, *Les États-Unis et la Société des Nations (1914–1946)* (Bern: Peter Lang, 2015).
11 Mark Blyth, *Austerity: The History of a Dangerous Idea* (New York: Oxford University Press, 2013); Wolfgang Streeck, *Buying Time: The Delayed Crisis of Democratic Capitalism* (London: Verso, 2017); Ruchir Sharma, *The Rise and Fall of Nations: Forces of Change in the Post-Crisis World* (New York: W.W. Norton, 2016).
12 Pankaj Mishra, *From the Ruins of Empire: The Intellectuals Who Remade Asia* (New York: Farrar, Straus & Giroux, 2012); Marie-Claire Bergère, *Sun Yat-sen* (Stanford: Stanford University Press, 1994), 293–351.
13 Hannah Arendt, *Thinking without a Banister: Essays in Understanding, 1953–1975* (New York: Schocken Books, 2018); Tracy Strong, *Politics without Vision: Thinking without a Banister* (Chicago: University of Chicago Press, 2012).
14 Samuel Moyn and Andrew Sartori, eds, *Global Intellectual History* (New York: Columbia University Press, 2013).
15 Frederick Cooper and Jane Burbank, *Empires and World History: Power and the Politics of Difference* (Princeton: Princeton University Press, 2011).
16 Said, *Representations of the Intellectual*.
17 Conrad, *What is Global History?* 185–204.
18 This extends the work in George Steinmetz, ed., *Sociology and Empire: The Imperial Entanglements of a Discipline* (Durham: Duke University Press, 2013). See also Ben Wildavski, *The Great Brain Race: How Global Universities and Reshaping the World* (Princeton: Princeton University Press, 2012).

Chapter 1

A NEW SYSTEM OF IMPERIAL GOVERNMENT: POLITICAL ECONOMY AND THE SPANISH THEORY OF COMMERCIAL EMPIRE, CA. 1740–50

Fidel J. Tavárez

> Everything we see in that great portion of the Spanish Monarchy (America) is revealing, in accordance with reason (a gritos de la razón), the necessity to introduce in its government a new method, so that such rich territorial possessions give us advantages that are proportional to the vastness of such expansive dominions and the beauty of their products.
>
> —*Nuevo sistema de gobierno económico para la América*[1]

The *Nuevo sistema de gobierno económico para la América* (ca. 1748), perhaps the most important reform proposal of the eighteenth-century Hispanic world, summarized its aims with the lines in the epigraph above. In a nutshell, the *Nuevo sistema* argued that the Spanish metropole had to ensure that it gained 'advantages' from its New World possessions. In so doing, the *Nuevo sistema* enjoined Spanish ministers to treat Spanish American territories as colonies, as dominions that produced cheap raw materials for the metropole and that consumed metropolitan manufactures. It was in this same spirit that the text encouraged Spanish ministers to govern, following a principle that any British and French colonial minister knew all too well, namely that 'the purpose of the colony is to benefit the *patria*, to whom it owes its existence'.[2] By insisting on subduing the colonies for the exclusive benefit of the metropole, the author of the *Nuevo sistema* was attempting to transform the Spanish Monarchy into a new kind of colonial commercial empire.

What inspired this insistence on creating a new system of imperial government in the New World? The answer to this question, of course, centrally involves the intellectual biography of the *Nuevo sistema*'s author: Melchor Rafael de Macanaz.[3] Most importantly, however, the *Nuevo sistema*'s reform proposals can be, in large part, attributed to the rise of a new kind of knowledge that contemporaries called political economy or the science of commerce. Macanaz posited that few of his predecessors understood the principles of this new science, for which reason he partly redeemed them of guilt for Spain's decline. In their time, Macanaz assured, the sciences of commerce were 'poorly developed'. It was only in the last century and a half, he continued, that political economy 'has reached the high level in which we see it today'.[4] Although Macanaz never put it in exactly these terms, he was implicitly admitting that political economy gave him the intellectual tools to begin to design a new commercial system that would make Spain the most powerful colonial empire in Europe. The argument that this chapter advances is that Spain acquired the language of empire – of a colonial commercial empire to be precise – with Macanaz starting in the 1740s, in the context of the rise of political economy as a new science of imperial power.[5]

Many readers will be surprised by the argument I have just proposed. Did not Spain, after all, possess a robust imperial discourse in 1492, when the Catholic monarchs decided to support the conquest of the newly 'discovered' islands in the Caribbean? Spain, according to most accounts, had become a colonial empire at the end of the fifteenth century, after the Catholic monarchs unified Castile and Aragon, after they conquered Granada and, most importantly, after they conquered the New World. As many accounts would have it, by the second half of the sixteenth century, Phillip II had managed to assemble the largest empire of his time, particularly after he added Portugal and its colonies to his dominion in 1580, creating an empire 'upon which the sun never set'. Seen from this perspective, Macanaz's suggestion concerning the need to create a new imperial system in the 1740s amounts to little more than a mere banality, for Spain had already subjected America to a robust form of imperial rule in the sixteenth century. This was especially the case considering all of the silver Spanish kings managed to extract from the viceroyalties of New Spain and Peru.[6]

This age-old perspective, however, has erred in equating conquest with colonial subjection and modern imperialism. We should be careful in making this analogy, for, as many scholars have argued, the early-modern Monarquía de España can be more accurately described, to use John H. Elliott's celebrated phrase, as a 'composite monarchy', as a polity comprised of multiple kingdoms and provinces with historic constitutions, rights, privileges, liberties and *fueros*.[7] A new generation of scholars has pushed even farther than Elliott, arguing not only that Spain was not a colonial empire, but also that it did not have a permanent or clearly defined centre. According to these scholars, Spain was a 'polycentric monarchy'.[8] This group of historians has transcended the old idea that the empire contained a pragmatically flexible bureaucracy, suggesting instead that flexibility may have been inherent to the jurisdictional nature of Spain, rather than a deviation from a strictly imperial logic.[9] In a monarchy of this sort, even conquered territories like the Indies were incorporated into a polycentric framework, which meant that local elites, not the metropole, benefitted from the economic exploitation of the New World. Spanish American territories, therefore, functioned as kingdoms and provinces, not colonies, of Castile.[10]

It was precisely this composite, jurisdictional and polycentric framework that Macanaz was putting into question in Spanish American territories. Macanaz posited that American territories could not function as autonomous domains if Spain were ever to become a powerful commercial empire. Instead, a commercial empire entailed converting Spanish American territories into colonies and Madrid into their metropole. At stake was not simply reducing the juridical status of the

New World from kingdoms and provinces to colonies, but also making the entire polity work in concert to improve its power. Above all, integration meant that the different territories of the monarchy could not engage in whatever economic activities its inhabitants deemed convenient. Instead, colonies had to produce raw materials, while the metropole had to produce manufactures for the consumption of all subjects.

The *Nuevo sistema* was only the first of a wave of subsequent court manuscripts that argued for the creation of a commercial empire. But, it is precisely because it was the first, and perhaps also the most important text to articulate this new imperial vision that we must pay close attention to it. The *Nuevo sistema*, of course, has been the subject of many studies. No worthy scholarly work on the Bourbon Reforms can do without discussing the *Nuevo sistema* in some detail. But, in this chapter, I seek to avoid the traditional lines of inquiry that historians have followed. I do not ask whether the *Nuevo sistema* reflected a mercantilist, liberal, neo-mercantilist or proto-liberal framework. Nor do I inquire into the worthiness, effectiveness or viability of its proposals. Rather, I seek to explain what Macanaz was attempting to do with the monarchy in putting forward his proposal for a new system of government in Spanish America. My goal is to attempt to grasp Macanaz's intentions by reading his proposals in the context of the many reform projects that surfaced in Bourbon Spain and in the context of the European-wide phenomenon of what we may call commercial statecraft, namely the idea that the advancement of commerce had become an essential component in the interimperial battle for power and preservation.

I hope to convince readers that Macanaz, like his intellectual heirs, was attempting to transform the Spanish composite or polycentric monarchy into a colonial commercial empire, and that political economy gave him the conceptual tools to put forward this new imperial vision. The implications of my argument, at least for the purposes of this anthology, are significant. My suggestion is not simply that an empire like Spain used Enlightenment political economy for imperial purposes, but that this science of commerce gave Spain the tools to begin to think of itself as an empire. To the extent that we can consider eighteenth-century political economy a social science, and there are many reasons not to do so, political economy was not simply enmeshed in European imperialism, but it actually gave it stimulus; indeed, it was the science of imperial preservation and power par excellence. With this suggestion, I hope to invite scholars to think of the social sciences not simply as bodies of knowledge that can and have been used for imperial purposes, but also as bodies of knowledge that have given birth to imperial visions.

A mere court manuscript written in the 1740s, the *Nuevo sistema* unexpectedly became a blueprint for imperial reform in the eighteenth-century Spanish Atlantic. Three interrelated ideas defined the imperial programme encapsulated in this text. The first was that Spain's American colonies must give advantages to its metropole, which, in short, meant that 'the purpose of the colony is to benefit the *patria*, to whom it owes its existence'.[11] The second idea dealt with the specific way in which the colonies could potentially benefit the metropole. The colonies had to provide the metropole with an abundant source of markets, which could only be accomplished by instituting a commercial system in which 'the entire consumption of the colonies should emanate precisely from the products of the *patria*'.[12] The third and last idea concerns the commercial policy that was best equipped to capture Spanish America's consumption: *comercio libre* (free internal trade). With free internal trade and reduced port duties, peninsular Spaniards would allegedly be able to sell their manufactures at cheaper prices and, as a consequence, undersell foreign competitors. Herein lay the chain of ideas that defined the Spanish theory of commercial empire.

The *Nuevo sistema* seems clear enough. But its apparent simplicity is deceptive, which can explain why historians have lost sight of some its most defining characteristics.[13] Even while many have long acknowledged the importance of the *Nuevo sistema* as the intellectual backbone of imperial reform, few scholars have taken the time to reconstruct the text's intellectual context. The task is difficult but urgent, particularly because the *Nuevo sistema* exercised a direct influence on some of the most far-reaching reform proposals of the time. In the second half of the eighteenth century, every significant minister read a version of this text. Likewise, every contemporary historian of the eighteenth-century Hispanic world has at one point or another engaged with the *Nuevo sistema*. Its importance, thus, cannot be overemphasized. In the following paragraphs, I will locate the *Nuevo sistema* in its proper context. In particular, I will reconstruct how and why the *Nuevo sistema* was written and how it circulated in administrative circles.

We shall begin with a brief inventory of the most important versions of the *Nuevo sistema*. While the first printed version of the *Nuevo sistema* dates to 1789, the manuscript versions allegedly date to 1743. The most important versions of this 1743 manuscript are located at the Biblioteca Nacional de España (BNE) and the Biblioteca del Palacio Real (BPR).[14] Additionally, portions of the *Nuevo sistema* also appeared in the second half of Bernardo Ward's *Proyecto económico*. There is a manuscript version of Ward's *Proyecto* at the BPR that dates to 1762, but there is also a print version that appeared in 1779.[15] Indeed, throughout the second half of the century, the *Nuevo sistema* was widely disseminated in the Hispanic world. It is important, nonetheless, to make a distinction between the earlier manuscript versions and the subsequent printed versions of the text. While the latter were concerned with wider dissemination among Spanish subjects from both sides of the Atlantic, the former intended to influence ministers and policymakers in the court. It is to these earlier manuscript versions that we shall pay most attention, for they served as the main inspiration for Spain's turn towards commercial empire.

Uncovering the origins of the 1743 manuscript versions inevitably entails deciphering its author. The task may not promise a great degree of certainty, but it is nonetheless important for reconstructing the work's context. While many of the manuscripts of the *Nuevo sistema* are signed by José del Campillo y Cossío, there are elements in the text that do not map very well with his earlier intellectual trajectory. Consider, for instance, Campillo's 1741 manuscript, *Lo que hay de más y menos en España*. It is true, Campillo admitted, 'that if we did not have the Indies there would not be as much money as there sometimes is in the Royal Treasury'.

But, it is also true, he continued, that, without the American territories, peninsular 'subjects would have more utility [for the state]', which, in turn, would ultimately give 'motive for Spain to build the factories that it lacks'.[16] Campillo was careful in making these suggestions, but he regretted, nonetheless, the negative effects that the possession of Spanish America ostensibly generated for the metropole. Something seems amiss, for just two years later the *Nuevo sistema* stated that 'it is evident that the very vast American dominions can produce the greatest benefits for Spain'.[17] Did Campillo change his mind so drastically in less than two years? Most likely, the answer to this question is no.

The principal reason for which Campillo was very probably not the author of the *Nuevo sistema* stems from his early commitment to the kind of military reason of state that predominated during the first half of the century. Like most of the ministers of his generation, Campillo came of age at a time when the king's most fundamental objective was to augment the health of the Royal Treasury. And, like the rest of his counterparts, Campillo was convinced that to become a formidable European power, Spain needed money (bullion), not colonial markets per se, for a bullion-rich nation could use this monetary abundance to expand its military capacity. Campillo's commitment to military expansion is clearly evident in his administrative trajectory. Since at least 1717, Campillo earned the favour of José Patiño, one of the most important ministers and military men of the early Bourbon Reforms.[18] During the next two decades, Campillo held multiple military posts, including some that required crossing the Atlantic.[19] By the time Campillo inherited the ministries (*secretarías*) of finance, war, the navy and the Indies between 1739 and 1741, he had had a long military career. A commitment to augmenting Spain's military capacity was Campillo's primary concern.

Who, then, could have authored the *Nuevo sistema*? Based on a manuscript located in the Real Academia de la Historia in Madrid (RAH), Barbara and Stanley Stein have suggested that the author of the *Nuevo sistema* was the prolific writer, thinker, minister and erudite scholar Melchor Rafael de Macanaz.[20] The manuscript in question, the *Discurso sobre la America española*, is almost identical to the *Nuevo sistema*, for which reason the Steins think that Campillo plagiarized Macanaz. Nonetheless, other than the fact that they have found the *Discurso* in the RAH, the Steins offer very little evidence to prove that Macanaz was indeed the original author. Although the Steins' suspicions are probably correct, a deeper textual analysis is necessary before arriving at any definitive conclusion.

One significant piece of evidence to further support Macanaz's authorship is another version of the *Nuevo sistema* held at the Instituto Valencia de Don Juan (IVDJ) in Madrid. The version at the IVDJ, titled *Nuevo sixtema para el perfecto gobierno de la América*, is also signed by Macanaz.[21] Most importantly, however, this version dates to 1719. This alone should be proof that Macanaz was the original author, and that he wrote the *Nuevo sistema* earlier in the century. But the 1719 date is improbable when considering some of the allusions the text makes. In particular, the *Nuevo sixtema* at the IVDJ alludes to a *visita* (visitation) that Antonio de Ulloa conducted in the mines of Potosí, for which he wrote some reports allegedly dating to 1647. In fact, these reports date to a century later, when

Antonio de Ulloa wrote some reports to Ensenada about the state of the mines. Furthermore, upon close inspection, it is evident that someone tampered with the *Nuevo sixtema* at the IVDJ. The text in question actually originally stated the more probable date for the reports: 1747. But, someone wrote a 6 over the 7 to make the 1719 date listed at the beginning of the manuscript plausible. To determine the correct date for the manuscript, it is therefore necessary to read the *Nuevo sixtema* at the IVDJ alongside the *Discurso* at the RAH and the many versions of the *Nuevo sistema* at the BNE and the BPR.

The most important piece of evidence in support of Macanaz's authorship is the already-mentioned allusion to Antonio de Ulloa. Macanaz indicated that, before writing the *Discurso*, he had read a set of letters written by Ulloa in 1747. 'I have in my power some letters that the visitor of the mines of Potosí wrote after the conclusion of his visit in 1747', he stated.[22] The 1743 Campillo manuscripts retained this allusion to Ulloa but omitted the year of the letters. Most likely, Macanaz was referring to the famous *Noticias secretas* that Ulloa and Jorge Juan wrote to the minister of war, the navy, finance and the Indies, the Marqués de la Ensenada, after their long sojourn in South America with the French expedition of scientists like Louis Godin, Pierre Bouguer and Charles Marie de La Condamine.[23] Although the purpose of the expedition was to determine the shape of the Earth, Ulloa and Jorge Juan had taken advantage of the opportunity to observe keenly the workings of Spanish American society, including the productivity of the mines and the nature of colonial commerce. Macanaz used the *Noticias secretas* to comment upon the decay of the mines of Potosí and the prevalence of foreign contraband trade in Peru. The important piece of information to keep in mind is that even though the Campillo manuscripts (dated in 1743) cited Ulloa, Campillo could not have possibly read the *Noticias secretas* until at least 1747 or 1748, at which point he was already deceased.

Undoubtedly, Macanaz seems like the most probable original author. He likely wrote the *Nuevo sistema* between 1747 and 1750. To be sure, these dates may seem difficult to accept, especially since Macanaz had been imprisoned in La Coruña between 1748 and 1760. But his indefatigable pen never stopped producing political tracts and advice papers while imprisoned. The *Nuevo sistema* was probably one of his most prized creations during this time. Still, why would Macanaz or anyone else circulate the *Nuevo sistema* as if Campillo were its author? There are at least three reasons that could explain this decision to circulate it with Campillo as its author: (1) Macanaz lived in exile in France since 1715 due to problems with the Inquisition; (2) Campillo died in 1743, so, if the manuscript was deemed heretical, there was no one to condemn or imprison; (3) Campillo also had the advantage of being one of the most respected ministers of Phillip V's reign. Most readers would have taken Campillo's ideas very seriously, which was not the case for Macanaz, a man who had not only lost favour in the court but also prestige among many of his peers. It is most probable, then, that at some point in the late 1740s or early 1750s someone came across Macanaz's manuscript. That person, whose identity we may never discover, wrote a new introduction and a table of contents, and then circulated the manuscript with Campillo as its author in order to stimulate a serious discussion among Spanish ministers about how to reform the monarchy's commercial system.

That Macanaz was likely the author of the *Nuevo sistema* should not be surprising. Macanaz had been one of the most innovative architects of the new Bourbon monarchy. Most importantly, he advocated for the elimination of the old *gobierno polisinodial* of the councils, insisting that the king did not have a duty to consult the councils before implementing policies that promoted national well-being. Instead, he called for the implementation of a ministerial form of government through the Secretarías de Estado y del Despacho Universal.[24] Similarly, Macanaz was an early architect of a unified Spanish monarchy, without autonomous kingdoms, that worked in concert to augment its power. It was in this line of thought that Macanaz participated in designing the Nueva Planta of 1714, which eliminated the historical constitution of the kingdoms of Aragón while implementing the intendancy system to improve the fiscal health of the monarchy. Finally, though he ran into problems with the Inquisition, and though after 1715 he lived in exile in France, Macanaz continued to serve the Spanish Monarchy in the capacity of adviser and ambassador at least until 1748, when he returned to Spain only to be imprisoned.[25] Through the many manuscripts that he forwarded to Phillip V and his ministers, Macanaz had developed some of the most far-reaching reform proposals in Spain, including, but not limited to, the implementation of a general single tax to replace consumption taxes and specific plans for the stimulation of commerce, agriculture and manufacturing.

Moreover, in an early manuscript, Macanaz had been one the earliest thinkers to put forward one of the key principles of the Spanish theory of commercial empire: the idea that it was markets rather than bullion that increased the nation's power. This manuscript, entitled *Auxilios para bien gobernar una monarquía católica* (ca. 1722), consists of twenty-two rules of prudence that a good Catholic monarch ought to follow. Amid many recommendations, from inspiring religiosity among subjects and governing with virtue to asserting the rights of the king vis-à-vis the papacy (regalism) and promoting the sciences, rule II stated that 'the mines of silver and gold, far from bringing opulence to the nation that possesses it, drag it into a state of misery'.[26] In fact, Macanaz stated, the unfounded pursuit of bullion 'is what populates the mines with auxiliaries, leaving agriculture, factories, and other more useful operations without teachers'.[27] If Spain continued pursuing silver relentlessly, 'we will be lords of our great mines, only to be slaves for the rest of European nations that lack them'.[28] Macanaz's solution was clear and straightforward. Rule V of the *Auxilios* declared that 'commerce is the principal sinew of the monarchy'.[29] Macanaz might not yet have emphasized the importance of harnessing American markets, but he had both critiqued Spain's bullionism and emphasized the importance of trade in stimulating economic improvement. This early work of Macanaz inaugurated an intellectual thread that continued through the *Nuevo sistema* and the rest of the treatises of commercial empire that followed.

Macanaz, of course, did not develop these ideas in a vacuum. There had been a long tradition of this anti-bullionist line of thinking in Britain, especially during the English Financial Revolution, which gave birth to the first credit-based circulating paper currency. In an insightful book, Carl Wennerlind has demonstrated that what gave impetus to the English Financial Revolution was a new vision of wealth that challenged the neo-Aristotelian conviction that the total wealth of the world was limited by the amount of bullion in circulation. The innovative thinkers around Samuel Hartlib (ca. 1600–1662), the Hartlibian circle, questioned the bullionist arguments of the neo-Aristotelians by positing that wealth was potentially infinitely expandable.[30] Like the neo-Aristotelians, the thinkers of the Hartlibian circle were concerned with solving the problem of the scarcity of money. But, the Hartlibian circle was not, in fact, interested in having enough money to maintain balance and harmony, as were the neo-Aristotelians.[31] Rather, they wanted to expand the quantity of money in England to stimulate and provide incentive for production and exchange. Without money and the potential for profit, people would simply not engage in productive activity. The solution, however, was not to acquire bullion through international warfare and privateering, as it had been for an earlier generation. Instead, England had to develop an alternate, non-metallic currency.

While it is not entirely implausible that Macanaz read and engaged with many of the works that inspired the creation of the Bank of England, he was mostly informed by the example of France, where the infamous Scottish political economist, financier and minister, John Law, attempted to create a paper currency and a French National Bank between 1716 and 1720.[32] In many ways, Law was an intellectual heir to the English Financial Revolution. He had not been directly involved in the planning of the Bank of England, but he was inspired by the English example to propose innovative solutions to the scarcity of money problem in Scotland. Law's solution was to create land banks that instituted a paper currency backed by land. Law believed that land banks were exceptionally stable systems because land, unlike bullion, did not decrease in value as its available stock increased.[33] In this respect, Law disagreed with some of the architects of the Bank of England, especially John Locke, who had argued that paper currency should be backed by bullion. The logic of a non-metallic currency, nonetheless, suggests the clear affinities that existed between the Bank of England and Law's projects for Scotland and France.

Despite his clear influence on Macanaz, Law was not an exemplary case to follow, for his financial schemes had collapsed miserably. Law's reputation, moreover, was not one that merited emulation. Although Macanaz lived in Paris at the time of the affair, he never made any references to Law's experiments in France. By the time he wrote the *Discurso* or *Nuevo sistema* in the late 1740s, his most likely interlocutor was the French minister and political economist Jean-François Melon, whose *Essai politique sur le commerce* (1734, expanded edition in 1736) was both widely read and translated in Spain.[34] As the former secretary of John Law, Melon defended his mentor's system, even while diverging from the infamous Scotsman in some respects. They shared, nonetheless, the conviction that to become wealthy and powerful a nation had to do more than simply pursue bullion; it had to trade and cultivate useful subjects.

Even though Macanaz had been proposing similar anti-bullionist ideas since the 1720s, it is clear that by the 1740s the work of Melon had become one of the main catalysts for rethinking Spain's commercial system. The author of the *Nuevo sistema*, whether Macanaz or someone else, often alluded to a certain 'philosopher' who critiqued Spain's insatiable desire for bullion; Melon was probably the philosopher in question. Moreover, in 1743 the first partial translation of Melon's work made its appearance in the Spanish press: Theodoro Ventura de Argumossa Gándara's *Erudicción política*.[35] And, while the *Erudicción* was not a faithful translation of the entirety of Melon's work, it surely carried many of the essential messages that the *Essai politique* had put forward, among which we can include both a conjectural history concerning the origins of competitive commercial society and the idea that 'one of the greatest mistakes that exist is to believe that the countries that abound in mines of gold and silver are the richest'.[36] Macanaz similarly asserted that with Spain's unrelenting pursuit of precious metals, 'the true treasure of the state, which is man, has disappeared with this cruel task'.[37] Indeed, Spanish ministers, like the rest of the European theorists of commercial society, were becoming profoundly intrigued by this anti-bullionist perspective, whose main suggestion was that wealth stemmed from labour, not money.

One of Melon's most fundamental innovations was to link the anti-bullionism of his predecessors with a comparative analysis of imperial commercial systems. Melon, following some incipient ideas developed by Locke, suggested that an unrelenting pursuit of bullion was not simply bad monetary policy, but that it captured the logic behind a detrimental kind of empire, whose sole goal was to conquer and subdue. This kind of empire was overcome by what he called the spirit of conquest. While the Romans had been the earliest example of this kind of empire, Spain, of course, was the clearest contemporary illustration. Spain's imperial apparatus was founded on an irrational and obsessive pursuit of mines. Indeed, while Spain was worried about extracting bullion from its American mines, the rest of Europe was reaping most of the benefits of its commerce. In his *De l'esprit des lois* (1748), Montesquieu would later reiterate the same idea. Decades later, Adam Smith repeated many of the insights that Melon had already elaborated in 1736, proposing that 'a project of conquest gave occasion to all the establishments of the Spaniards in those newly discovered countries. The motive which excited them to this conquest was a project of gold and silver mines.'[38]

The idea of the spirit of conquest served Macanaz well when he designed his new system of government. Like Melon in 1736, in the 1740s, Macanaz wrote that 'the lust for mines came about after the conquests'.[39] Macanaz, however, did not go as far as Melon, who suggested that Spaniards had destroyed Amerindians deliberately in order to take over American mines. For Macanaz, the near evisceration of Amerindians was the product of war, not of Spain's deliberate attempt to annihilate all natives. But he was critical of Spaniards' actions in the New World, nonetheless. He argued that 'el espíritu guerrero' (the warring spirit) that predominated during the reign of Charles V had been necessary at the time because only a few Spaniards faced the challenge of battling millions of Indians. After the Conquest, however, this warring spirit had become obsolete, in spite of Spaniards' inability to recognize this.[40] As Macanaz suggested, during the Conquest, 'it was necessary to utilize all the severity of war in order to intimidate and contain those barbarians [Indians] with the impression of Spanish courage'. But, this warring spirit was taken too far 'until killing the wretched Indians'.[41] 'To inopportunely conserve the spirit of conquest, and to prefer dominion over the benefits and utilities of commerce ... ruined the accomplished conquests,' he continued.[42] In sum, consumed by a 'warring spirit', Spaniards had failed to understand that trade was more useful than conquest and the possession of vast mines.[43]

While Macanaz never stated explicitly why he had placed his faith entirely on commerce, his reasons are not difficult to adduce, especially considering that he shared many of the views of his intellectual interlocutors. Melon, for instance, began his analysis about the relationship between commerce and power by discussing the historical origins of commercial society.[44] For Melon, the most important historical turning point took place when the nations of the world ceased to trade in order to obtain necessities, a kind of trade which they defined as barter or reciprocal commerce. But, while commercial reciprocity could only take place among equals, once societies became unequal, reciprocity ceased to be possible, and competition and rivalry became the rules of the day.[45] Macanaz certainly shared this perspective but added that Spain had an advantage over every other empire: large colonial markets. Spanish ministers had until then failed to realize this key advantage. Even though Spain had 'the most abundant consumption in the world within the king's dominions ... only twenty percent of what our Indies consume stems from the products of Spain'.[46] That Spain was handing out its markets to foreign nations was no trivial matter, for 'powerful nations are rich or powerful only in relation to one another'.[47] In foregoing its American markets, then, Spain was not simply losing wealth but also ceding power to its competitors.

How, then, could Spain improve its trade in order to bring about economic improvement and outperform its competitors? For Macanaz, the main culprit of Spain's inability to control its own colonial markets was the old *Carrera de Indias*, which he saw as a commercial system that basically stimulated British and French industry. Ever since the beginning of the Spanish War of Succession in 1700, the British and the French had been vying for control over the old fleets and galleon system. In theory, the Spanish-controlled *Carrera de Indias* was supposed to supply the manufactures that the New World needed. In practice, however, the peninsula's manufacturing base did not have the capacity to supply the New World with even the most basic necessities. This meant that Spanish-authorized merchants had to rely on foreign goods from foreign merchants to carry out the *Carrera de Indias* and the commercial fairs that took place in Xalapa and Portobelo. Up until the Treaty of Utrecht in 1713, the French had enjoyed significant advantages. But in 1713, Spain was forced to recognize the presence of a yearly *Navio de Permiso* carrying 500 tons of British goods and the *Asiento* granting the British a monopoly over the provisioning of slaves in Spanish America. Over the course of the first half of the eighteenth century, the French and the British would continue fighting to conquer Spanish American markets. If not through legal means, as was the case in 1713, the British and French both sought a portion of American markets by engaging in illicit trade (contraband).[48] Gaining control over Spain's American markets, hence, was Macanaz's main goal.

Macanaz's alternative to the old *Carrera de Indias* was *comercio libre*, which he saw as a true panacea for Spain's ills. The improvement of commerce had also been part of the intellectual arsenal of previous ministers, but Macanaz, unlike his predecessors, linked commerce to freedom. As he insisted, it was of utmost importance 'to think of liberty as the soul of commerce, without which it [commerce] could not prosper nor live'.[49] It was for this very reason that Macanaz thought that the old fleet and galleon system produced *estanco* (stagnation or lack of circulation) and prevented the empire from harnessing its productive powers in concert. In fact, commercial liberty 'is the soul of all the improvements which we argue will occur in Spain's agriculture, manufactures and other significant matters'.[50] Most important for the purposes of erecting a commercial empire was the fact that with commercial freedom 'illicit commerce will be in great measure eliminated, particularly in all of those types of textiles [or products] that will be produced in Spain'.[51] In eliminating contraband, then, the metropole would gain control of its American markets.

Naturally, Macanaz's project for *comercio libre* entailed significant reforms to Spain's commercial system. Rather than yearly fleets and galleons departing from Cádiz, Macanaz suggested that Spaniards from all kingdoms and provinces of the peninsula should be allowed to trade directly with American ports. Spaniards, hence, would be able to depart to the Indies during any time of the year and from any Spanish port in *navios sueltos* (unattached vessels) or convoys.[52] Macanaz's new system must have seemed chimerical to many. Indeed, he was suggesting not only that Spaniards should be able to travel freely to the Americas to trade, but also that no duties should be charged upon departure. Here was the most threatening aspect of Macanaz's system, for it apparently tinkered with royal rents. But Macanaz was not foolish, and he knew that he had to assure the king that his coffers would remain healthy. Hence, he suggested that duties would be collected only upon arrival from the Indies. In fact, because duties would now be collected upon return, Macanaz suggested that all ships had to re-enter Spain through La Coruña for subjects of northern Spain, and through Cádiz for subjects from the rest of the peninsula.

Macanaz was not interested in regaining control over American markets simply to siphon bullion to the peninsula. Since he thought that wealth came from productive labour and agriculture, Macanaz instead suggested that it was necessary to think of commerce 'as the principal foundation of all the other interests of the Monarchy, for it [commerce] revitalizes agriculture, the arts, factories and the manufactures of industry'.[53] Later in the work, Macanaz repeated the aforementioned maxim even more forcefully. He stated that commerce should 'be the instrument and means to foment the other branches that constitute the wealth of a nation and that create its prosperity'.[54] In sum, deploying the notion of a 'new system', Macanaz held that *comercio libre* was the basis for 'good politics and reason of state', in an age where commerce and economic improvement, not money or military capability, determined the relative power of a nation.[55]

Conclusion

Macanaz's new system had many more dimensions, among which we can cite the institution of a new administrative apparatus in the New World. However, we should keep in mind a few of the most important tenets of commercial empire that Macanaz put forward in the 1740s: (1) to become powerful Spain had to acquire markets, not bullion, (2) Spain had an abundant source of markets in the colonies, and (3) the best way to control colonial markets was to implement *comercio libre* between the metropole and the colonies. According to Macanaz, what would come about as a result of this new government was a highly integrated commercial system in which the metropole would use American raw materials to produce cheap manufactures, which it could then use to control American markets and become the most powerful commercial state of Europe. With these proposals, Macanaz was not simply encouraging his ministerial peers to reform the empire. More precisely, he was calling for the creation of a Spanish commercial empire as a replacement for an obsolete composite monarchy.

To conclude, a few words about Macanaz's economic ideas are in order. The fact that he advocated for free internal commerce but retained the allegedly mercantilist concern with the balance of trade has done much to perplex historians who have sought to categorize him as either a mercantilist or a liberal thinker. To resolve this seeming paradox, some have resorted to unholy concoctions like neo-mercantilism or proto-liberalism. This chapter has tried to show that none of these categories do justice to what Macanaz was attempting to do. To fully grasp the *Nuevo sistema*'s proposals, it is necessary to understand them in the context of the bitter imperial commercial rivalries of the eighteenth century, the rise of political economy as a science of power and the polycentric Hispanic political culture that Macanaz sought to replace with his new imperial programme. Thus, Macanaz's new system of imperial government is best understood as a theory of commercial empire that came to fruition as a result of his interaction with some of the most important writings on political economy in the eighteenth century, particularly the work of Jean-François Melon. This, in turn, suggests that political economy did not simply serve imperial purposes, although this was certainly the case as well. Rather, in the Hispanic world, political economy was the intellectual seed that gave imperialism life.

Notes

1 José del Campillo y Cossío, *Nuevo sistema de gobierno económico para la América* (Mérida: Universidad de los Andes, Facultad de Humanidades y Educación, 1971), 67. While there are many versions of this text, including some in manuscript form, I will cite this modern edition throughout the chapter.
2 Ibid., 77.
3 While most historians have assumed that José del Campillo y Cossío was responsible for writing the *Nuevo sistema*, its most likely author was Melchor Rafael de Macanaz, one of the most prolific thinkers and ministers during the reign of Phillip V. I will explain the significance of this fact later in the chapter.

4   Campillo, *Nuevo sistema*, 68.
5   I owe this formulation in part to Sophus A. Reinert. His rigorous treatment of the imperial and competitive/political origins of political economy has shaped many of the arguments of this chapter. Sophus A. Reinert, *Translating Empire: Emulation and the Origins of Political Economy* (Cambridge: Harvard University Press, 2011); Sophus A. Reinert and Pernille Røge, *The Political Economy of Empire in the Early Modern World* (Basingstoke: Palgrave Macmillan, 2013).
6   For classic accounts of the Spanish empire, see Clarence Henry Haring, *The Spanish Empire in America* (San Diego: Harcourt Brace Jovanovich, 1985); William S. Maltby, *The Rise and Fall of the Spanish Empire* (Basingstoke: Palgrave Macmillan, 2009); John H. Elliott, *Imperial Spain, 1469–1716* (London: Penguin, 2002).
7   J. H. Elliott, 'A Europe of Composite Monarchies', *Past & Present* 137, no. 1 (1992): 48–71.
8   Pedro Cardim, Tamar Herzog, José Javier Ruiz Ibañez and Gaetano Sabatini, eds, *Polycentric Monarchies: How Did Early Modern Spain and Portugal Achieve and Maintain a Global Hegemony?* (Eastbourne: Sussex Academic Press, 2012).
9   For the older interpretation of the monarchy's flexible bureaucracy, see John Leddy Phelan, 'Authority and Flexibility in the Spanish Imperial Bureaucracy', *Administrative Science Quarterly* 5, no. 1 (1960): 47–65; Colin M. MacLachlan, *Spain's Empire in The New World: The Role of Ideas in Institutional and Social Change* (Berkeley: University of California Press, 1988).
10 On the jurisdictional nature of the Spanish Monarchy, see Pablo Fernández Albaladejo, *Fragmentos de monarquía: Trabajos de historia política* (Madrid: Alianza Editorial, 1992); Jean-Frédéric Schaub, *Le Portugal au temps du Comte-Duc d'Olivares, 1621–1640: Le conflit de juridictions comme exercice de la politique* (Madrid: Casa de Velázquez, 2001).
11 Campillo, *Nuevo sistema*, 77.
12 Ibid., 80.
13 Scholars have sought to explain the *Nuevo sistema* as a project that merely reflected either mercantilist or pragmatic convictions. Miguel Artola, 'Campillo y las reformas de Carlos III', *Revista de Indias* 12 (1952): 50–79; Josefina Cintrón Tiryakian, 'Campillo's Pragmatic New System: A Mercantile and Utilitarian Approach to Indian Reform in Spanish Colonies of the Eighteenth Century', *History of Political Economy* 10, no. 2 (1978): 233–57.
14 There are many versions of this manuscript at the BNE. See, for example, Mss. 10543 V.1. For the manuscript at the BPR, see Mss. II/1132.
15 Bernando Ward, *Proyecto económico, en que se proponen varias providencias, dirigidas a promover los intereses de España, con los medios y fondos necesarios para su plantificación* (Madrid: Por D. Joachin Ibarra, Impresor de Cámara de S.M., 1779).
16 José del Campillo y Cossío, 'Lo que hay de más y menos en España', in *Dos escritos políticos*, ed. Dolores Mateos Dorado (Oviedo: Junta General del Principado de Asturias, 1993), 95.
17 Campillo, *Nuevo sistema*, 60.
18 On Patiño, see Ildefonso Pulido Bueno, *Jose Patiño: El inicio del gobierno político-económico ilustrado en España* (Huelva: Artes Gráficas Andaluzas, 1998).
19 For biographical information about Campillo, see the critical introductions written by the editors of the *Nuevo sistema* and *Dos escritos políticos*.
20 Barbara H. Stein and Stanley J. Stein, *Silver, Trade, and War Spain and America in the Making of Early Modern Europe* (Baltimore: Johns Hopkins University Press, 2000), 221–26.

21 IVDJ-Mss. 26-III-39 – Macanaz, *Nuevo sixtema económico para el perfecto govierno de la América* (1719).
22 RAH-Sign. 9-26-7/4998 – Macanaz, *Discurso sobre la America española* (ca. 1747), fn. 82.
23 Kenneth J. Andrien, 'The Noticias Secretas de America and the Construction of a Governing Ideology for the Spanish American Empire', *Colonial Latin American Review* 7, no. 2 (1998): 175–92.
24 And even while he supported the continuation of the council of Castile, he did so by proposing fundamental changes to the functioning of this old governing body. See Concepción de Castro, 'La Nueva Planta del Consejo de Castilla y los pedimentos de Macanaz', *Cuadernos de Historia Moderna* 37 (2012): 23–42.
25 For a biography of Macanaz, see Carmen Martín Gaite, *El proceso de Macanaz: Historia de un empapelamiento* (Madrid: Siruela, 2011).
26 Melchor Rafael de Macanaz, *Auxilios para bien gobernar una monarquía católica* (Madrid: Imprenta de D. Antonio Espinosa, 1789 [ca. 1722]), 41. The original manuscript sits at the Biblioteca Nacional de España.
27 Ibid., 43.
28 Ibid., 47.
29 Ibid., 65.
30 Carl Wennerlind, *Casualties of Credit: The English Financial Revolution, 1620–1720* (Cambridge: Harvard University Press, 2011), ch. 2.
31 Andrea Finkelstein, *Harmony and the Balance an Intellectual History of Seventeenth-Century English Economic Thought* (Ann Arbor: University of Michigan Press, 2000).
32 On John Law, see Antoin E. Murphy, *John Law: Economic Theorist and Policy-Maker* (Oxford: Clarendon Press, 1997).
33 John Law, *Money and Trade Considered: With a Proposal for Supplying the Nation with Money* (Glasgow: R. & A. Foulis, 1750 [1705]). Law had developed his ideas on land banks in more detail in an earlier work. See John Law, *John Law's 'Essay on a Land Bank,'* ed. Antoin E. Murphy (Dublin: Aeon Publishing, 1994 [1704]).
34 On Melon's influence in Spain, see Jesús Astigarraga, 'La dérangeante découverte de l'autre: Traductions et adaptations espagnoles de l'*Essai politique sur le commerce* (1734) de Jean-François Melon', *Revue d'histoire moderne et contemporaine* 57, no. 1 (2010): 91–118.
35 Argumossa Gándara, *Erudicción política, despertador sobre el comercio, agricultura, y manufacturas, con avisos de buena policía, y aumento del Real Erario* (Madrid, 1743).
36 Ibid., 1.
37 Campillo, *Nuevo sistema*, 74.
38 See Adam Smith, *The Wealth of Nations* (New York: Bantam Dell, 2003 [1776]), ch. 7, part 2, 715.
39 Campillo, *Nuevo sistema*, 74.
40 Ibid., 72.
41 Ibid., 73.
42 Ibid., 72.
43 For an elaboration of this perspective, see ibid., 143–44, 209.
44 Melon's book, in turn, was following the steps of his mentor John Law, who also developed a theory about the historical origins of commercial society. See Law, *Money and Trade Considered*, 6–19.
45 Melon famously illustrated this point with a conjectural history of commercial society, in which three islands of equal economic standing gradually became unequal and

began to compete for power. Jean-François Melon, *Essai politique sur le commerce* (1736), 2–9.
46 Campillo, *Nuevo sistema*, 70.
47 Ibid., 71.
48 Geoffrey J. Walker, *Spanish Politics and Imperial Trade, 1700–1789* (Bloomington: Indiana University Press, 1979); John Robert Fisher, *The Economic Aspects of Spanish Imperialism in America: 1492–1810* (Liverpool: Liverpool University Press, 1997).
49 Campillo, *Nuevo sistema*, 94.
50 Ibid., 146.
51 Ibid., 149.
52 Ibid., 151.
53 Ibid., 95.
54 Ibid., 153.
55 Ibid., 156.

Chapter 2

POOR MAO'S ALMANACK? EMPIRE, POLITICAL ECONOMY AND THE TRANSFORMATION OF SOCIAL SCIENCE

Sophus A. Reinert[1]

Writing a memorandum for the Austrian authorities in Habsburg Milan in the late 1760s arguing for the need to institute a *ministro di Economia*, and no doubt promoting his own candidacy for just such a post, the Lombard reformer Francesco Maria Carpani observed how the 'great Monarchies' of his age had come to 'embrace diverse Provinces, Realms, and Nations, and, proportionally to their extension, require that the administration of their finances be simplified' for 'expansion necessitates greater expenses'. Yet the political-economic problem of empire he confronted was not merely quantitative, in that larger territories required more work to manage, but qualitative, in that the administrative work itself became more complex:

> The Earth is divided into different climates and situations, landlocked and maritime, flat and mountainous, and mankind (the Philosophers unite everyone according to the same principles) differs according to climates and governments in thinking, in language, in customs, and in laws, the Codes of all nations emerging from the different events, circumstances, needs, and revolutions suffered in the past. Monarchies extend in various climates from South to North, and over maritime and landlocked nations, inhabiting high mountains and vast plains, which one cannot force to think the same way, to speak the same language, subject to the same laws, bend to the same customs, diets, and dress.[2]

Imperial polities, in short, had expanded far beyond natural and cultural confines widely understood, simultaneously necessitating the accumulation of local contextual knowledge regarding unfamiliar places and the development of administrative procedures able to harness them for centrally defined purposes of what Carpani called 'political economy', whether in terms of infrastructure, institutionalized taxation or industrial policy. The city-state of Milan owed its historical wealth to a sustained governmental capacity to capitalize on the varied resources and regional specialities of Lombardy, and the problem of 'political economy' facing the immense territorial polities of his age lay, Carpani argued, in replicating that success in a vastly larger and, importantly, more varied world. His point, as such, was less to 'simplify' the economic administration of Habsburg lands – encompassing at least fifteen languages and six recognized religions – than to make their daunting diversity manageable.[3] He had no doubts that 'the Economic Science makes richer Conquests, than that of Arms', which itself anyway had come to depend only on 'money' but it required the information management of a truly imperial political economy to stave off decline and usurpation at the hands of one's 'enemies'.[4]

The problem adumbrated by Carpani haunted legislators across the European world, and often with even greater urgency. The lands he had in mind might have been vast and varied, but the Habsburg project after all remained resolutely continental at the time compared to the great thalassocracies of the age; its first, and short-lived, overseas colony was established on the Nicobar Islands only in 1778.[5] Whether observing regional realities or vast oceanic empires, early modern European writers demonstrated a remarkably widespread preoccupation with the role of contextual knowledge in political economy and its relationship to questions of power and empire, with examples ranging from the Castilian institution of the *visita* to Faustian undertakings in the tradition of the Piedmontese renegade Jesuit Giovanni Botero's *Universal Relations*, in contexts ranging from late Renaissance Naples to the Scottish Enlightenment and the New World in the Age of Revolutions.[6] The development of a codified discipline of political economy in effect cannot be understood without reference to Europe's process of interstate competition and context of overseas expansion.[7] Crisply annotating his personal copy of the anonymous but soberly self-descriptive *True Constitutional Means for Putting an End to the Dispute Between Great-Britain and the American Colonies*, which was published in 1769, Benjamin Franklin, who was soon to become a Founding Father of the United States, lamented the arrogance of certain British pamphleteers in proposing to legislate for the farthest-flung corners of their empire: the 'folly,' as he put it, 'of thinking to make Laws for a Country so unknown'.[8]

Not surprisingly, the rich historical relationship between empire and knowledge has been the subject of sustained attention by scholars in recent years, and what follows aims to contribute to this historiography by considering more carefully the tortuous emergence and eventual transformation of the term 'social science' around the turn of the eighteenth century against the backdrop of imperial preoccupations with knowledge and political economy in the early modern European world. Though the phraseology of 'social science' is habitually associated with the work of Émile Durkheim and Max Weber around the turn of the nineteenth century, it originally developed out of a very different Enlightenment concern with problems of war, empire, injustice and schemes precisely like those elucidated by Carpani. Indeed, social science initially adopted not merely the concerns but also the analytical language of earlier political economy. The term's first known occurrence was in the first edition of Abbé Emmanuel Sieyès' 1789 pamphlet *What is the Third Estate?*, and it came to enjoy currency at the time as a moral guide to the new world order and even a synonym for politics in the wake of the French

Revolution.⁹ And, though meant to overcome influential traditions of 'jealous' political economy and pave the way for a brighter future for mankind as such – a larger project of which the *Declaration of the Rights of Man and of the Citizen* was a crucial product[10] – the term was quickly hijacked by the very national prejudices it sought to transcend. Indeed, it might even inadvertently have aggravated the pathology of global imbalances it sought to alleviate. And, as it turns out, the very same Franklin who lamented British intellectual overextension played a crucial if hitherto largely unknown role in this process.

Early modern political economy was certainly a polyvalent discipline, but it was conceptually bound to imperial logics even when, as in the small states of central and Northern Europe, it was seen explicitly as providing an alternative to territorial empires. A core tenet of the administrative tradition known as cameralism was, in effect, that the qualitative improvement of one's territories and the wise management of one's affairs might make worldly flourishing achievable without resort to violent conquests.[11] Where many, if not most, saw a golden ticket to temporal greatness in the dreadful interaction of economic efficiency and spatial expansion, others framed their visions of political economy in precisely such anti-imperial terms, seeing in intensive economic competition a bloodless alternative to conquests.[12] But even the most peaceful doctrine at the time had, in one way or another, to contend with the existence, and threat, of de jure and de facto empires. The relationship between political economy and imperialism was thus hardly transparent, and certainly not uniform, but a clear impetus is identifiable in many of the more influential works of the period towards their synergy; success in great power politics required the mobilization of resources drawn from imperial dominions, formal or informal, which in turn demanded careful studies of foreign lands and contextually calibrated policies to bear fruit.[13] In the eyes of thinkers and statesmen across the Old World and its imperial corollaries, the lethally competitive process of early modern state-formation necessitated ever more exhaustive and efficient quests for funds and resources to invest in industries and pay for troops and navies. Empires were the subjects and often the goals of political economy, but simultaneously the discipline's sites for practical and theoretical observation, experimentation and application. The connection between knowledge, political economy and empire was, in a particularly callous if popular expression, self-reinforcing.[14]

Political economy – as a theoretical discipline and as an administrative practice – was in other words refined by the very imperialism it facilitated, as encounters, examples, experiences and anecdotes from Europe's imperial past and present provided the conceptual raw materials for the codification of territorial governance on a planetary scale.[15] This vision of knowledge as an enabler of empire was, in one form or another, institutionalized across the European world, and its manifest success might in hindsight have obfuscated its conceptual novelty. A case from the very origins of the imperial arms race in early modern Europe, that of the ill-fated English Muscovy Company, might serve to remind us of what was at stake in the transition. The company was chartered to establish trading relations via the yet undiscovered Northeast Passage to Russia and China in the 1550s as a means of counteracting an ongoing economic crisis and launch England's imperial project, and Edward VI and the merchants of London sent Sir Hugh Willoughby and three ships laden with unsold textiles northwards in 1553.[16] Willoughby had, in accordance with contemporary patronage practices, been chosen because he was 'trusty and faithfull', but odds are he had never set foot on a ship before, let alone seen the aurora borealis, and apparently nobody had told him that Novaya Zemlya might get cold in December.[17] Though one ship indeed made landfall near present-day Arkhangelsk, Willoughby and two ships sailed aimlessly around the Barents Sea before attempting to winter on the Kola Peninsula.[18] Russian fishermen eventually found their frozen corpses with the spring thaw, still bundled in the colourful woollen cloths they had hoped to peddle in far-away Cathay.[19] A 1576 Admiralty hearing put the problem succinctly; 'for lacke of knowledge', Willoughby's crews 'were frozen to deathe'.[20]

Trade, navigation and empire, in short, required – and in turn acquired – contextual knowledge. A similar process was observable in the neighbouring 'sciences of man' as Europeans learnt to look out into the world in order to look deep inside themselves, a moment in intellectual history of which the myth of the noble savage and nineteenth-century anthropology might be the most durable relics.[21] Needless to say, these were lessons that early modern imperialists – and English ones most successfully of all – would take to heart in the coming years.[22] Just as the need for success in imperial political economy was explained in terms of existential competition with 'enemies', as Carpani put it, so political economy itself was conceptualized in emulative terms at the time. Not only did writers invest national and regional pride in questions of theoretical primacy and innovation, but also the popularity of national discourses of political economy in foreign markets came to be correlated with perceived comparative successes in imperial rivalries. The number of translations of political economy between European languages exploded in the wake of the imperial and truly global Seven Years War, and, in absolute terms, the discipline itself came to occupy a progressively larger share of the European book market in the second half of the eighteenth century (part and parcel of what Steven L. Kaplan and I have called 'The Economic Turn').[23] There can, in short, be no doubt that the mainstream of eighteenth-century political economy within and between European states was galvanized by this emulative imperial discourse.[24]

But there were of course multiple and often competing forms of 'empire' operational in the early modern European imagination, from political references to empires whether British, Spanish or Vandal through more theoretical concepts such as James Harrington's 'Empire of the Lawes' to ever more metaphorical usages like John Dryden's 'Empire of Love' and simultaneously imperative and abstract dominions such as 'the empire of the Devil' warned against by theologians.[25] And the same subject could, synchronously, be the locus of very different forms of imperial authority. Papal political economists of the late eighteenth century were, for example, puzzled, if also empowered, by the multiplicities of empires at their disposal, and by how they could make up for the Holy See's shrinking territorial claims through the expansion of its spiritual and economic 'empires'.[26]

Endless debates similarly ensued in early modern Europe over what exactly one could claim an empire over, most famously perhaps with regards to dominions over the sea.[27] It was in this imperial maelstrom that 'social science' took shape, its millenarian aim to establish an empire to end all others, an 'empire', as many contemporaries began referring to it as, 'of humanity'.[28]

This underlying conceptual nebulosity of empire is itself significant for appreciating eighteenth-century 'social science' and its relationship to contemporary practices of imperial political economy. For, much like empires, economic works too could take many forms across many genres, from the theoretical to the prescriptive, from the hermetic to the popular and 'social science' related to them all, albeit in different ways and for different purposes.[29] As Michael Sonenscher has shown, the meta-discipline of 'social science' emerged in late-eighteenth-century France out of timeless debates over the just relationship between morality and politics that had been galvanized by revolutionary concerns with human rights, yet its precise meaning long remained elusive. The Parisian journal *L'Historien* noted in 1795 that though 'we do not have a very clear idea of the difference between social science and political economy', one could perhaps 'think of political economy as social science applied to administration and legislation of agriculture, manufacturing, trade, public works, navigation, taxation, or all the means required to make families subsist and nations prosper'.[30]

Scholars, the present one included, have tended to think of political economy largely in terms of economic theories and policies relating to the first part of *L'Historien*'s definition – in other words, that part most closely relevant for Carpani's project or Adam Smith's definition of 'political economy' as 'a branch of the science of a statesman or legislator' (what Joseph A. Schumpeter referred to as 'the history of economic analysis').[31] Yet, the second part of the definition, 'the means required to make families subsist and nations prosper', also related to questions of political economy, specifically to the vexing relationship, explicitly explored since antiquity, between *oikonomia*, the classical tradition of household management, on the one hand, and the economic management of a polity, on the other – the bridge, so to speak, between Xenophon's *Oeconomicus* and *Poroi*, his treatise on individual household management, on the one hand, and his proposal for increasing Athenian revenues, on the other.[32]

Publications at both ends of such political-economic 'social science' were increasingly circulated in the eighteenth-century world, but on surprisingly different scales and for rather divergent scopes that are relevant for the problematique at hand. On the high end of the spectrum, Adam Smith's 1776 *Inquiry into the Nature and Causes of the Wealth of Nations* would by 1850 have seen a total of 94 editions, 107 if one counts truncated editions, in at least 8 languages.[33] By comparison, the undoubtedly most popular work on the other end, Benjamin Franklin's 1757 *The Way to Wealth*, saw more than 1,100 appearances in 26 languages by the mid-nineteenth century.[34] Indeed, it was so popular that no work relating to economic habits or ideas would be close to matching its dissemination before the 1964 publication of the *Quotations from Chairman Mao Tse-tung*.[35] To present Franklin's short piece on self-help, published in the last ever edition of his celebrated *Almanack* under the title 'Father Abraham's Speech', as an effort in 'social science' might seem overly convenient, but it was indeed presented as the exemplar of precisely the lower end of 'social science' devoted to 'a wise economy' even in the second half of the nineteenth century.[36]

An assemblage of aphorisms collected and intertwined with a moralizing narrative, *The Way to Wealth* was composed in response to the fiscal pressures of the Seven Years War and identified the path to individual, communal and plausibly even worldly melioration in a personal commitment to virtues of industry and thrift.[37] Franklin's contribution to the discipline that soon would be known as 'social science' therefore stood at an oblique angle to the more theoretical traditions of 'political economy' that dominated European debates in the eighteenth century, not to mention Carpani's concerns regarding the importance of contextual knowledge for the political economy of empire. In fact, one of the reasons for the longevity and success of Franklin's particular vision of virtuous capitalist behaviour was its ability precisely to transcend the sort of circumstantial nuance he himself thought necessary for practical political economy. The extraordinary international dissemination of *The Way to Wealth* represented the empire of an idea of human peace and progress based on virtuous economic pursuits rather than a territorial empire as such, and the extent to which important future readers of Franklin's work would emphasize its anti-imperial nature is striking given the author's own vexed adherence to imperialism.[38] And, given the revolutionary nature of eighteenth-century 'social science', it was a far better representative of that still negotiated and contested discipline than more traditional bestsellers of theoretical political economy at the time.

The late Robert Wokler often emphasized the extent to which this 'central science of modernity' reneged on the Enlightenment's values during the course of the nineteenth century, ceasing to be a 'science of legislation for the promotion of human happiness' built on a discourse of 'rights' and aimed at 'changing the world' to instead become a 'modern social science' set on the preservation of the status quo.[39] This story has, so far, only been told in relation to French history and thinkers, but at the time it was equally valid for other parts of Europe as well, particularly so on the Italian Peninsula. In the wake of the Jacobin uprisings in Italy, for example, a paradox emerged from the very core of Italian political economy when some began to sense the discipline's inherent definitional contradictions as it had been pursued in early modern Europe. Its laudable quest for human welfare and happiness had been derailed by narrow national prejudices, and the very ruthlessness of international competition the discipline seemed to rely on and encourage by necessity undermined the well-being of humanity as such. 'Social science' was a means of squaring the proverbial circle. And although they offered new insights, these new social scientists drew on a rich intellectual tradition stretching back to the conceptualization of political economy as a science of happiness derived from a general notion of human rights in Italy.[40]

It was in this context that the Salernitan Jacobin revolutionary Matteo Angelo Galdi opened his extraordinary and entirely neglected 1797–98 *Political-Economic Relationships Between Free Nations* by observing that 'social science currently shapes the study of all true friends of the liberty of nations', explaining that it aimed at nothing less than 'overthrowing the monstrous edifice of tyranny and superstition, and restoring to man all the energy to which he by nature is susceptible, to accompany him on the great career that he has left to go to in the state of happiness'. The new discipline of 'social science' was a discipline born from 'the great revolution' that finally would put 'universal public rights and the rights of peoples' into practice, crucially by overcoming Europe's imperialist past and the 'bloody wars' that had 'immolated millions of men' over 'some uninhabited reefs in the East and West Indies', to put an end to the 'eternal state of war' and 'reciprocal jealousies' tearing mankind apart. The first task of the new social science therefore lay in capitalizing on the 'destruction' and 'most violent crises' of the revolutionary period to provide a more solid foundation of the 'great social relationships, that is the politico-economic relationships, between nations'. Only this could pave the way for 'justice', 'eternal peace' and 'universal happiness' in the world.[41]

The brave new world violently brought about by the French Revolution and its global reverberations necessitated a 'social science' that accommodated the highs and lows of political economy – the Smiths and the Franklins so to speak – within a rigorous ethical framework in which projects for individual and national betterment did not come at the expense of humanity writ large. There was something undeniably millenarian about this movement, and as the nineteenth century progressed, writers came to adopt a far more operational definition of social science. Though there were calls for 'political economy' to 'give way to social science', and others warned of confusing the two and reducing everything to a science of 'happiness', the secular trend from revolutionary idealism to disenchanted pragmatism was evident.[42] By the time Francesco Trinchera annotated the bestselling lectures of the Carraran-Genevan revolutionary politician and academic Pellegrino Rossi in 1843, 'political economy' was indeed absorbed by 'social science', but its aim had become that of establishing the 'relationships that exist between the duties imposed by the national economy, and the high mission of the State'.[43] Not only did political economy as such emerge as the pre-eminent social science, but, in the minds of many, it had also come to usurp it entirely.

As the Sicilian economist Placido de Luca had put it, 'the triumph of social science' lay in 'reconciling' the principles of 'individuality' and 'society', yet only for the purposes of the 'preservation and improvement of all the parts constituting the social body'.[44] The problem, of course, lay in defining the boundaries of said body, which quickly had receded from Galdi's expansive vision of a species-wide global body social to the narrower confines of international competition that had characterized European history and, under the aegis of nationalism, would mar it so starkly in the nineteenth and twentieth centuries. Works such as Franklin's *The Way to Wealth* played an intriguing role in this process because of their inherently protean qualities. Poor Richard's exhortation to be diligent and frugal could be – and indeed *was* – marshalled to the cause of both the old and new conceptions of 'social science', to further the cause of cosmopolitan improvement as well as national greatness, and his industrious vision was quickly emulated for the same imperial reasons that had driven earlier notions of political economy.

Not only that, but the geographical dissemination of its ethos similarly suggests that the sort of 'social science' originally intended to attenuate global differences might have helped exacerbate them instead. The international discourse of political economy, improvement and industriousness indeed remained a predominantly 'Western' phenomenon in the period before 1850.[45] Franklin's work, which in one reading might be considered the most widely published statement of peaceful industry at the time, circumnavigated the world, but though it played a role in the globalizing process of the time, it was itself far from globalized.[46] *The Way to Wealth* appeared in Breton, Bulgarian, Croatian, Czech, Danish, Dutch, English, Finnish, French, Gaelic, German, Greek, Hungarian, Icelandic, Italian, Norwegian, Polish, Portuguese, Romanian, Romansch, Russian, Slovak, Slovenian, Spanish, Swedish and Welsh, but seemingly in no non-European language. Geographically speaking, *The Way to Wealth* was mostly published in the industrializing parts of the European world; out of more than 1,100 known appearances in the period, only five were south of the equator. Even at their most anti-imperial, in short, the subject matters of political economy and 'social science' remained far more global than their disciplinary diffusion; while capitalism increasingly connected people and resources around the world in the eighteenth and nineteenth centuries, its ethos long remained a prerogative of the industrializing core. And where some, in the tradition of Jean-Baptiste Say, hailed Franklin's doctrine of 'social science' as a means to transcend the logics of empire, others explicitly hailed it as a way of making subjects more industrious and thus getting ahead in international competition, with virtuous workers serving as weapons of great power politics.[47] It was in this spirit that *The Way to Wealth*'s physical publications eventually became truly global in the second half of the nineteenth century. A Japanese translation of *The Way to Wealth* was published at the time of the country's own period of industrialization and attempt to find a place in the sun during the Meiji Restoration, and a dual French-Chinese edition appeared in Beijing in 1884.[48]

And it was perhaps in China that the paradox of Enlightenment 'social science' found its most extreme expression two centuries later. Though, given the unexpected and subterranean paths of intellectual history, it is perhaps not entirely surprising that the chapter devoted to the ethics of labour in Mao's *Little Red* came eerily close to echoing Franklin's *The Way to Wealth*. Communist Mao's regard for ostensibly capitalist Franklin might seem paradoxical, but he repeatedly extolled that mercurial Founding Father in public speeches for being 'self-taught' and making great scientific contributions without formal academic qualifications – a 'newspaperseller, yet he discovered electricity'.[49] More intriguingly, however, Mao admitted to having read, in his youth, of '[heroes] of capitalism' such as 'Confucius, Napoleon, Washington, Peter the Great', and so on, adding,

> I had also read a biography of Franklin. He came from a poor family; afterwards, he became a writer, and also conducted experiments on electricity. ... He talked about man being a tool-making animal. ... Afterwards, Marx put forward the view that man is a tool-making animal.[50]

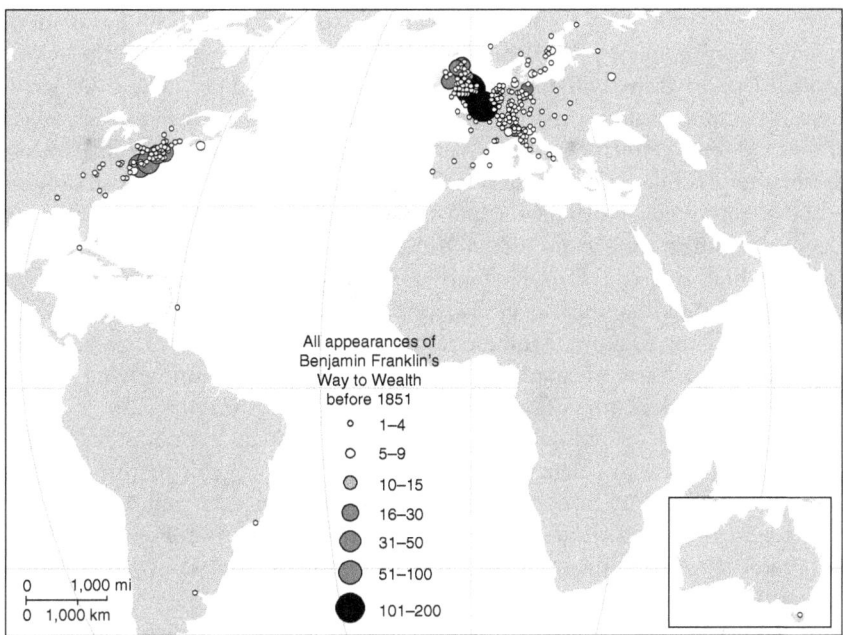

Map 2.1 All known appearances of Benjamin Franklin's *The Way to Wealth* before 1851.

What exactly Mao meant by these references may never become clear, but he continued, in one of his Franklinian speeches, to argue, somewhat quixotically on the eve of the Cultural Revolution, that 'we must read a few books. There is a great difference between reading because of the necessities of our present struggles, and reading aimlessly.'[51] Reading Franklin was neither a frivolity nor a capitalist sin, for Poor Richard had been a proto-Marxist exemplar of man's productivity and tool-making ingenuity, free from bourgeois burdens such as pedigree or education. An avatar of commercial society, and at the time already the face of the US $100 bill, Franklin had, appropriately for advocates of dialecticism, become a Maoist communist requisite.[52] For all his vitriol against bourgeois 'paper tigers', Mao realized that a polity's success and security in the international agon had come to depend on matching productive capacities with one's contenders. No doubt he remembered Karl Marx and Friedrich Engels's stipulation in *The Communist Manifesto*,

> The Bourgeoisie ... compels all nations, on pain of extinction, to adopt the bourgeois mode of production; it compels them to introduce what it calls civilization into their midst, i.e. to become bourgeois themselves. In one word, it creates a world after its own image.[53]

Even explicit resistance to capitalism required the adoption, to a greater or lesser extent, of its unforgiving work ethic. World politics had become a process of competitive productivity, in which, given the ruthless nature of international rivalries encapsulated by Carpani, the ethos and 'social science' of *The Way to Wealth* came to transcend its ideological origins and, ultimately, overturn its ostensibly cosmopolitan mission. 'To make China rich and strong needs several decades of intense effort,' Mao preached, 'which will include, among other things, the effort to practice strict economy and combat waste, i.e., the policy of building up our country through diligence and frugality.' And, curiously, Mao's choice of disciplinary labels for the project at hand was nothing else but 'social science', through which one could 'understand and change society and carry out social revolution'.[54] Franklin's unlikely global apotheosis can, under this lens, be located in Mao's heir Deng Xiaoping's influential yet plausibly apocryphal declaration that 'to get rich is glorious', through which the quotidian habits underlying the two great competing ideologies of the twentieth century became one.[55]

Here, perhaps, lay ultimately the empire of political economy as master-discipline of the social sciences – not necessarily a bourgeois empire, as Marx had envisioned it, but rather a globalizing stipulation that political existence increasingly depended on the competitive administration of economic life. It was the organic development of Carpani's earlier intuition that knowledge, empire and political economy were forever intertwined in the crucible of international competition. Political economy was first codified and institutionalized as a coherent field of discourse in relation to ongoing imperial rivalries in early modern Europe, and, in the minds of some of its earliest proponents, 'social science' emerged out of the perceived necessity of reconceptualizing said political economy to overcome international discord and socialize the relationships not only between people but also between peoples. Bestselling texts like Franklin's *The Way to Wealth* were written – and later appropriated across large parts of the world – to point a way towards a more sociable future. Yet the way in which such 'social science' was emulated and institutionalized globally ultimately followed the blackguard logic of empire too, amounting to a resolute rejection of Galdi's cosmopolitan idealism in favour of Carpani's traditional realism. Through social science's power over the realm of individual agency, the agonistic politics of international competition expanded beyond the sphere of high policies to become embedded in the very habits of the quotidian. It is a world that cannot fail to seem familiar to us, for it is our own, born from the ashes of Enlightenment social science.

Indeed, amid pressing preoccupations with the future of the world order at the dawn of the twentieth century, the Pistoiese philosopher and eventual fascist Alessandro Chiappelli pointed to the very same passages of Franklin as Mao later would to epitomize neither capitalism nor communism, but modernity as such: 'Aristotle could say that man by nature is a citizen, an evident truth in the ancient world; and for the same reason Franklin could define him an artificer, an equally evident truth in the modern world.'[56] This was a striking attenuation of Marx's original argument that 'the real meaning of Aristotle's definition is that man is by nature citizen of a town. This is quite as characteristic of classical antiquity as Franklin's definition of man as a tool-making animal is characteristic of Yankeedom.'⁵⁷ What to Marx seemed quintessentially American had, also because of the extraordinary influence of Franklin's work, become universal and 'modern' by the twentieth century. But, as soon would be clear, if the modern man in Franklin's image was an artificer of his own fortune, his preferred architectural style was polyvalent at best, embracing not only the National Mall in Washington, DC, but the Forbidden City in Beijing as well. Enlightenment social science had, as such, indeed helped establish an 'empire' comprehending the world entire, but it was ultimately a realm of agonistic toil and not cosmopolitan entitlements. Carpani would not have objected.

This is, of course, not to say that the original, explicitly anti-imperial notion of 'social science' in favour of which Franklin was marshalled early on died without a fight, and laments regarding the discipline's failure to live up to its moral promise of unifying humanity have reappeared over the centuries up to our present day.⁵⁸ Writing in 1834, the rural economist Giuseppe Romanazzi of Bari put this sentiment eloquently:

> Once it had destroyed the edifice of the Middle Ages, social science resolved itself in simple doctrines of public economy, temporarily, we hope, even though this can be an oscillation that can last for centuries, before one sees it relax, and extend itself to more natural and wider boundaries.⁵⁹

Needless to say, that time – and the 'Empire of Humanity' it promises – has yet to arrive, and in the meantime the filiations of 'social science' inherited from the Enlightenment remain both numerous and, at times, contradictory. What is certain is that we still very much live in a world in which the exigencies of productivity – whether for reasons of international competitiveness, material melioration or simply conspicuous consumption – influence the daily lives of the world's inhabitants like few other things. As a fixture of the modern condition, it was championed by the polar extremes of our long-reigning ideological spectrum, capitalist Franklin and communist Mao, and will doubtlessly continue to shape coming chapters of our disparate global histories. Indeed, the power of human productivity and of ideas to unleash it and give it purpose has been, for centuries now, the greatest force in the world. If this is to continue, we must become even more attentive to the fact that these global histories are entirely interwoven, that we, for the moment, have only one planet and that our survival and our flourishing might well require the more peaceful, more sustainable and more equally distributed ways to wealth imagined by the first social scientists. For it to be possible, just as the science of political economy that emerged from the first age of empire and spatial expansion gave way to the 'social sciences' in reaction to epochal revolution, so too the 'social sciences' that have developed hand in hand with our own age of globalization will again have to transform in reaction to the Anthropocene turmoil we face – not merely as citizens of competing polities, but as the increasingly threatened inhabitants of a single pale blue dot. If not, the danger is that the current chapter of our common story will inexorably yield to a conclusion.

Notes

1. I would like to thank Kenneth E. Carpenter for creating the incredible bibliography of Benjamin Franklin's *The Way to Wealth* informing parts of this work, Michael Hemment for the affiliated website http://waytowealth.org/ and Scott Walker of the Harvard Map Collection for the maps. I have analysed the bibliography at length in Sophus A. Reinert, 'The *Way to Wealth* around the World: Benjamin Franklin and the Globalization of American Capitalism', *American Historical Review* 120, no. 1 (2015): 61–97. For assistance at the New York Public Library, I am grateful to Kyle R. Triplett. For comments and criticisms I would like to thank Jeremy Adelman, the participants of the PIIRS colloquium on Empire and Social Science out of which this essay grew and, in particular, Robert Fredona. Finally, though to make a rather different argument, some of the following passages draw on the discussion of early 'social science' in Sophus A. Reinert, *The Academy of Fisticuffs: Political Economy and Commercial Society in Enlightenment Italy* (Cambridge: Harvard University Press, 2018), particularly 367–72.
2. Francesco Maria Carpani, 'Discorso sopra la necessità di un Controllore, e dell'incumbenza del medesimo', Archivio di Stato di Milano, Milan, Italy, *Atti di Governo 11, Commercio, Parte Antica, Cart. 3, P.G., 1740–1769*, 2r. On Carpani, see Carlo Capra, 'Un precursore delle riforme: Francesco Maria Carpani (1705–1777)', in *L'Europa tra illuminismo e Restaurazione: Scritti in onore di Furio Diaz*, ed. Paolo Alatri (Rome: Bulzoni, 1993), 115–55.
3. On the variegated nature of the Habsburg Empire, see Charles W. Ingrao, *The Habsburg Monarchy, 1618–1815*, 2nd edn (Cambridge: Cambridge University Press, 2000).
4. Carpani, 'Discorso sopra la necessità di un Controllore', 2r, 6v, 7v. On early modern information management in relation to political economy, see recently Jacob Soll, *The Information-Master: Jean-Baptiste Colbert's Secret State Intelligence System* (Ann Arbor: University of Michigan Press, 2009). On commerce as a form of warfare at the time, see Sophus A. Reinert, *Translating Empire: Emulation and the Origins of Political Economy* (Cambridge: Harvard University Press, 2011) and, for an earlier Milanese analysis of the phenomenon in similar terms, Sebastiano Franci, 'La guerra senza sangue', ed. Pietro Verri, Fondazione Mattioli, Milan, *Archivio Verri*, 380.4, published in a more toned-down form as 'Alcuni pensieri politici', in *Il Caffè, 1764–1766*, eds Gianni Francioni and Sergio A. Romagnoli (Turin: Bollati Boringhieri, 1993), 143–50.
5. Heinrich Sieveking, 'Die Kaiserliche Flagge auf den Nikobaren: Ein Beitrag zur Kolonialgeschichte', *Ostasiatische Rundschau* 5–6 (1940): 111–12.
6. For an impressionistic sample, see Giovanni Botero, *Delle relationi universali*, 4 vols. (Rome: Ferrari, 1591–1596); Antonio Serra, *A Short Treatise on the Wealth and Poverty of Nations (1613)*, trans. Jonathan Hunt, ed. Sophus A. Reinert (London: Anthem, 2011), 129 and *passim*; Sir James Steuart, *An Inquiry into the Principles of Political Oeconomy: Being an Essay on the Science of Domestic Policy in Free Nations*, 2 vols. (London: A. Millar & T. Cadell, 1767), vol. 1, 3. On the *visita*, see among many others, Stafford Poole, *Juan de Ovando: Governing the Spanish Empire in the Reign of Phillip II* (Norman: University of Oklahoma Press, 2004), 116 and *passim*.
7. For practical cases of such interactions, see the essays in Sophus A. Reinert and Pernille Røge, eds, *The Political Economy of Empire in the Early Modern World* (Basingstoke: Palgrave Macmillan, 2013).

8   Benjamin Franklin, marginalia in Anonymous, *The True Constitutional Means for Putting an End to the Dispute Between Great-Britain and the American Colonies* (London: T. Becket and P.A. de Hondt, 1769), 14, New York Public Library, New York, *KF 1769. It was a sentiment that very much framed Franklin's approach to political economy in both theory and practice; see, for example, his much later letters to Jan Ingenhousz (16 May 1783) and the Duc de Deux-Ponts (on or after 14 June 1783), both in Benjamin Franklin, *The Papers of Benjamin Franklin*, eds Leonard W. Labaree, et al., 41 vols. (New Haven: Yale University Press, 1959–2014), vol. 40, 8–13 and 163 respectively.

9   Emmanuel Sieyès, 'What is the Third Estate?' (1789), in *Political Writings*, ed. Michael Sonenscher (Indianapolis: Hackett, 2003), 92–162, 115; Robert Wokler, 'The Enlightenment and the French Revolutionary Birth Pangs of Modernity', in *The Rise of the Social Sciences and the Formation of Modernity: Conceptual Change in Context, 1750–1850*, eds Johan Heilbron, Lars Magnusson and Björn Wittrock (Dordrecht: Kluwer, 1998), 35–76, 43–7; Cheryl B. Welch, 'Social Science from the French Revolution to Positivism', in *The Cambridge History of Nineteenth-Century Political Thought*, eds Gareth Stedman Jones and Gregory Claeys (Cambridge: Cambridge University Press, 2011), 171–99. On the origins of 'social science', see further Keith Michael Baker, 'The Early History of the Term "Social Science"', *Annals of Science* 20 (1964): 211–26; Brian William Head, *Ideology and Social Science: Destutt de Tracy and French Liberalism* (Dordrecht: Martinus Nijhoff, 1985); Robert Wokler, 'Ideology and the Origins of Social Science', in *The Cambridge History of Eighteenth-Century Political Thought*, eds Mark Goldie and Robert Wokler (Cambridge: Cambridge University Press, 2006), 688–709, particularly 691–3.

10 On which see Lynn Hunt, *Inventing Human Rights: A History* (New York: W.W. Norton, 2007) and, for caveats, Samuel Moyn, *Human Rights and the Uses of History* (London: Verso, 2014). On early modern economic jealousy, see Istvan Hont, *Jealousy of Trade: International Competition and the Nation-State in Historical Perspective* (Cambridge: Harvard University Press, 2005), 340.

11 On the importance of contextual knowledge for Cameralism, see Reinert, *Translating Empire*, 234–45, 249; Alix Cooper, *Inventing the Indigenous: Local Knowledge and Natural History in Early Modern Europe* (Cambridge: Cambridge University Press, 2007). Similar arguments were, needless to say, fielded across the early modern European world, and not always in opposition to imperialism. For a transatlantic example, see John Lauritz Larsen, *Internal Improvement: National Public Works and the Promise of Popular Government in the Early United States* (Chapel Hill: University of North Carolina Press, 2001).

12 The classic expression of this more peaceful analysis remains Albert O. Hirschman, *The Passions and the Interests: Political Arguments for Capitalism before Its Triumph* (Princeton: Princeton University Press, 1997); Albert O. Hirschman, 'Rival Views of Market Society', in *Rival Views of Market Society and Other Recent Essays* (Cambridge: Harvard University Press, 1992), 105–41. On Hirschman, see Jeremy Adelman, *Worldly Philosopher: The Odyssey of Albert O. Hirschman* (Princeton: Princeton University Press, 2013).

13 This sentiment is certainly representative of the majority of works present in Kenneth E. Carpenter, *The Economic Bestsellers Before 1850* (Boston: Kress Library of Business and Economics, Harvard Business School, 1975), now updated in Erik S. Reinert, Kenneth Carpenter, Fernanda Reinert and Sophus A. Reinert, '80 Economic Bestsellers before 1850: A Fresh Look at the History of Economic Thought', *The Other*

Canon Foundation and Tallinn University of Technology Working Papers in Technology Governance and Economic Dynamics 74 (2017).

14 Sophus A. Reinert, 'Rivalry: Greatness in Early Modern Political Economy', in *Mercantilism Reimagined: Political Economy in Early Modern Britain and its Empire*, eds Phil Stern and Carl Wennerlind (Oxford: Oxford University Press, 2014), 348–70. See similarly Hamish Scott, 'The Fiscal-Military State and International Rivalry during the Long Eighteenth Century', in *The Fiscal-Military State in Eighteenth-Century Europe: Essays in Honour of P.G.M. Dickson*, ed. Christopher Storrs (Aldershot: Ashgate, 2009), 23–53, particularly 47.

15 This process could even be evident across the career of a single writer and agent of empire. See, for example, the case of the Bristol merchant and writer John Cary discussed throughout Reinert, *Translating Empire*.

16 Robert Thorne, 'A Declaration of the Indies and Lands Discovered, etc.', in *The Principal Navigations, Voyages, Traffiques and Discoveries of the English Nation*, vol. 1, eds Richard Hakluyt and Edmund Goldsmid (Edinburgh: E. & G. Goldsmith, 1885), 212–16; Richard Eden, 'Preface to the Reader', in *The Decades of the Newe Worlde or West India … Wrytten in the Latin Tounge by Peter Martyr of Angleria and Translated into Englysshe by Rychard Eden* (London: Powell [for Sutton], 1555). The classic account of the foundation of what soon would be known as the 'Muscovy Company' remains T. S. Willan, *The Early History of the Russia Company, 1553–1603* (Manchester: Manchester University Press, 1956), particularly 1–5. On the contemporary crisis, see Robert Brenner, *Merchants and Revolution: Commercial Change, Political Conflict, and London's Overseas Traders, 1550–1653* (London: Verso, 2003), 7. Though long infamous, the episode has recently generated interest among popular historians, see Kit Mayers, *North-East Passage to Muscovy: Stephen Borough and the First Tudor Explorations* (Stroud: The History Press, 2005) and James Evans, *Merchant Adventurers: The Voyage That Launched Modern England* (London: Weidenfeld & Nicolson, 2013).

17 Edward VI of England, 'The Copie of the Letters Missive, Which the Right Noble Prince Edward the Sixt Sent to the Kings, Princes, and Other Potentates, Inhabiting the Northeast Partes of the Worlde, toward the Mighty Empire of Cathay, at Such Time As Sir Hugh Willoughby Knight, and Richard Chancelor, with Their Company, Attempted Their Voyage thither in the Yeere of Christ 1553 and the Seuenth and Last Yeere of His Raigne', in Hakluyt and Goldsmid, *Principal Navigations*, vol. 1, 231–2; see also J. [Iosif Khristianovich] Hamel, *England and Russia: Comprising the Voyages of John Tradescant the Elder, Sir Hugh Willoughby, Richard Chancellor, Nelson, and Others*, trans. John Studdy Leigh (London: Richard Bentley, 1854), 5–6.

18 The logbook is reproduced in Hakluyt and Goldsmid, *Principal Navigations*, vol. 1, 234–7.

19 For the note, see British Library, London, United Kingdom, 'Sir Hugh Willoughby's voyage for the discovery of Cathay, in 1553', Cotton MS, Otho E VIII, f. 16r. The event eventually became the stuff of legend across Europe, see Daryl W. Palmer, *Writing Russia in the Age of Shakespeare* (Aldershot: Ashgate, 2004), 28–9. It has been suggested that the crews in effect died of carbon monoxide poisoning rather than cold, see Eleanora C. Gordon, 'The Fate of Sir Hugh Willoughby and His Companions: A New Conjecture,' *Geographical Journal* 152, no. 2 (1985): 243–7.

20 See the deposition of James Alday relating to the expedition of Sir Hugh Willoughby, The National Archives, Kew, UK, High Court of Admiralty, 13/22 ff. 99d-101v. The passage is often quoted from Willan, *Early History of the Russia Company*, 5, but the

archival reference there given is at best antiquated. See further Sophus A. Reinert, 'Authority and Expertise at the Origins of Macro-economics', in *Antonio Serra and the Economics of Good Government*, eds Rosario Patalano and Sophus A. Reinert (Basingstoke: Palgrave Macmillan, 2016), 112–42.

21 Key historiographical works remain, from different perspectives, Ronald L. Meek, *Social Science & The Ignoble Savage* (Cambridge: Cambridge University Press, 1976); Christopher Fox, Roy S. Porter and Robert Wokler, eds, *Inventing Human Science: Eighteenth-Century Domains* (Berkeley: University of California Press, 1995); Joan-Pau Rubiés, *Travellers and Cosmographers: Studies in the History of Early Modern Travel and Ethnology* (Aldershot: Ashgate, 2007). On the longevity of this tradition, for example in relation to the discipline of anthropology, see, among others, the essays in Benoît de l'Estoile, Federico Neiburg and Lygia Sigaud, eds, *Empires, Nations, and Natives: Anthropology and State-Making* (Durham: Duke University Press, 2005).

22 On the role of science and knowledge in the success of British imperialism, see, among many, many others, Richard Drayton, *Nature's Government: Science, Imperial Britain, and the 'Improvement' of the World* (New Haven: Yale University Press, 2000) and Margaret C. Jacob and Larry Stewart, *Practical Matter: Newton's Science in the Service of Industry and Empire, 1687–1851* (Cambridge: Harvard University Press, 2006). For caveats, see William J. Ashworth, 'Rostow's Ghost: Science, Culture and the British Industrial Revolution', *History of Science*, 56 (2008): 249–74.

23 Steven L. Kaplan and Sophus A. Reinert, eds, *The Economic Turn: Recasting Political Economy in Enlightenment Europe* (London: Anthem, 2019).

24 Reinert, *Translating Empire*. On this war see, among others, Daniel Baugh, *The Global Seven Years War, 1754–1763* (London: Routledge, 2011). On the transformative power of related expenses, see still John Brewer, *The Sinews of Power: War, Money, and the English State, 1688–1783* (Cambridge: Harvard University Press, 1988) and Hont, *Jealousy of Trade*, 340.

25 James Harrington, *The Common-Wealth of Oceana* (London: Streater, 1656), 11; John Dryden, 'Epistle Dedicatory', in *The State of Innocence and the Fall of Man: An Opera* (London: J. Tonson, 1735); François-André-Adrien Pluquet, *Dizionario delle eresie*, 6 vols. in 3, trans. and rather heavily ed. Tommasio Antonio Contin, 2nd edn (Venice: Giovanni Francesco Garbo, 1771–1772), vol. 3, 216. On early modern ideologies of empire, see still Anthony Pagden, *Lords of All the World: Ideologies of Empire in Spain, Britain, and France, ca.1500–ca.1800* (New Haven: Yale University Press, 1998); David Armitage, *The Ideological Origins of the British Empire* (Cambridge: Cambridge University Press, 2000).

26 Prominent writers in this tradition include Claudio Todeschi, *Saggi di agricoltura, manifatture, e commercio …* (Rome: Casaletti, 1770); Claudio Todeschi, *Pensieri sulla pubblica felicità* (Rome: Casaletti, 1774); Paolo Vergani, *Della importanza e dei pregi del nuovo sistema di finanza dello Stato Pontifico* (Rome: Lazzarini, 1794). On papal economists at the time, see, among others, Luigi del Pane, *Lo stato pontificio e il movimento riformatore del Settecento* (Milan: A. Giuffrè, 1959). The point regarding empires in different spheres was clearly made already by St. Augustine of Hippo's disciple St. Prosper of Aquitaine; see his *Carmen de ingratis*, vol. 2, ed. Charles T. Huegelmeyer (Washington DC: Catholic University of America Press, 1962), 40–2, 46. For similar observations, see Johann Georg Keyssler, *Travels through Germany, Bohemia, Hungary, Switzerland, Italy and Lorrain*, 4 vols., 2nd edn (London: Linde, 1756–1757), vol. 2, 6.

27 On this debate, see still Richard Tuck, *The Rights of War and Peace: Political Thought and the International Order from Grotius to Kant* (Oxford: Oxford University Press, 2001), and for its prehistory Robert Fredona, 'Angelo degli Ubaldi and the Gulf of the Venetians: Custom, Commerce, and the Control of the Sea Before Grotius', in *New Perspectives on the History of Political Economy*, eds Robert Fredona and Sophus A. Reinert (Cham: Palgrave Macmillan, 2018), 29–73. For a perhaps unintentionally witty dismissal of the whole debate, see Louis Joseph Plumard de Dangeul [misleadingly presented as the translation of a certain John Nickolls], *Remarques sur les avantages et les desavantages de la France et de la Gr. Bretagne, par rapport au commerce, & aux autres sources de la puissance des états* (Leiden [but Paris], 1754), 144. For an eighteenth-century overview of the historiography, see Paolo Todeschi, 'Sul Dominio del mare', in *Opere*, 3 vols. (Rome: Casaletti, 1779), vol. 2, cxlix–clxxvi.

28 This vocabulary of imperial humanity was widespread, particularly with regards to penal reforms, imperial economic injustices and emerging abolitionist sentiments; see, for example, John Coakley Lettsom, 'On the Howardian Fund and Prison Charities', *The Gentlemen's Magazine* (London: John Nichols, 1757), vol. 57, 464; Benjamin Franklin, 'The Colonist's Advocate: VII', in *Papers*, vol. 17, 52–5, 53; William Bradford to Luigi Castiglioni, 10 August 1786, praising Cesare Beccaria's work as a vehicle of 'the empire of humanity', in Luigi Castiglioni, *Viaggio negli Stati Uniti*, 2 vols. (Milan: Marelli, 1790), vol. 2, 23–5; Jullien to Benjamin Franklin, 13 February 1779, in *Papers*, vol. 28, 533–4; Benjamin Rush to John Coakley Lettsom, 18 May 1787, in *Letters of Benjamin Rush* (Philadelphia: American Philosophical Society, 1951), 417; Thomas Clarkson, *The History of the Rise, Progress, and Accomplishment of the Abolition of Slave-Trade by the British Parliament*, 2 vols. (London: Longman, Hurst, Rees, & Orme, 1808), vol. 1, 545, establishing an idiom influential well into the nineteenth century; see, for example, [Lucius A. Hine?], 'Our Coloured Population: A Negro State', *The Quarterly Journal and Review* [Cincinnati] 1, no. 3 (1846): 199.

29 For recent work on more literary genres of early political economy, see, among many others, Catherine Gallagher, *The Body Economic: Life, Death, and Sensation in Political Economy and the Victorian Novel* (Princeton: Princeton University Press, 2008); Richard T. Gray, *Money Matters: Economics and the German Cultural Imagination, 1770-1850* (Seattle: University of Washington Press, 2008); Carl Wennerlind, *Casualties of Credit: The English Financial Revolution, 1620-1720* (Cambridge: Harvard University Press, 2011).

30 Michael Sonenscher, '"The Moment of Social Science": The *Decade Philosophique* and late Eighteenth-Century French Thought', *Modern Intellectual History* 6, no. 1 (2009): 121–46, 129–31.

31 Adam Smith, *An Inquiry into the Nature and Causes of the Wealth of Nations*, ed. Edwin Cannan, prefaced by George J. Stigler (Chicago: University of Chicago Press, 1976), 449. Key interpretative texts regarding Smith's definition remain Donald Winch, *Adam Smith's Politics: An Essay in Historiographic Revision* (Cambridge: Cambridge University Press, 1978); Knud Haakonssen, *The Science of a Legislator: The Natural Jurisprudence of David Hume and Adam Smith* (Cambridge: Cambridge University Press, 1981). For Joseph A. Schumpeter's phrase, see *A History of Economic Analysis*, ed. Elizabeth Boody Schumpeter (New York: Oxford University Press, 1954), 199. For recent calls to expand the confines of political economy, see Emma Rothschild, 'Arcs of Ideas: International History and Intellectual History', in *Transnationale Geschichte: Themen, Tendenzen und Theorien*, eds Gunilla Budde, Sebastian Conrad and Oliver Janz (Göttingen: Vandenhoeck & Ruprecht, 2006),

222; Sophus A. Reinert, 'Lessons on the Rise and Fall of Great Powers: Conquest, Commerce, and Decline in Enlightenment Italy', *American Historical Review* 115 (2010): 1420–1.

32 Xenophon, *Oeconomicus: A Social and Historical Commentary*, trans. and ed. Sarah B. Pomeroy (Oxford: Oxford University Press, 1995); Xenophon, *Xenophon's Poroi: A New Translation*, trans. and ed. Ralph Doty (Lewiston: Edwin Mellen, 2003).

33 Carpenter, *The Economic Bestsellers Before 1850*, 22, building on Charles J. Bullock, *The Vanderblue Memorial Collection of Smithiana: An Essay* (Boston: Baker Library, Harvard Graduate School of Business Administration, [1939]). For further work on the international influence of Adam Smith's *Wealth of Nations*, see Cheung-Chung Lai, ed., *Adam Smith across Nations: Translations and Receptions of the Wealth of Nations* (Oxford: Oxford University Press, 2000); Kenneth E. Carpenter, *The Dissemination of the Wealth of Nations in French and in France, 1776–1843* (New York: Bibliographical Society of America, 2002); Keith Tribe et al., eds, *A Critical Bibliography of Adam Smith* (London: Pickering & Chatto, 2002).

34 Benjamin Franklin, 'Poor Richard Improved, 1758 [*The Way to Wealth*]', in *Papers*, vol. 7, 326–50, text on 340–50, on which see Reinert, 'The *Way to Wealth* around the World' and http://waytowealth.org, last accessed 27 February 2019.

35 Mao Tse-Tung, *Quotations from Chairman Mao Tse-Tung* (San Francisco: China Books and Periodicals, 1990), on which see now the essays in Alexander C. Cook, ed., *Mao's Little Red Book: A Global History* (Cambridge: Cambridge University Press, 2014).

36 Ambroise Clément, *Essai sur la science sociale: économie politique—morale éxperimentale—politique théorique* (Paris: Guillaumin, 1867), 65.

37 See among others Reinert, 'The *Way to Wealth* around the World' as well as Jill Lepore, 'The Way to Wealth', in *The Story of America: Essays on Origins* (Princeton: Princeton University Press, 2012), 44–58. Truth be told, Franklin had expressed the quintessence of the *Way to Wealth* already in the opening line of his 1748 *Advice to a Young Tradesman*, which began with the statement 'remember that Time is Money' and ended by maintaining that 'the Way to Wealth, if you desire it, is as plain as the Way to Market. It depends chiefly on two Words, Industry and Frugality.' See Benjamin Franklin, 'Advice to a Young Tradesman, Written by an Old One', in *Papers*, vol. 3, 306–8.

38 See, for example, Jean-Baptiste Say's influential usage of Franklin's *Way to Wealth* in Richard Whatmore, *Republicanism and the French Revolution: An Intellectual History of Jean-Baptiste Say's Political Economy* (Oxford: Oxford University Press, 2000), 117 and Michael Sonenscher, *Before the Deluge: Public Debt, Inequality, and the Intellectual Origins of the French Revolution* (Princeton: Princeton University Press, 2007), 334–48. On Franklin and empire, see Carla Mulford, 'Early Modern Imperialism, Traditions of Liberalism, and Franklin's Ends of Empire', in *Benjamin Franklin's Intellectual World*, eds Paul E. Kerry and Matthew S. Holland (Madison: Farleigh Dickinson University Press, 2012), 25–42 and now Carla Mulford, *Benjamin Franklin and the Ends of Empire* (Oxford: Oxford University Press, 2015).

39 Wokler, 'Ideology and the Origins of Social Science', 707–9.

40 See, among others on this tradition, Vincenzo Ferrone, *La società giusta ed equa: Repubblicanesimo e diritti dell'uomo in Gaetano Filangieri* (Rome-Bari: Laterza, 2003); Antonio Trampus, *Il diritto alla felicità: Storia di un'idea* (Rome-Bari: Laterza, 2008).

41 Matteo Angelo Galdi, *Dei rapport politico-economici fra le nazioni libere* (Milan: Presso Pirotta e Maspero stampatori-librai, year 6 [1797 or 1798]), 'avviso ai lettori'

and 3–8, 12; on Galdi, see Maria Rosa Strollo, *L'istruzione a Napoli nel 'decennio francese': Il contributo di Matteo Angelo Galdi* (Naples: Liguori, 2003).

42 Nicola Giuseppe Corvaia, *La bancocrazia*, 2 vols. (Milan: A. Ubicini, 1840), vol. 1, 253; Fabio Invrea, *Discorsi sulla pubblica ricchezza ossia sopra di quanto la costituisce sulla di lei origine, aumento, e ripartizione* (Genoa: Ferrando, 1846), 100–1, misquoting Karl Heinrich Rau, *Lehrbuch der politischen Oekonomie*, 3rd edn, 3 vols. in 5 (Heidelberg: C.F. Winter, 1837–1851), vol. 1, 47 to make his point. Rau had warned of turning political economy into '*Staatswissenschaft*', not 'scienza sociale'. Curiously, the first known reference to 'social science' in the English language was William Thompson's 1824 *Inquiry into the Principles of the Distribution of Wealth most Conducive to Human Happiness* (London: Longman et al., 1824), viii–ix, which essentially equated it with 'the art of social happiness'. On this see Wokler, 'Ideology and the Origins of Social Science', 702.

43 Francesco Trinchera in Pellegrino Rossi, *Corso di economia politica, prima versione italiana con note di Francesco Trinchera arricchita dalla giunta della storia dell'economia di Ch. H. Rau e da due articoli del cav. Luigi Blanch*, 2 vols. (Naples: Dallo stabilimento del Guttemberg, 1843), vol. 2, 263. On Rossi, see now the essays in Michele Finelli, ed., *Pellegrino Rossi: Giurista, economista e uomo politico (1787–1848)* (Soveria Mannelli: Rubbettino, 2011).

44 Placido de Luca, *Dell'utile o svantaggio che producono all'industria i privilegi: memoria estemporanea pel concorso alla cattedra di economia e commercio nella R. Università degli studii di Catania*, 2nd edn (Naples: Matteo Vara, 1841), 5–6.

45 E.g. Reinert, *Translating Empire*; Andrew Sartori, 'Global Intellectual History and the History of Political Economy', in *Global Intellectual History*, eds Samuel Moyn and Andrew Sartori (New York: Columbia University Press, 2013), 111–33.

46 On this heuristically significant difference, see David Armitage, 'Is there a Pre-History of Globalization?', in *Foundations of Modern International Thought* (Cambridge: Cambridge University Press, 2013), 33–45. On the power of circumnavigation, see Joyce E. Chaplin, *Round About the Earth: Circumnavigation from Magellan to Orbit* (New York: Simon & Schuster, 2012).

47 Benjamin Franklin, *Mezzo facile di pagare le imposizioni ossia la scienza di Riccardo Saunders* (Turin: Francesco Prato, 1797), 5–6, recalling a Petrarchan discourse of decline and political economy discussed in Reinert, 'Lessons on the Rise and Fall of Great Powers'. See similarly Benjamin Franklin, 'The Way to Wealth', *Nova-Scotia Magazine* 4, no. 10 (1791): 603.

48 Imai Terako, 'Nihon ni okeru Furankurin no juyō—Meiji jidai', *Tsudajuku daigaku kiyō* 2–4 (1982): 1–39. I am grateful to Garon, *Beyond Our Means*, 388, fn. 30 for this reference; Benjamin Franklin, *La Science du Bonhomme Richard; ou le Chemin de la Fortune* (Beijing: Collège de Tungwen, 1884).

49 Mao Tse-tung, 'Remarks at the Spring Festival: Summary Record. 13 February 1964', 208, as well as 'Talk on Questions of Philosophy. 18 August 1964', 220 and again 'Speech at Hangchow. 21 December 1965', 237, in *Chairman Mao Speaks to the People: Talks and Letters, 1956–1971*, trans. John Chinnery and Tieyun, ed. Stuart Schram (New York: Pantheon Books, 1974).

50 Mao, 'Talk on Questions of Philosophy', 220, probably referencing Karl Marx, *Capital*, ed. Ernest Mandel, trans. Ben Fowkes (London: Penguin, 1981), vol. 1, 444, fn. 7, plausibly paraphrasing Benjamin Franklin in James Boswell, *The Journal of a Tour to the Hebrides with Samuel Johnson* (London: Baldwin, 1785), 25 or *The Life of Samuel Johnson*, 2 vols. (London: Baldwin, 1791), vol. 2, 199.

51 Mao, 'Talk on Questions of Philosophy', 221.
52 For example, ibid., 228.
53 Karl Marx and Friedrich Engels, *The Communist Manifesto*, ed. Gareth Stedman Jones (London: Penguin, 2004), 224.
54 Tse-Tung, *Quotations from Chairman Mao Tse-tung*, 73, 186, 204.
55 On the importance of this phrase, see, among others, Wei-Wei Zhang, *Transforming China: Economic Reform and Its Political Implications* (Basingstoke: Palgrave Macmillan, 2000). Western readers have felt similarly about things, and even Paul W. Conner's *Poor Richard's Politicks* (New York: Oxford University Press, 1965), 65, concluded at the height of the Cold War by asking whether 'Moscow' might not 'be more congenial to a reincarnate Franklin than modern Philadelphia'.
56 Alessandro Chiappelli, *Leggendo e meditando* (Rome: Dante Alighieri, 1900), 239.
57 Marx, *Capital*, vol. 1, 444, fn. 7, referring to Franklin above and Aristotle, *Politics*, book 1, 1253a.
58 See for variations John Hobson, quoted and discussed in Gregory Claeys, *Imperial Sceptics: British Critics of Empire, 1850–1920* (Cambridge: Cambridge University Press, 2010), 272, and Wokler, 'Ideology and the Origins of Social Science', 707–9 and the role played by 'social science' at different times in the nineteenth and twentieth centuries in Mark Mazower, *Governing the World: The History of an Idea* (London: Penguin, 2012), 95–100, 292.
59 Giuseppe Romanazzi, *Note e considerazioni sull'affrancazione de' canoni e sul libero coltivamento del tavoliere di Puglia* (Naples: Tramater, 1834), 104. See similarly John Hobson, quoted and discussed in Claeys, *Imperial Sceptics*, 272, and Wokler, 'Ideology and the Origins of Social Science', 707–9.

Chapter 3

UTILITARIANISM AND THE QUESTION OF FREE LABOUR IN RUSSIA AND INDIA, EIGHTEENTH–NINETEENTH CENTURIES

Alessandro Stanziani

The attempt to identify the forms of coercion and bondage that existed in eighteenth- and nineteenth-century Russia and India raises several intellectual and political questions, starting with the policies that were adopted by the British towards these countries. The English abolitionist movement began its rapid development in the 1780s. Prior to 1820, the movement was mainly concerned with abolishing the slave trade; until that date, it did not focus on the abolition of slavery itself. In any event, the British values of freedom and the protection of human rights were deemed universal.

At the same time, this universalist view was shattered when it came to India. In the late eighteenth and early nineteenth centuries, most observers and colonial elites were convinced that the forms of dependence existing in India did not come under the heading of slavery: they were domestic relationships and in any case 'traditional'. This approach fit well with the need to manage the Empire and India in particular,[1] where British control was still precarious, as the wars against the Marathas, Mysore, and the Sikhs, among others, demonstrated. Nevertheless, the debate over how to qualify the forms of dependence and labour in India intensified in the first half of the nineteenth century and intersected with the debate over orientalism, on the one hand, and the forms of sovereignty (direct rule, indirect rule, protectorate), on the other.[2]

The issues raised by Russia were at once similar and different. The specific features of serfdom were open to discussion when compared with those of colonial slavery; at the same time, as the abolitionists had no direct control in the case of Russia, they could do little but attempt to influence British diplomatic attitudes towards the country.

The political economists of the time, Jeremy Bentham in particular, took part in these debates; free labour was compared with bondage in terms of utility and efficiency as well as broader ethical principles. The problem, as Bentham saw it, lay precisely in choosing between two ways of thinking: first was the universalist approach, which meant adopting the same principles everywhere – in Britain, India and Russia – thereby providing the grounds on which labour and its institutions should be evaluated. The other, more particularist approach, was open to distinctions among these three places. In the end, Bentham opted for the first approach; yet surprisingly (at least compared with the images we have of it today), he thought that Russian serfdom offered an interesting solution to the problem of labour control. It was precisely in Russia that he invented his Panopticon. From that point, he went on to adopt complex, shifting attitudes towards India. We are going to retrace the development of these approaches, together with the various ways they were interpreted until around the mid-nineteenth century, not only in intellectual circles but also and above all amongst the colonial elites themselves. Henceforth, the influence of utilitarianism in India became a springboard for thinking about more general issues, starting with the role of knowledge as a tool for empire-building and colonial control. The aims of political economy, especially utilitarianism, were decidedly universalist: the same categories and interpretive models were valid throughout the world. It would be a mistake to assume, however, as subaltern studies has often maintained, that this universalism was accepted from the outset by colonial elites to justify their imperial constructions. As we shall see, notably in the case of India, the universalist attitude encountered opposition from another approach, which stressed the importance of local specificities. This form of 'orientalism' also deserves to be discussed, without equating it a priori with Edward Said's approach. Indeed, this knowledge was used not only to 'invent' an Indian reality to better control it; on the contrary, it openly questioned the wisdom of putting so much effort into transforming India, thus lending a sort of 'legitimacy' to its local customs, including slavery. In short, while it is important to view utilitarian political economy as a form of knowledge that played an essential role in building the British empire, it by no means identified, and thereby justified, only one form of imperial construction. The question therefore consists in explaining how and why, among the possible solutions to empire-building and bondage that were compatible with utilitarian principles, some prevailed over others, and to what extent the local context in Russia, India and even England helped to reshape those political and economic solutions and utilitarian thought itself.

Periphery and Freedom: The Invention of the Panopticon in Russia

Samuel Bentham, Jeremy's brother, arrived in Russia in 1780 as a naval engineer. He first worked for an English manufactory in St. Petersburg and then toured the Ural Mountains in 1781–2, before entering the service of Prince Potemkin in 1784. The prince was at this time Catherine's lover and close adviser, and he owned country estates and numerous factories. He was also directly involved in the ongoing Russian expansion, east to Poland and south to Crimea. The government was then devoting much attention to the development of a short stretch of Black Sea coast that it had secured from Turkey in 1774. These ambitions generated tensions and conflicts with the Ottoman Empire, and an alliance with Britain was part of the Russian strategy. It was thus not by chance that Potemkin asked Samuel Bentham to manage one of his estates, located in the Krichev district of Belorussia. In fact, the estate was the principal supplier to naval stores in the Black Sea. Bentham's main task was to build ships for Potemkin; to this end, he made an appeal to twenty skilled workers from Britain. Unfortunately, these workers showed little respect for instructions or work schedules, and while their foremen complained about the lack of discipline, they too disobeyed Bentham's instructions.[3]

It was in this context that Jeremy, who had joined his brother a few months earlier, wrote numerous letters that took up these problems and called for an improvement in the system of labour surveillance, particularly regarding the work of the foremen. Indeed, the estate lacked the skills needed for building ships. Bentham's brother thus suggested that they bring English skilled workers to Krichev. When twenty skilled workers arrived on the estate in 1785, disciplinary problems quickly surfaced.[4] Jeremy Bentham noted 'a lack of discipline and order among the workmen'.[5,6] The letters addressed the well-known problem of how to supervise the supervisors; these letters were subsequently assembled into the Panopticon letters, published first in 1791.[7] They show that Jeremy was impressed by the virtues of the Panopticon principle elaborated by his brother:

> Relative to a house of correction ... it occurred to me that a plan of a building, lately contrived by my brother, for purposes in some respects similar, and which, under the name of the Inspection house, or the Elaboratory, he is about erecting here, in Krichev, might afford some hints for the above establishment. ... To say all in one word, it will be found applicable, I think, without exception, to all establishments whatsoever, in which, within a space not too large to be covered or commanded by buildings, a number of persons are meant to be kept under inspection.[8]

Nonetheless, the shared project of the Bentham brothers and Potemkin – to build a Panopticon on Potemkin's estate – fell through, because he sold the estate in 1787, which led Jeremy Bentham to return to England. Jeremy's contribution was to generalize his brother's project,[9] making it applicable outside of Russia and incorporating it into his general approach to the organization of labour. He first extended the idea of an office of labour surveillance to prisons, then to schools, and finally to hospitals – and to all situations in which the problem of supervision arose.

The prison project, then, was first of all a project for labour surveillance, and the unskilled serfs were less of a concern than the skilled foremen. The project was not a reaction to the indiscipline of Russian serfs, but, on the contrary, was a response to the behaviour of English foremen and skilled workers. Russia thus inspired Bentham with a model of labour organization and surveillance that could be applied in Europe, and in England, in particular, as he suggested in his correspondence. Most of the countless interpretations of the Panopticon, including Foucault's, go wrong precisely because they overlook this context and hence the link between prison and labour, on the one hand, and free and forced labour, on the other. At the same time, it should be stressed that the Panopticon was not the reaction of an English liberal confronted with an absolutist system and forced labour. For Bentham, after all, the point was precisely to improve the surveillance and labour efficiency of English wage workers. According to Bentham, it was not the condition but rather the duration of the obligation that constituted the real difference between free and unfree labour. The living conditions of a free worker were not necessarily better than those of a slave or serf. Jeremy Bentham's starting point, to be sure, was an idea that resonated powerfully with his sense of morality: that it was better to put prisoners to work than let them vegetate and that such an approach would facilitate prisoners' progressive reintegration into society. Yet he could not resist straying from this rationale and returning to the utilitarian calculation that new forms of surveillance and organization could and should make prison labour profitable.[10] From there it was but a short step to start thinking about ways to maximize prisoner productivity. At first he proposed to rationalize prisoners' diet: they should not become malnourished or else their productivity would diminish. Yet Bentham thought mostly in terms of amounts and was not embarrassed to suggest that prisoners be given spoiled food mixed with fresh food (within reasonable limits, to avoid abrupt drops in labour productivity).[11] He seemed excited at the thought that prisoners could be made to work fifteen hours and more without their wanting to leave their jobs, as wage labourers did.

Identifying 'free' labour

Such an attitude was all the more widespread because at that time, the notion of 'free' labour was not the one we are accustomed to now. In eighteenth- and nineteenth-century Britain, wage earners were considered domestics and were above all supposed to provide a service.[12] The labour of servants was usually conceived as a master's property, and property consisted in the service rather than in the body or person of the captive. According to Bentham, 'The master alone is considered as possessing a property, of which the servant, in virtue of the service he is bound to render, is the object; but the servant, not less than the master, is spoken of possessing or being invested with a condition.'[13] The legal status of labour provided the common ground upon which the organizational concerns of the firm (or the estate) and the relief system for the poor lay. In fact, insubordination or failure to comply with workshop production rules was presented as a breach of contract without notice, and as such was liable to sanctions under criminal law.[14] Criminal-law control over labour was aimed at reducing both turnover and supervision costs,[15] and limiting turnover was also one of the main aims of the Poor Laws. This link is crucial in the broad history of labour and labour institutions in Britain, as well as in the particular history we are dealing with here, that is, the origin of the Panopticon. In both cases, labour surveillance was at centre stage. In 1782, a bill known as Gilbert's Act was adopted that allowed neighbouring parishes to group together for Poor Law purposes and set up poorhouses under a board of guardians. This occurred just around the time when Samuel and Jeremy Bentham moved to Russia, and they closely followed this debate. The Krichev experience confirmed for Jeremy the necessity of reforming both the workhouses and the Poor Laws. The passage of this bill also explains why critiques of Poor Laws and the Panopticon project emerged concurrently in public debates of the mid-1780s. Only the 'indigent' and disabled were supposed to receive relief, Jeremy Bentham argued, while the 'ordinary poor' had to settle down and find employment.[16]

It was exactly during these same years, the 1770s and the 1780s, that antislavery activity intensified at the same time as a profound transformation in English attitudes towards the poor was taking place. These issues remained connected until, under pressures of widespread hostility towards both coerced labour and public relief, the apprenticeship system of slavery was introduced in the colonies in 1833–34 and a new Poor Law was passed in 1834.[17] Following the suggestions of Bentham and others since the 1780s, reformers made a sharp distinction between the 'natural poor' and the indigent (unable to work), and only the latter were permitted to benefit from poor relief. In intellectual and public debates of the time, poor relief, the general condition of labour, and the question of slavery and serfdom were tightly linked. More than just 'efficiency' was at stake (hence Adam Smith's and others' assertions that wage labour was more productive and efficient than forced labour); public order, vagrancy and social welfare were equally important.

Bentham was not exceptional in advancing these ideas. For example, his friend Admiral Jonas Hanway, founder of the Magdalen Hospital, applied the same principles to the navy and workhouses. He transformed the prison into a place of highly productive forced labour and then exported that model to the working world at large. To discipline wage labour in ways similar to forced labour was thus a widespread goal in nineteenth-century Britain, and the Panopticon was only one of many proposed methods.

Indeed, these orientations found roots not only in debates about slavery, serfdom and the guilds in the eighteenth century and in Bentham's approach but also in the building of empires. After all, Russia was not a British colony; how did the political economy of utilitarianism confront the question of labour and freedom in places like India?

Utilitarianism in India

Utilitarianism's relationship with India has received much more attention than its dissemination in Russia. This was probably due to the imperial dimension of their connection and all the debates relating to it. In the 1970s, the cultural turn, and in particular Geertz, Foucault, Said and subaltern studies, stressed the relationship between culture and power. Starting from this premise, British rule in India was viewed above all as control over language. Many historians and social scientists have talked about 'kidnapped language' and language-based or 'cultural' dependence, and so forth. According to this view, Western perceptions of the 'other' reduce civilization to positively valued institutions, behaviours and accomplishments associated with the West.[18] Within this context, utilitarianism in India has been viewed as a major expression of this attitude, consisting of imposing rules, legal notions and criminal codes in order to control India. I will discuss this view and show that, in the case of both Russia and India, individual and institutional experiences in the Indian subcontinent had a considerable impact on utilitarianism and the British notions of labour, rights and sovereignty. Indeed, the evolution of the Masters and Servants Acts in Britain was influenced not only by Bentham's experience in Russia but also by the British experience in India. The ideals and approaches to the law[19] formulated by Bentham and James Mill as well as the famous utilitarian analysis of status and contract were to a large extent inspired by Indian regulations and jurisprudence.[20] The underlying question was whether legal and economic categories could apply universally or whether they had to be rooted in local culture. In 1782, just before his experience in Russia, Bentham urged lawmakers to take the conditions peculiar to India into account before trying to impose British rules.[21] He agreed that the laws of England should serve as the standard; at the same time, he pointed out that, unlike Russia and Canada, Bengal was so completely different from England that a transfer of British law could not be achieved in toto.

The transfer of British values and institutions to India became in fact a core issue in political debates and administrative governance between the 1760s and the 1810s.[22] The conquest of India was still unstable, as the wars against the Marathas and Mysore testify. Attitudes within the East India Company (EIC) as well as in Parliament varied considerably. Some, prompted by the political and military instability, advocated a cautious approach; others, on the contrary, demanded more direct intervention and expansion justified by warfare, trade security and, last but not least, the need to abolish slavery in the Indian interior. The outcome of these approaches, together with the fierce resistance of Indian states and populations, was a patchwork of institutional and practical solutions; they varied according to the field (law, economy, culture, lower or higher education, criminal or commercial law, trade or labour), the geographical area concerned (Southern India, Northern India, the Malabar Coast, etc.), and, of course, the individuals concerned. Thus, while the EIC inherited many Mughal and post-Mughal legal institutions such as the *Qazi* courts (appellate courts),[23] parliamentary committees agreed that 'no Conclusion can be drawn from the English law, that can be properly applied to the Manners or State of this Country (India), with the exception of plans for the eradication of banditry'.[24]

Indeed, it was not a question of governance in India alone; during those same years, British criminal law was the focal point of an intense intellectual and political debate at home. Reformers opposed Edmund Burke and his conservative allies, demanding a fundamental change in the criminal justice system, which was accused of being arbitrary and highly irrational.[25] This debate overlapped with the debate over the laws to be adopted in India. Both Burke's *Reflections on the Revolution in France* (1790) and William Jones's enthusiasm for Hindu civilization, expressed in his project to compile a digest of Indian law, reasoned in terms of the uniqueness of a culture (Indian, English or French) to argue against revolution and in favour of colonialism.[26]

Burke led the prosecution in the impeachment trial of Warren Hastings, the first governor-general of India, in which he accused the EIC of violating 'the eternal laws of justice' through treaty violations, arbitrary and despotic government, and acts of corruption. He called for stricter parliamentary control over the company and protection of indigenous laws. This latter demand was made in opposition to Hastings's attempt to codify Hindu and Muslim law with a view to incorporating them in Anglo-Indian legal administration. In fact, Burke was openly attacking the association of ideas linking India with oriental despotism.

Bentham sought to criticize this view: in his opinion, deciding the question of British influence and Indian 'specificity' was secondary to establishing good laws everywhere. He associated India with oriental despotism and encouraged a radical reform of its laws in accordance with utilitarian principles. It was from this standpoint that he condemned Indian forms of slavery.[27]

Indeed, in the 1770s, Warren Hastings, the governor-general of India, and the Provincial Council of Patna issued a declaration limiting the right of masters over their slaves to no more than one generation.[28] Yet as late as March 1808, the Joint Magistrate J. Richardson denounced the continuing tolerance of slavery in India.[29] No official action was undertaken, except to keep a register of slaves.[30] The British anti-slavery movement thus claimed it was necessary to expand the abolitionist campaign to India. Supporters of local customs and pragmatic colonial elites replied that what existed in India was not real slavery, but merely forms of family dependence and domesticity. They won the backing of the English planters in India, who claimed that their enterprises were not comparable to the plantations in the West Indies. Even within the abolitionist movement, many held that bondage in India was different from slavery, either because they genuinely believed it or for tactical reasons, that is, to stop the transatlantic slave trade first. The fact that there was nothing in the subcontinent comparable to the transatlantic slave trade – the use and trade of slaves in and from India took place on land and was therefore much more difficult to quantify and control – also helped to support this view.

Although Bentham never worked out a detailed analysis of the Indian system, his systematic approach to the law met with some success among younger, enthusiastic utilitarians. Meanwhile, British rule in India was gradually consolidated after the Napoleonic Wars. The final defeat of the Marathas in 1818 transformed Bombay into a major centre under company rule. Then, after two decades of stability, a new offensive took place, bringing about the annexation of Corg (1834), Mandvi (1839), Kolaba (1840), Surat (1842), Sind (1843) and Punjab (1849). The first question that arose in this context was which type of governance should be adopted for the newly annexed states: direct rule or a subsidiary system. As an officer of the EIC, James Mill criticized the latter solution for failing to provide the strong centralization required for military purposes.[31] He also began drafting a systematic utilitarian legal agenda for India. Mill thought Mughal feudal law had to be replaced by British law[32] and he was convinced that poverty and ignorance could be cured by framing the right laws. From this perspective, India was a tabula rasa that could be moulded by utilitarianism. In the years following the Napoleonic Wars, these ideas seemed to be assimilated into a wider trend among British rulers in India looking for ways to make local administration more efficient. Contrary to Mill's views, however, in the eyes of most British elites in India, efficiency was linked much less to abstract principles of utilitarianism than to law enforcement.[33] In other words, whenever there was a conflict between abstract justice and practical sovereignty, priority should be given to the latter. This meant that Islamic law should be preserved – even if it went against certain British principles of justice – as long as it guaranteed compliance with the rules. This policy nevertheless proved difficult to put into practice: by the 1820s, the Indian courts had been reorganized several times and numerous digests of Indian law had been produced. Even so, uncertainty continued to surround judicial procedures in the 1830s; no less than nine different systems of civil procedure were simultaneously in effect in Bengal before 1859.[34] The Draft Penal Code of 1837, irrespective of its alleged amendments to the old order, not only acknowledged that, as of 1837, the 'technical terms and nice distinctions borrowed from Mohammedan Law are still retained', but kept the indigenous names for various facets of the company's judicial system.

The young John Stuart Mill took a position in this debate. John Stuart had been brought into the EIC's India House by his father James at the age of seventeen, after having been instilled with his father's Benthamite ideas. He believed that local customs and chiefs must submit to British rule.[35] Like Bentham before him, the younger Mill concluded that what India needed was a penal code, rather than a hodgepodge of existing laws. The only escape from darkness for Indians was to be led through a long and arduous process of tutelage by those more advanced. During the 1830s, however, his thinking was gradually changed by two interrelated events: first, he was confronted by opposition from the EIC and British officials who refused to subjugate local customs; second, the military campaign in Mysore and the difficulties the British encountered in overcoming local resistance convinced Mill to adopt more pragmatic attitude towards local elites.[36]

At the same time, according to Mill, this general orientation in defence of indirect rule could not apply to questions of slavery. He wrote in a dispatch that 'the custom of permitting Brahmins to purchase Domes for the cultivation of their lands, it be permitted by Government, is liable to gross abuse'. And he complained to the government of Calcutta that the abolition of slavery in India 'seems still to be very defective'.[37] He reiterated this position in 1842 when he denounced the fact that the sultan of Sharja and the imam of Muscat had violated the treaty of 1839 abolishing the slave trade with the African Somali tribe.[38] A year later, he expressed his regret that the practice of kidnapping children had been allowed to linger on within the EIC's possessions.[39]

Indeed, the abolition of slavery in India was linked to several factors: first, the passage from apprenticeship to freedom in other British colonies led the abolitionist movement to focus on India; second, the EIC came under increasing criticism concerning its fiscal autonomy, its use of slaves and its monopoly on trade, all of which were contrary to liberal principles. Further support came from the Americas, where abolitionists criticized slavery in the South as well as in India and accused Britain of hypocrisy on both sides – in India for tolerating slavery and in the United States for financing the slave trade. Thus, in 1839 the British India Society was founded, and it immediately set about attacking slavery as a cause of human suffering along with famines. The society adopted a global approach: its leaders argued that the abolition of slavery in India would improve local conditions, eradicate famine and help to promote abolitionism in the Americas.[40] For most participants, the issue of Indian slavery was not just about abolitionism but also about the rule of the EIC and India's future within a reconfigured imperial system.

Even though slavery was officially outlawed in India in 1843, local governors and elites espoused quite different attitudes depending on their own definition of slavery. For example, debt bondage was systematically excluded from it and therefore tolerated.[41] The government of Madras and other provincial British governments captured fugitive slaves and labourers and sent them back to their masters. Finally, as in other British dominions, the official abolition of slavery in India was followed by extremely coercive rules regarding vagrants, issued in the name of public order and economic growth as an antidote to poverty.

Conclusion

Initially, Enlightenment and later utilitarianism and liberal thought were all faced with a fundamental dilemma compelling them to choose between freedom, morality and ethics, on the one hand, and labour and sovereignty, on the other. The dilemma involved the status of 'free' labour and the role of law in relation to the economy. Economic rationality, born of the Glorious Revolution in Britain and the French Revolution and further developed during the first half of the nineteenth century, had trouble reconciling these elements. In this environment, it was not unreasonable for Bentham to take an interest in Russian serfdom in order to reform the Poor Law in Britain; this did not mean he considered the British workers serfs, but simply that Western and Eastern Europe were confronted by common problems of labour and surveillance, public order and the economy. Bentham's ideal of rational law based upon utilitarian principles provided the umbrella to discuss India, Canada and Russia within the same theoretical approach. It was no accident that the British Parliament debated the abolition of slavery in the colonies and the reform of the Poor Law and the apprenticeship system at the same time. Slaves were emancipated but placed under a system of temporary apprenticeship; as a result, the apprenticeship system was radically transformed (and finally abolished) in Britain and, consequently, the Poor Law, too, entered a new phase. Historians have artificially separated these debates, according to their own interests and fields – the history of labour, of slavery and so forth – whereas in the archives and in reality, they were all parts of a single problem. In England, the Poor Law was reformed, and the abolition of slavery was gradually accepted, even as the navy and the poor houses continued to make use of coerced labour. In India, slavery was tolerated in the name of indirect rule, while the transfer of British institutions raised widespread scepticism if not hostility not only among various Indians but also among the British colonial elites themselves.

The relationship between labour and authority was crucial in this context. The whole debate centred on the question of how to increase productivity – through tighter controls or enhanced worker incentives. They were seen as the only available options, but it was impossible to link either one entirely to forced labour or wage labour. Although it might seem that serfdom involved coercion and wage labour involved freedom, the debates show precisely the opposite: the partisans of reformed (but not abolished) slavery and serfdom advocated giving slaves and serfs more responsibility; they maintained that free wage labour entailed far greater surveillance costs. This led to the adoption of apprenticeship in the colonies and an even longer 'transition' period in Russia, before as well as after the official abolition of serfdom. In the colonies, the difference between slavery, apprenticeship and indentured contracts was clear in the legal statutes, but much less obvious in the implementation of rules and social practices.[42] In opposition to these uncertain attitudes, most radical reformers considered coercion to be definitively less profitable than free labour and advocated a complete transformation of labour institutions and practices. Yet, paradoxically, they did not hesitate to adopt coercive methods in order to impose reforms. This occurred in Russia as well as in the European the idea of colonies. The idea of coercion for a good cause was to meet with increasing success in the late nineteenth and twentieth centuries.

Notes

1 On these debates, among others: Andrea Major, *Slavery, Abolitionism and Empire in India, 1772–1843* (Liverpool: Liverpool University Press, 2012); Indrani Chatterjee, *Gender, Slavery and Law in Colonial India* (New Delhi: Oxford University Press, 1999).
2 On this point: Lauren Benton, *A Search for Sovereignty: Law and Geography in European Empires, 1400–1900* (Cambridge: Cambridge University Press, 2010).
3 Jeremy Bentham, *The Correspondence of Jeremy Bentham*, 12 vols., ed. Timothy L. S. Sprigge (London: Athlone Press, 1968–2006), vol. 2, 504; *The Works of Jeremy Bentham*, 11 vols., ed. John Bowring (Edinburgh: William Tait, 1838–1843), vol. 10, 161. See also Simon Werrett, 'Potemkin and the Panopticon: Samuel Bentham and the Architecture of Absolutism in Eighteenth-century Russia', *The Philosophic Age Almanac 9* (1999, special issue: *The Science of Morality: Jeremy Bentham and Russia*): 106–35; Ian R. Christie, *The Benthams in Russia, 1780–1791* (Oxford: Berg, 1993).
4 Ibid.
5 Bentham, *Correspondence*, vol. 3, 498.
6 Ibid., 503, 509–12.
7 Jeremy Bentham, *'Panopticon': or, the Inspection-House; Containing the Idea of a New Principle of Construction Applicable to Any Sort of Establishment, in which Persons of Any Description are to be kept under Inspection; and in Particular to Penitentiary-Houses, Prisons, Houses of Industry, Workhouses, Poor Houses, Manufactures, Madhouses, Lazarettos, Hospitals, and Schools; with a Plan of Management Adopted to the Principle; in a Series of Letters, Written in the Year 1787, from Crechoff in White Russia, to a Friend in England*, 2 vols. (London: T. Payne, 1791).
8 Jeremy Bentham, *The Panopticon Writings*, ed. Miran Bozevic (London: Verso, 1995), letter 1.
9 Bentham, *Correspondence*, vol. 4, 40.
10 Jeremy Bentham, *The Rationale of Punishment* (1830), reprod. in Bowring, *Works of Jeremy Bentham*, vol. 1, 439.

11 Janet Semple, 'Foucault and Bentham: A Defence of Panopticism', *Utilitas* 4, no. 1 (1992): 105–20, in particular at 130–1.
12 Alessandro Stanziani, *Bondage: Labor and Rights in Eurasia, from the Seventeenth to the Twentieth Century* (New York: Berghahn, 2014).
13 Jeremy Bentham, *Principles of Morals and Legislation*, ch. 43, sec. 1, para. 1433, in Bowring, *Works of Jeremy Bentham*, vol. 1.
14 George J. Barnsby, *Social Conditions in the Black Country, 1800–1900* (Wolverhampton: Integrated Publishing Services, 1980).
15 Michael Huberman, *Escaping from the Market: Negotiating Work in Lancashire* (Cambridge: Cambridge University Press, 1996).
16 Jeremy Bentham, 'Essay II. Fundamental Positions in Regard to the Making Provision for Indigent Poor', in *Essays on the Subject of the Poor Law* (1796), reproduced in *The Collected Works of Jeremy Bentham Writings on the Poor Law*, ed. Michael Quinn (Oxford: Clarendon Press, 2001), 39.
17 On this link, see David Brion Davis, *The Problem of Slavery in the Age of Revolution, 1770–1823* (New York: Oxford University Press, 1999); Robert Blackburn, *The Overthrow of Colonial Slavery, 1776–1848* (London: Verso, 1988).
18 Christopher Lloyd, *The Structures of History* (Oxford: Blackwell, 1993); Paul Griffith, 'Ethnocentrism as Act of Kidnapping: The Procrustean Complex in the West', *American International Journal of Social Science* 1, no. 2 (2012): 59–70; Roy Preiswerk and Dominique Perrot, *Ethnocentrism and History: Africa, Asia and Indian America in Western Textbooks* (New York: Nok. Print, 1978).
19 Kartik Kalyan Raman, 'Utilitarianism and the Criminal Law in Colonial India: A Study of the Practical Limits of Utilitarian Jurisprudence', *Modern Asian Studies* 28, no. 4 (1994): 739–91.
20 On the impact of the Indian experience on Britain: Eric Stoke, *The English Utilitarians and India* (Oxford: Oxford University Press, 1959).
21 Jeremy Bentham, 'Essay on the Influence of Time and Place in Matters of Legislation', in Bowring, *Works of Jeremy Bentham*, vol. 2, 171.
22 Alessandro Stanziani, *Bâtisseurs d'Empires: Russie, Inde et Chine à la croisée des mondes* (Paris: Liber, 2012) and *Seamen, Migrants and Workers. Bondage in the Indian Ocean World, Eighteenth-Nineteenth Centuries* (New York: Palgrave Macmillan, 2014).
23 Tapas Kumar Banerjee, *Background to Indian Criminal Law* (Calcutta: Orient Longman 1963), 130; Harald Fischer-Tiné and Michael Mann, eds *Colonialism as Civilizing Mission* (London: Anthem Press, 2004).
24 'Extract of the Proceedings of the Committee at Kishan Nugar (28 June 1772)', in 'Seventh Report from the Committee of Secrecy' (6 May 1773), in *House of Commons Sessional Papers of the Eighteenth Century*, ed. Sheila Lambert (1975), 348 (hereinafter 'Seventh Report').
25 Elie Halevy, *The Growth of Philosophic Radicalism*, trans. Mary Morrist (London: Faber & Faber, 1972); Douglas Hay, *Albion's Fatal Tree: Crime and Society in Eighteenth Century England* (London: Pantheon Books, 1975); Daniel Lieberman, *The Province of Legislation Determined: Legal Theory in Eighteenth Century England* (Cambridge: Cambridge University Press, 1989).
26 Jones to Arthur Lee, 1 October 1786, in *The Letters of Sir William Jones*, ed. Garland Cannon (Oxford: Oxford University Press 1970), vol. 2, 712.
27 Lea Campos Boralevi, *Bentham and the Oppressed* (New York: Walter de Gruyter, 1984); Fred Rosen, *Bentham, Byron and Greece: Constitutionalism, Nationalism, and Early Liberal Political Thought* (Oxford: Clarendon Press, 1992).

28 IOR (India Office Library and Records, London): BRC (Bengal Revenue Consultations) 16 August 1774, n. 442, letter from the Provincial Council at Patna to Warren Hastings, 4 August 1774.
29 IOR, Bengal Judicial Consultations, P/132/21.
30 IOR, Bengal Judicial Consultations, P/132/57.
31 *British Parliamentary Papers* (1831–32), XIV, 16 February 1832.
32 James Mill, *The History of British India* (London: James Madden, 1858 [1818]).
33 C. E. Grey and E. Ryan, 'Some Observations on a Suggestion of a Code of Law', submitted 13 September 1830 to the governor-general in council. Bentick to Grey and Ryan, *British Parliamentary Papers* VI (9 October 1831): 144.
34 Sandra den Otter, 'Law, Authority and Colonial Rule', in *India and the British Empire*, eds Douglas Peers and Nandini Gooptu (Oxford: Oxford University Press, 2012), 168–90, in particular 179. See also Elizabeth Kolsky, *Colonial Justice in British India: White Violence and the Rule of Law* (Cambridge: Cambridge University Press, 2010); Martin Wiener, *An Empire on Trial: Race, Murder and Justice under British Rule, 1870–1935* (Cambridge: Cambridge University Press, 2009).
35 John Stuart Mill, 'Essays on Equality, Law, & Education', in *Collected Works of John Stuart Mill*, [orig. 1825, ed. John Robson], eds Stefano Collini (Toronto: University of Toronto Press, 1984), vol. 21, 83.
36 Lynn Zastopul, 'India, J.S. Mill and Western Culture', in *J.S. Mill's Encounter with India*, eds Martin Moir, Douglas Peers and Lynn Zastoupil (Toronto: University of Toronto Press, 1999), 111–48; Robin Moore, 'John Stuart Mill and Royal India', in ibid., 87–110.
37 IOR, John Stuart Mill, Political dispatch to India, 13 February 1838, E/4/753, 909–12.
38 IOR, John Stuart Mill, Political dispatch to Bombay, 21 September 1842, E/4/1071, 335–45.
39 IOR, John Stuart Mill, Political dispatch to Bombay, 18 October 1843, E/4/1074 54–6.
40 IOR, British India Society, *British India: The Duty and Interests of Great Britain, to Consider the Condition and Claims of Her Possessions in the East: Addresses Delivered before the Members of the Society of Friends, at their Yearly Meeting, Devonshire House, Bishopsgate Street, on the 1st of June, 1839* (London: Johnston & Barrett, 1839).
41 Gwyn Campbell and Alessandro Stanziani, eds, *Debt and Bondage in the Indian Ocean, 18th–21st Centuries* (London: Pickering & Chatto, 2013).
42 Alessandro Stanziani, 'Local Bondage in Global Economies: Servants, Wage Earners and Indentured Migrants in Nineteenth Century France, Britain and the Mascarenes', *Modern Asian Studies* 47, no. 4 (2013): 1218–51.

Chapter 4

GEOGRAPHY AND THE RESHAPING OF THE MODERN CHINESE EMPIRE

Shellen Wu

The Development and Progress in Tibet is the Inevitable Result of History. The development and progress in modern Tibet results from the innate logic of its social and historical environment, and has its roots in China's progress in a larger context. Its development is in line with the advance of world's modern civilization.[1]

PRC White Paper, 2013

Reading through the White Papers issued by the Chinese government in recent years, particularly regarding Tibet, Xinjiang and the disputed island of Diaoyutai/Senkaku, it may feel as though one has stepped back in time to the golden age of historicism in the nineteenth century, when claims of historical inevitability would have no more raised eyebrows than positivist views of science and progress advancing at the vanguard of civilization. The People's Republic of China (PRC) has issued these position papers on territory and sovereignty with deadly earnestness, reflecting stances which arise neither from Marxism nor its hybrid forms in the era of reform and opening. Most media accounts in recent years have vaguely attributed these views to resurgent nationalism. Yet, in itself nationalism does not fully account for the fact that since the collapse of the Qing dynasty in 1911 Han Chinese have viewed areas populated by other ethnic groups as inseparable and inviolable parts of the Chinese national body. The logical extension of nationalism should be the expulsion of ethnic minorities and their territories from the Chinese national boundaries. In reality, the opposite happened. Nationalism and other theoretical models from the social sciences, based almost exclusively on Western historical development, thus offer a very limited explanation of contemporary Chinese territorial claims and strategic aims.

It is my contention that China's modern territoriality dates from the twilight years of the Qing dynasty, when the collapsing dynasty left an ideological vacuum on the question of empire. The 1910s swept away not only the Qing, but no less than four other historically land-based empires, including the Ottoman Empire, Austria-Hungary, the German Empire and Imperial Russia. Against the tide of nation states in the twentieth century, only China was able to reconstitute its borders to retain most of the territorial reach of the multi-ethnic Qing Empire. Geography played an essential role in this reconfiguration of empire under the guise of the nation state, and until one incorporates imperial territoriality into the conceptualization of Chinese nationalism, the issuances of the PRC state council would continue to appear both incomprehensible and the anachronistic proclamations of a bygone age. Forged during a century of civil wars and foreign invasion, the geopolitical discourse of modern China combined a long-held tradition in geography, foreign influence and the twentieth-century revision of geography's role in the creation of a nation upon the territorial foundations of the Qing Empire.

Postcolonial theorists have long pointed to historicism as one means for Western liberals to reconcile the rhetoric of equality and rights in the metropole with the exclusion inherent in imperialism by keeping colonial subjects on tutelage indefinitely in the waiting rooms of History.[2] At the same time, as Dipesh Chakrabarty has argued, the very social sciences, developed in Europe in the context of imperialism, became universalized and naturalized as the lens for non-Western cultures to understand capitalist modernity.[3] The social sciences reinforced and propagated European conceptions of territoriality, sanctified in the development of international law (international in the sense that European and later Americans applied it everywhere they had a presence, but not in the reverse). The conditions of reciprocity and universality stretched only so far as European diplomats would countenance for 'our European international law'.[4] In the twentieth century, the political theorist Carl Schmitt saw international law and the modern world order in a line of direct descent from ancient Greece and the products of Western thought from the Age of Discovery to the Congress of Vienna in 1815.[5]

In the event, it was hardly coincidental that the American missionary W. A. P. Martin (1827–1916) was responsible for the translation into classical Chinese of both Henry Wheaton's *Elements of International Law* and the first science textbooks while serving as the headmaster of the officially sponsored Interpreter's College (Tongwenguan) in Beijing in the 1860s. Science and international law formed the two key aspects of what the West saw as its defining features and the foundations of its superiority to the rest of the world. If the process of translation underlay imperialism, however, the empirical evidence in China points to a different trajectory than that proposed by postcolonial theorists. Translation in China occurred not only across linguistic, legal and cultural/material divides, but also on a temporal level, incorporating modern science and the discourse of civilization to the terms and practices from the Chinese historical tradition.

The dynamic of a proffered equality in the indefinite future applied even in places with a long historical and geographical tradition, like China and India. Nevertheless, nineteenth-century imperialism and the Marxist influence on Chinese historiography in the twentieth century has resulted in the almost complete occlusion of the influence of China's own imperial past on its modern process of state-making. From his earliest works, Prasenjit Duara placed the impact of Western capitalism's penetration into the Chinese countryside and the extension of state control into rural society as the two key historical processes of the twentieth century.⁶ Influenced by the postcolonialists, Duara saw the marquee role of History in the imperialism discourse as tempered by the simultaneity of the nation state and empire in the rise of Western powers.⁷ In other words, he viewed the rise of the nation state and empire not as two separate and mutually exclusive phenomena but entwined processes that set off against one another in dialogue.

A sacrosanct belief in nationhood coeval with the realities of empire most notably played out in the Japanese empire, particularly in the brief history of the Japanese-controlled 'Manchu' puppet regime in Manchukuo.⁸ Duara had thrown down the gauntlet, and historians of modern Japan have eagerly followed up on his study of Manchukuo to examine the multifaceted practices and contradictions of the Japanese empire.⁹ In China studies, on the other hand, the nation and rise of nationalism has continued to be the paradigmatic norm in framing the history of twentieth-century China, in large part because imperialism became associated exclusively with the West and Japan. Yet, the limits of the nation as a framework of understanding modern Chinese history becomes apparent the minute we step back and examine a map of China: Chinese boundaries today, with the lone exception of outer Mongolia, follows closely the territorial outlines of the Qing Empire. How are we then to make sense of this disjuncture between historical interpretation and the geographical reality of empire?

In China and in the West descriptive geography both predated and incorporated aspects of later offshoots such as geology, botany and ethnography. A strong geographical tradition in China dates back to the fourth century BC when the 'Tributes of Yu' (*Yugong*) section of *The Book of History* (*Shang Shu*) divided the country into nine provinces and carefully documented the topographical geography of each province as well as their natural fauna and mineral production. From the Warring States period (475 BCE–221 BCE) rulers saw maps as the expression of their authority over territory. From the late Ming/Qing transition in the early seventeenth century, a number of scholars devoted considerable attention to political geography, travelling extensively in frontier regions to collect information firsthand. In one notable example, the early Qing polymath Gu Yanwu (1613–1683) travelled widely across the empire in his later years and collected materials for his studies on historical geography and epigraphy.¹⁰ Gu's particular attention to recording the historical evolution of localities and place names exemplified *yange dili*, which roughly translates to historical geography in English, methodologically combining linguistic and historical analysis in a uniquely Chinese textual geographical tradition. Following the historical precedence, the great Qing encyclopaedic compendium *Siku Quanshu* grouped geography under the overarching category of history.

During Qing rule, the needs of empire-building channelled geographical research into the empirical study of border peoples and their customs. Laura Hostetler has shown in her study of gazetteers and Miao albums commissioned by local officials that the Qing state used mapping and ethnographical studies in ways similar to contemporaneous premodern states in Europe.¹¹ These sources used in the governing of frontier territories arguably served similar or analogous purposes as European geographical compendiums in the nineteenth century. In the first half of the nineteenth century, Wei Yuan took up the problem of geography to compile a comprehensive vision of the world, placing China into a global context.[12] The resurgent interest in geography was linked to the issue of foreign policy and how to deal with neighbouring states like India and through India the ascendant British empire.

As late Qing officials like Wei Yuan, Lin Zexu and Xu Jiyu turned to Western geographical texts to compile knowledge about the world, geography in the West was transitioning from a natural science to a social science.[13] By the 1890s, the German geographer Friedrich Ratzel (1844–1944) had already moved onto a synthesis of history, geography and the study of human civilization. Ratzel's larger body of works drew heavily upon the connections between history and geography and contributed to the nascent field of anthropology by demanding that all societies be studied historically.[14]

Ratzel's American disciple, Ellen Churchill Semple (1863–1932), became one of the first faculty members in the geography department at the University of Chicago. Semple helped to disseminate geography in the United States as a holistic combination of history and civilization. In her most famous work, which names Ratzel in the title, Semple argued: 'A broad territorial base and security of possession are the central guarantees of national survival.'[15] Semple falls into a group of thinkers in the late nineteenth and early twentieth centuries from across the social sciences and on both sides of the Atlantic who sought causal links between the environment, history and the development of civilizations. A wide range of intellectuals, including Thomas Henry Huxley, Ellsworth Huntington, Oswald Spengler, Karl August Wittfogel, and *Annales* historians like Lucien Febvre and Marc Bloch, shared this common interest in crossing disciplinary boundaries to find universal laws of historical development.[16] Many of these figures expressed overt racism in their works, which became deeply embarrassing to subsequent generations of social scientists. But the underlying idea of a grand explanation for civilization continued to exert influence in the social sciences into the twenty-first century. In the preface to Samuel Huntington's 1996 book, he rather humorously referred to the unprecedented amount of public interest that accompanied the publication of his original essay, 'Clash of Civilizations', in *Foreign Affairs* in 1993.[17] What he didn't mention was his place in the unbroken intellectual lineage from the late nineteenth century of social scientists in pursuit of a theory of civilization.[18]

The interest in theories of civilization spanned the globe. Turn of the twentieth-century writers and reformers like Liang Qichao (1873–1929), steeped in both the classical tradition and open to new ideas from the West, acknowledged the early Qing contributions of writers like Gu Yanwu to political geography. Theories of state-formation articulated in the twentieth century have focused almost exclusively on European case studies. Yet from the late Qing, officials and other commentators actively sought out alternative state models while engaging with the reinterpretation of China's own imperial past.[19] In the transition from Qing to

Republican China, geography remained a staple subject in primary and secondary schools, while commercial presses rolled out large numbers of gazetteers, atlas collections and textbooks. Travel accounts, particularly to frontier areas, borrowed heavily from earlier Qing works, and a new genre dealing specifically with travel abroad also retained rhetorical conventions from earlier writings. Those clamouring for the adoption of 'modern' geography, however, simply did not see this abundant literature as science. By the 1930s, a new generation, including students who had returned after studying abroad, viewed *yange dili* as unscientific. In the clamour to adopt a 'scientific' geography, few Chinese writers at the time or since recognized the retention of imperial tropes and concerns in their writings.

For Chinese revolutionaries the territorial expanse of the Qing presented a problem. How does this vast, multi-ethnic land expanse fit into a discourse of the nation? Historical and geographical reconceptualization offered one solution. By the turn of the twentieth century, the prominent Chinese reformer/journalist/ intellectual Liang Qichao tied geography to new ideas about the nation state when he wrote about world geography and linked China to a newly formulated 'Asia'.[20] Liang wrote extensively on history and geography, linking the two fields together with the development of civilization.

Liang has become a magnet for scholarship precisely because he reflected so many of the broad intellectual trends of his times – from social Darwinism to new ideas of race, nationalism and empire. In his writings, as in earlier Chinese compendiums of knowledge, Liang placed geography under the general heading of history. He separated China into two geographical components: the eighteen provinces of the traditional heartland and the dependent regions (*shubu*) including Manchuria, Mongolia and Tibet.[21] Liang took it as a given that the geographical differences within China, divided along three main river systems and different climate zones, also reflected the racial characteristics of the ethnicities populating these regions. For Liang, the 'people of Asia' with whom the Chinese had interaction included only those successfully incorporated into the Qing Empire (the Tibetans, Mongols, Tongus, Xiongnu, Manchu and the Han), a concept that corresponded to the territorial extent and constituency of what he was configuring as the modern Chinese nation.[22] As the reification of culture and civilization, geography played a leading role in these accounts. Liang Qichao did not reject empire in favour of nationalism so much as advocated the retention of empire under the umbrella of Chinese nationalism.

As this 'new' geography gained popularity across Asia in the age of imperialism, geography began to be conflated with new notions of race, historical progress and civilization. The prominent intellectual and promoter of the Westernization of Meiji Japan, Fukuzawa Yukichi (1835–1901), for example, published an essay in 1885, 'Escape from Asia', which ruthlessly criticized Korea and China as the backward elements of East Asia. Fukuzawa went on to develop these early ideas into a theory of civilization.[23] For Fukuzawa, the advanced West stood at the top of the pyramid of civilizations, while in Asia, backward Korea and China did not qualify as civilized. Geography played a prominent role in the Meiji educational reforms as well as in discussions about civilization and social classification.[24] As Japan pulled away from Asia, Chinese intellectuals themselves began to see geography and more importantly, science, as an integral part of what qualified a people as civilized, even as Chinese learning lost its once central place in the Japanese discourse of civilization.[25] The newspaper *Hubei Xuebao*, published by Chinese students who had studied in Japan, contained numerous translations of Japanese writings on geography.[26] A piece in 1903 pointed out: 'Of the matters of importance to the country, not one is not related to political geography.'[27] Another piece in 1903 highlighted geography's expansive boundaries bridging the humanities and the sciences.[28] Most of these writers mentioned the broad areas of knowledge included in geography and that as a discipline it bridged the natural and social sciences. A 1903 essay translated from Japanese in the *Hubei Xuebao* pointed out the ancient origins of geography as a means to record and list natural phenomena. Nowadays, the article argued, geography had expanded to include (1) the relationship between the earth and heavenly bodies, (2) explanation of life and humankind, (3) the relationship between animals, minerals and humans, (4) industry and its political organization and (5) diplomatic relations.[29]

In turn of the century China, with the threat of imperialism looming over political crisis, and a pervasive sense of gloom among the gentry elite of the country, the promotion of geography was seen as a way to inculcate patriotism among the young and educate the general populace. References to geography invariably took on social Darwinian undertones. In 1902 the progressive paper *Xinmin Congbao* published an article entitled, 'The relationship between Geography and Civilization'.[30] The article discussed among other things why people in tropical regions did not develop civilization and promoted the idea that human evolution depended not only on material conditions but also on the triumph of the spirit. World civilizations, including China, the author pointed out, only developed on relatively flat terrain, mostly on plains.

The following year, in 1903, the *Xinmin Congbao* ran a series on geography, stating that 'the biggest question of the twentieth century is the future existence of China as a country'.[31] The writer defined imperialism geographically. The author saw the expansion of European empires as the direct result of political stasis on the European continent itself. Since Europe by and large was already settled politically, expansion by necessity must come at the margins of the world in relation to Europe. For the writer, European territorial ambitions posed a keen danger for countries like China, which stood to lose to the overwhelming wealth and power of the West. The danger of annihilation, the destruction of the country or *guo*, loomed large in these articles. Such writings circulated in China leading to the rise of an entire genre of *wangguo* literature, which Rebecca Karl has argued, reflected the 'modern process of racial, linguistic, cultural, and political annihilation'.[32] The proliferation of this particular genre of writing had its roots in the previous decades of reforms and the sense of futility and failure following the Sino-Japanese War. Karl has emphasized that the very coinage of the concept of 'Asia' was related to the social Darwinian dynamic of the era and that both Chinese and Japanese intellectuals saw the world as aligned between colonized and the colonizers.

Liang's formulation of Asia clearly shows that the social Darwinian undertones of these writings on geography opened the way to the new discourse of race. The journal *Nüxue Jiangyi*, aimed at educating women, published a series on geography in 1905, which included a section on race. The anonymous writer (most likely a man) divided the ethnicities in China into four large groups and in addition, a group 'which is resistant to acculturation', the Tibetans, 'an entirely barbarian people'.[33] Granted, according to this 'geographical' analysis, even among the Han, the northerners lacked stamina, the people in the middle resisted all law and order, and only the southerners qualified to become good citizens. According to an article translated from the Japanese, which appeared in the *Beiyang Gongbao* in 1903, geography used to be merely descriptive. With the rise of science, geography had become crucial as a gateway science.[34] According to a writer for the student publication *Hubei Xuesheng Jie*, 'There are many who cry that China will cease to be (*wan*) like India and Egypt and that China would also be colonized by the white man.'[35] Another article in the *Hubei Xuesheng Jie* argued that contemporary geographers were at fault for not making clear and explicit the relationship between geography and nationalism. Such oversight could prove fatal in a time of national vulnerability.[36] The overriding concern of these writers involved imperialism and its threat to China's sovereignty and continued independence.

Whether commentators termed these outlying regions *waifan* or *shubu*, long before an explicit discourse of frontier territories or *bianjiang* became the vogue during the Japanese invasion in the 1930s, various writers of textbooks for children and explanatory articles for adults differentiated between a predominantly Han core region and those culturally and ethnically different areas on the outer rim of the core region. The threat of imperialism and of China's political and economic crisis may have played out in hand-wringing and desperate appeals to avoid the fate of *wanguo*, but in the same breath such writers turned the imperialist dynamic on the 'uncivilized' peoples of *waifan*. What we see, then, was an entire spectrum of civilization in the newly articulated Asia. The West, as the agents of science and technology, occupied a separate category. The Japanese thinker and reformer Fukuzawa Yukichi may have wished to separate Japan from its backward neighbours China and Korea, but at the same time, Chinese intellectuals were equally eager to adopt the language of civilization, which would exclude the peoples of the *waifan* even as their territories would become the necessary space for the expansion of the Han majority.

Japanese encroachment in the northeast and the eventual invasion in the 1930s provided a further catalyst to geography's disciplinary revival. In the 1920s and 1930s, Japanese geographers carried out detailed studies of Chinese geography, not just in the northeast, but also in the rest of the Chinese mainland. These studies, fitting in with the broad expansion of geography into related areas of study, not only mapped out the mainland, but also provided information on transportation, taxation and local customs – Japanese geographers answered Ratzel's challenge to study geography and civilization as a holistic, interrelated field of study. As the Japanese invasion proceeded from the northeast to the rest of China, ideas about the geographical justification of empire circulated among Chinese readers. As the abundance of translations from Japanese demonstrates, in the early twentieth century Japan had become a central conduit of ideas from the West, at the same time itself looking to European empires for inspiration.[37] Japan had very little historical experience with the administration of an empire. China, however, had two thousand years of imperial policies and an equally ancient geographical tradition to draw from.

The efforts of early-twentieth-century geographers resulted in the formation of independent geography departments in Chinese universities starting in the 1920s. The flagship publication, *Dili Xuebao* (*Journal of Geographical Sciences*), began publication in 1934. From the first issue, articles in the journal on climate, soil studies and demography demonstrated a turn to empirical and fieldwork-based analysis as the foundation for the 'New' geography.[38] Despite all the calls for the formation of a modern Chinese geography, the line between politics and science was often blurred. In reality there was frequently little other than stylistic differences between the message coming from various right-leaning societies, whose publications advocated for the development of the Chinese frontier, and the research agenda of scientific institutions.

Starting in 1937, Japanese invasion and the formal start of war further spurred geographers to contribute to the war effort in any way possible. On 1 April 1941, the Institute of Geography debuted the inaugural issue of *The Journal of Geography* (*Dili*) from Beipei, a small town outside of Chongqing, where Academia Sinica (the precursor to the Chinese Academy of Sciences (CAS) in the pre-1949 years) and the China National Geological Survey had taken wartime refuge. The journal and other publications, from geographical textbooks to atlases and historical works, were part of a fundamental spatial reconceptualization of China stretching from the late Qing to 1949 and beyond. The space of China now included not just the two-dimensional surface of the earth, but also extended above to the skies, beyond land to the oceans, and below to the depths of the earth.

The ever-present threat of war and of Chinese defeat bubbled just beneath the rhetoric of a scientific geography. One of the leading geographers in the country, Huang Guozhang (1896–1966), contributed the preface to the inaugural issue of *The Journal of Geography*. Like many of his fellow scientists, Huang had received his training overseas. A Hunan native, Huang had received his graduate degree in geography from the University of Chicago and returned to China in 1928 to take up a teaching post in Nanjing. After the Japanese invasion, like many leading intellectuals of patriotic leanings, he retreated with the Nationalist (GMD) army into the interior and helped to found the Geographical Institute in Chongqing in December of 1939.[39] Huang began his preface by acknowledging the ancient roots of geography in both the West and in China, although in his view, Chinese geography stagnated and failed to go through the revolutionary changes the field had undergone in the West in the nineteenth century. As a result, in his view, Chinese geography had only started to catch up when Chinese students began to study abroad in large numbers.

According to Huang, 'Modern geography seeks to establish the principles of the relationship between mankind and the earth. Geography is not only a theoretical science, but also a discipline that seeks to address practical ways of improving people's lives. It is particularly important to the education of citizens of the nation.'[40] For Huang, geography could serve as a compass for both China's diplomatic efforts and its domestic policy. All organisms compete to survive and must adapt to their environment, according to Huang, but mankind goes a step further, to not only adapt to the environment but also exploit its value.[41] For Huang, since the start of the War of Resistance against the Japanese, geographical education had become all the more important and played a vital role in inciting an up-swelling of national fervour. Even with the forced move to Sichuan, incomplete library of reference materials and transportation difficulties, geographers at the Institute of Geography continued their research efforts. *The Journal of Geography*, Huang stated, amplified those efforts by broadcasting them to a broader reading public, targeting in particular university students, middle school geography teachers and all those with an interest in geographical research.[42]

The founding of the *Journal of Geography*, as well as a number of other academic and popular geographical journals from the 1930s and 1940s, attested to the popularity of the field. Yet, beyond the rhetoric of empiricism and science, these journals focused unmistakably on the frontier areas: the northeast, northwest and southwest. Commentators explicitly connected these regions to the Japanese invasion and imperialist encroachment. The northeast briefly became the focus of an intellectual fad in the 1930s; when Japanese occupation closed off the region, interest turned to the northwest. Finally, invasion and the retreat of the wartime regime to Sichuan made the southwest and its link to Southeast Asia vital to the war effort.

GMD official Zhu Jiahua (1893–1963), a geologist by training who entered politics in the 1930s, encouraged and supported the research emphasis of the Institute of Geography and the China Geological Survey on frontier regions. In particular, Zhu attempted to foster the building of a party structure in the northwest, including Xinjiang.[43] The political strategic thinking behind this plan was to counter the growing popularity and spread of the Communist Party from their base in Yanan in the northwest. Given a reprieve by the war from the GMD's relentless pursuit and suppression campaigns, from the 1940s the Communist party had begun to implement land reform and political organization in the arid and poverty-stricken northwestern area around their main base. Driven to the northwest by exigency and near annihilation in Jiang's last 'Bandit Suppression Campaign', the growing influence of the Communist base now ironically appeared to reinforce the writings of geopolitical writers, including Halford Mackinder's disciple, the British geographer and geopolitician James Fairgrieve, that future military threats to the Chinese heartland would come from central Asia and the vast flat stretches of land to the west.

Both during the war and after the Japanese surrender, the GMD Ministry of Agriculture and Forestry, in conjunction with the Ministry of Defense and the military, formulated detailed plans of land reclamation and established local bureaus and model farms.[44] These farms were located in the remaining areas of Free China during the war and explicitly designated as experimental areas for future agricultural and rural renewal. With the end of the war, the GMD took over Japanese-run collective farms in the northeast in 1945 and planned for the extension of these communes to the frontier areas in Mongolia, Xinjiang, Qinghai, Gansu and Tibet. For party bureaucrats these collective farms would accomplish the double role of providing employment for demobilized soldiers and reinforce Chinese sovereignty on the frontiers. On paper at least, proposals for these reclamation districts featured utopian plans for hospitals, manufacturing plants, recreational facilities, movie theatres and, for spiritual uplift, theatre troupes. Not surprisingly, the reality differed dramatically from the paper proposals. Yet, taken in conjunction with the scientific agenda of major research institutes, these plans offered a vision for rural renewal by setting up laboratories for social engineering. In the ideal world such frontier farms would become the experimental zones for agrarian renewal. The crushing demands of war, however, made insurmountable the obstacles to their successful implementation.

Geopolitics served as the geographical justification for conquest and expansion not only for the Japanese, but also offered Chinese intellectuals a means to reconcile the competing claims of empire and nation. The Japanese emulated the Germans and published a journal devoted to geopolitics.[45] At the same time, in April 1940 the political scientist Lin Tongji, historian Lei Haizong and writer and literature professor Chen Quan, along with a motley group of twenty-six of China's leading humanists joined together to found the journal *Zhan Guo Ce* (*Warring States Policies*) devoted to geopolitical writings in Kunming in the southwestern province of Yunnan.[46] Both the Japanese and the Chinese journals looked to the German intellectual tradition with admiration. The Japanese journal was innocuously named *Chiagaku Zashi* (*The Journal of Geography*). In contrast, the Chinese journal was named after the Warring States period of ancient China. In 1941, the geographer Sha Xuejun published an article in which he compared Hitler's rapid conquest of the European continent to the Qin state's vanquishing of rival states in the late third century BCE.[47] Sha was loosely affiliated with the group of intellectuals who published the journal *Zhan Guo Ce* and like them saw the ongoing war as a defining moment in world history. Chinese history deeply coloured Sha's understanding of the European war and not the reverse.

Historians entered the fray to add moral and historical weight to the cause of Chinese sovereignty over the empire. In 1948 the historian and oracle bone expert Ding Shan (1902–52) published a slim volume titled *Geography and the Rise and Fall of Chinese Civilization* (*Dili yu zhonghua minzu zhi shengshuai*). In the work, Ding argued that geography is the key to history and civilization, a conclusion that the eminent historian Gu Jiegang (1893–1980) reinforced in the preface he penned to the work. Ding broke no new ground in connecting historical development and geography. Gu Jiegang himself had written extensively on historical geography beginning in the 1920s and in 1938 had co-authored a work of historical geography entitled, *A History of Change in China's Frontier Regions*.[48] The historical geographer Tan Qixiang (1911–92) and Gu Jiegang, like their Western intellectual counterparts, used history to legitimize conquest and incorporate imperial territories into the national body.[49]

Ding based his argument on his detailed knowledge of Chinese history. First, Ding pointed out that geographical differences led to cultural divisions. Starting with the First Emperor's unification of China, Ding argued, Chinese rulers overcame geographical barriers and accomplished forced cultural homogenization. For Ding, the pinnacle of the Han dynasty's achievements came with the emperor Han Wudi's sponsorship of Zhang Qian's westward expeditions and wars of conquest in western regions. These military campaigns, however, exposed the Han race (*minzu*)'s reliance on the power of horses, leading to Ding's second major point: the importance of horses in warfare and in the rise and demise of the early dynasties.

Next, Ding turned to the north-south differences in Chinese geography, which over the long term he viewed as contributing to an unfortunate north-south tension in Chinese history.[50] Ding pointed to the successive southern remnants of northern empires. For Ding, these historical examples merely illustrated the aphorism that 'those who live by mountains live off the mountains. Those who dwell by water live off water. All humans depend upon nature for their livelihoods. Countries, too, must rely on geography's protection to ensure their independence.'[51] Moving rapidly through dynasties, Ding saw as the Qing's greatest accomplishment its capable management of the border regions and Tibet.[52] For Ding Shan, the Qing's demise could be traced to its loss of control of productive power. The industrial revolution unleashed for the West a burst of dynamic impetus which brought down the Qing much as the powerful horse riding, nomadic peoples of the northwestern regions ran roughshod over the sedentary agricultural peoples of the Chinese cultural heartlands in the Han and Tang dynasties.

Ding posited that, in the history of the Chinese civilization, external forces caused crises. Before the Opium War, he argued, these external pressures frequently originated from the deserts of the northwest; after the Opium War, they arrived over the seas.[53] Ding cited Halford Mackinder's student, James Fairgrieve, and his 1915 work, *Geography and World Power*. Fairgrieve's work had been translated into Chinese in 1938, with a second edition coming out in 1939. Although the book shows a shallow understanding of China's history and geographical situation, it proved popular with Chinese readers. The very brevity and vagueness of Fairgrieve's discussion of China allowed his Chinese readers room for interpretation. In the short section on China, Fairgrieve made a standard geo-determinist argument, pinpointing Beijing and Xian as the two key entries into China from the northwest and the terminus of future railway lines across the northern China plateau, the core of central Asia. Ding slightly altered Fairgrieve's assessment by equating the Japanese invasion from the northeast with historical invasions of the Chinese heartland from the northwest. In these final pages of his work, it becomes clear why in 1948 Ding wrote this condensed volume on geography's role in shaping Chinese history. Time and again over the course of Chinese history, Ding argued, these border regions posed a strategic threat to Chinese civilization, one that if left unchecked spelt its doom. Written after the Japanese surrender, Ding already saw beyond the current war to the potential source of future conflict. At stake was nothing less than the fate of Chinese civilization.

Conclusion

The creation of modern Chinese geography contains multiple strands: a strong tradition in historical geography which became submerged but still influential in the twentieth century; conflicting views about the role of science and scientism dating back to the late Qing; and the political and physical contingencies resulting from the Japanese invasion. These currents cut across the twentieth century into the twenty-first. In China the process of translation took place not only from Western geography and through Japanese intermediaries but also between its own historical past and the present. The Qing state developed mining in Yunnan Province in the southwest with policies that allowed troops to settle the newly opened areas with their families, with the proceeds of mining paying for the costs of empire.[54] In the far west, the Qing followed its conquest of the new territories (the literal meaning of Xinjiang) with large-scale plans for military colonization.[55] The demands and constraints of empire created policy discussions and debates well before the arrival of a Western discourse of imperialism.

From 1949 the PRC's consolidation of power finally established stability for social scientists to safely conduct research in the frontier regions. The formation of an interdisciplinary committee for exploration at the CAS in 1956 created the institutional structure for scientists across various disciplines to collaborate on fieldwork and research. Along similar lines as the CCP's economic planning, the CAS interdisciplinary committee established five-year plans and divided their research into macro regions. The research agenda largely continued the wartime focus on border regions in the northeast, the northwest and the southwest.[56]

The newly established Communist state continued frontier settlement programmes first initiated or planned under the previous regime. At the same time, during the heyday of Sino-Soviet cooperation in the 1950s, the central Academy of Sciences sponsored the translation of Soviet works that harshly condemned geopolitics as the tool of American imperialism.[57] In particular, these essays pinpointed and savaged the implicit racism of geo-determinism. Geographers had seen themselves as patriots contributing to the nationalist war effort, but starting in the early 1950s, their wartime writings made them the prime targets of anti-rightist political campaigns. The geographers had long clamoured for their inclusion among the physical scientists in the Academy of Sciences, but their persecution during the Cultural Revolution aligned their fates with the humanists. In the end, their services were seen as less useful to the state than the physicists who might contribute to the nuclear programme and the geologists who surveyed for oil and other natural resources. The PRC preserved the empire but destroyed the social scientists who had articulated its discourse. The PRC executed plans of forced settlement and frontier development that the high Qing state and certainly the GMD regime never had the wherewithal to implement. Even as individual lives and an entire generation were sacrificed, the empire endured.

Huang Guozhang, one of the founders of the wartime Institute of Geography, committed suicide with his wife in 1966; noted human geographers Hu Huanyong and Li Xudan were labelled counter-revolutionaries in the 1950s and spent years in jail before being rehabilitated in the 1980s. Political scientist Lin Tongji, who received his PhD from UC Berkeley, was labelled a rightist in 1958. More 'fortunate' members of that cohort of social scientists, including the geographer Sha Xuejun and Zhang Yintang, lived out the rest of their lives in exile in Taiwan and the United States, respectively. The litany of tragic fates is at once a sombre reminder of individual powerlessness against the relentless political upheavals in twentieth-century China and an intimation of a much larger epistemological shift at work since the nineteenth century, shaped by evolving ideas about the state, empire and science.

Notes

1. English version of White Paper on 'Development and Progress of Tibet', issued by the Information Office of the State Council of the People's Republic of China, 22 October 2013, http://www.china.org.cn/government/whitepaper/node_7192768.htm
2. Dipesh Chakrabarty, *Provincializing Europe: Postcolonial Thought and Historical Difference* (Princeton: Princeton University Press, 2000), 8.
3. Ibid., 29.
4. Lydia Liu, 'Translating International Law', *The Clash of Empires: The Invention of China in Modern World Making* (Cambridge: Harvard University Press 2004), 124; Rune Svarverud, *International Law as World Order in Late Imperial China: Translation, Reception and Discourse, 1847–1911* (Leiden: Brill, 2007), 106; Richard S. Horowitz, 'International Law and State Transformation in China, Siam, and the Ottoman Empire during the Nineteenth Century', *Journal of World History*, 15, no. 4 (2004): 445–86.
5. Carl Schmitt, *The Nomos of the Earth in the International Law of the Jus Publicum Europaeum*, trans. G. L. Ulmen (New York: Telos Press, 2006).
6. Prasenjit Duara, *Culture, Power, and the State: Rural North China, 1900–1942* (Stanford: Stanford University Press, 1988), 3–4.
7. Prasenjit Duara, *Rescuing History from the Nation* (Chicago: Chicago University Press, 1997), 19.
8. Prasenjit Duara, *Sovereignty and Authenticity: Manchukuo and the East Asian Modern* (Lanham: Rowman & Littlefield, 2003), 179–80.
9. Yoshihisa Tak Matsusaka, *The Making of Japanese Manchuria, 1904–1932* (Cambridge: Harvard University Press, 2001); Louise Young, *Total Empire: Manchuria and the Culture of the Wartime Imperialism* (Berkeley: University of California Press, 1998), particularly 307–98; Mariko Asano Tamanoi, 'Knowledge, Power, and Racial Classifications: The "Japanese" in "Manchuria"', *The Journal of Asian Studies* 59, no. 2 (2000): 248–76; Jun Unchida, *Brokers of Empire: Japanese Settler Colonialism in Korea, 1876–1945* (Cambridge: Harvard University Press, 2011).
10. Willard J. Peterson, 'The Life of Ku Yen-wu (1613–1682)', *Harvard Journal of Asiatic Studies* 29 (1969): 201–47.
11. Laura Hostetler, *Qing Colonial Enterprise: Ethnography and Cartography in Early Modern China* (Chicago: University of Chicago Press, 2001); Laura Hostetler, 'Qing Connections to the Early Modern World: Ethnography and Cartography in Eighteenth Century China', *Modern Asian Studies* 34, no. 3 (2000): 623–62.
12. Matthew Mosca, *From Frontier Policy to Foreign Policy: The Question of India and the Transformation of Geopolitics in Qing China* (Stanford: Stanford University Press, 2013), 273–4.

13 Jakub Grygiel, *Great Powers and Geopolitical Change* (Baltimore: Johns Hopkins University Press, 2006), 15.
14 Andrew Zimmerman, *Anthropology and Antihumanism in Imperial Germany* (Chicago: University of Chicago Press, 2001), 204.
15 Ellen Churchill Semple, *Influences of Geographic Environment on the Basis of Ratzel's System of Anthro-Geography* (New York: Henry Holt & Company, 1911), 139.
16 William Rowe, 'Owen Lattimore, Asia, and Comparative History', *Journal of Asian Studies* 66, no. 3 (2007): 759–86.
17 Samuel Huntington, *The Clash of Civilizations and the Remaking of World Order* (New York: Simon & Schuster, 1996), 13.
18 This interest in 'civilization' was not exclusive to the West, as shown by Tessa Morris-Suzuki, 'The Invention and Reinvention of "Japanese Culture"', *Journal of Asian Studies* 54, no. 3 (1995): 759–80.
19 Zhaoguang Ge, 'Absorbing the "Four Borderlands" into "China": Chinese Academic Discussions of "China" in the First Half of the Twentieth Century', *Chinese Studies in History* 48, no. 4 (2015): 331–65.
20 Liang Qichao, 'Zhongguoshi xulun', in *Yinbingshi wenji dianxiao*, eds Wu Song, et al. (Kunming: Yunnan jiaoyu chuban she, 2001), vol. 3, 1620.
21 Ibid., vol. 3, 1802.
22 Rebecca Karl, *Staging the World: Chinese Nationalism at the Turn of the Twentieth Century* (Durham: Duke University Press, 2002), 152.
23 Yukichi Fukuzawa, *An Outline of a Theory of Civilization*, trans. David Dilworth and G. Cameron Hurst III (New York: Columbia University Press, 2009).
24 Kären Wigen, *A Malleable Map: Geographies of Restoration in Central Japan, 1600–1912* (Berkeley: University of California Press, 2010), 171; David Howell, *Geographies of Identity in Nineteenth-Century Japan* (Berkeley: University of California Press, 2005), 131.
25 Douglas Howland, *Translating the West: Language and Political Reason in Nineteenth Century Japan* (Honolulu: University of Hawaii Press, 2002), 33.
26 Chinese students translated or sometimes plagiarized Japanese works, often themselves loose translations of Western works. See Joshua A. Fogel, ed., *The Role of Japan in Liang Qichao's Introduction of Modern Western Civilization to China* (Berkeley: University of California Press 2004), in particular Marianne Bastid-Bruguiere, 'The Japanese-Induced German Connection of Modern Chinese Ideas of the State: Liang Qichao and the *Guojia lun* of J.K. Bluntschli', 105–24 and Ishikawa Yoshihiro, 'Liang Qichao, the Field of Geography in Meiji Japan, and Geographical Determinism', 156–76.
27 *Hubei Xuebao*, no.1 (4) (1903): 28.
28 *Hubei Xuebao*, no. 1 (1) (1903): 31.
29 *Hubei Xuebao*, no. 1 (14) (1903): 35.
30 China's New Citizens (pen name), 'Dili yu wenmin zhi guanxi', *Xinmin Congbao*, no. 1 (1902).
31 Guan Yun, 'Zhongguo yu wan yi wenti lun', *Xinmin Congbao*, no. 4 (1903).
32 Karl, *Staging the World*, 69.
33 *Nüxue Jiangyi*, no. 8 (1905).
34 'Zhuanjian: dili xue xinyi Jiangxi fa', *Beiyang Gongbao*, no. 149 (1903).
35 Li Buqing, 'Zhongguo dili yu shijie zhi guanxi', *Hubei Xuesheng Jie*, no. 1 (1903).
36 Yang Zijiang (a pseudonym, very common during this period for expressing revolutionary views), 'Dili', *Hubei Xuesheng Jie*, no. 5 (1903).

37 William Beasley, *Japanese Imperialism, 1894–1945* (New York: Oxford University Press, 1987), 252.
38 The push for empiricism was taking place across a variety of science and social science disciplines. See Grace Shen, 'Taking to the Field: Geological Fieldwork and National Identity in Republican China', *Osiris* 24, no. 1 (2009): 231–52; Tong Lam, *A Passion for Facts: Social Surveys and the Construction of the Chinese Nation-State, 1900–1949* (Berkeley: University of California Press, 2011), 3.
39 Huang Guozhang, *Dili*, no. 1 (1) (1941): 3.
40 Ibid., 1.
41 Ibid., 2.
42 Ibid., 3.
43 Academia Sinica archives, Zhu Jiahua papers, 301-01-15-018; ibid., 301-01-15-019.
44 Academia Sinica archives and the GMD Party Archives both contain materials related to these *tunken* plans.
45 Gerry Kearns, *Geopolitics and Empire: The Legacy of Halford Mackinder* (Oxford: Oxford University Press, 2009), 20.
46 Jiang Pei, *Zhanguo cepai: Sichao yanjiu* (Tianjin: Tianjin renmin chubanshe, 2001), 11–12.
47 Sha Xuejun, 'Jinri zhi deguo' ('Today's Germany'), *Readers Digest* (*Duzhe wenzhai*), no. 1 (1941): 25–32.
48 Gu Jiegang and Shi Nianhai, *Zhongguo Jiangyu Yangeshi* (Shanghai: Shangwu Chubanshe, 1938).
49 Peter Perdue, *China Marches West: The Qing Conquest of Central Eurasia* (Cambridge: Harvard University Press, 2005), 336, 384.
50 Ding Shan, *Dili yu zhonghua minzu zhi shengshuai* (Shanghai: Dazhongguo tushu ju, 1948), 30.
51 Ibid., 40.
52 Ibid., 64.
53 Ibid., 72.
54 James Lee, 'State and Economy in Southwest China, 1250–1850' (PhD diss., University of Chicago, 1987), 223–9.
55 Perdue, *China Marches West*, 342–7.
56 Sun Honglie, et al., eds, *Zhongguo ziran ziyuan zonghe kexue kaocha yu yanjiu* (Beijing: Shangwu yinshu guan , 2007); Zhang Jiuchen, *Ziran ziyuan zonghe kaocha weiyuan hui yanjiu* (Beijing: Kexue chubanshe, 2013).
57 Zhongguo dili xuehui zhishi bianji weiyuanhui (Chinese Geographical Society Geographical Knowledge Editorial Committee), *Guanyu zichan jieji dili sixiang de pipan* (*Critique of Bourgeois Geographical Thinking*) (Shanghai: Xin zhishi chubanshe, 1955); Soviet Academy of Sciences Geographical Research Institute, ed., *Wei mei di fuwu de zichan jieji dilixue* (*Bourgeois Geography in the Service of American Imperialism*), trans. Tian Meng (Beijing: Zhonghua shuju, 1952).

Chapter 5

THE PERIPHERY'S ORDER: OPIUM AND MORAL WRECKAGE IN BRITISH BURMA

Diana Kim

Periphery, n. 3. The region, space, or area surrounding something; a fringe, margin. Now chiefly: the outlying areas of a region, most distant from or least influenced by some political, cultural or economic centre.
Oxford English Dictionary 2014[1]

While the word periphery denotes a remote and weak location, for recent scholarship on Empire, it connotes a vibrant site of inquiry. Across the social sciences, there is a large body of literature that takes peripheries seriously with interdisciplinary stakes ranging from the intellectual activism of amplifying muted voices of the past to decentring attention from imperial cores and their binary opposition to colonies in favour of hybridity to the critical task of challenging dominant narratives and reflexively questioning the very categories by which scholars regard imperial pasts and presents.[2] A particular strength to current research on peripheries has come from what Dipesh Chakrabarty terms the hermeneutic tradition in the social sciences.[3] This tradition, writes Chakrabarty, 'produces a loving grasp of detail in search of an understanding of the diversity of human life worlds. It produces what may be called "affective histories" … [and] finds thought intimately tied to places and to particular forms of life.'[4] By contrast, peripheries have received less attention from a more analytic tradition in the social sciences. That is, compared with how much has been gained through the production of affective histories, social scientists have thought less lovingly about how to harness details and diversity for explanatory purposes.

This chapter begins to remedy this asymmetry by exploring the explanatory value of non-European peripheries in studies of Anglo-European Empire. The first part addresses the following question: What are the analytical promises and pitfalls of focusing on 'a fringe, margin' in order to say something more general about imperial orders? I draw examples from recent scholarship on opium in nineteenth- and twentieth-century Southeast Asia that highlights the importance of situated actors and ideas in the 'Far East' colonies, especially of Burma and the Philippines, to transformations in imperial and global prohibition regimes. My aim is to clarify the ways by which students of opium and Empire are beginning to articulate an explanatory vocabulary for how – under what conditions and by what mechanisms – local developments at peripheries shaped, influenced or even caused major anti-opium movements and legislative changes occurring afar.[5]

The second part of this chapter presents an illustrative event in 1890s British Burma that helps specify how peripheries matter. During the early years of this decade, a Royal Commission on Opium was tasked with evaluating whether India's export trade should be halted as well as the possibilities of prohibition. The Royal Commission was, according to John Richards, 'one of the great Victorian inquiries devoted to the Indian Empire' and much ink has been spilt on how the commission's final report delivered a 'devastating blow to the hopes of the anti-opium reformers in Britain' in its endorsement of the status quo legal opium market and denial of any 'extensive moral and physical degradation by opium' in India.[6] However, few have paid adequate attention to the exceptional status of Burma in this report, which not only acknowledged opium harms unique to this province but also endorsed strong state controls over opium sales and consumption unparalleled elsewhere in the Empire.[7] I argue that the sources of this differential treatment lie in the local expertise asserted among bureaucrats on the ground in Burma, which was forcefully injected into centres of power as authoritative administrative categories, as building-blocks for imperial policy knowledge. As suggestive evidence, I demonstrate situated bureaucrats crafting a notion of 'moral wreckage' concerning opium-consuming Burmans; how much this language dismayed the Royal Commission and yet figured into its assessments of Burma's exceptional status; and how these developments at the periphery generated the conditions of possibility for prohibition in Burma, with repercussions for the British Indian Empire as well.

In seeking to situate peripheries more firmly in an analytic tradition of social science, this chapter understands Empires as complex and nested sites of knowledge production. Throughout, my use of the word 'periphery' is not in reference to something fixed or essential, but rather to a putatively small part in a large composite – a part that, to return to its ordinary English language use – appears as 'a fringe, margin' to a more general imperial order.[8] In the process of specifying the ways by which developments in the former influenced the latter, this chapter also hints at ways of considering the creative capacities of peripheries in terms of generating authoritative theories and categories of their day and, more broadly, illuminating the imperial origins of social science.

Opium and Empire

In 1990, Carl Trocki worried that for students of nineteenth-century Southeast Asian politics 'the story of the opium trade and its role in the entire imperial century has been almost totally neglected'.[9] Much has changed over the past two decades with a growing interdisciplinary body of scholarship attentive to how the rise and fall of opium trades entwined with the making of colonial states and imperial structures in Southeast Asia. We know much more about the relationships between commercial opium and the development of peasant economies, labour productivity, the growth of colonial capitalism, and financial support for territorial expansion missions, the building of administrative infrastructures, as well as coeval dynamics of opium regulation and social control.[10]

Building upon this growing literature on opium *within* Southeast Asia, a new generation of scholarship highlights the significance of developments concerning opium to the imperial world *beyond* the region. For example, Anne Foster has argued that the British, French, Dutch, as well as the latecomer American empire's ideas about the 'civilizing mission of imperialism' at once drew upon and were reconfigured through local debates on the viability of opium sales revenue and ethics of opium consumption in Southeast Asia.[11] Daniel Wertz's lucid study of American opium policymaking in the Philippines shows how situated Protestant missionaries and evangelical reformers served as powerful forces behind colonial opium prohibition laws in 1906, which had ramifications for both US narcotic policy and international drug treaties. Not only did moral crusaders led by figures like Bishop Charles Henry Brent successfully agitate in the Philippines for the first complete ban on nonmedical opium in a Southeast Asian colony, but their legislative victories also spurred the first international conferences on drug trade control, by 'provid[ing] the global anti-opium movement, which had previously been vocal and active but had precious few tangible results to show for it, with some badly needed momentum'.[12] In turn, Wertz contends, the earliest US federal narcotic laws, such as the 1909 Smoking Opium Exclusion Act, were 'prompted by American calls for international conventions on narcotics control, calls that had their root in prohibition policies in the Philippines'.[13]

Most recently, the large repercussions of seemingly small opium debates within and concerning Southeast Asian colonies have been suggested in Ashley Wright's rich monograph on the state regulation of opium consumption in British Burma.[14] Expanding Robert Maule's pioneering work on the dilemmas that the poppy production in the Federated Shan States posed for early twentieth-century British drug diplomacy, Wright demonstrates how interdepartmental negotiations concerning the Trans-Salween Shan States and opium supply worked to clarify the ambiguities of Burma's constitutional relationship to India and Britain after separation in 1935.[15] This status clarification would subsequently affect the respective positions and modes of participation of each in the League of Nations, the International Labour Organization and other nascent transnational entities.

On the one hand, these recent works demonstrate clear hermeneutic value to exploring the local opium politics of Southeast Asia. Close attention to the cacophony of opium-anxious American voices in a newly conquered Philippines makes audible soft variations of morality, fiscal interest and protection on a general theme of early-twentieth-century progress. Not only does this diversity illuminate fissures within liberal imperial ideas about law's relationship to government and commerce, but such detail also provides a fine-grained lens or even unique window into the lived experiences of actors in their own historical time. Moreover, as Maule and Wright show, to the extent that local decisions for opium policy in a geographically remote place of minor political significance (like the Shan States at the edge of Burma, part of an administratively 'backward' province of India) came to matter a great deal for Britain, the politics of the periphery also refract the dense and multicentric institutional structures of European Empire's overseas rule.

On the other hand, there are several analytical challenges to linking local actors, ideas and occurrences to larger ideational and institutional configurations. First, the opium colonies of Southeast Asia represented economic and geopolitical peripheries in the world of opium economy and international drug diplomacy efforts, at least until the first decade of the twentieth century.[16] Given their marginal status, how can one demonstrate the causal impact of what happened in the Philippines upon US federal policy change and global drug regime formation? Wertz acknowledges this difficulty, tempering the extent to which he argues that American Protestant missionaries in the Philippines and their networks effected grand transformations; 'on an international level, the anti-opium movement *only catalysed* a process of systematizing and rationalizing the control of far-off colonies' (emphasis added).[17] Also, other than missionaries, there were many other stakeholders involved in the regulatory debates, local and otherwise. Traders and merchants, local administrators, religious authorities other lobby groups as well as medical practitioners abounded – both on the ground and entwined in professional and social alliances branching out from the colony. How can one tell who mattered more and why? Certainly, the American missionaries were certainly not the first to agitate for anti-opium legislation concerning 'native' consumption; prior proponents include British excise officials in Burma and Japanese administrators in Formosa. In this sense, how does one parse out the extent to which what happened in the Philippines in the 1900s generated changes elsewhere from the antecedent efforts in other parts of Southeast Asia? That is, how does one disentangle the effect of one seemingly marginal development in a periphery from other forces at the fringe? In sum, periphery-based explanations face issues of relative scale, overdetermination and infinite regress as analytical problems.

Additional challenges concern the distinctive nature of peripheries. Careful studies highlight the peculiarities of opium politics for each Southeast Asian colony, both in terms of demographic, ethnic and racial, institutional variation and the self-perceptions of actors at the time. For instance, Wright shows that opium regulations in late-nineteenth-century British Burma followed differential regional and social approaches based on context-specific factors such as the lagged annexation of Upper Burma, indirect rule arrangements in the Shan States, the special tin mining productivity in Tenasserim and the population distribution and imagined hierarchies among Burmans, non-Burman 'natives' and migrant Chinese and Indians. Burma was also special due to its 'imbedded position in multiple networks', which were 'both imperial, connecting Burma to India to Britain, and more broadly transnational, linking Burma to China and the United States of America'.[18] Moreover, the uniqueness of British Burma was something explicitly articulated by contemporaries, as Wright shows through the 1895 final report of the Royal Commission on Opium. 'Since Burma was a province of British administered India it was included in the Commission's investigation, but it was also clearly understood that in the context of British India, Burma was a *special case*'[original emphasis] – a case in which, unlike any other part of India, the extraordinary harm to local inhabitants was acknowledged and, contrary to most parts of Southeast Asia in the 1890s, strict top-down controls on opium sales and consumption were placed.[19]

Given the exceptional qualities of British Burma as such, what can this 'special' or deviant case yield for the purpose of explaining more general developments of opium and British India?[20] More precisely, if peripheries reveal oddities, then how can they say something general or generalizable about Empire and imperial orders? One way to begin to address these questions is to understand the relationship between peripheries and Empire as 'mutually constitutive', to borrow Jeremy Adelman's language, in ways that allow for 'broader, blurred, and curving lines of causality'.[21] The following section seeks to do so by considering the antecedent conditions to the peculiarities of British Burma that Wright rightly emphasizes, tracing the emergence of a seemingly authoritative idea of special Burman vulnerabilities in a way that helps elucidate how causality travels within constituted ties.

Morally wrecked: From periphery to Empire

In 1893, William Gladstone's Liberal government agreed to appoint a Royal Commission to investigate the nature of the opium industry in India and its trade economy. The commission was in part a concession to anti-opium forces and their lobbyists in Britain who decried 'the system by which the Indian opium revenue is raised [as] morally indefensible'.[22] The commission's conclusions, however, unequivocally denied opium's harm for India and endorsed the existing system of production and export.[23] Scholars have pointed to several factors that conditioned this conclusion, which include Gladstone and the Earl of Kimberley's biases (especially due to the latter's involvement in appointing the commission's members as secretary of state for India), the backgrounds and social ties of individuals who sat on the commission's panel (which comprised a pro-opium majority), the evidence and witnesses the commission utilized (with limited input from 'native' populations), as well as the contested authority of medical science (and those who espoused faulty theories linking opium's efficacy against malaria).[24]

Against a well-known backdrop of the Royal Opium Commission's defence of opium in and for India, what has gone relatively underappreciated is the way in which the commission acknowledged the special harms of opium in Burma. While the commission, in its final report published in 1895, would deny the 'extensive moral and physical degradation by opium' within the British Indian Empire, it acknowledged the opposite in Burma. During a five-month tour of the region and China, and among the near thousand witnesses interviewed, the Royal Commission spent merely ten days, speaking with only thirty-seven individuals in Burma, hinting at the relatively minor significance of this province to British imperial opium considerations at the time. Then how – under what conditions and in what ways – did Burma come to figure as an exception to the Indian state of opium harm?

On 19 December 1893 at the Government House in Rangoon, the chairman of the Commission, James Lyall sought an audience with Donald Smeaton, the financial commissioner of Burma at the time. Lyall wished to question Smeaton on an 'exceedingly strongly worded document' that the latter had written, which Lyall pronounced as 'for an official paper, exaggerated and sensational in tone'.[25] It was a document that Lyall foresaw as one which, 'when it comes into the possession of a certain part of the English public will be much used and much relied upon'.[26]

Smeaton's document was prosaically titled *Note by the Financial Commissioner on the extent to which Opium is consumed in Burma and the effects of the Drug on the People*.[27] It contained a summary report of the first colony-wide inquiry conducted on 'the extent and effects of opium-smoking and opium-eating in Burma'.[28] It was a 'systematic and thorough inquiry', prided Smeaton, based on 'reports for all Commissioners, Deputy Commissioners, from the Inspector General of Police, for the Inspector General of Prisons, from certain superintendents of jails, and from a few non-official gentlemen'.[29] According to this colonial administrator, there was a 'general consensus in opinion' in Burma that 'the evil effects of opium on mind and body are much more marked in Burmans than in other races' and that as a result, crime in the colony was on the rise.[30] Numerically:

> [Of] the total number of families in Lower Burma about 11 percent have fathers who are habitual opium-smokers or eaters ... and 24,624 (individuals) or nearly 29 percent, have probably taken to crime, that is to say, are either convicted criminals, or are known, or are believed to be pursuing a career of crime.[31]

The phrase 'taken to crime', Smeaton clarified, referred to a Burman's morphing into a *beinsa*. In its Anglicized transliteration, the Burmese word *beinsa* was used by local officials as a label that referred interchangeably to both a special sort of criminal act and an actor associated with opium. By no means a violent individual, a *beinsa* was known as an opium-smoker who would steal from his family and others close to him, not out of malice but rather because his use of the narcotic left him enervated, indigent and prone to vice.[32]

In Smeaton's account, the focus on Burman families and their fathers emphasized how crimes caused by opium were small but unusually salient on this micro-social level. For the expert colonial official who saw these people directly and witnessed their metamorphoses, the seemingly moderate scale of this offence belied its extremely dangerous nature. In the context of Burma, *beinsa* crimes represented a large social problem, 'likely to lead to a great demoralization of the people', Smeaton argued. He cited corroborating district reports from other local administrators, such as Deputy Commissioner H. L. Tilly of Upper Chindwin. Tilly reported that a 'general slackness, both physical and *moral*' [emphasis added] could be seen among Burmans after consuming opium.[33] The inspector general of police, Major S. C. F. Peile also wrote about how 'in too many instances one has only to scratch the opium-eater or smoker to come on the criminal'.[34] Once convicted, 'the Burman resembles a mummy, always apathetic and downhearted, besides being quite disorderly in his habits'.[35] Not all were convicted, however. Most were not. Surgeon-Major P. W. Dalzell added a description of the everyday *beinsa*, explaining how his 'downward course' occurred.[36] 'With the love of ease that is characteristic of the race, the listlessness induced by the drug is intensified, and in the process of time honest labor is given up, nourishment is irregularly taken, the appetite for proper food abates, while that for the drug is stimulated.'[37] This Burman, Dalzell made plain, 'becomes a social outcast and is obliged to consort with those who are themselves addicted to the vice'.[38]

This was what it meant to be 'morally wrecked' in Burma, Smeaton explained in his *Note*.[39] He could provide many examples of the 'morally wrecked' which included:

> Kaing Hla Phru, son of Rhauk Phwe, deceased, was a rich merchant; became opium-smoker. His father tried all in his power to make him leave off opium, but of no avail. He did no work, and died a confirmed opium-smoker in the lifetime of his father.
>
> Shwe Tha, aged 23, son of Aung Rhe, advocate, passed his Middle School examination and was preparing for his entrance examination; took to opium smoking and left off all study. His father tried his best to reform his son, but of no avail, and when he could not get any money for opium, he used to take away anything he could lay hold of. The father was obliged to send him away.
>
> Htun Aung Gyaw, son of Ah Thu Ke, merchant; became opium-smoker, and when he could not get money from his parents he commenced stealing from his parents, and when they died he inherited their valuable properties, which he soon squandered; lastly, he sold his house, and became so poor that no one would receive him and was obliged to go away to the district.
>
> Re Phaw, son of Ka La, merchant, deceased, was doing a good business, dealing in piece goods from Calcutta; became opium-smoker, stopped all his work, and devoted all his time in smoking opium, and spent all his money in opium and gambling, and died in a wretched state.[40]

And the list went on. Commonly, these accounts were 'the evidence of fathers, which is very clear in establishing opium as the cause', of 'doing no work', '[leaving] off all study', 'stealing from … parents', and '[dying] in a wretched state'. To those in the colony, the 'morally wrecked' were well known to injure their family and kin.

The Commission was sceptical of this assessment. Chairman Lyall drew attention to a table presented in Smeaton's document, 'given in para[graph] four of the Note'.[41] This table depicted the Burman opium-consuming population in Arakan.

Lyall asked Smeaton: 'Do you not think that the heading, "physically or morally wrecked" is sensational?'[42] The heading that perturbed Lyall was for the number of 'morally wrecked' consumers based on whether they had 'taken to Crime'.[43] From

Table 5.1 'Statistical Table' of Opium Consumption, Arakan Division, Lower Burma (1893)

District	Extent of Local Inquiry	Population of selected Localities	Consumers of Opium			Percentage of Consumers to Total Population examined	Number of Consumers physically or morally Wrecked			Percentage of those physically and morally Wrecked to Total Number of Consumers
			Smokers	Eaters	Total Consumers		Physically	Morally (taken to Crime)	Total	
Akyab	23 circles, 110 villages	133,623	1,899	2,643	4,542	3·4	1,969	682	2,651	58
Kyaukpyu	Greater part of district	140,000 (approximate)	1,624	2,208	3,832	3·7	2,000 (approximate)	912	2,912	76
Sandoway	19 villages	12,000 (approximate)	161	133	294	2·5	Not stated	196	196	67
Total, Arakan Division	—	285,623	3,684	4,984	8,688	3·	3,969	1,790	5,759	66

Courtesy of From Surgeon-Major, P. W. Dalzell, Officiating Inspector-General of Jails, Burma to Donald Smeaton, Financial Commissioner, Burma, no. 6966-300 (December 2, 1891), ROC, vol. 2, 552.

Lyall's perspective, this heading also seemed to make the assumption 'that every man who is found to be an opium-consumer and has been suspected or convicted of crime has come to it through opium'.[44] The chairman probed, 'Do you not think that is a most extravagant assumption?'[45] What evidence, Lyall wanted to know, did this local official have to prove that crime and 'moral wreckage' occurred as a result of opium consumption in Burma?

'My evidence is chiefly hearsay,' Smeaton replied.[46] But such hearsay, he bluntly stated, represented 'the facts reported by district officers and superintendents of jails' and the only way of knowing colonial circumstance.[47] According to Smeaton, the regular channels through which the transient chairman accustomed to European and Indian institutions might collect information were both unavailable and unreliable as 'petty crime, petty thefts' taken by the opium-smoking Burman 'would hardly come within the cognizance of a criminal court at all'.[48] These *beinsa* were peculiar crimes that had an individual thieving 'from his own father's or mother's or mother-in-law's house, reaping crops from other people's paddy fields ... robbing from stacks and taking clothes and food'.[49] Smeaton assured Lyall that such 'cases do not come out in criminal courts' but were 'the kind[s] of offence[s] that the Burmans understand when they call the subject "morally wrecked"'.[50] In other words, there was an opium problem in Burma that was real, felt and known by those in the colony.

Smeaton further invoked the authority of situated experience to explain the causes of the 'morally wrecked' and their crimes. He unequivocally asserted that 'the crime is the effect of the consumption of opium, and not the cause'.[51] Lyall directly challenged this point: 'May it not be the other way?'[52] That is, the chairman wondered whether criminals were simply more prone to using opium and that an established criminal class in Burma – those 'law-breaking, and vicious, and self-indulgent people' – were naturally taking to opium.[53] Smeaton dismissed this possibility. 'What you call the effect is the cause. It is *after* [emphasis added] a man has taken to opium that he takes to crime.'[54] He assured Lyall and other visiting commission members that his claim to knowledge was not his personal opinion – 'I can give hardly any personal experience myself,' Smeaton admitted – but that of hearsay from colonial officials and 'the weight of the Burmese evidence'.[55] The financial commissioner relied confidently on the sum of the two.

Modest officials in Burma claimed an immodest sort of expertise. It allowed them to countenance direct observations as the unique and authoritative form of colonial knowledge. For no one else could quite speak in the same way, for example, about the minute and almost nondescript moral violations that the Burmans themselves called *beinsa* and considered crimes. Perhaps no other agent of Empire cared to replicate the minutiae of routine tasks or even lay claim to the mundane details that everyday administration yielded. Nonetheless, the consolidated product represented a powerful means for colonial rule. And it appears that this group of local officials successfully persuaded imperial politicians and policymakers to acknowledge the special circumstances of British Burma and alter colonial law and policy accordingly.

On 1 January 1894, a new system of regulations formally forbidding the consumption of opium by Burmans was introduced.[56] This was an unprecedented level of intervention and interference into colonial opium markets for British India as well as Europe-governed Southeast Asia in general. As Wright points out, given the way by which Burma was administratively nested in multiple institutional settings, implementing a sumptuary interdiction in Burma entailed changes in legal rules under the All-India Opium Act I of 1878. Officializing an exception in Burma was likely a highly unwelcome proposition, not least because of the precedent it might set for other parts of British India, thus giving momentum to anti-opium agitators. Just three years earlier in 1891, the Government of India had refused to sanction the colonial government's proposal for prohibition, not persuaded that 'the evil to be removed (was) as great as … depicted'.[57] In order to convince the governor-general in council for Bengal to amend the law, the chief commissioner of Burma could not merely state that 'public opinion in Burma was unanimous in holding that opium is specially deleterious to men of Burmese race'.[58] It was necessary, insisted the law-making body in Bengal, to have the statement 'supported by unquestioned facts and statistics'.[59]

It was only after Smeaton's *Note* was submitted to Bengal that its council agreed to formally authorize opium consumption restrictions and sales controls in Burma.[60] To be clear, I do not mean to suggest that these documents persuaded men like Lyall or the Royal Commission to regard Burma differently from other parts of India, nor that they necessarily caused legal policy reforms for Burma's exceptional status. Rather, local officials like Smeaton and their claimed expertise generated the conditions of possibility for these changes in external perceptions and formal institutions to occur. This influence is observable, in part in how 'morally wrecked' Burmans were nonetheless acknowledged in the commission's final report.

This influence can also be seen in how, over time, the value of administrative expertise became weighted in favour of direct observation and ethnographic acumen. In the process of submitting the 'facts and statistics' required by Bengal, the chief commissioner of Burma Alexander MacKenzie – even as he sent over Smeaton's *Note* and the bulk of the 1891 colony-wide reports on which the *Note* was based – caustically stipulated that 'I attach very minor importance to the collection of statistics at any precise point in time.'[61] 'With all deference to the view taken by the Government of India,' MacKenzie tempered, his expertise on opium derived from 'the consensus of voices condemning it, extending as this does through a long series of years, and emanating as we know from authorities of every shade of opinion, official and non-official, European and native'.[62] The chief commissioner made sure that the Bengal Council understood his opinion of the trifling value of such numbers 'when we have before us indisputable evidence as to the results of the personal knowledge and experience of such a cloud of witnesses'.[63] And indeed, what would remain with those far from Burma and become part of imperial discourse were not the numbers and statistics per se, but rather the containing labels like 'morally wrecked' and other fragments of locally crafted administrative vocabulary. As he approved the legal changes for Burma for 1894, the secretary of state for India would echo what had become a common refrain, that is, of the 'specially deleterious' effects of the drug upon the vulnerable Burman were 'doubtless'.[64] In this sense, the local officials in Burma made it possible for others in the British Indian Empire to articulate the need for and to justify reforms, even as they might worry about the novel and stringent nature of the new regulatory regime.[65]

Conclusion

Charles Tilly once suggested that the engaged social scientist cares about 'big structures, large processes, and huge comparisons'. If so, then how does training our gaze on Empire's edges help (or hinder) the ways by which we explain big structures of domination, large processes of change and make huge comparisons across imperial orders? This chapter has grappled with this question by considering the pitfalls and possibilities for a causal vocabulary through which to explain how non-European peripheries matter for studies of European Empire. To make the case for peripheries as providing the conditions of possibility for large-scale ideational and institutional reforms, I have presented an episode from the late-nineteenth-century British efforts to prohibit opium in Burma. Specifically, this chapter has traced how local administrators in this peripheral province of the British Indian Empire laid claim to a unique and specialized expertise on opium crimes and their causes, in ways that not only contradicted, but further challenged imperial knowledge of opium's effects and regulatory imperatives.

Notes

1   *Oxford English Dictionary Online*, 2014, Oxford University Press, http://www.oed.com/view/Entry/141021 (accessed 15 September 2014).
2   See essays in Frederick Cooper and Ann Laura Stoler, eds, *Tensions of Empire: Colonial Cultures in a Bourgeois World* (Berkeley: University of California Press, 1997); Christine Davis and Michael Kennedy, eds, *Negotiated Empires: Centers and Peripheries in the Americas, 1500–1820* (New York: Routledge, 2002); Lauren Benton and Richard Ross, eds, *Legal Pluralism and Empires, 1500–1850* (New York: New York University Press, 2013). For more sustained engagements with peripheries as an analytical category, see Jack Greene, *Peripheries and Center: Constitutional Development in the Extended Polities of the British Empire and the United States, 1607–1788* (Athens: University of Georgia Press, 1986); as 'laboratories' for metropolitan modernity and science, see Gwendolyn Wright, *The Politics of Design in French Colonial Urbanism* (Chicago: University of Chicago Press, 1991); Helen Tilley, *Africa as a Living Laboratory: Empire, Development, and the Problem of Scientific Knowledge, 1870–1950* (Chicago: University of Chicago Press, 2011).
3   Dipesh Chakrabarty, *Provincializing Europe: Postcolonial Thought and Historical Difference* (Princeton: Princeton University Press, 2008 [2000]), 18.
4   Ibid.
5   See Peter Hedstrom and Richard Swedberg, 'Studying Mechanisms to Strengthen Causal Inferences in Quantitative Research', in *The Oxford Handbook of Political Methodology*, eds Box-Steffensmeier, et al. (Oxford: Oxford University Press, 2008), 4, for mechanisms defined as 'precise, abstract, and action-based explanations, which

show how the occurrence of a triggering event regularly generates the type of outcome to be explained'.
6. John Richards, 'Opium and the British Indian Empire: The Royal Commission of 1895', *Modern Asian Studies* 36, no. 2 (2002): 375, 378. Selected commentary and analyses of the Royal Opium Commission include Joshua Rowntree, *The Opium Habit in the East: A Study of the Evidence given to the Royal Commission on Opium, 1893–1894* (London: P. S. King & Son, 1895); Kathleen Lodwick, *Crusaders against Opium: Protestant Missionaries in China, 1874–1917* (Lexington: University of Kentucky Press, 1996), 85–108; Paul Winther, *Anglo-European Science and the Rhetoric of Empire* (Oxford: Lexington Books, 2003).
7. But see Ashley Wright, *Opium and Empire in Southeast Asia: Regulating Consumption in British Burma* (Basingstoke: Palgrave Macmillan, 2014), especially ch. 4–5 (61–94).
8. I recognize the epistemological, methodological and normative stakes in calling a non-European location a periphery, although I do not discuss them here.
9. Carl Trocki, *Opium and Empire: Chinese Society in Colonial Singapore, 1800–1910* (Ithaca: Cornell University Press, 1990), 5.
10. See James Rush, *From Opium to Java: Revenue Farming and Chinese Enterprise in Colonial Indonesia, 1860–1910* (Ithaca: Cornell University Press, 1990); Ian Brown, 'The End of the Opium Farm in Siam, 1905–7', in *The Rise and Fall of Revenue Farming: Business Elites and the Emergence of the Modern State in Southeast Asia*, eds John Butcher and Howard Dick (New York: St Martin's Press, 1993), 233–45; Jan Van Ours, 'The Price Elasticity of Hard Drugs: The Case of Opium in the Dutch East Indies, 1923–1938', *Journal of Political Economy* 103, no. 2 (1995): 261–79; Richards, 'Opium and the British Indian Empire', William Jankowiak and Daniel Bradburd, eds, *Drugs, Labor and Colonial Expansion* (Tucson: University of Arizona Press, 2003); Carl Trocki, 'Opium and the Beginnings of Chinese Capitalism in Southeast Asia', *Journal of Southeast Asian Studies* 33, no. 2 (2003): 297–314; Derek MacKay, *Eastern Customs: The Customs Service in British Malaya and the Opium Trade* (London: Radcliffe Press, 2005); Anne Foster, 'Prohibition as Superiority: Policing Opium in Southeast Asia, 1898–1925', *International History Review* 22, no. 2 (2000): 253–73 and 'Opium, the United States, and the Civilizing Mission in Colonial Southeast Asia', *Social History of Alcohol and Drugs* 24, no. 1 (2010): 6–19; Wright, *Opium and Empire*.
11. Foster, 'Prohibition as Superiority', 7.
12. Daniel Wertz, 'Idealism, Imperialism, and Internationalism: Opium Politics in the Colonial Philippines, 1898–1925', *Modern Asian Studies* 47, no. 2 (2013): 469.
13. Ibid., 470.
14. Wright, *Opium and Empire*. See especially ch. 8: 'Separation, Negotiation, and Drug Diplomacy: 1935–1939' (126–46). The entwined interests and legal conundrums surrounding opium production in and export from the Shan States have been detailed in two articles by Robert Maule in 'The Opium Question in the Federated Shan States, 1931–1936: British Policy Discussions and Scandal', *Journal of Southeast Asian Studies* 23, no. 1 (1992): 14–36; 'British Policy Discussions on the Opium Question in the Federated Shan States, 1937–1948', *Journal of Southeast Asian Studies* 33, no. 2 (2002): 203–24.
15. Ibid.
16. Economically, the value of opium's commercial life in British Burma and the Philippines was dwarfed against the backdrop of the great China–India trade. On the relative scope of the regional opium trade, see Kitri Chaudhuri, 'Foreign Trade and Balance of Payments (1757–1947)', in *The Cambridge Economic History of India*, vol. 2

(ca. 1757–ca. 1970), eds Dharma Kumar and Meghnad Desai (Cambridge: Cambridge University Press, 1983), 804–77. Epistemologically, Anglo-European knowledge of opium's 'oriental' significance was mostly drawn from China and India based on prior encounters with domestic poppy cultivation and large-scale opium manufacturing in the latter, as well as the former population's popular consumption On eighteenth- and early-nineteenth-century European perceptions of opium's special significance in India and China, see Amar Farooqui, *Smuggling as Subversion: Colonialism, Indian Merchants, and the Politics of Opium, 1790–1843* (Oxford: Lexington Books, 1998); Frank Dikötter, et al., *Narcotic Culture: A History of Drugs in China* (Hong Kong: Hong Kong University Press, 2004).

17 Wertz, 'Idealism, Imperialism, and Internationalism', 470.
18 Wright, *Opium and Empire*, 152.
19 Ibid., 9.
20 On deviant cases, see Alexander George and Andrew Bennett, *Case Studies and Theory Development in the Social Sciences* (Cambridge: MIT Press, 2004), 114–15.
21 Jeremy Adelman, *Republic of Capital: Buenos Aires and the Legal Transformation of the Atlantic World* (Stanford: Stanford University Press, 1999), 4.
22 Hansard, House of Commons Debate (30 June 1893), vol. 14, 591.
23 Richards, 'Opium and the British Indian Empire', 378.
24 Lodwick, Crusaders against Empire; Martin Booth, *Opium: A History* (New York: St Martin's Press, 1998); Richards, 'Opium and the British Indian Empire'; Winther, *Anglo-European Science*; Wright, *Opium and Empire*.
25 Question no. 8081 (19 December 1893), Royal Opium Commission Final Report (hereafter ROC), vol. 2, 230.
26 Question no. 8080, in ibid.
27 Donald Smeaton, 'Note by the Financial Commissioner on the extent to which Opium is consumed in Burma and the effects of the Drug on the People' (27 April 1892), ROC, vol. 2, 539–47.
28 Council of the Chief Commissioner, Burma, 'Resolution' (29 August 1891), no. 10E.
29 Ibid.
30 Ibid., 543.
31 Ibid.
32 Ibid.
33 From H. L. Tilly to name unknown, Commissioner of the Central Division, no. 855-44 (1 December 1891), ROC, vol. 2, 590.
34 From S. C. F. Peile, officiating inspector general of police to Hebert Thirkell White, chief secretary to the chief commissioner, Burma, no. 532-109M (22 January 1892), ROC, vol. 2, 605.
35 Name unknown, Superintendant of Jail, Sandoway, quoted in Smeaton, 'Note by the Financial Commissioner'.
36 From Surgeon-Major, P. W. Dalzell, Officiating Inspector-General of Jails, Burma to Donald Smeaton, Financial Commissioner, Burma, no. 6966-300 (2 December 1891), ROC, vol. 2, 605.
37 Ibid.
38 Ibid.
39 Ibid., 539.
40 Ibid., 554.
41 Ibid., 552.
42 Ibid.

43 Smeaton, 'Note by the Financial Commissioner'.
44 Question no. 8091 (19 December 1893), ROC, vol. 2, 230.
45 Question no. 8092, ibid.
46 Question no. 8090, ibid.
47 Smeaton, 'Note by the Financial Commissioner'.
48 Question no. 8095, ROC, vol. 2, 230.
49 Ibid.
50 Ibid.
51 Question no. 8092, ibid.
52 Ibid.
53 Question no. 8090, ibid.
54 Ibid.
55 Ibid.
56 C. G. Bayne, revenue secretary to the chief commissioner, Burma, 'Note on the System of Opium Administration in Burma' (9 December 1893), ROC, vol. 2, 479.
57 From Government of India to Sir Alexander MacKenzie, Chief Commissioner, Burma, letter no. 3166 (29 July 1891), ROC, vol. 2, 537.
58 Ibid.
59 Ibid.
60 On 18 March 1893, the *Revised Opium Rules for Regulating the Matters Specified in Sections 5 and 13 of the Opium Act 1878,* namely, the possession and use of opium was printed in the *Burma Gazette.* Publication in this government journal was a prerequisite for official documents to have the force of law.
61 Alexander MacKenzie, Chief Commissioner, Burma, 'Minute', enclosure no. 1 to 'Further Papers regarding the use of Opium by Burmans' (30 April 1892), ROC, vol. 2, 537.
62 Ibid.
63 Ibid.
64 Lord Wodehouse, 3rd Earl of Kimberley, secretary of state for India to Government of India (31 August 1893), no. 112 (Revenue), appendix XL, ROC, vol. 2, 488.
65 Government of India, Finance and Commerce Department, Separate Revenue-Opium to Chief Commissioner, Burma (20 June 1893), no. 2567, appendix L, ROC, vol. 2, 650.

Chapter 6

CUSTOM IN THE ARCHIVE: THE BIRTH OF MODERN
CHINESE LAW AT THE END OF EMPIRE

Matthew S. Erie[1]

Enter the archive

The late Qing reforms occurred during a period of epochal crisis: war with Japan and aggression by the Eight-Nation Alliance as well as domestic turmoil in the form of the anti-Manchu, anti-imperialist Boxer Rebellion. Against this backdrop of external war and internal disintegration, reforms became increasingly robust and comprehensive. The limited Self-Strengthening movement (1861–95), which sought to modernize military and economic institutions, was replaced by the New Policies reforms (1898–1912). The New Policies programmes targeted broader reforms, including dismantling China's legal system that had survived with revision since the seventh-century CE Tang Dynasty. Chinese law was excoriated as the source of Chinese weakness against foreign and internal forces. The Great Qing Law Code was faulted for its lack of sophistication, for not separating substantive and procedural law and for not distinguishing civil law from criminal law. Local corruption and chronic injustice under the law were the wellsprings of popular discontent.

The turn of the century was a period of intense intellectual foment as foreign ideas, mainly filtered through Japan, including sovereignty, constitutionalism, state theory and international law, radically transformed thought regarding the relationship between ruler and ruled in the Qing court.[2] Legal reform centred around debates to abolish the Great Qing Law Code and write a constitution based on foreign or Japanese models.[3] To build a modern legal system, Qing reformers began the process of drafting civil law codes, inspired by German and French civil law via the Japanese experience of legal modernization. As part of its legal modernization, the Qing reformers commenced a little-observed social scientific project to collect the 'customs' of Chinese people to serve as raw material for civil law codes, hereinafter 'the Project'.

The Project deserves attention for several reasons. It was the earliest systematic study conducted by the Chinese on foreign law. The study took the form of review and analysis of the Japanese civil law system as well as European continental precedents. At the same time and as a result of emulating foreign templates, the

Project turned inward by constructing an archive of Chinese customs. Chinese customs were to provide the raw material for writing modern civil law codes. Hence emulation did not mean imitation; the goal was to write laws tailored to Chinese society. To carry out the Project, jurist-officials operated through the imperial bureaucracy and trained local experts to collect, catalogue and analyse the customs. Lawyers became quasi-ethnologists. The Project was an interdisciplinary effort, not unlike the 'ethnographic state'[4] in colonial British India that created caste as the explanatory paradigm of Indian society through census, map and archive.[5] Although regarded as a failure, the methodologies and institutions that the Project established became the cornerstones of a modern legal science in China.

The Project has implications well beyond the history of Chinese law. It shows Qing reformers generating disciplines that crossed traditional boundaries of 'domestic'/'foreign', 'premodern'/'modern' and 'jurist'/'field administrator' that were part of a broader reconfiguration of Chinese statehood at the turn of the century. That is, the Project was not only utilitarian (i.e. collecting customs to write civil law codes) but epistemological as well. It established mechanisms of social science to order the production of knowledge. In the process, it demonstrates a careful adaptation of law, from Japanese and European experiences, for a specific Chinese modernist purpose. Qing lawyers did not just 'cut and paste' from the Japanese experience but employed custom in the context of China's legal culture.

More broadly, the Project affords an entry into understanding the relationship between legal studies, as a social science, and empire. I argue that the creation of custom or customary law is a technique of government universal to empire. The Chinese case underscores the ambivalence of custom and its archive, however. This ambivalence operates across several contradictions which I map out in this chapter: (i) custom as resource and not foil to modernity, (ii) reformers turning to law to reform, just as much as to preserve, the empire, and (iii) custom as generative of 'global' social sciences that nonetheless assumed varied forms in different settings (e.g. anthropology and legal studies).

Taking these contradictions in turn, the collection of the customary law of colonial subjects has long served to legitimate the imposition of imperial law. As Paul Kramer (this volume) shows, however, the relationship between knowledge and possession is not isomorphic. In the spirit of such counter-conventionalism, the Project challenges 'colonial governmentality'[6] as customs were collected not just for ethnic others 'over there', but for the dominant group as well, the Manchu-Han body politic. The Qing Empire was singular among early-twentieth-century empires in that it featured an expansive state ruling over non-Han peoples through a distinct ideology of culture and civilization: Confucianism. Qing documentation of frontier peoples through ethnographic writings is well documented.[7] The Project, however, archived not only the customs of Muslims, Mongolians, Tibetans and other populations at the borders of the Qing Empire, but also those of the Han at the 'centre'. *All* of these practices were interpellated as 'custom'.

Next, the jurist-officials who led the custom surveys were trying to reform and not just sustain the Qing Empire. Their position was thus ambiguous. As historian Thomas Mullaney has written of social scientists during the early communist period, such 'establishment intellectuals'[8] were not just handmaidens of political will. Similarly, the Qing legal reformers tried to lead the state, rather than being led by it. The proposed constitutional changes of the jurists would have altered the relationship between the emperor and the sovereign state. Consequently, the Project shows nascent social science not just reproducing but shaping the political power that sustains it.

Third, the use of custom as an object of study assumed its most familiar form in colonial anthropology. The late Qing reform, however, invoked custom as part of a global circulation of ideas about law and fin de siècle legal science. Whereas the Qing had developed notions of empire prior to its encounter with Western imperialism (see Wu, this volume), modernizing Qing jurists developed second-hand knowledge of European law primarily through the Japanese after 1900. Japanese translations of continental civil law were instrumental to Qing reformers. The language of legal modernity was taken up by reformists in different empires, French, German, Japanese and Chinese. Appropriation was not just one way from West to East but characterized by incessant reinvention. 'Custom' was part of this conceptual translation of law.

The late Qing legal reforms blur the distinctions by which empires are usually regarded as antithetical to nations. Classical studies assume empires are hierarchical, vertically structured and constituted by heterogeneity, whereas nations are egalitarian, horizontally structured and constituted by sameness.[9] Recent scholarship refutes such distinctions, proposing that building empire and nation may proceed in tandem, that imperial projects may be framed in nationalist terms and vice versa.[10] Although the Qing Empire collapsed in 1912 and the Project was never completed, it survived the empire and was carried out in various forms by the Republican government and the communists. The way in which the Project ordered and classified difference and the disciplines that created such knowledge were selectively replicated by the governments of successive Chinese nation states. In other words, while the Project's explicit goal was to mine Chinese customs for legal resources, in retrospect, it founded a unique trans-regime social scientific endeavour to order China's multi-ethnic diversity and cohere the state. The effort was born not with the emergence of the nation, but at the end of the empire. As the Chinese notion of nation reflects inheritance from its imperial past, its difficulties in ruling non-Han peoples can be traced to the genesis of order and law during the archiving of custom.

Custom as keystone: Law, ethnography and empire

The Great Qing Law Code that governed the Qing Empire (est. 1636) was chiefly concerned with penal and administrative matters, rather than civil matters. Compiled in 1740, it consisted of 436 statutes and some 1,800 sub-statutes.[11] The Great Qing Law Code was based, in part, on the Tang Code, compiled in 653 CE. Legal historians have observed the remarkable degree of continuity of the law codes during the two millennia of the imperial period.[12] Imperial law was characterized by not just chronological consistency but also spatial or geographic uniformity. The Qing, however, led by the Manchu, based in northeastern China, was an expansionist state. In the southwest, the Qing conquered Yunnan Province in 1662.[13] Farther west, the Qing solidified control over Tibetan areas in Amdo and Kham in 1724 and 1728, respectively,[14] and quelled Muslim rebellions in Gansu Province in 1862–77.[15] The Qing engaged in a protracted campaign against the Mongolians, destroyed the Zunghar Khanate and annexed Xinjiang Province in the far northwest in 1760.[16]

To incorporate these multi-ethnic borderlands, the Qing adopted a number of different strategies, including installing imperial institutions and relying on local forms of authority.[17] The 'New Qing History' has demonstrated that while the Great Qing Law Code was applied to the borderlands, the Qing did not force assimilation on non-Chinese populations.[18] The Qing established legal institutions like the Court of Colonial Affairs (*Lifanyuan*) to deal with Mongols, Tibetans and Turkic Muslims.[19] These courts implemented Qing law while allowing non-Han legal specialists, for instance, qadis in Xinjiang, to handle most familial matters in accordance with Islamic law.[20]

The New Policies reforms led to a rethinking of the place of law, its sources and institutions, in governing the empire, including the non-Han frontiers. At the turn of the century, not only the Qing but also empires from Spanish America to British India underwent a reconfiguring of power through law. Historian Lauren Benton has argued that empires employed legal pluralism, 'the formal mapping of imposed and indigenous law' as a colonial project.[21] Benton defines legal pluralism not as normative diversity, which is composed of 'elusive subjective beliefs' but as 'jurisdictional conflicts' whereby vaguely defined legal authorities exercise power to regulate and administer sanctions over particular actions or people.[22] Centrally, Benton's definition does not distinguish between state law and non-state law or customs. I depart from Benton's approach by arguing that the articulation of 'law' versus 'custom' was central to the exercise of imperial authority.

In the early twentieth century, the category of 'custom' or 'customary law' was invoked in the service of empire. Often, it was the nascent social science of anthropology that grew out of a complex relationship with colonial projects in the Pacific, Africa and Asia, that identified custom as a source of social sanction among colonized groups. The founders of anthropology produced knowledge about non-European peoples through practices congruent with those of empire-building, and law was a central category to be observed/constructed.[23] Bronislaw Malinowski's *Crime and Custom in Savage Society* (1926) sought to extract principles (e.g. exchange) governing behaviour among Melanesians.[24] Isaac Schapera, working in Botswana, recorded native law for the explicit purpose of indirect rule.[25] Also basing their ethnographies in Africa, Max Gluckman conducted a study on Lozi courts to understand their administration of justice[26] and Paul Bohannan studied courts of the Tiv.[27] Other anthropologists foregrounded the customary rules of household, kinship and clan.[28] With the exception of Malinowski, these anthropologists founded British structural-functionalism and were heavily influenced by A. R. Radcliffe-Brown, and thus their analyses often sought to explicate the jural rules that cohered social groups.[29] The category of law was thus central to the birth of empire through anthropology and its demarcating of difference: customary law/colonial law, popular law/state law or unofficial law/official law.

While the assumptions underlying their interpretations varied, many of the founders subscribe to a sharp distinction between 'law' and 'custom' – even in the face of countervailing empirical data.[30] Law was defined narrowly as court enforced. Custom, on the other hand, was diffuse and resided in the ambient social and psychological atmosphere, 'the sum total of rules, conventions, and patterns of behavior', as Malinowski wrote.[31] The distinction nonetheless was somewhat specious for neither 'law' nor 'custom' assumed written form, they had no external existence outside their embodiment in the 'memory of people'.[32]

China had a different set of disciplinary tools to study custom as a supplement to imperial rule than Western anthropology.[33] Anthropology was a relative latecomer to the social scientific production of knowledge in service to empire. Rather, it was Qing jurists who objectified custom as a tool of governance. In examining the Qing case, the traditional distinction in Chinese political philosophy has been between *fa* (law) and *li* (rite). Whereas *fa* was a positivist notion of law as deriving from the ruler for purposes of punishment, *li* determined ordered relationships (e.g. ruler/ruled, father/son) along with core precepts such as filial piety and justice. Confucius famously developed a systematic theory of *li* and denigrated *fa*.

As to whether traditional Chinese law included a third source of legality, in addition to *li* and *fa*, namely 'custom' (e.g. *zongfa*) is debatable. Legal scholar Liang Zhiping has argued there was a thick exchange between the Great Qing Law Code and custom that took the form of *xiangli* (rural rules), *suli* (conventional practices), *xianggui* (rural regulations) and *tuli* (localized rules) in the areas of marriage, property, inheritance, sale, rent, mortgage and debt.[34] Likewise, legal historians have identified the widespread use of contracts and 'popular' forms of property ownership in developing a theory of a laissez-faire state in promoting economic development indirectly through enforcement of such unofficial instruments.[35]

Historian Jérôme Bourgon, however, has taken issue with the thesis that the Qing looked to custom as a source of civil law. He argues that customary law is a Western invention that entered China only during the late Qing and was exploited by Republican reformers.[36] Bourgon's analysis is compelling, perhaps more than he knew. His argument can be 'pushed back' to apply to the late Qing, but with qualifications. The Qing began the process the Republican tried to carry through: using customs for the purpose of writing legal codes pursuant to continental law theory. The difference was that the Qing operated under a different set of assumptions, including the integrity and viability of the empire, and an imperial world view that, albeit challenged, still held at the centre.

Customary law/modern law

The Project transformed the category of 'custom' or 'customary law' as a basis for law. Chinese reformers looked to Meiji Japan in constructing a modern constitution and civil code.[37] Debates in Japan over legal modernization[38] found new resonance in China. Beginning in 1904, cabinet ministers of the Qing government established the Bureau for the Revision of the Laws (*xiuding falüguan*), hereinafter 'the Bureau.' The Bureau had two main responsibilities under Qing law reform: first, collect, compile and systemize Qing law for either the purpose of deletion or revision, and second, translate foreign laws.[39] The mandate of the Bureau was expansive, including civil, commercial and criminal fields of law. Debates about transforming the empire into a constitutional government, along with overlapping debates about education and examination and financial institution reform, provided impetus to the Project. The generic term *xiguanfa* was borrowed from the Japanese *kanshuhou* or 'customary law' as one of the key concepts developed through the Project. As with *zhimindi* ('colony') (see Dudden, this volume), 'customary law'[40] belonged to a legal-political lexicon that translated Western concepts through words that used Chinese characters, but which gained new meanings following Japanese modernization. The Chinese then re-acquired these neologisms.[41]

The late Qing survey aimed to collect and document the body of customs in traditional Chinese culture. The survey planning began in 1907 and fieldwork began the year later.[42] Each province established a survey bureau (*diaochaju*) at the prefectural and county levels under which a legal system department (*fazhike*) implemented the actual fieldwork. Even Xinjiang, which was not formally made a province until 1884, established a survey bureau in 1909.[43] The first survey was focused on commercial affairs customs and the second on civil affairs customs. The survey of commercial affairs customs began in the southeastern provinces, known at the start of the twentieth century as the engine of Chinese commerce. The survey[44] was directed at collecting data on the social strata of businessmen, the size and operation of markets, systems of registration for businessmen, trademarks, employment, agencies, mortgaging and so on.[45] The survey's dependence on the coordination of local officials resulted in inconsistencies.[46]

The second survey that dealt with civil affairs customs saw a greater degree of regulation, standardization and bureaucratization. The customs survey was part of a broader effort to adopt empirical methods of management, such as the census, to improve governance in the face of foreign pressures.[47] In 1909, in preparation for the survey, the Bureau issued 'The Regulations on the Civil Customs Survey in Ten Articles' (*Diaocha minshi xiguan zhangcheng shitiao*), hereinafter 'the Regulations'.[48] The Regulations gave general guidelines on both the administration and the content of the civil customs survey. The Regulations specified that local businessmen and gentry, in consultation with surveyors from the relevant level survey bureau would conduct fieldwork; officials dispatched from the Bureau would oversee the surveys (articles 3 and 4). The Bureau regulated even the minutiae of methodology. Survey teams had a standardized set of observation protocols specifying methods of data collection, the duration of surveys, the type of ink and paper to be used on forms and so on.[49] A time limit was set for all surveys that would be submitted to the relevant level survey bureau and then to the Bureau (article 5). As was typical of the practices of the New Policies reforms, the surveys enlisted the resources of local business and commerce groups, thereby co-opting non-state actors and civil society for the purpose of strengthening the state.[50]

The organization and composition of the survey and their questionnaire documentation registers a disconnection from the categories solicited in the Regulations. The Regulations specifically cite the drafting of the civil law, that is the Great Qing Civil Law Draft, as the reason for the surveys. While the first part of the Great Qing Civil Law Draft, which was completed in 1911, and which includes three sections on the general part, debt and property, has a traditional German five-part division, the Regulations themselves do not privilege Western taxonomy in organizing Chinese customary law. Article 7 specifies, 'The names of the laws cannot be compromised. The common sayings cannot be systematized by the surveyors. In order to avoid a proliferation of confusion, the sounds of the common sayings must be preserved and reported accurately.' The Bureau sought to confer upon itself, and not the fieldworkers, the responsibility of translating the customs into areas of law consonant with modern Western jurisprudence. Not unlike British anthropologists in colonial Africa and India, Chinese legal reformers faced the difficulty of translating so-called premodern laws into terms cognizable under Western law.

In perhaps the defining debate of legal anthropology, Max Gluckman employed universalist (Western) terms in his analysis[51] whereas Paul Bohannan sought to retain native categories in what he called the 'folk system' of interpretation.[52] The Qing reformers' solution to the problem was typically Chinese – to foreclose any question by administrative fiat in the form of a rule. However, while the Regulations preferred 'indigenous' terms, the questionnaire used for the surveys was organized along the lines of the five-field German civil law tradition. Bourgon argues that the questionnaire was divided into the parts of German law 'without any concession to Chinese local practices or previous official law'.[53] This view may be overstated. While the questionnaire shows the five-field division, within each field there are specifically Chinese customs. For instance, the general part, chapter 1, includes 'customs related to people's groups' (*yu renji tuanti you guanxi de xiguan*) such as 'Buddhist monks' and nuns' fungible property' (*seng-ni de maimai chanye*); part 4, chapter 6 is 'kinship committees' (*qinshuhui*) and chapter 7 is 'family support relations' (*fuyang zhi guanxi*); and part 5, chapter 2 is entitled 'clan pedigree inheritance' (*zongtiao zhi jicheng*). Still, Bourgon's point that the survey design excludes many customary practices (e.g. the sale contracts that warranted servile bonds) is well taken.

From the completed surveys that survive, there is evidence that non-Western taxonomies prevailed in the collection of customary law. Part of the reason for this may be the considerable time constraints under which the survey[54] was conducted in order to use survey results for drafting the codes. Many of the completed surveys were divided into five parts (*bu*): popular customs (*minqing fengsu*), the customs used by local gentry to attend to matters (*difang shenshi banshi xiguan*), civil customs (*minshi xiguan*), commercial customs (*shangshi xiguan*) and procedural customs (*susong xiguan*). Parts were further subdivided into types (*lei*), categories subdivided into items (*kuan*), items subdivided into terms (*xiang*) and terms subdivided into sub-terms (*mu*).⁵⁵ Completed questionnaires followed the same structure. For instance, an excerpt from a questionnaire on popular customs⁵⁶ (item three 'professions', term four 'business') reads as follows:

> Question 11. Does each place have a chamber of commerce? What kind of things do its organizers do? What about its funds?
>
> Answer. Cai Village, Guangxu period year 34 [1909], created a business affairs committee to prevent the smuggling of silver, foreign monies, copper, and bank notes, to prevent waste, and such things. According to the town's convention, gentry and merchants do their duty expecting no rewards.
>
> Question 12. What are the common names of the businessmen?
>
> Answer. The proprietors are called landlords, the people who run things are called managers, and the youth who study are called apprentices.
>
> Question 13. What about businesses' records of using brokers?
>
> Answer. All small merchant enterprises that deal in livestock, chickens, and ducks specifically have records of using brokers.
>
> Question 14. Which businesses must temporarily [work with] petty officials?
>
> Answer. Large brokers, small brokers, steelyard businesses, pipe stores, department stores, banks, grain shops, poultry shops, banquet halls, cotton businesses, wholesale grain shops, oil businesses, fresh fruit shops, and porters.

As shown by the questions and responses, the questionnaires are designed to elicit specific and local data that can be compared within and across regions. The questions are not coded with Western terminology but adhere closely to 'local knowledge'. Working under considerable time pressure, the Bureau collected in total 828 volumes.⁵⁷ Surveying was stopped in 1911 with the decline of the empire.

'Grand Shen' and the making of modern law

The career of the great legal reformer of the late Qing period Shen Jiaben (1840–1913), known as 'Grand Shen', sheds light on the development of a modern legal science in the late Qing period and the place of customary law in it. Shen Jiaben was a product of the imperial education and examination system and a career jurist-official who became the Head of the Bureau at the age of sixty. His position, however, was ambivalent.⁵⁸ His aim was to strengthen the empire internally as well as in regard to foreign powers, but to do so, he sought to radically alter the nature of the government through law. As the architect of the Project, he oversaw the greatest reform in the two-thousand-year history of Chinese law.

While Shen Jiaben oversaw the translation of Western laws for Chinese purposes, he sought to harmonize Chinese tradition and Western law.⁵⁹ As foreign powers legitimized extraterritoriality on the weakness of Chinese law, the principal aim of legal reform led by Shen Jiaben was to modernize Chinese legal institutions to provide equality to Chinese and foreigners alike under unified imperial law.⁶⁰ The ultimate goal of legal reform was a constitutional government with judicial independence, meaning that administrative officials could no longer exercise judicial control.⁶¹

Shen Jiaben saw the survival of medieval corporal punishments in the Qing Code, such as death by dismembering (*lingchi*), public beheading for display (*xiaoshou*) and guilt due solely to a relationship with the offender (*yuanzuo*) as a bar to China's entrance to a modern league of nations. Within a span of ten years (1905–10), Shen Jiaben revised the Great Qing Law Code by abolishing 344 provisions, which became the basis for the Current Criminal Law (1909), and drafted the Criminal and Civil Affairs Procedural Law (1906), the Great Qing New Criminal Law (1907), the Great Qing Criminal Procedural Law Draft (1910) and the Civil Procedure Law Draft (1910).⁶²

In both methodology and substance, Shen Jiaben sought to use indigenous non-state or 'unofficial' resources to reform formal state law. Shen Jiaben's approach to textual analysis and criticism (*kaoju*) was widespread among Qing literati. *Kaoju* emphasized practical affairs over the idealist philosophy (*lixue*) of the Song and Ming periods. Although he initiated extensive legal scholarly exchange with Japan, Shen Jiaben's approach to the revision of legal texts was based on classical Chinese exegesis.⁶³ In a comparative law frame, Japanese and Western models were used as references to understand the divergence between ancient Chinese and modern Western legal systems and not to be transplanted *in toto*. He wrote, 'Not to skillfully investigate Chinese law's principles and its merits and demerits, and only mix in Western law is akin to a mutual misrecognition of their complementarity. [Only by studying both Chinese and Western law can we] safely hope to return to the path.'⁶⁴ He saw customary law as a source of legal modernization of equal weight, and indeed, an alternative source of legal modernization to wholesale Westernization.

Shen sought to develop native talent while learning from Japan and the West. He employed foreigners who resided in China as researchers, but realized he could not depend exclusively on foreigners. He established China's first modern law school staffed solely by Chinese, the *Falü xuetang* in Beijing in 1906.⁶⁵ At the same time, through the Bureau, he funded overseas study for Chinese law students. He believed such institutions and intellectual links would assist the modernization effort. So while the impetus to collect customary law was exogenous and based on Japan's experience, that is, the 'custom becomes written law' model,⁶⁶ the material sought was wholly endogenous.

Shen Jiaben and others regarded the body of Chinese customary law as a viable resource-rich pool for law reform. As legal scholar Sui Hongmin writes, customary law was one solution to the 'desire to pursue the best law most suitable to the condition and standards of the Chinese people'.⁶⁷ One of the customary law reports, 'The Anhui Constitutional Government Survey Bureau Edited and Submitted Civil Affairs Customs Answers, 1908–1911', reflects the prevailing view at the time

> Custom is law's origin. All countries east and west believe in customary law's efficacy and adopt it as the material for written law. China was the first to

become civilized. The popular sentiments and customs include those that carry on as before from remote antiquity as well as those that gradually change. Their present value is in fabricating law codes. Following the detailed spirit of the survey, customs are the preparatory measures for legislation.[68]

However, such sources of customary law had to be transformed: from local to state-wide, from status-bound and hierarchical to contractual and equal, and from charismatic to bureaucratic and rationalistic. The legislation and codification process, although based partially on the customary law material, would greatly alter their nature, scope and legal effects. Despite the quantity of customs gathered in the final year of the Qing dynasty, the Great Qing Civil Law Draft did not include much of customary law; rather, German legal principles and even the Chinese code of etiquette played more significant roles.[69]

Assessing custom as imperial classification

The empire-wide Project to collect customs for purposes of legal modernization was never completed. Where it was supposed to find most traction (e.g. the Great Qing Civil Law Draft), its presence was minimal. Yet in some respects, the Project survived the empire. The Republic government, which succeeded the Qing, reinterpreted customs as the *volk* or spirit of the people of the new nation (*minzu*) and continued the Project. The Beiyang government continued the Project under the reconstituted Bureau in 1919. In 1930, the Nanjing government's Ministry of Justice published its survey results, an abridged version of which contains some 3,432 customs. The communists would once again reinterpret custom in lines with the thought of Marx, Lenin and Lewis Henry Morgan to serve as a criterion of 'ethnic minority' (*shaoshu minzu*). The nation-wide 'ethnic identification' (*minzu shibie*) classification scheme of the 1950s which constructed China's fifty-five officially recognized minorities[70] was thus, in some ways, prefigured by the Project. Custom was reassigned to 'minority'. The Han majority no longer had custom, but rather, 'law'.[71]

The Project marked a turning point in governance in China as empire and foreshadowed China as nation. The Project was a fulcrum through which reformers like Shen Jiaben balanced seemingly competing concerns: Western and Chinese, imperial and local, empire and nation. The turn of the century witnessed a global circulation in the idea of custom. As deployed by Western colonial powers, custom was a tool for administration of colonies. The social scientific form custom-based studies assumed was most predominantly that of anthropology. As in the case of British India, a detailed ethnography of customs was basic to 'almost every form of executive action'.[72] Anthropology thus distilled social rules that were codified and used to govern colonial subjects. In addition to its utilitarian value, there was a second, ideological, purpose to custom in colonial anthropology. It served as a source of legitimization for rule when contrasted to 'modern' law.[73]

Here, the Chinese case complicates imperial classification projects that privilege the example of Western imperialism (and demonize anthropology along the way). All practices, institutions and rules of both Chinese and non-Chinese peoples within the Qing Empire were labelled as custom. Rather than legitimating the rule of a Western minority over a non-Western population and landmass by imposing 'enlightened' law over custom-bound masses, the Qing (themselves a minority) applied the category to the majority Han in addition to minority groups, including those on the state's periphery. In calling all such practices 'custom' regardless of majority/minority distinctions, the law reformers effaced the traditional distinction between empire and nation.

Crucially, the mobilization of custom was not a result of an anthropological survey but of legal categories. Despite inveterate depreciations of lawyers in China, jurists led the modernization programmes at the end of the Qing Empire. Legal science was the 'cutting edge', so to speak, of the social sciences.[74] Yet it was directed not just at old laws and legal institutions but also at the broader system of government. It is suggestive that Shen Jiaben, who oversaw the Project, has experienced a kind of revival in modern China since the 1989 Tiananmen massacre, which calls for pragmatic constitutional reform in the face of the Chinese Communist Party's monopoly on power.[75] For lawyers in China, past and present, deriving authority from the state does not necessarily mean that one's agency is tied to that of the regime.

Ultimately, as customs were based on locality or groups (whether defined by profession, ethnicity or region), there was a built-in tension in using them as guidelines for writing laws that apply to all subjects of the empire. To modify Benedict Anderson, the legal reformers could not stretch 'the short, tight skin of the [custom] over the gigantic body of the empire'.[76] One solution, as realized by the successors to the successors of the Qing, the communists, was to adopt broad civil law language in their national laws. Broad provisions could be narrowly defined by legislative bodies at the sub-national level (e.g. provinces, prefectures, counties and cities). Unfortunately, in so doing, legal modernization under the communists has seen a counter-Project such that laws are mainly devoid of the substance of rules that bind groups at the local level. The insensitivity of law to the traditions and practices of minorities, such as Tibetans and Muslims, has been one factor leading to widespread ethnic discontent in the modern era.

Notes

1 Research conducted for this chapter was funded by a Princeton Institute for International and Regional Studies Postdoctoral Fellowship and a Henry Luce Foundation/ACLS Program in China Studies Postdoctoral Fellowship. The author would like to thank the organizers, discussants and participants of the 'Empire and the Social Science' symposium, especially Jeremy Adelman and Rachel Price. Further, the author thanks Glenn Tiffert for reviewing an earlier draft. All mistakes are the author's.

2   Suzanne Ogden, 'Chinese Concepts of the Nation, State, and Sovereignty' (PhD diss., Brown University, 1974); 'Sovereignty and International Law: The Perspective of the People's Republic of China', *New York University Journal of International Law and Politics* 7, no. 1 (1974): 1–32; Douglas R. Reynolds, *China, 1898–1912: The Xinzheng Revolution and Japan* (Cambridge: Harvard University Press, 1993); Jonathan K. Ocko and David Gilmartin, 'State, Sovereignty, and the People: A Comparison of the "Rule of Law" in China and India', *The Journal of Asian Studies* 68, no. 1 (2009): 55–133.

3   Peter Zarrow, 'Constitutionalism and the Imagination of the State: Official Views of Political Reform in the Late Qing', in *Creating Chinese Modernity: Knowledge and Everyday Life, 1900–1940*, ed. Peter Gue Zarrow (New York: Peter Lang, 2006), 51–82.

4   Nicholas B. Dirks, *Castes of Mind: Colonialism and the Making of Modern India* (Princeton: Princeton University Press, 2011).

5   Bernard S. Cohn, 'The Census, Social Structure and Objectification in South Asia', in *An Anthropologist among Historians and Other Essays*, ed. Bernard S. Cohen (Delhi: Oxford University Press, 1987), 224–54.

6   David Scott, *Refashioning Futures: Criticism after Postcoloniality* (Princeton: Princeton University Press, 1999).

7   See, for example, Laura Hostetler, *Qing Colonial Enterprise: Ethnography and Cartography in Early Modern China* (Chicago: University of Chicago Press, 2001).

8   Thomas Mullaney, *Coming to Terms with the Nation: Ethnic Classification in Modern China* (Berkeley: University of California Press, 2011), 11.

9   Ernest Gellner, *Nations and Nationalism* (Ithaca: Cornell University Press, 1983); Eric Hobsbawm, *Nations and Nationalism since 1780: Programme, Myth, Reality* (Cambridge: Cambridge University Press, 1992); Max Weber, 'The Nation', in *Nationalism*, eds John Hutchinson and Anthony D. Smith (Oxford: Oxford University Press, 1994), 21–5.

10 Gary Wilder, *The French Imperial Nation-State: Negritude and Colonial Humanism between the Two World Wars* (Chicago: University of Chicago Press, 2005); Antoinette Burton, ed., *After the Imperial Turn: Thinking with and through the Nation* (Durham: Duke University Press, 2003); Peter Fitzpatrick, *Modernism and the Grounds of Law* (Cambridge: Cambridge University Press, 2001).

11 Derk Bodde, 'Basic Concepts of Chinese Law: The Genesis and Evolution of Legal Thought in Traditional China', *Proceedings of the American Philosophical Society* 107, no. 5 (1963): 377.

12 See, for example, Phillip M. Chen, *Law and Justice: The Legal System in China, 2400 BC to 1960 AD* (New York: Dunellen Publishing, 1973).

13 Charles Patterson Giersch, *Asian Borderlands: The Transformation of Qing China's Yunnan Frontier* (Cambridge: Harvard University Press, 2006).

14 Melvyn C. Goldstein, 'The Dragon and the Snow Lion: The Tibet Question in the 20th Century', in *China Briefing, 1990*, ed. Anthony J. Kane (Boulder: Westview Press, 1990), 129–67.

15 Jonathan N. Lipman, *Familiar Strangers: A History of Muslims in Northwest China* (Seattle: University of Washington Press, 1997).

16 James A. Millward, *Beyond the Pass: Economy, Ethnicity, and Empire in Qing Central Asia, 1759–1864* (Stanford: Stanford University Press, 1998).

17 Evelyn S. Rawski, 'Presidential Address: Reenvisioning the Qing: The Significance of the Qing Period in Chinese History', *Journal of Asian Studies* 55, no. 4 (1996): 833–4.

18 Pamela Kyle Crossley, *Orphan Warriors: Three Manchu Generations and the End of the Qing World* (Princeton: Princeton University Press, 1990); Mark C. Elliott, *The*

Manchu Way: The Eight Banners and Ethnic Identity in Late Imperial China (Stanford: Stanford University Press, 2001).

19 June Teufel Dreyer, *China's Forty Millions: Minority Nationalities and National Integration in the People's Republic of China* (Cambridge: Harvard University Press, 1976), 9–10.

20 Huan Tian, 'Governing Imperial Borders: Insights from the Study of the Implementation of Law in Qing Xinjiang' (PhD diss., Columbia University, 2012); Ildikó Bellér-Hann, *Community Matters in Xinjiang, 1880–1949: Towards a Historical Anthropology of the Uyghur* (Leiden: Brill, 2008).

21 Lauren Benton, *Law and Colonial Cultures: Legal Regimes in World History, 1400–1900* (Cambridge: Cambridge University Press, 2002), 253.

22 Lauren Benton and Richard J. Ross, 'Empires and Legal Pluralism: Jurisdiction, Sovereignty, and Political Imagination in the Early Modern World', in *Legal Pluralism and Empires, 1500–1850*, eds Lauren Benton and Richard J. Ross (New York: New York University Press, 2013), 5.

23 Sally Falk Moore, 'Certainties Undone: Fifty Turbulent Years of Legal Anthropology, 1949–1999', *Journal of the Royal Anthropological Institute* 7, no. 1 (2001): 3–5; John L. Comaroff and Jean Comaroff, 'Introduction: The Portraits of an Ethnographer as a Young Man', in *Picturing a Colonial Past: The African Photographs of Isaac Schapera*, eds John L. Comaroff, Jean Comaroff and Deborah James (Chicago: University of Chicago Press, 2007), 5; Sally Falk Moore, ed., *Law and Anthropology: A Reader* (Malden: Blackwell Publishing, 2005), 67–76; Sally Engle Merry, *Colonizing Hawai'i: The Cultural Power of Law* (Princeton: Princeton University Press, 2000), 7–8; John Kelly, 'Gordon Was No Amateur: Imperial Legal Strategies in the Colonization of Fiji', in *Law and Empire in the Pacific: Fiji and Hawai'i*, eds Sally Engle Merry and Donald Brenneis (Sante Fe: School of American Research Press, 2004), 61–100; Annelise Riles, 'Law as Object', in Merry and Brenneis, *Law and Empire in the Pacific*, 187–212.

24 Bronislaw Malinowski, *Crime and Custom in Savage Society* (New York: Harcourt, Brace & Co., 1926).

25 Isaac Schapera, *A Handbook of Tswana Law and Custom: Compiled for the Bechuanaland Protectorate Administration* (London: Oxford University Press, 1938).

26 Max Gluckman, *The Judicial Process among the Barotse of Northern Rhodesia* (Manchester: University of Manchester, 1955).

27 Paul Bohannan, *Justice and Judgment among the Tiv* (Prospect Heights: Waveland Press, Inc., 1957).

28 Meyer Fortes, *The Web of Kinship among the Tallensi* (Oxford: Oxford University Press, 1949); E. E. Evans-Pritchard, *Kinship and Marriage among the Nuer* (Oxford: Oxford University Press, 1951).

29 For instance, in his study of kinship terms, Radcliffe-Brown identifies three types of rules that order relationships: personal sentiment or affective element, etiquette and jural rules (i.e. 'rights' and 'duties'). See A. R. Radcliffe-Brown, 'Introduction', in *African Systems of Kinship and Marriage*, eds A. R. Radcliffe Brown and D. Forde (London: Oxford University, 1950), 11. He further makes rules constitutive of kinship itself. See Radcliffe-Brown, 'Introduction', 13.

30 Gluckman, *Judicial Process*, 163–70; Schapera, *Handbook*, 35–6; Bohannan, *Justice and Judgment*, 57. Notably, Malinowski rejected this distinction and in fact placed 'law' as a subset of the category of 'custom'. See Malinowski, *Crime and Custom*, 54.

31 Ibid., 51.

32 Schapera, *Handbook*, 37.

33 Japan at the start of the twentieth century was the conduit for China's introduction to the early theories of anthropology, including evolutionism, diffusionism and historical-particularism. See Gregory Eliyu Guldin, *The Saga of Anthropology in China: From Malinowski to Moscow to Mao* (Armonk: M.E. Sharpe, 1994), 23. It was not until the 1920s that Chinese scholars such as Cai Yuanpei, who studied abroad in Germany, developed ethnology as a social science in China. See Guldin, *The Saga of Anthropology in China*, 30.

34 Liang Zhiping [梁治平], *Qingdai Xiguanfa: Shehui Yu Guojia (Qing Customary Law: Society and State)* (Beijing: Zhongguo Zhengfa Daxue Chubanshe, 1996), 38, 129–30.

35 Kathryn Bernhardt and Philip C. C. Huang, eds, *Civil Law in Qing and Republican China* (Stanford: Stanford University Press, 1994); Madeleine Zelin, Jonathan K. Ocko and Robert Gardella, eds, *Contract and Property in Early Modern China* (Stanford: Stanford University Press, 2004).

36 Jérôme Bourgon, 'La coutume et le droit en Chine à la fin de l'empire', *Annales. Histoire, Sciences Sociales* 54, no. 5 (1999): 1073–107; Jérôme Bourgon, 'Uncivil Dialogue: Law and Custom Did Not Merge into Civil Law under the Qing', *Late Imperial China* 23, no. 1 (2002): 50–90; Jérôme Bourgon, 'Rights, Freedoms, and Customs in the Making of Chinese Civil Law, 1900–1936', in *Realms of Freedom in Modern China*, ed. William C. Kirby (Stanford: Stanford University Press, 2005), 84–112.

37 Legal reform in Meiji Japan sought to hybridize Japanese tradition with an emulation of European continental law. By the end of the nineteenth century, Japan had a modern legal system with trained lawyers, an independent court system and a codified law. However, as procedures for civil and criminal adjudication developed, traditional forms yielded to Western patterns as can be seen in the drafting of the 1890 Code of Civil Procedure. In 1888, under French and German assistance, the First Diet was wracked by debate regarding family law and succession. While most of the code provisions had been drafted to consider customary practices, many of the premises underlying them were incompatible with Japanese tradition. See John O. Haley, *Authority without Power: Law and the Japanese Paradox* (New York: Oxford University Press, 1991), 4, 75; Frank K. Upham, *Law and Social Change in Postwar Japan* (Cambridge: Harvard University Press, 1987), 11–12.

38 Western-trained legal reformer Yatsuka Hozumi (1860–1912), who was initially enamoured with positive notions of law, eventually found the basis for Japanese sovereignty in the family and ancestor worship. On the new legislation, he claimed, 'Civil Code enacted, filial piety destroyed.' See Richard H. Minear, *Japanese Tradition and Western Law: Emperor, State, and Law in the Thought of Hozumi Yatsuka* (Cambridge: Harvard University Press, 1970). Noda Yoshiyuki, a legal scholar known for his culturalist view of law, describes a system of social rules that he calls 'custom' borrowing from Lévy-Bruhl, or in Japanese *giri*, defined as interpersonal rules of conduct attuned to social status. He finds that even after the reception of rationalist law, affective or emotive *giri* still regulates the social life of Japanese. Noda Yoshiyuki, *Introduction to Japanese Law* (Tokyo: University of Tokyo Press, 1976), 174, 175, 180.

39 The Guiding Measures for the Revision of the Laws by the High Officials for Legal Revision, 1907, state that before the laws can be revised, a survey covering foreign laws, the Qing Code of etiquette (*lizhi*), and civil and commercial customs must be conducted. Traditional Chinese sources of criminal law were excluded, and thus foreign models predominated in the field of criminal law. Specifically, the foreign penal codes translated were those of France, Germany, Holland, Russia, Japan,

Belgium, United States, Sweden and Finland. Li Guilian [李贵连], *Shen Jiaben Pingchuan (Commentary on Shen Jiaben's Legacy)* (Nanjing: Nanjing University Publishers, 2005), 115–16.

40 Bourgon notes that before legal modernization in Meiji Japan, the root word *shu kan* had, since antiquity, meant individual habits, but underwent semantic revision during this period. See Bourgon, 'Rights, Freedoms', 94. The contemporary usage of the word *shu kan* means both personal and social customs, although the former more so. The flipped term *kan shu* means social custom only. The contemporary Chinese definition of *xiguan* is 'custom; usual practice; *habitus*; convention' and *xiguanfa*, 'common law; customary law; consuetudinary law'. See Bianxie zubian (Editorial Group), ed., *Hanying Falü Cidian (A Chinese-English Law Dictionary)* (Beijing: China Commercial Press, 1995), 863.

41 Lydia Liu, *Translingual Practice: Literature, National Culture and Translated Modernity – China 1900–1937* (Stanford: Stanford University Press, 1995); Pei Yu [裴钰], 'Bu Jiang "Riben Hanyu" Jiu Bu Neng Shuohua? (If You Do Not Speak Japanese-Chinese, Can You Speak?)', *Lianhe Zaobao (Joint Morning Report)*, 9 February 2009.

42 The traditional date is 1907 or 1908. Hu Xusheng, citing the Hubei Survey Bureau Legal System Department First Survey Subject List, dates the beginning of the survey to 1904. Hu Xusheng [胡旭晟], '20 Shiji Qianqi Zhongguo Zhi Minshangshi Xiguan Baogaolu Ji Qi Yiyi (Daixu) (An Article in Lieu of a Preface: The Abstracts of the Report on Civil and Commercial Customs of the Early Part of the 20th Century and Its Significance)', in *Minshi Xiguan Diaocha Baogao Lu (Abstracts of the Report on Civil Affairs Customs)*, eds Hu Xusheng [胡旭晟], Xia Xinhua [夏新华] and Li Jiaofa [李交发] (Beijing: Zhongguo Zhengfa Daxue Chubanshe, 2000), 2.

43 Sui Hongming [眭紅明], 'Qingmo Minchu Minshangshi Xiguan Diaocha Zhi Yanjiu (Research on the Late Qing and Early Republican Civil and Commercial Affairs Survey)' (PhD diss., Nanjing Normal University, 2004), 39.

44 The guiding rules for the first survey, directing its contents and methods, were the Law Bureau's *Regulations on the Survey of Provincial Commercial Customs*. The date of the rules is most likely 1909. See Sui, 'Research'.

45 Li, *Commentary*, 163.

46 The Bureau for the Revision of the Laws' *Regulations for the Commercial Customs of Every Province* provided guidance for the survey, enumerating, for example, the types of businesses that should be recorded and what type of information should be elicited from each business. Hu Xusheng dates the document to March 1909 *Minshi Xiguan Diaochao Baogaolu (Abstracts of the Report on Civil Affairs Customs)* (Beijing: Zhongguo Zhengfa Daxue Chubanshe, 2000), 1067.

47 Tong Lam, *A Passion for Facts: Social Surveys and the Construction of the Chinese Nation-State, 1900–1949* (Berkeley: University of California Press, 2011).

48 Xiuding falüguan (Bureau for the Revision of the Laws), 'Diaocha Minshi Xiguan Zhangcheng Shitiao (Regulations on the Civil Customs Survey in Ten Articles)', in *Diaocha Minshi Xiguan Wenti (Civil Customs Survey Questions)* (Beijing: Xiuding falüguan shuayin (Printed by the Office of the Revision of Laws), 1909), 1–3. As to the date of the Regulations, article 3 specifies that the Regulations were announced in 1909.

49 Hu, 'An Article', 3.

50 Prasenjit Duara, *Rescuing History from the Nation: Questioning Narratives of Modern China* (Chicago: University of Chicago Press, 1995), 150.

51 Gluckman, *Judicial Process*, 254.

52 Bohannan, *Justice and Judgment*, 4.
53 Bourgon, 'Rights, Freedoms', 98.
54 This includes the translation of all foreign laws. This work was begun in earnest in 1907 but largely went unfinished. The survey of the Chinese code of etiquette included conducting archival research in the Bureau of the Study of Principles (*lixueguan*) along with the local gazetteers.
55 Hu, 'An Article', 3.
56 The following is an excerpt from the *Collection of Reports on Popular Sentiments and Customs*. See Li, *Commentary*, 165–6.
57 Sui, *Research*, 45.
58 Marie Seong-Hak Kim, *Law and Custom in Korea: Comparative Legal History* (Cambridge: Cambridge University Press, 2012), 62.
59 Following the Opium War (1839–1842), China was forced to sign what has collectively become known as the 'Unequal Treaties,' which, among other things, conferred extraterritorial rights in China to foreign powers. By the time Shen Jiaben assumed power in the Qing judiciary, a long list of foreign powers had extraterritorial claims including Japan, Britain, France, the United States, Germany, Austria, Russia, Portugal, Italy, the Netherlands, Belgium, Denmark, Sweden and Norway. See Turan Kayaoğlu, *Legal Imperialism: Sovereignty and Extraterritoriality in Japan, the Ottoman Empire, and China* (Cambridge: Cambridge University Press, 2010), 151.
60 This strategy backfired. Foreign powers adapted through various countermeasures, one of which was establishing counsellor courts. The United States Congress, for example, passed an act in 1906 creating the US Court for China that gave the US judiciary exclusive jurisdiction over all American citizens in China. See Teemu Ruskola, 'Colonialism without Colonies: On the Extra Territorial Jurisprudence of the U.S. Court for China', *Law & Contemporary Problems* 71, no. 3 (2008): 217–42.
61 Xiaoqun Xu, 'The Fate of Judicial Independence in Republican China, 1912–37', *China Quarterly* 149 (1997): 2–3; Li, *Commentary*, 454.
62 Xu, 'The Fate of Judicial Independence', 2, fn. 7; Howard L. Boorman, 'Biographical Dictionary of Republican China' (New York: Columbia University Press, 1970), 98–9.
63 Not to overstate the point that the methodology of legal reform was that of classical Chinese legal scholarship, from 1906 to 1910, Shen Jiaben sent Chinese jurists to Japan to survey Japanese legal modernization. He employed several Japanese legal experts such as Okada Asatarō, his chief criminal law advisor who imitated German legal analysis. Thus, many of those working under Shen Jiaben were Western-trained. At the same time, while Shen Jiaben advocated the consultation of Japanese legal experts, his writings show he did not necessarily listen to their opinions. See Li, *Commentary*, 152–4.
64 Ma Jianhong [马建红], 'Huidao Shen Jiaben Chaoyue Shen Jiaben: Zhongguo Fazhi Xiandaihau Daolu Fansi (Return to Shen Jiaben, Surpass Shen Jiaben: A Reconsideration of the Road of China's Legal Modernization)', in *Lunwenji: Shenjiaben Falü Sixiang Yanjiu (A Collection of Essays: Research on Shen Jiaben Legal Thought)*, ed. Ma Zhibing (Beijing: Zhongguo fazhi chubanshe, 2003), 288.
65 Boorman, 'Biographical Dictionary', 97.
66 Sui, *Research*, 22, fn. 4.
67 Ibid., 30.
68 Ibid., 28–9.

69 Zhang Sheng [张生], 'Qingmo Minshi Xiguan Diaocha Yu 'Daqing Minlü Cao'an De Bianzuan (The Late Qing Survey of Civil Customs and the Compilation of the Qing Civil Code Draft)', *Faxue yanjiu (Legal Studies Research)* 1 (2007): 125.
70 Mullaney, *Coming to Terms*.
71 The category *Hanzu xiguan* (Han customs) is rarely used in Chinese. The variant *Hanzu xisu* (Han conventions) is more common which suggests that *xiguan* has become semantically linked to ethnic minorities in the communist period.
72 Nicholas B. Dirks, 'Castes of Mind', *Representations* 37 (1992): 67–8.
73 Elizabeth A. Povinelli, *The Cunning of Recognition: Indigenous Alterities and the Making of Australian Multiculturalism* (Durham: Duke University Press, 2002); John L. Comaroff, 'Colonialism, Culture, and the Law: A Foreword', *Law & Social Inquiry* 26 (2001): 305–14.
74 Martin Chanock wrote: 'Law is the cutting edge of colonialism.' Martin Chanock, *Law, Custom and Social Order: The Colonial Experience in Malawi and Zambia* (Cambridge: Cambridge University Press, 1985), 4.
75 Shiping Hua, 'Shen Jiaben and the Late Qing Legal Reform (1901–1911)', *East Asia* 30, no. 2 (2013): 121–38.
76 Benedict Anderson, *Imagined Communities: Reflections on the Origin and Spread of Nationalism* (London and New York: Verso, 1983), 86.

Chapter 7

NITOBE INAZO AND THE DIFFUSION OF A KNOWLEDGEABLE EMPIRE

Alexis Dudden

This chapter premises a significantly underappreciated intellectual accomplishment of the early stages of the Japanese empire. In 1911, a man named Nitobe Inazo designated the terms for 'colony' and 'colonization' that are still in use in Japanese today, and he also put the final touches on a full course of instruction at Japan's most prestigious school – the University of Tokyo – for students there to learn about the nation's growing empire and its workings. He called the field 'colonial policy studies' (植民地政策学).

Over the next three decades, many of Nitobe's students and his students' students would become Japan's colonial leaders in positions ranging from colonial officials and bureaucrats to teachers themselves of colonial policy studies at universities in Japan and in the empire's outposts, such as Seoul and Taipei. Collectively, their efforts would disseminate knowledge of the 'colonial' – from the people involved in hydraulic projects and languages – that was recursively defined as useful for the Japanese empire's proper expansion and functioning. The approach epitomized social science's best practices of the day, replete with quantifiable evidence, statistical analysis and generalized claims, all of which Nitobe pithily summed up on his classroom blackboard at the University of Tokyo at the start of class each day: 'Colonization is the spread of civilization.'[1] One of his most famous disciples was Yanaihara Tadao who, like his teacher, converted to Christianity and was often described by contemporaries as a 'humanist'. As chair of colonial policy studies at the University of Tokyo during the 1930s, Yanaihara continued Nitobe's legacy by stressing the importance of knowing the colonial terrain as a rational object so that the science of 'planting people' – the literal translation of Nitobe's expression for 'colonization' – would be carried forward into the future on the colonial subjects' own terms.[2]

The year 1911 was the same year that the Carnegie Endowment for International Peace named Nitobe Inazo the first Japanese exchange professor to the United States, switching him with Hamilton Wright Mabie, a prominent essayist for the leading weekly magazine, *The Outlook*. Mabie delivered lectures throughout Japan on topics such as 'American Ideals' and 'American Culture and Life'. Although Nitobe's establishment of colonial policy studies within Japan and his selection by the Carnegie Endowment as point person to spread thoughtful awareness about Japan in the United States were not causally related, taken together on a shared historical plane they bring into relief Nitobe's chief intention for Japan at the time: that the nation's growing Eurasian-Pacific empire make mutually intelligible sense to the world's other imperializing nations as common practice. To this end, in positive – and positivistic – ways he urged: 'As our countrymen continue to think about the word "colony" they become enlightened about the concept of colonial enterprise. These days, national prestige and national strength depend on overseas expansion, and the idea of colonization has reached our nation's people.'[3]

Nitobe's challenge was to create a disciplined approach to this 'idea' among those who would shape colonization's trajectory from its centre in Tokyo as well as in its imperial locales. Although he remains known primarily as the author of *Bushido: The Soul of Japan* (1900) and by his self-styled moniker, 'the bridge across the Pacific', Nitobe's life and work with regards to the academic formation of colonial policy studies nonetheless also defines him as the intellectual architect of Japanese colonization writ large. His efforts, moreover, remain critical for understanding how international social science practices and norms became normative in the Japanese empire, which, in turn, made the empire make 'sense' to its outsiders.

A number of impediments block an appreciation of Nitobe's significance in the colonial mix as it were, stemming in no small measure from a historiographic preoccupation with Nitobe's more attention-grabbing accomplishments that overshadow his stamp on the *intellectual* history of the Japanese empire.[4] For example, in the early days of Japan's overseas expansion, colonial economic output shaped the narrative about Nitobe, particularly the development schemes that he put into practice in Taiwan which famously quadrupled sugar output during the Japanese colony's first few years.[5] Later on, Nitobe would lead Japan's delegation to the League of Nations, becoming one of the League's under-secretaries, guiding matters such as resolution of the Aland Island dispute, the promotion of racial equality principles and the creation of transnational intellectual property practices (including international library loan). Nonetheless, Nitobe's visions for the rational organization and mediation of colonized places and people during the formative years of the Japanese empire demonstrate the significance that he himself placed on a universalistic understanding of how best to know, analyse and foster sustained growth in and among such spaces. In a word, he remains responsible for a socially scientific approach to colonial policy, and its reach would spread throughout Japan's empire until its violent collapse in 1945.[6]

An additional hurdle stems from a historiographical tendency to insert a solid conceptual break between Japan's premodern internal expansions and assimilation policies and the nation's modern history of empire-building.[7] To be sure, many features of the global industrial system that arrived together with American and European gunships in the nineteenth century tore much asunder in Japanese society. At the same time, however, critical elements of existing social, political and economic orders made it possible for Japanese leaders to refract some of the powerful new international rules and practices for labour, trade and commodity extraction that confronted them – and which rendered many places and people ripe for colonization – and use them to transform their nation into one of the world's imperializing nations by the outset of the twentieth century.[8] In this vital way, Japan differed from the rest of Asia, becoming an imperializer rather than imperialized.

Nitobe Inazo's personal history aligns him metonymically with these larger trends. His grandfather, Tsuto's success at building canals across a wide swath of unused land in northern Japan's Sambongi plain in the 1850s secured the family's reputation for agricultural engineering in key ways.[9] Two decades later in the midst of the greatest upheaval to confront Japan in centuries – unrest that would end the Tokugawa shogun's rule and re-introduce the emperor to policymaking – advisors to the new emperor Meiji ensured that Tsuto's grandson, Inazo, be named to a group of specially recruited young men to attend a new agricultural development school established in 1875 in Japan's first colony, Hokkaido. As elaborated later in this chapter, the curriculum at the Sapporo Agricultural College – today Hokkaido University – included courses that would have made sense to Tsuto such as 'geometrical drawing', yet also instructed things unforeseen in Tsuto's time such as 'military drills' to prepare young men to 'clear natives' from the land.[10] Notably, the American advisers hired to guide the post-revolutionary government in Tokyo in its newly created bureaucracy, the Colonial Development Office, introduced these subjects, defining their content and aim. In short, what Nitobe and other students would study in Sapporo became elemental to Japanese people's future understanding of their own empire in new ways. Nitobe himself understood this shift explicitly, explaining his choice for the term for 'colony' and 'colonization': 'Would it suffice to name (Japan's) newly occupied territories with old expressions? No, it is better to use a new term.'[11]

Also related – and perhaps at the heart of the difficulty of grasping the social sciences' place in the construction of the Japanese empire – are barriers that have redirected the focus away from the American imprint on this history as well as America's direct encouragement of Japan's imperial expansion in general. For varying reasons, in 1945 American politicians and strategists moved immediately to claim the total victory over Japan in American terms alone even though it had been very much an Allied effort that brought down the Japanese empire.[12] Americans worked together with Japanese officials under the US-led occupation, and their efforts jointly worked to deny rationality to Japan's modern history of empire as well as its knowledgeable origins. Historian Yukiko Koshiro insightfully observes that at this juncture 'the Japanese began living in *sengo*, a state of postwar reflection on the nation's "humbling" defeat by the United States alone'.[13] Looked at differently, what many call 'victor's justice' to describe the American determination of Japan's war criminality also was a matter of 'victor's denial' most clearly with regards to the intellectual underpinnings of the Japanese empire.

In compelling ways, therefore, the American historian William Appleman Williams' urgent challenge to US historians in the 1950s remains useful in this context. As is well known, in face of preferred exceptionalist notions of spreading 'American freedom' through American expansion, Williams charged his students and readers instead to understand that, beginning with the late nineteenth century's closing of the American frontier, US foreign policy intentionally spread empire to secure areas for new capital investment and reliable markets.[14] Understanding the ways in which American officials, educators and missionaries introduced practical, scientifically organized knowledge of American 'colonization' strategies to Japan in the 1870s and 1880s brings a significant and tangible component of this history and its effects into relief. It demonstrates, moreover, that this moment blends seamlessly into Japan's perpetuation of such a rational approach for knowing its own expanding empire, at once making clear the importance of the social sciences' presumed universality and how power functioned through them in early-twentieth-century empires.

In 1870, the recently revolutionized Japanese government hired the American Commissioner of Agriculture, Horace Capron, as an adviser to its newly created Colonial Development Bureau. At the time, the young Meiji regime famously sought 'knowledge from throughout the world' and employed Europeans and Americans to guide the nation's refashioning, selecting those whom Japanese leaders believed best matched Japanese conditions.[15] England and France were the world's leading imperial powers of the day, yet the Meiji bureaucrats decided that American experience in internal colonization best mirrored the challenges they faced in Hokkaido, Japan's first colony, claimed for the nation only the year before. Indigenous inhabitants – the Ainu, Nivkh and Orok people – had lived for roughly 20,000 years scattered throughout the territory that newcomers from the 'mainland' – as Japan's older islands soon became known – would begin to claim as their own. Practical knowledge for coping with these developments challenged Meiji leaders. Hokkaido itself is roughly the size of the state of Utah in American terms, yet conceptually for Japan its incorporation into the nation was as large as the Louisiana Purchase had been in the development of the United States, essentially doubling the country's size overnight. Meiji officials established a new bureaucracy to take charge, the *Kaitakushi*, a name variously translated as the Hokkaido Development Office or the Colonial Development Bureau, and they hired Capron to advise its goals. Capron's experience as the ranking official in Washington in charge of America's frontier expansion, among other things, appealed greatly, as did his time as a soldier which included being not only the oldest Union cavalry officer during the American Civil War but also an earlier special presidential appointment to 'remove' Native Americans from Texas following the Mexican–American War. Between 1870–1, the Meiji government paid Capron the astronomical consultancy fee of $10,000 (roughly $250,000 today) to travel to its new Hokkaido colony and formulate a proper course of action.

Capron's vision for how the Japanese government should proceed in cultivating this territory prevailed despite various domestic political crises that unfolded in the mix. Not insignificantly, people in Hokkaido today still refer to these as Japan's 'frontier days', often by way of recounting their families' frontiersmen lineage in ways strikingly similar to Americans in the nation's western states. The history involved could not be more straightforward, and in important ways is tied directly to the implementation of a social sciences approach for organizing this space for colonization. In 1876, through Capron's counsel, the Japanese government contracted William S. Clark, then president of the Massachusetts Agricultural College (today University of Massachusetts at Amherst), to move to Hokkaido and create a similar school in the colony's new capital at Sapporo where a new cadre of young Japanese would learn the proper techniques for colonizing Hokkaido.

Nitobe Inazo was enrolled in the school's second year, and fifteen years later, in 1893, teaching at what by then was renamed the Imperial Agricultural College, he waxed nostalgic about the school and Japan's original colonial moments in ways that usefully set the scene:

> The War of Restoration Over, the Japanese Government turned its attention to more peaceful pursuits. It began to divert the overflowing energies of the warrior class and the superabundant strength of the oppressed peasantry into new channels of industrial warfare and conquest ... (to) the northern frontier of the Empire and a land endowed with magnificent natural resources as yet untouched by human hand, the new Imperial Government wisely began to extend its fostering care.[16]

Nitobe's recollection of Hokkaido lying pristine and in need of proper 'care' reveals better than anything the sum total of how he and the social scientific approach to the world that he espoused viewed the unfolding of empire in general: either in terms of a rationalizing, masculinizing process disciplining a virginal space in which 'natives' and 'aboriginals' remained in some sort of Edenic state or – and increasingly important to Japanese colonial officials as the nation expanded its reach – as already inhabited places, whose populations needed a firm, 'civilizing' hand. Significantly, William Penn and Henry George were writers whose influence Nitobe felt deeply.

Described consistently as 'Japan's greatest internationalist', Nitobe was at once an educator, author and statesmen, similar in many ways to Woodrow Wilson, who became one of his heroes. Not unimportantly, however, and in ways not dissimilar to the enduring myth – 'If President John F. Kennedy had not been shot the United States would not have gone to war in Vietnam' – in American self-narration, Nitobe died just as Japan withdrew from the League of Nations in 1933 (he was no longer in Geneva, but his opinions were still actively sought). In practical terms, therefore, Japan's 'greatest internationalist' remains historically clean in terms of Japan's disavowal of the League and the nation's subsequently disastrous total war for imperial gain (1931–1945) without *himself* ever having had to decide whether or not to publicly protest what transpired. Historiographically, therefore, Nitobe remains the leading 'internationalist', rather than an 'imperialist'.

These details remain important because the theoretical understandings of modern colonial empire and rationally conceived agricultural sciences would group together these disparate forms under the rubric of 'civilization', 'cultivation' and 'development'. Nitobe's solidly American-backgrounded understanding of modern colonizing practice led him to do a complete translation of William Penn's works and to analyse the colonization of Pennsylvania, endeavours that progressed logically from his studies with American teachers in Sapporo in the 1870s and 1880s.

Henry George's theories would similarly influence his understanding of social and political economy. In short, everything that went along with Nitobe's designation of the most important 'key word' of them all – 'colony' and 'colonization studies' – came from Nitobe's insistence on getting their deep meanings 'right', reflexively speaking.

A campus on the New England institutional model of the day appeared on Hokkaido's newly created capital at Sapporo's otherwise 'blank' terrain. Beginning in the late 1870s the curriculum at the Sapporo Agricultural College included instruction in English for all grades, farm management, math and engineering with special focus on topographical surveying and levelling, upper level courses in 'Universal History' and the 'History of Civilization', and military drills to prepare students to become officers in the nation's newly formed frontier militia, the Tondenhei (屯田兵), whose teachers taught techniques learnt in the American Indian Wars.

Many of the students at the school came from families that had been of samurai rank before the abolition of this class system in 1873. For the most part, the government swallowed the students' fees with the contractual understanding that upon graduation the student would assume a post in the Tondenhei and/or also would teach at the school or one of its developing offshoot academies. Nitobe Inazo never ranked at the top of his class in terms of academic performance – during his first year he averaged an 80 per cent compared to his equally famous classmate, the great social thinker Uchimura Kanzo, who averaged close to a 90 – yet more than any other graduate of the school he fully imbibed its world view, making its core teachings his life's work and a reality throughout the growing Japanese empire.[17]

Fast forward twenty years into the first and second decades of the twentieth century, and the Japanese were referring to Hokkaido as a 'home' island, having added the 'outer territories' of Taiwan, the southern half of Sakhalin island and Korea to the growing empire. At this juncture, Nitobe's introduction at Japan's best university of a socially scientific course of study for knowing these places as well is key.

What was at stake for Japan? Many of the same things that were at the heart of governance for the other colonial powers whose ranks the Meiji leaders were determined to join. With regards to the disciplines and discourses that these collective colonizing efforts created, Timothy Mitchell's explanation of how power works in this context remains most incisive. In Mitchell's understanding, it was a 'world where political power ... operates always to appear as something set apart from the real world, effacing a certain, metaphysical authority'.[18]

Thus, it is not an overstatement to suggest that in 1911 when Nitobe Inazo published his still little-known essay of great importance – 'On the Term "Colony"' – he was a man on a mission.[19] The essay appeared a year after Japan's full annexation of Korea, and Nitobe explained that through this action as well as the previous expansions of the Japanese empire, the Japanese were fluently practising the international politics of empire. His essay's contention was that an unfortunate lack of appreciation for such monumental developments persisted in Japanese society, a flaw he saw best evinced in the inconsistent ways in which Japanese expressed the term for 'colony' in Japanese. He argued that in order for Japan to declare itself a full colonial power – which he argued in thoroughly positive terms – there must be a consensus on how to render its name in order to make the policies and the knowledge undergirding it fluent to the international community.

At this historical juncture in Japan, courses about the colonies seemed to appear overnight at vocational schools whose graduates would become bureaucratic functionaries in Japan's newly acquired overseas colonies, at elite prep schools whose students would guide the creation of imperial policy writ large during the decades to come, as well as at the most prestigious universities whose ranks would lead Japanese policy through 1945. In this milieu, Nitobe took charge and created the full-fledged discipline of 'colonial policy studies' to drive home its central tenet: 'Colonization is the spread of civilization' (植民は文明の伝播).

In his essay on naming the 'colony', Nitobe made clear that readers would understand that the Japanese usage was discrete from the Chinese's:

> So that there wouldn't be any doubt about whether this European word ... had first been translated into Chinese (or Japanese), I consulted many French-Chinese and English-Chinese dictionaries. The Chinese language lacked 'colony' as a meaningful term until very recently (and it) is not yet commonly used in our neighboring country.

Nitobe's insistence that Chinese lacked the term that Japanese would now define for the Chinese-character sphere at once elevated Japan above China – still remarkable in regional power politics terms in 1911 – and connected Japan to the imperializing nations whose society Nitobe sought. He continued:

> As our countrymen continue to think about the word, they become more enlightened about the concept of colonial enterprise. These days national prestige and national strength depend on overseas expansion, and the idea of colonization has reached our nation's people.[20]

At this juncture, Nitobe took a stand, urging the government to adopt a rendering for 'colony' that he believed best captured the imperialist practice and thus best translated Japan's projects back into the Euro-American contexts in which he wanted Japan to make sense:

> The word 'colony' first reached our countrymen's ears from the English and the Dutch ... the *Doeff-Haruma Japanese-Dutch Glossary* was published between 1855 and 1858. I have looked up the word in this dictionary yet have found no Japanese translation for the Dutch '*zie Volplanting*'. Isn't it odd that the Japanese scholars helping Doeff could not come up with the term '*shokumin*' (literally, 'planting people')? Did they lack sufficient knowledge? Did they simply avoid it because it was a word that had not been used before? ... Beginning in 1862, the word '*colony*' appeared in Hori Tatsunosuke's *English-Japanese Dictionary*.[21]

Two phonetically identical variants of 'colony' and 'colonial' (*shokumin*) existed in Japanese at the time of Nitobe's writing (explaining why he was making such a push for consistency but also intelligibility, recursively speaking); 'to plant people' (植民) and 'to increase people' (殖民). As its chief policy promoter, Nitobe wanted his government to rationalize and internationalize the practice by designating Japan's efforts as 'planting people' (植民):

> Regardless of its general use, the Chinese characters for 'planting people' are used in the vernacular but not yet officially. ... (Whenever) names of places like Korea, Taiwan, or Karafuto (now, Sakhalin) are mentioned ... they are referred to as 'new additions to the empire'. Does it suffice to name these newly occupied territories with old expressions? Wouldn't it be better to use the new term – *shokumnichi* (植民地)?[22]

Simply put, Nitobe argued that 'planting people' captured the contemporary European meaning and best translated Japanese policy abroad, defining the arena where he wanted to be understood. Form mattered, and now that Japan was a legitimate imperialist (accomplished by its 1910 takeover of Korea if not earlier), Nitobe wanted his nation to make sense.

The tendency, therefore, to uphold Nitobe Inazo in a separate chamber of history from Japan's Pan-Asianist imperialists of the 1930s, has fostered rigid walls between the political and theoretical creation of Japan's empire and the knowledge-oriented repression that occurred therein. His intellectual followers have insisted on a sort of faith in the reasoning that no blurring of lines took place between the carving out of empire and the scientific control of totalitarian policies.

This tendency – and it pertains to several other architects of the empire as well – continues to make it difficult to internationalize the history of Japanese imperialism, which is why consideration of how Japan's practice meshed with others continues to be urgently needed. In the first half of the twentieth century, Japan, China, Russia, England, France, the United States and Germany would likely have vied over the territories that brought them to the wars they fought, but Nitobe defined Japan's imperialist expansion as an informed, knowledgeable social science and political practice at its outset.

Contemporary events in Japan and Northeast Asia make real the need for a broad re-examination of the history of the Japanese empire. An unfortunate yet enduring feature of international histories of empire fails Japan and Japanese society: that of measuring Japan's imperialist experience as different from a supposed norm (a combination of British, French, American and Dutch experience and to a lesser extent German and Italian as well). A logic that measures Japan against a Western standard continues at once to overlook Japan's empire and/or presumes that anyone interested should insert Japan's case into the prevailing theoretical models – models that, on the one hand, claim to be international and/or global in scope, yet, on the other hand, do not incorporate Japan in their formulation.

Specific examples in otherwise excellent studies of empire include Jane Burbank and Fred Cooper's recent *Empires in World History* and Michael Hardt and Antonio Negri's *Empire*.[23] The former refers to the Japanese empire only when it comes into confrontation with the 'standard' practitioners (chiefly the French and the English in Southeast Asia) but not in its own generative moments, while the latter does not even offer a historical point of entry for any in the non-West to actively participate in this debate or in the origins of globalism. Consequently – and to greater and lesser degrees – for matters of Japan and empire and global studies, Dipesh Chakrabarty's elaboration of the nation continues to ring a little too true: Japanese experience remains consigned to an 'imaginary waiting room of history'.[24]

Emphatically, this observation is an attempt neither to ignore differences nor to take cheap shots. Rather, it remains an effort to raise questions about what we collectively get away with when we write 'global' and even 'empire'. In a word, failure to incorporate Japan's modern history of empire writ large into the global calculus sustains conditions within Japan *today* that have generated a persistent and destabilizing thread in modern Japanese society and historiography, which those determined to 'write away' Japan's twentieth century manipulate to their benefit. At once Japanese scholars determined to engage Japan in the bigger picture continue to be branded 'communist', 'Marxist', or simply 'not Japanese', while others are able to shrug and explain along the lines of 'we just did what everyone else was doing'.

Expressing such reasoning in the 1920s or even in the 1950s may have made sense. Today, however, the real-life, ongoing 'blowback' from Asians victimized by the Japanese empire and war (in Chalmers Johnson's sense of the term) sets up an 'us versus them' binary that claims something called history as its rallying cry yet is increasingly empty of content. Scholars of Japan's empire who work with broader histories regularly have to begin over again with basics, which sustains a perfect storm that works to the benefit of those who would deny the violence that went hand in hand with the unfolding of Japan's empire: those determined to 'dignify' the nation's ancestors through history counter that anything to the contrary is a 'masochistic' view of the nation's past. This negates specific atrocities and structures and throws the onus back on those seeking dignity through having their particular history meaningfully recorded, politicizing everything in the present tense.

Interrogating empire and the social sciences thus offers a productive possibility for overcoming this conundrum. In clear ways, in the late nineteenth century Japan's leaders endeavoured to incorporate Japan into the global project of empire by 'rewriting' the nation. The creation of the modern social sciences was axiomatic to this, and the discourses that arose with them in the late nineteenth/early twentieth century would make Japan make new international sense at a time when the rest of Asia was being carved up and/or eyed for colonial takeover: in other words, not making sense left a place/nation ripe for the imperialist urge. The language that Japan's leaders created to describe, know and explain Japan's rapid industrialization, mass militarization and territorial expansion was intelligible to an international audience. At the same time – and critically – such terms were consistent with traditional Japanese practices and the nation's new aspirations.

Thus, while these new discourses were not more important than the military strength needed to conquer places and people to build the empire, they confirmed Japan's place in the international history of global, industrial empire.

Notes

1 Nitobe Inazo Zenshu Henshu Iinkai (NIZHI), *Nitobe Inazo Zenshu* (Tokyo: Kyobunkan, 1970), vol. 4, 7–10.
2 In English, see Susan C. Townsend, *Yanaihara Tadao and Japanese Colonial Policy: Redeeming Empire* (Richmond: Curzon, 2000) for discussion of Yanaihara coming into conflict with the military over the extent of Japan's expansion. Yanaihara would resign from academia between 1937 and 1945, returning to the University of Tokyo after the war to a new chair in international economics and developmental economics. Ultimately, he served as president of the university from 1951–1957.
3 NIZHI, *Nitobe Inazo Zenshu*, vol. 4, 353; some of the translations included here of Nitobe's texts appeared in my *Japan's Colonization of Korea: Discourse and Power* (Honolulu: University of Hawaii, 2005).
4 Most famously, in 1900 Nitobe published *Bushido: The Soul of Japan* (Philadelphia: Leeds & Biddle, 1900), which would be included in most mentions of Nitobe thereafter, during his lifetime and beyond.
5 Sugar remained significant to Taiwan's economy even after Japan's empire collapsed in 1945. Although far less important to the country's economy today – down to less than 1 per cent of GDP in 2014 compared to over 50 per cent in 1952 – economic historians credit this commodity as well as Nitobe Inazo's techniques for raising it as a critical source of capital accrual.
6 It remains important to understand that even though the empire collapsed in 1945, important features of social science practices would extend into the post-imperial future. For example, Nitobe's student, Yanaihara Tadao, reorganized colonial policy studies into course on developmental economics.
7 In English, the most lucid counter to this persistent theme is David Howell, *Geographies of Identity in Nineteenth Century Japan* (Berkeley: University of California, 2005); and also, Karen Wigen, *The Making of a Japanese Periphery, 1750–1920* (Berkeley: University of California Press, 1995).
8 For the best analysis in English of Japan's economic system on the eve of the modern era, see Tetsuo Najita, *Visions of Virtue in Tokugawa Japan: The Kaitokudo Merchant Academy of Osaka* (Honolulu: University of Hawaii, 1997).
9 On the Nitobe family history, see Ota Yuzo, '*Taiheiyo no hashi*' *toshite Nitobe Inazo* (Tokyo: Misuzu Shobo, 1987).
10 The Sapporo Agricultural College, *The Sapporo Agricultural College* (Sapporo, Hokkaido, 1893).
11 Nitobe Inazo, 'Shokumin naru Meiji ni tsukite', *Hogakkai Zasshi* 29, no. 2 (1911): 12.
12 Rana Mitter, *Forgotten Ally: China's World War II, 1937–1945* (New York: Houghton Mifflin, 2013); Yukiko Koshiro, *Imperial Eclipse: Japan's Strategic Thinking about Continental Asia before August 1945* (New York: Cornell University Press, 2013).
13 Ibid., 11.
14 Begin with William Appleman Williams, *The Tragedy of American Diplomacy* (New York: W.W. Norton, 2009 [1959]); see also Andrew Bacevich, 'Tragedy Renewed: William Appleman Williams', *World Affairs* 171, no. 3 (2009): 62–72.

15 In English, see Kenneth Pyle, *The New Generation in Meiji Japan: Problems of Cultural Identity, 1885–1895* (Stanford: Stanford University Press, 1969).
16 Nitobe Inazo, *The Imperial Agricultural College of Sapporo, Japan* (Sapporo, Hokkaido: Imperial College of Agriculture, 1893), 1.
17 For these and all other details of the school's functioning, see the *Annual Report of the Sapporo Agricultural College*, Kaitakushi and Hokkaido-cho (published between 1877 and 1886). Nitobe's grades are included in the *Second Annual Report*, 124.
18 Timothy Mitchell, *Colonising Egypt* (Berkeley: University of California Press, 1991).
19 Nitobe, 'Shokumin naru Meiji ni tsukite'.
20 Ibid.
21 Ibid.
22 Ibid.
23 Jane Burbank and Fred Cooper, *Empires in World History* (Princeton: Princeton University Press, 2011); Michael Hardt and Antonio Negri, *Empire* (Durham: Duke University Press, 2000). The clearest example, however, remains Patrick Wolfe's statement in his otherwise comprehensive and thought-provoking review essay for the *American Historical Review*, 'History and Imperialism: A Century of Theory, from Marx to Postcolonialism', 102, no. 2 (1997): 388–420, which explains in its second footnote that 'for reasons of space, Japanese imperialism will not be discussed'.
24 Dipesh Chakrabarty, *Provincializing Europe: Postcolonial Thought and Historical Difference* (Princeton: Princeton University Press, 2000).

Chapter 8

MODERN IMPERIALISM AND INTERNATIONAL LAW:
CARL SCHMITT AND ERNST RUDOLF HUBER ON THE
'INTERNATIONAL LEGAL ORDER OF GREAT SPACES'

Joshua Derman[*]

Theorizing imperialism in Weimar and Nazi Germany

Over the past decade, the German jurist Carl Schmitt (1888–1985) has received a renewed wave of attention for his writings on imperialism and American foreign policy.[1] This phenomenon owes much to the rediscovery of his Weimar-era articles on international law, such as 'The Rhineland as an Object of International Politics' (1925) and 'The USA and the International Legal Forms of Modern Imperialism' (1933), as well as to the recent English translation of his last major work, *The Nomos of the Earth in the International Law of the Jus Publicum Europaeum* (1950).[2] In these texts Schmitt presented a trenchant critique of 'modern imperialism', by which he meant the efforts of Western powers to extend their power at a time when prior strategies of conquest no longer seemed practical or politically acceptable. It was characteristic of modern imperialism, he argued, that the institutions and verbiage of international law had replaced territorial aggrandizement as the decisive means of projecting political influence. Legal machinations not only helped obscure power interests but also served to 'morally paralyse' the victims of imperialism by inducing them to accept the justifications under which they were dominated as legitimate.[3]

The historical conjuncture of the early twenty-first century has proven to be especially propitious for the revival of Schmitt's themes. In the aftermath of the 2003 US invasion of Iraq and the George W. Bush administration's 'global war on terror', debates about 'liberal empire', humanitarian intervention and globalization have provided a context in which Schmitt's work has found new readers.[4] What has been largely absent from these discussions and appropriations, however, is an effort to situate his critique of imperialism within the context of his support for National Socialism.[5] For Schmitt was not merely a noted diagnostician of hegemonic power relations; he was also the most prominent theorist and intellectual propagandist of the Nazi New Order among his contemporaries. On 1 April 1939, only a few weeks after the dismemberment of Czechoslovakia, Schmitt delivered a public lecture in which he called for legally partitioning the world into multiple continental *Großräume* or 'great spaces'. The prototype for this kind of international legal order, he argued, was the 'original' Monroe Doctrine of 1823, which demanded recognition for a continental space (the Western hemisphere), imbued by a politically awakened people (the United States) with a specific political idea (republicanism), that excluded interventions by extrahemispheric powers (Russia and the Holy Alliance). Germany, or any other *Reich* with its own distinctive political ideology, he counselled in the published version of his lecture, *The International Legal Order of Great Spaces*, would do well to claim its own continental zone and exclude outside interventions.[6]

Though it is unlikely that Schmitt's writings made a causal impact on the course of Nazi foreign policy, they did succeed in staking out – or at the very least anticipating – two key concepts in the regime's propaganda. On 28 April 1939, only a few weeks after Schmitt introduced his theory of great spaces, Adolf Hitler rebuffed an American request for Germany to clarify its foreign objectives by declaring, in a speech to the Reichstag, that Germany would assert its own Monroe Doctrine for Europe. On several occasions throughout the Second World War, the German foreign minister, Joachim von Ribbentrop, similarly sought to discourage American intervention by invoking a Monroe Doctrine as applied to Europe.[7] The notion of a globe divided into great spaces, which Schmitt did so much to popularize, was widely discussed by German jurists and economists during the war, who, for all their reservations concerning the 'legal' aspects of his proposed order, nonetheless commended him for providing a concept that succinctly evoked a world order in which German hegemony over Europe went unchallenged.[8]

Schmitt began his career as a diagnostician and critic of the 'modern imperialism' of the Western democracies, most notably the United States, yet by the eve of the Second World War he had become a vigorous defender of an 'international legal order' that seemed to promote the very kind of regional hegemony that he once decried. Was Schmitt simply recommending that Nazi Germany emulate the conduct of its rivals? If so, then why did he insist that an international legal order of great spaces would have nothing in common with the 'imperialism of global humanity' (*Welt- und Menschheitsimperialismus*) allegedly pursued by the Anglo-Saxon powers?[9] This chapter seeks to illuminate Schmitt's changing understanding of 'imperialism' by tracing his usage of the concept between 1925 and 1939. It argues that Schmitt reworked his concept of imperialism in response to political imperatives, such that his critique of modern imperialism, advanced between the mid-1920s and early 1930s, became mostly irrelevant to him by the outbreak of the Second World War. A theory of imperialism which had been framed to accentuate Germany's victimhood in the aftermath of the First World War was discarded in favour of an alternate vision – one that better suited Schmitt's aims of legitimating Nazi ideology and foreign policy.

For some of Schmitt's contemporaries, the discrepancies between his early critique of modern imperialism and his subsequent endorsement of great spaces constituted an aporia of political significance. During the Second World War, one of Schmitt's most talented students, the law professor Ernst Rudolf Huber (1903–

1990), came to suspect that his mentor's incoherencies were symptomatic of the regime's broader failure to articulate a compelling vision of European order.[10] This chapter concludes by considering how Huber tried, in vain, to recast Schmitt's international legal order of great spaces in a form that would be convincingly anti-imperialistic. Huber's attempts to reconcile the propaganda of the Nazi New Order with its barbarous reality, and the nature of his disillusionment once he belatedly grasped the impossibility of his task, present a striking case study in the response of German intellectuals to totalitarianism – a response delivered, so to speak, from the 'belly of the beast'.[11]

The Rhineland and modern imperialism

Schmitt's interest in theories of imperialism was awakened during his time as a professor at the University of Bonn, where he taught from 1922 to 1928.[12] The political fate of the Rhineland, whose western bank had already been occupied by Allied troops during the Armistice period, was the focus of considerable debate at the Paris Peace Conference that ended the First World War. The French delegation mooted the possibility of turning the Rhineland into an independent state, while many political associations in France went further and advocated that it be directly annexed. Under pressure from the United States and Britain, France eventually settled for a fifteen-year Allied occupation of the Rhineland and its demilitarization in perpetuity. In January 1923, when Germany was ruled to have defaulted on its reparations of coal and timber, France and Belgium extended the ambit of their military occupation by sending troops into the neighbouring Ruhr industrial region. The Ruhr occupation, which coincided with a heightened period of French-sponsored Rhenish separatism, lasted until July 1925.[13] These occupations and interventions, which undermined the sovereignty of the German state without fully abrogating it, outraged Schmitt. In his view, they represented the application of novel imperialistic methods to a European population.

One of the distinctive features of modern imperialism, according to Schmitt, was that it sought to gain control over other countries without resorting to territorial conquest. A number of factors had, in his view, helped motivate this transformation of imperialism since the late nineteenth century. As a consequence of the rise of popular sovereignty and nationalism, liberal states had grown increasingly reluctant to assimilate foreign populations and confer on them the rights of citizenship. The rhetoric of self-determination, in vogue since the end of the First World War, also made it politically unacceptable to treat other countries as mere 'objects' of international negotiation. In search of alternatives to annexation, modern imperialist powers discovered new strategies for undermining the sovereignty of other nations. They availed themselves of the protectorate, which purported to leave the government of a 'half-civilized' country intact while assuming responsibility for its foreign relations; they leased territory for bases and settlements; and they took over the colonies of their defeated adversaries through the mandates system of the League of Nations. But there was another, less transparent way for Western powers to extend their influence: they could claim to recognize the independence of other nations while simultaneously authorizing interventions into their domestic affairs under exceptional circumstances.[14]

A contemporary example of imperialism through emergency interventions was the unilateral declaration of Egyptian independence, issued by the British government in 1922, which ended the country's status as a protectorate but reserved for Britain the right to intervene at its own discretion to defend the Suez Canal, foreign interests and minorities, the Sudan, and Egypt itself against outside aggression.[15] Even more significant, from Schmitt's point of view, were 'intervention treaties' (*Interventionsverträge*) signed by two contracting parties, a legal innovation he credited to the United States. As a condition for receiving its independence after the Spanish American War, Cuba was required to incorporate into its constitution the Platt Amendment, which permitted the United States to intervene to maintain, in its words, 'a government adequate for the protection of life, property, and individual liberty'. Newly independent Panama signed a treaty that entitled the United States to intervene in defence of the canal at any time.[16] Schmitt regarded intervention treaties as 'the most important tool' of 'modern, fundamentally economic imperialism'.[17]

What Schmitt meant by 'economic imperialism' (*ökonomischer Imperialismus*) is open to multiple, though not necessarily incompatible, interpretations. On some occasions he appears to have endorsed the contemporary view that capitalists were the agents driving modern imperialism. According to newspaper accounts of his unpublished lecture, 'Ideas of World Peace', which he delivered to the Association of Catholic Academics in Münster on 13 October 1925, Schmitt came to the conclusion that 'this [American] imperialism subordinates the political to the economic, that it views the state as an annex or subsidiary tool [*Hilfsinstrument*] of big companies'.[18] For the most part, however, Schmitt refrained from engaging with any of the voluminous contemporary literature on the economic causes or motivations of European imperialism.[19] More often than not, he identified modern imperialism as 'economic' simply to distinguish it from other methods of projecting state power beyond national borders. Though modern imperialism might avail itself of opportunities for armed intervention, it was principally characterized by the fact that 'economic means of power take the place of military ones'.[20] By taking charge of the fiscal apparatus of foreign countries, exploiting their capital and natural resources, and flooding their markets with imported goods, liberal democratic countries could enjoy the economic and strategic benefits of military conquest without bearing the associated burdens.[21]

Last but not least, modern imperialism was distinctive for Schmitt by virtue of its determination to monopolize the vocabulary in which it was described. The legal arrangements characteristic of modern imperialism typically employed concepts that were deliberately vague and indeterminate and were framed in such a way that only the imperial power could interpret and apply them. Even if interventions took place only infrequently, the fact that an outside power had acquired the right to determine the meaning of key concepts, such as 'the protection of foreign interests, the protection of independence, public order and security, the maintenance of international treaties, etc., defined the norm of an imperial relationship.[22] In 1933, when Schmitt returned to this topic in an article on modern American imperialism, he captured the relationship between imperialism and linguistic hegemony in the following memorable phrase: 'In the case of a historically significant imperialism, it is not only the military and naval armaments that matter, not only the economic and financial wealth, but also the ability to determine the content of political and legal concepts.'[23]

Schmitt believed that all the characteristics of modern imperialism were evident in the Allied occupation of the Rhineland. Instead of annexing or detaching the Rhineland, as might have been the outcome in a nineteenth-century war, the subversion of German sovereignty after the First World War took place through the legal institution of the Treaty of Versailles. While Schmitt did not explicitly say that this imperialism had been carried out at the behest of capitalist interests, he observed that the workings of the multinational Inter-Allied Rhineland High Commission mimicked some of the features that were typical of the modern capitalist economy:

> Today we are experiencing the first, highly dangerous attempts to transfer modern methods of industrial and financial practice onto the political life of the state, and to hide the real power relationships in a system of shell companies and fictitious foundations, thereby making them invisible. The characteristic of the time lies in the fact that the real ruler remains hidden, that he no longer rules but merely wants to 'control'.[24]

Finally, Schmitt emphasized that the Treaty of Versailles incorporated vague concepts and clauses whose alleged violation could be cited to justify intervention. It neither specified the full amount of reparations owed by Germany, nor placed any meaningful restrictions on the Allies' right to impose discretionary sanctions. It left the size and competencies of the occupying forces undefined and permitted the Allies to do anything they felt necessary to safeguard them. While parts of the Rhineland were to be evacuated after five years if specified conditions were 'faithfully fulfilled', the treaty failed to indicate who would judge whether the conditions were met.[25] Schmitt regarded the Treaty of Versailles as an American-style 'intervention treaty', designed to be interpreted and applied by imperialist powers who wished to legitimize their domination in legal and moral terms.

Global arbitration and modern imperialism

Modern imperialism, as Schmitt first described it in reference to the Rhineland in the mid-1920s, was an Anglo-American project to undermine the sovereignty of independent states, chiefly through means of 'intervention treaties' that gave legal justification for foreign interventions into their domestic affairs. However, by the early 1930s the course of international politics seems to have assuaged his anxieties that something like the Ruhr occupation could happen again. 'The

American method of intervention treaties has up until now remained essentially restricted to the Americas,' he noted. 'The United States has no interest, at least not for the moment, in extending this practice to other continents.'[26] Following the departure of the last Allied troops from the Rhineland in 1930, and the moratorium on reparations payments in 1932, Schmitt may have concluded that the Treaty of Versailles no longer functioned as an effective vehicle for legitimizing interventions. In any case, the intervention treaty now appeared to Schmitt as a historical artefact of Western imperialism, rather than a current threat.

Schmitt's final elaboration of his theory of modern imperialism appeared in his 1933 article, 'The United States and the International Legal Forms of Modern Imperialism', based on a lecture he delivered at the University of Königsberg in the previous year. Schmitt began by discussing how the United States exploited 'intervention treaties' and conventions of diplomatic recognition to extend its regional influence at the end of the nineteenth century.[27] Then, in a departure from his earlier writings, he called attention to the methods the United States had employed to establish itself as the 'arbiter of the world' (*Schiedsrichter der Welt*), a phase of American foreign policy that began with President Woodrow Wilson's decision to enter the war on the side of the Entente in 1917.[28] Schmitt had previously depicted modern imperialism as operating through legally sanctioned interventions into the domestic affairs of other states. By the end of the Weimar Republic a subtle shift had taken place. For Schmitt, modern American imperialism now signified an effort to intervene in conflicts *between* states. Like a judge in a court of arbitration, or a referee in a sporting match, the United States was claiming for itself the right to decide the international disputes of others. The main legal instrument through which the United States arrogated itself this authority, Schmitt argued, was the Monroe Doctrine.

In 'The United States and the International Legal Forms of Modern Imperialism' Schmitt emphasized that the United States had not always used the Monroe Doctrine to advance an expansive conception of its role in the world. In 1823 President James Monroe famously announced that the United States would oppose all attempts at further colonization in the western hemisphere, and he warned European powers not to infringe on the independence of the new republics of Latin America; in exchange, the United States would refrain from involving itself in the internal affairs of European nations. Over the course of the following century, Schmitt argued, the inviolability of the western hemisphere became a principle enshrined in international law, even as the political meaning of the Monroe Doctrine remained in flux for the United States. At the turn of the twentieth century, President Theodore Roosevelt divested the Monroe Doctrine of its 'defensive' character by invoking it to justify the occupation of neighbouring Latin American states. Finally, in the aftermath of the First World War, Woodrow Wilson and his successors devised new ways of appropriating the letter or the spirit of the Monroe Doctrine to advance the new global ambitions of the United States.[29]

According to Schmitt, the Monroe Doctrine gained new relevance in part due to the League of Nations, whose founding document, the Covenant, declared that the doctrine's validity remained unaffected by any competencies assigned to the League. Though the United States never joined the League, numerous Latin American countries who had signed 'intervention treaties', or whose sovereignty was otherwise circumscribed by American policies, became voting members. By recognizing the Monroe Doctrine, the League renounced any claim to intervene in American affairs, while the United States retained the ability to influence disputes among European nations through the representation of its Latin American proxies.[30] Schmitt claimed that the Monroe Doctrine's spirit also pervaded one of the more recent and noteworthy international agreements that the United States helped create, the Kellogg Pact of 1928. In the words of the pact, signatories pledged to 'condemn recourse to war for the solution of international controversies, and renounce it, as an instrument of national policy in their relations with one another'. In the Kellogg Pact, Schmitt perceived a recrudescence of what he called the 'strange elasticity and flexibility' of the Monroe Doctrine.[31] While it purported to condemn war 'as an instrument of national policy', the pact permitted its signatories to wage wars for the furtherance of *international* policy, that is, for ostensibly liberal humanitarian goals, or for the purpose of self-defence or the defence of existing treaties. The pact implicitly gave the United States license to determine for itself when and where these exceptions obtained.[32] 'Just as the Monroe Doctrine lies in the hands of the United States', Schmitt argued, 'so it can take the position vis-à-vis the Kellogg Pact that suits a world power: that it is the one who defines, interprets, and applies it. ... If that is the case, then the Kellogg Pact could acquire a function for the Earth that the Monroe Doctrine has had for the American continent.'[33]

Woodrow Wilson's invocation of human rights, the Entente's wartime propaganda and the assertion of German liability for war damages in the Versailles Treaty signified for Schmitt the end of an era in which limited, nonmoralizing wars had been the norm. Departing from the classic practice of treating all parties to a war as legally equal, the Kellogg Pact, in the hands of the United States, would brand some belligerents as lawbreakers.[34] In the mid-1920s Schmitt had tried to show that modern imperialist powers did not annex other countries; instead, they opted for economic means of exploitation that left state sovereignty nominally intact. Now he wanted to argue that 'imperialist great powers' did not fight 'wars', either, but preferred to engage in operations that could be classified as 'execution, punitive expedition, peaceful measures to defend treaties, international policing and protection of freedom'.[35] Once the United States had claimed the right to discriminate legitimate belligerents from criminals, or even to determine whether a state of war existed at all, its power as 'arbiter of the world' would be unmatched.

Imperialism as universalism

The first phase of Schmitt's theorizing about imperialism was distinguished by his preoccupation with a 'modern imperialism' that subverted the traditional concepts of sovereignty and war in the service of extending political influence. Schmitt mobilized the concept of modern imperialism to unmask the power interests of the Western democracies and stimulate moral outrage at Germany's treatment under the Treaty of Versailles. Once he commenced his legal and propagandistic work on behalf of the Nazi regime, however, his usage of 'imperialism' shifted in significant ways. After 1933 he invoked 'imperialism' not primarily to indict Nazi Germany's antagonists, but rather to justify its actions in the court of public opinion. This was a reactive tactic that aimed to rationalize and justify the regime's domestic and foreign policies. Whatever Nazi Germany had done at home or abroad, he implied, was legitimate because it was *not* imperialistic. The concept of modern imperialism largely disappeared from his writings, and he began to speak of 'imperialism' tout court, a project he associated with any great power that endorsed 'universalism' as an ideology. Finally, his understanding of the relationship between law and imperialism began to change. Whereas international law had previously figured in his account as a tool or enabler of modern imperialism, it now appeared as a potential bulwark against the imperialist tendencies of either liberalism or Marxism.

It seems most plausible to explain these conceptual shifts as part of Schmitt's concerted effort to direct his rhetoric away from merely criticizing the post-Versailles international order and towards endorsing the specific content of National Socialist ideology. The first evidence of this strategy can be found in his 1936 article 'National Socialist Legislation and the Reservation of "Ordre Public" in International Private Law'. In this short text, notable for its enthusiastic endorsement of Nazi racial discrimination, Schmitt set out to explain why the Nuremberg Laws, unlike the legislation of the Soviet Union, did not challenge traditional European notions of marriage, family, property or inheritance. Nazi Germany had no intention of imposing racial distinctions on the citizens of other nations, he asserted. It only reserved the right to determine who counted as a German national:

> National Socialist law does not encompass the world or humanity, nor does it intend to do so. That is a main difference as compared with Bolshevik law. It is *not universal, not international, not imperialistic, not aggressive*. It is not the law of a world revolutionary class. It does not claim to be the most advanced stage of law for all of humanity, which needs to be foisted on all other states, with force if necessary. Ours is a *völkisch* law. In emphasizing the *völkisch* character of its own or any other legal order, it returns to the only possible basis of any conceivable international law, and of any conceivable private law, namely, to the *foundation of mutual regard and mutual respect for the uniqueness of each Volk*.[36]

In Schmitt's telling, the racial legislation of Nazi Germany aimed to protect the *völkisch* character of the national community against the influx of universalizing ideas and tendencies. In that way, for Schmitt, espousing racism constituted the antithesis to imperialism *qua* universalism, whether liberal or Marxist.[37] The Nuremberg Laws made no claim to decide who was a Briton, Frenchman or Japanese, but only to legally determine who counted as a German: 'This thoroughly defensive, *völkisch* character – as opposed to the imperialistic, humanity-encompassing, aggressive character of Bolshevik legal thought – is the hallmark of our National Socialist legislation.' In accordance with the anti-Semitic dictum that Jewishness was inimical to any truly *völkisch* existence, Schmitt excluded Jews from the 'mutual respect' that was supposed to be accorded to each *Volk*.[38]

In his justification for the Nuremberg Laws, Schmitt made no reference to any specific restructuring of the European or global international order, though by the late 1930s he seems to have concluded that some kind of transformation was inevitable. In *The Turn to a Discriminating Concept of War*, a paper he delivered in late 1937, Schmitt argued that contemporary liberal jurisprudence had effectively discarded the tenets of classical international law without positing anything more substantial than a few nebulous ideas of world government; there was no going back to the traditional understanding of international law, but also no clear sign of what lay ahead.[39] Over the course of the following year, the foreign policy of Nazi Germany underwent a dramatic transformation. Austria, the Sudetenland and Memel were annexed; a so-called 'Protectorate' of Bohemia and Moravia was established; and a treaty of protection was signed with the newly independent state of Slovakia. Writing in the spring of 1939, Schmitt felt compelled to make sense of these developments and construct a theory of international law that would legitimize them. To do so, he would have to find a way to justify the fact that Germany had annexed some states and parts of states, and hollowed out the sovereignty of others by placing them under its 'protection'. This would require him to abandon his earlier critique of modern imperialism and find a way of reclaiming the Monroe Doctrine, the only conceivable international legal precedent for partitioning the world, from the imperialism with which he had previously associated it.

There is no indication in Schmitt's writings that he planned to appropriate the Monroe Doctrine for Germany prior to the spring of 1939. During the Weimar Republic, Schmitt had pessimistically observed that the erosion of small states' sovereignty was the trend of contemporary international relations: as a consequence of modern Western imperialism, 'probably ... only a few continents or other giant complexes will remain as bearers of real sovereignty, thanks to their own Monroe Doctrines'.[40] But while Schmitt may have been prescient about these developments, it would be a mistake to interpret his comments as evidence that he looked forward to the monopolization of sovereignty on the part of 'a few continents' in the late 1920s. Back then, Schmitt insisted that Germany should resist becoming the victim of imperialistic Monroe Doctrines. Not large enough to be a world power, but not small enough to be absorbed into the political orbit of another state, Germany would have to decide 'whether it will preserve its will to political existence, or whether it will let itself be psychically and morally worn down, so that it consents to satisfy foreign leviathans with its own flesh and blood'.[41] This was a call for the reassertion of German sovereignty, especially when it came to the status of the demilitarized Rhineland, but not yet a demand that Germany claim its own continental dominion among the other great powers. Eleven years after making this declaration, Schmitt felt compelled to execute an about-turn and justify Nazi Germany's new status as the 'leviathan' of Europe.

Schmitt was reluctant to define the concept of imperialism too precisely in his 1939 brochure *The International Legal Order of Great Spaces*. But he was determined at least to demonstrate that his proposed international legal order – and in particular the great space assigned to the German *Reich* – was not going to emulate the imperialism that he associated with the twentieth-century United States.[42] According to Schmitt, the American turn to imperialism had commenced with 'dollar diplomacy'. By facilitating the penetration of private capital into the economies and public finances of Latin American countries, Theodore Roosevelt and his successors distorted the original Monroe Doctrine, a 'defensive resistance against the interventions of spatially foreign powers', into 'the justification for capitalist imperialism'.[43] Schmitt strongly implied that Germany's relationship to the other states in its great space would be different, though he failed to explain why or how. 'While "imperialism", since the end of the nineteenth century, has become an expression that is often abused – frequently in the form of a mere catchword – to characterize economic-capitalist methods of colonization and expansion,' he observed, 'the word *Reich* has remained free of this stigma', and thus recommended itself as a name for the polity at the heart of Germany's great space.[44] The second phase of American imperialism had been inaugurated by Woodrow Wilson's campaign to impose liberal political and economic ideology across the globe.[45] Nazi Germany, in contrast, would know its place – both literally and figuratively.

In his critique of modern imperialism from the mid-1920s, Schmitt had condemned Britain and the United States for depriving other nations of their full sovereignty and autonomy through international legal arrangements. Yet his international legal order of great spaces proposed to do just the same to the smaller nations of central and eastern Europe: the *Reich*, rather than the sovereign state, would henceforth serve as the privileged subject of international law. Unlike even the 'original' Monroe Doctrine, which claimed to defend the American states against extrahemispheric threats to their independence and territorial integrity, Schmitt's scheme attached no priority to safeguarding the autonomy of the nations within its great space.[46] How could this discrepancy be justified? Since liberal jurisprudence and the League of Nations had already degraded traditional conceptions of state sovereignty and autonomy, Schmitt argued, Germany ought not to be blamed for abandoning them as well. The United States might have once promoted the 'political idea' of republicanism within its great space, but Germany would promote something else – not the independence and autonomy of its subject states, but rather the independence and segregation of racial groups. Nazi Germany would protect Germans of foreign nationality while simultaneously 'respecting' the individuality of each *Volk* within its great space, with the exception of the Jews, whom Schmitt considered fundamentally 'foreign' (*artfremd*). Taken together, these principles represented the distinctive 'political idea' of the German great space: 'The rejection of all assimilation, absorption, melting pot ideals.'[47] Rather than assimilate its subjects to a dominant culture or ideology, or allow them to mix freely, the German *Reich* would enforce *völkisch* identity and separateness. 'While "imperium" often has the meaning of a universalistic – and hence *übervölkisch* – construction that encompasses the world and mankind,' he observed, 'our German *Reich* is fundamentally determined in terms of the *Volk* and is a fundamentally nonuniversalistic legal order based on respect for the individuality of every *Volk*.'[48] While attempting to distance himself from imperialism, Schmitt had ironically constructed an international legal order that was based on the same kind of vague, indeterminate concepts (great space, *Volk*, intervention) that he formerly associated with the foreign policy of the modern United States.

Ernst Rudolf Huber on imperialism, great spaces and international law

Schmitt's ham-handed attempts to distinguish his international legal order of great spaces from the imperialism of the Western democracies did not go unnoticed by his contemporaries. In January 1940, a leading Swiss newspaper called attention to his discussion of imperialism, only to dismiss it as nothing more than a cynical attempt to justify Germany's new status quo through retrospective legal manipulations:

> Schmitt makes an effort to prove that this notion of great spaces has nothing to do with imperialism. But his proof is a failure. *The drive for Lebensraum is only a new form of imperialism*, and his attempt to anchor *Lebensraum* in international law is one of those attempts, well known in the history of constitutional and international law, to let power appear in the guise of law.[49]

The law professor Ernst Rudolf Huber, one of Schmitt's protégés and a leading theorist of the public law of the Third Reich, was determined to extract something meaningful from his mentor's efforts. The challenge facing German jurists, as Huber saw it, was to explain why the Nazi New Order would not practice the kind of modern imperialism that Schmitt had imputed to the Western democracies. 'The decisive problem for political theory as well as legal theory', he declared in 1941, 'is how to distinguish the idea of the *Reich*, in its turn toward the principle of great spaces, from the imperialism of others, against which we have honestly and uprightly fought.'[50] The legitimacy of the Nazi New Order seemed to hang in the balance.

Huber was one of Schmitt's closest and most talented students. After completing his dissertation in 1927 at the University of Bonn under Schmitt's supervision, he went on to assist his former teacher by advising military officers in the circle around Chancellor Franz von Papen and by drafting a legal justification for President Hindenburg's deposition of the Prussian government. Huber joined the Nazi Party in the spring of 1933 and subsequently received chairs in law at the universities of Kiel, Leipzig and Straßburg. He rapidly attained the reputation of being one of the leading theorists of 'constitutional law' (such as it existed) in Nazi Germany.[51] In April 1939 Huber participated in the conference where Schmitt presented his ideas on great spaces for the first time, but missed hearing him deliver the paper.[52] Huber soon read the published version, which he subjected – along with Schmitt's other Nazi-era writings on international law – to close analysis and constructive criticism, in a lengthy review essay as well as in his own wartime writings on the fate of the German *Reich*.

Rather than accept that Schmitt had deliberately contradicted himself to justify the *faits accomplis* of Nazi foreign policy, as this chapter has argued, Huber insisted that Schmitt's Nazi-era theories were the outcome of an intellectual development that bridged the political caesura of 1933. Schmitt's attraction to the idea of great spaces, he claimed, had been motivated by his growing appreciation for the achievements of American imperialism. The rise of the United States to global power had made such an impression on him that, by the end of the Weimar Republic, he was capable of expressing 'recognition, if not admiration, for [its] "authentic and grand imperialism"'.[53] The virtue of Schmitt's international legal order of great spaces was that it precluded imperialist hypocrisy by granting legal recognition to the special status of great powers. As Huber put it, 'Schmitt's international legal theory of great spaces acknowledges the reality of imperialism as a legal fact of the matter, and seeks to make it into the basis of a new system of international law.'[54]

At the same time, Huber refused to believe that Schmitt could have so readily abandoned the sense of justice that led him to condemn modern imperialism in the first place. '[Schmitt] himself fought in the name of the law, with great decisiveness, against the coercive conditions of Versailles and the imperialism of the democracies,' Huber insisted, 'and it is obvious that he has no intention of viewing a power situation as a legal state of affairs simply because it exists.'[55] The problem with imperialism was that it was unjust and exploitative. What would make the international legal order of great spaces any different? 'Although Schmitt does not discuss it in detail,' Huber suggested, 'I believe that I understand him correctly when I say that, in his view, the aspect of *order* transforms and elevates the power system of imperialism into the legal system of the notion of great spaces.'[56] Huber conceived this order in legal and moral terms. Only if the German *Reich* offered leadership instead of domination, only if it were based on fixed principles rather than the cynical exploitation of legal institutions – in other words, only if the internal structure of the great space lived up to the ideals of the law could it exempt itself from the charge of imperialism. In contrast with Western imperialism, which 'concealed itself behind sonorous clichés about the equal rights of all nations', Germany would accept the responsibility that came with its hegemonic position in Europe, namely, the duty to promote 'the economic, cultural, and political existence of European *Völker*'.[57] That meant acknowledging national identity and aspirations through some form of 'hegemonic federalism', even if the *Reich* constrained the sovereignty of the states within its great space.[58] 'The just exercise of power will be the criterion for distinguishing between the old imperialism and a true international legal order of great spaces,' Huber declared.[59]

Huber's published writings exuded optimism about the possibility of realizing such a 'legal' order. By 1943, however, his lectures were expressing overt criticism of the regime's conduct of foreign affairs. In a speech titled 'The Idea of the *Reich* and

International Law', delivered in Metz and Saarbrücken, Huber took the regime to task for failing to establish a just and equitable international order. The exploitative connotations inherent in Schmitt's concept of great spaces, he suggested, were predictive of Nazi Germany's behaviour towards the occupied countries of Europe:

> The much used and much abused word 'great space' lends itself to various misunderstandings, as if the only thing that mattered were acquiring the space along with its strategic possibilities, bases, starting positions and lines of defense, with its commercial relationships, its natural resources, its industrial capacity, its volumes of labor power, and its agricultural exploitability. One can perhaps conquer the world with such materialistic spatial thinking – but one cannot rule it in such a way, and one cannot establish a lasting, stable order. Such materialism of great spaces would be merely another word for the old imperialism – and it might be all sorts of things, but it would not be law.[60]

By the winter of 1944–45 Huber was prepared to admit that the Nazi New Order had failed to offer an appealing alternative to the 'old imperialism' of the Western democracies. In a lecture manuscript on 'The General Theory of the *Volk* and State', he singled out the 'materialism of great spaces' (*Großraum-Materialismus*) as a root cause of Germany's impending defeat:

> Make no mistake, this kind of materialism of great spaces exists not only among others. We possess various dangerous tendencies in this direction, and various failures of our policy can be traced to a materialistic misunderstanding of the idea of great spaces. The true idea of the *Reich* does not demand the exploitation of *Völker* through a dominating imperium, but rather bases itself on the recognition of national individuality and on the just ordering of *Völker* into a pacified community.[61]

Huber was bold enough to acknowledge that the *Reich* had advanced its own imperialistic interests under the banner of an ideology of great spaces. But he made no mention of Nazi Germany's persecution or mass murder of the Jews, who were evidently denied a future in his *völkisch* conception of European order.

Huber could hardly be classified as an oppositional intellectual under National Socialism. Yet in his attempts to make sense of Schmitt's writings on imperialism, we witness how a convinced supporter of Nazi Germany struggled with the contradictions of an 'international legal order of great spaces', and in the process grew increasingly alienated from the regime.[62] As a student in Bonn in the mid-1920s, Huber had been enthralled by Schmitt's analysis of the situation of the Rhineland, in which the power interests of the Allied powers became visible to him as if magnified through a powerful lens.[63] Schmitt's critique of modern imperialism was charged with the language of moral indignation. 'Modern imperialism has developed new methods of domination and exploitation that eschew blatant political annexation ([i.e.] protectorates, mandates, lease and intervention treaties),' Schmitt declared in 1925. 'The application of these methods to *Völker* – and parts of *Völker* – of European culture and education would be no less an injustice than blatant violation through political annexation.'[64] Huber expected that Schmitt's proposal for a new international legal order would redress some of these iniquities. But by the end of the war he had lost confidence that either Schmitt or the regime regarded great spaces as a matter of moral justice. Far too late, Huber began to realize the contradictions inherent to a foreign policy of 'anti-imperialist imperialism'.[65] It seems unlikely that a comparable reckoning ever took place for Schmitt.

Notes

* This author wishes to express his gratitude to Jeremy Adelman and the other participants in the symposium 'Empire and the Social Sciences' at the Princeton Institute for International and Regional Studies in March 2014. Research for this chapter was supported by a General Research Fund grant (16400514/C5993) from the Hong Kong Research Grants Council.
1 See, for example, William Rasch, 'Human Rights as Geopolitics: Carl Schmitt and the Legal Form of American Supremacy', *Cultural Critique* 54 (2003): 120–47; William Rasch, ed., 'World Orders: Confronting Carl Schmitt's *The Nomos of the Earth*', special issue, *South Atlantic Quarterly* 104, no. 2 (2005); Louiza Odysseos and Fabio Petito, eds, *The International Political Thought of Carl Schmitt: Terror, Liberal War and the Crisis of Global Order* (Abingdon: Routledge, 2007); and Carl Melchers, *Carl Schmitt als 'Imperialismustheoretiker': Zur Renaissance der Vorstellung von der imperialen Souveränität der Vereinigten Staaten* (Saarbrücken: VDM Verlag Dr. Müller, 2008). See also G. L. Ulmen, 'American Imperialism and International Law: Carl Schmitt on the US in World Affairs', *Telos* 72 (1987): 43–71.
2 Carl Schmitt, 'Die Rheinlande als Objekt internationaler Politik', in *Frieden oder Pazifismus? Arbeiten zum Völkerrecht und zur internationalen Politik, 1924–1978*, ed. Günter Maschke (Berlin: Duncker & Humblot, 2005), 26–50; Carl Schmitt, 'USA und die völkerrechtlichen Formen des modernen Imperialismus', in ibid., 349–77; Carl Schmitt, *The Nomos of the Earth in the International Law of the Jus Publicum Europaeum*, trans. G. L. Ulmen (New York: Telos, 2003). An English version of Schmitt's 1933 article on the United States and modern imperialism has recently been published under the title 'Forms of Modern Imperialism in International Law', trans. Matthew Hannah, in *Spatiality, Sovereignty and Carl Schmitt: Geographies of the Nomos*, ed. Stephen Legg (Abingdon: Routledge, 2011), 29–45.
3 Carl Schmitt, 'Völkerrechtliche Probleme im Rheingebiet' (1928), in Maschke, *Frieden oder Pazifismus?*, 263.
4 For critical perspectives on this trend, see David Chandler, 'The Revival of Carl Schmitt in International Relations: The Last Refuge of Critical Theorists?' *Millennium* 37, no. 1 (2008): 27–48; and Benno Gerhard Teschke, 'Fatal Attraction: A Critique of Carl Schmitt's International Political and Legal Theory', *International Theory* 3, no. 2 (2011): 179–227.
5 An important exception is William Scheuerman, *Carl Schmitt: The End of Law* (Lanham: Rowman & Littlefield, 1999), ch. 6, which argues that Schmitt's Nazi-era theorizing was the outcome of a growing desire to emulate American imperialism. On theories of imperialism in – and about – Nazi Germany, see Marcus Llanque, 'Der nationalsozialistische Imperialismus im Lichte der zeitgenössische Theoriebildung',

in *Imperialismus in Geschichte und Gegenwart*, ed. Richard Faber (Würzburg: Königshausen & Neumann, 2005), 101–21.
6 Carl Schmitt, 'Völkerrechtliche Großraumordnung mit Interventionsverbot für raumfremde Mächte: Ein Beitrag zum Reichsbegriff im Völkerrecht', 4th edn. (1941), in *Staat, Großraum, Nomos: Arbeiten aus den Jahren 1916–1969*, ed. Günter Maschke (Berlin: Duncker & Humblot, 1995), 269–371. All passages from 'Völkerrechtliche Großraumordnung' cited in this chapter also appeared in the first edition, which was published in April 1939.
7 See Lothar Gruchmann, *Nationalsozialistische Großraumordnung: Die Konstruktion einer 'deutschen Monroe-Doktrin'* (Stuttgart: Deutsche Verlags-Anstalt, 1962); Joseph W. Bendersky, *Carl Schmitt: Theorist for the Reich* (Princeton: Princeton University Press, 1983), ch. 12; and Mathias Schmoeckel, *Die Großraumtheorie: Ein Beitrag zur Geschichte der Völkerrechtswissenschaft im Dritten Reich, insbesondere der Kriegszeit* (Berlin: Duncker & Humblot, 1994).
8 On Schmitt and his rivals, particularly in the SS, see Ulrich Herbert, *Best: Biographische Studien über Radikalismus, Weltanschauung und Vernunft, 1903–1989* (Bonn: Dietz, 2011), 271–98.
9 Schmitt, 'Völkerrechtliche Großraumordnung', 291.
10 For earlier discussions of Huber's critical engagement with Schmitt's international thought, see Jörg Fisch, Dieter Groh and Rudolf Walther, 'Imperialismus', in *Geschichtliche Grundbegriffe: Historisches Lexikon zur politisch-sozialen Sprache in Deutschland*, eds Otto Brunner, Werner Conze and Reinhart Koselleck (Stuttgart: Klett-Cotta, 1982), vol. 3, 230–1; Schmoeckel, *Die Großraumtheorie*, 73–4, 168–9, 211–14; Maschke, ed., *Staat, Großraum, Nomos*, 361; and Reinhard Mehring, *Carl Schmitt: Aufstieg und Fall* (Munich: Beck, 2009), 420–1.
11 The phrase is taken from the title of Michael Stolleis's essay, 'In the Belly of the Beast: Constitutional Legal Theory (*Staatsrechtslehre*) under National Socialism', in *The Law under the Swastika: Studies on Legal History in Nazi Germany*, trans. Thomas Dunlap (Chicago: University of Chicago Press, 1998), 87–101.
12 On Schmitt's analysis of the predicament of the Rhineland, see Peter M. R. Stirk, 'Carl Schmitt's Enemy and the Rhetoric of Anti-Interventionism', *European Legacy* 8, no. 1 (2003): 21–36; and William Rasch, 'Anger Management: Carl Schmitt in 1925 and the Occupation of the Rhineland', *New Centennial Review* 8, no. 1 (2008): 57–79.
13 Margaret Macmillan, *Paris 1919: Six Months that Changed the World* (New York: Random House, 2003), 158, 167–75, 194–203; Eberhard Kolb, *The Weimar Republic*, 2nd edn., trans. P. S. Falla and R. J. Park (London: Routledge, 2005), 47–9, 63.
14 Schmitt, 'Die Rheinlande als Objekt internationaler Politik', 27–30.
15 Ibid., 29; Schmitt, 'Völkerrechtliche Probleme im Rheingebiet', 263.
16 Carl Schmitt, 'Die Rheinlande als Objekt internationaler Politik', 29; 'Die Kernfrage des Völkerbundes' (1926), in *Frieden oder Pazifismus?*, 122–4; 'Völkerrechtliche Probleme im Rheingebiet', 263.
17 Schmitt, 'Die Kernfrage des Völkerbundes', 123.
18 'Weltfriedensideen', *Kölnische Volkszeitung*, 2 November 1925. Similar language appeared in another report of Schmitt's lecture, 'Vortrag der Vereinigung kath. Akademiker: Carl Schmitt über Weltfriedensideen', *Westfälischer Merkur*, October (n.d.), 1925. These clippings can be found in Nachlass Carl Schmitt, RW 265, nr. 21317, Landesarchiv Nordrhein-Westfalen, Duisburg.
19 On the origins of this debate, see Richard Koebner, 'The Concept of Economic Imperialism', *Economic History Review* 2, no. 1 (1949): 1–29. The only theorist

specifically targeted in Schmitt's writings was his erstwhile Bonn colleague Joseph Schumpeter, who argued in 'The Sociology of Imperialisms' (1918/19) that modern capitalism was inherently anti-imperialistic. See 'Die Kernfrage des Völkerbundes', 96, fn. 35; 'Der Begriff des Politischen' (1927), in ibid., 218; *Der Begriff des Politischen: Text von 1932 mit einem Vorwort und drei Corollarien* (Berlin: Duncker & Humblot, 2002), 77; 'USA und die völkerrechtlichen Formen des modernen Imperialismus', 349; and 'Großraum gegen Universalismus' (1939), in *Positionen und Begriffe im Kampf mit Weimar—Genf—Versailles 1923-1939* (Berlin: Duncker & Humblot, 1994), 341–2.

20 Schmitt, 'Die Kernfrage des Völkerbundes', 96.
21 Schmitt, 'Die Rheinlande als Objekt internationaler Politik', 31.
22 Ibid., 29.
23 Schmitt, 'USA und die völkerrechtlichen Formen des modernen Imperialismus', 365.
24 Schmitt, 'Die Rheinlande als Objekt internationaler Politik', 34.
25 Ibid., 32–3.
26 Schmitt, 'USA und die völkerrechtlichen Formen des modernen Imperialismus', 359.
27 Ibid., 356–9.
28 Ibid., 356.
29 Ibid., 351–5.
30 Ibid., 360–2. Schmitt previewed this argument in 'Der Völkerbund und Europa' (1927), in *Frieden oder Pazifismus?*, 243–4.
31 Schmitt, 'USA und die völkerrechtlichen Formen des modernen Imperialismus', 355.
32 Schmitt, 'Der Völkerbund' (1930/31), in *Frieden oder Pazifismus?*, 342–3; *Der Begriff des Politischen* (1932), 51–2. See Scheuerman, *Carl Schmitt*, 151.
33 Schmitt, 'USA und die völkerrechtlichen Formen des modernen Imperialismus', 364.
34 Schmitt, *Der Begriff des Politischen* (1932), 37, 50–2, 77–8.
35 Carl Schmitt, 'Der Völkerbund und das politische Problem der Friedenssicherung' (1930), in *Frieden oder Pazifismus?*, 322, fn. 68.
36 Italics in the original. Carl Schmitt, 'Die nationalsozialistische Gesetzgebung und der Vorbehalt des "ordre public" im Internationalen Privatrecht', *Zeitschrift der Akademie für Deutsches Recht* 3 (1936): 206.
37 This point is clearly made in Scheuerman, *Carl Schmitt*, 159–61. Schmitt would refer to the Soviet Union as an 'imperialist' power on only a few subsequent occasions. See Carl Schmitt, 'Die letzte globale Linie' (1943), in *Staat, Großraum, Nomos*, 447; and 'Strukturwandel des Internationalen Rechts' (1943), in *Frieden oder Pazifismus?*, 670.
38 Ibid. See also Carl Schmitt, 'Die deutsche Rechtswissenschaft im Kampf gegen den jüdischen Geist', *Deutsche Juristen-Zeitung* 41, no. 20 (1936): 1198–9.
39 Carl Schmitt, 'Die Wendung zum diskriminierenden Kriegsbegriff', in *Frieden oder Pazifismus?*, 518–97; 'Völkerrechtliche Großraumordnung', 306.
40 Schmitt, 'Die Kernfrage des Völkerbundes', 79. This geopolitical prognosis was already widely shared by German commentators. As Friedrich Naumann observed during the First World War, 'Sovereignty, that is freedom to make decisions of wide historical importance, is now concentrated at a very few places on the globe. ... The spirit of large-scale industry and of super-national organisation has seized politics. People think, as Cecil Rhodes once expressed it, "in Continents". Friedrich Naumann, *Central Europe*, trans. Christabel M. Meredith (London: P. S. King, 1916), 4.
41 Schmitt, 'Völkerrechtliche Probleme im Rheingebiet', 264–5.
42 'An analysis of this concept of imperialism and its extensive literature would go beyond the scope of our presentation, and must be reserved for another investigation',

he remarked in a footnote, and never returned to the topic. Schmitt, 'Völkerrechtliche Großraumordnung', 297, fn. 61.
43 Ibid., 280-1, 284.
44 Ibid., 297.
45 Ibid., 285.
46 On this point, see John P. McCormick, 'Carl Schmitt's Europe: Cultural, Imperial and Spatial Proposals for European Integration, 1923-1955', in *Darker Legacies of Law in Europe: The Shadow of National Socialism and Fascism over Europe and its Legal Traditions*, eds Christian Joerges and Navraj Singh Ghaleigh (Oxford: Hart, 2003), 138; and G. L. Ulmen, 'Translator's Introduction', in *The Nomos of the Earth*, 23.
47 Schmitt, 'Völkerrechtliche Großraumordnung', 294-5. As evidence of these intentions on the part of Nazi Germany, Schmitt cited two sources: Hitler's 20 February 1938 speech to the Reichstag, which asserted that Germany would 'protect' ethnic Germans outside its own borders; and the German-Polish Joint Declaration on Minorities of 5 November 1937, in which the signatories pledged to respect the desire of their respective national minorities to maintain their own languages, political associations and schools.
48 Schmitt, 'Völkerrechtliche Großraumordnung', 296-7.
49 'Großraumordnung mit Interventionsverbot', *Neue Zürcher Zeitung*, 25 January 1940. Nachlass Carl Schmitt, RW 265, nr. 20067.
50 Ernst Rudolf Huber, *Bau und Gefüge des Reiches* (Hamburg: Hanseatische Verlagsanstalt, 1941), 51.
51 Mehring, *Carl Schmitt*, 178, 264-7, 291-8, 418-24; Ewald Grothe, '"Sehnsucht nach einem Gespräch." Die Korrespondenz zwischen Carl Schmitt und Ernst Rudolf Huber 1926-1981', in Carl Schmitt and Ernst Rudolf Huber, *Briefwechsel 1926-1981*, ed. Ewald Grothe (Berlin: Duncker & Humblot, 2014), 13-40.
52 Ernst Rudolf Huber to Carl Schmitt, 29 April 1939, in *Briefwechsel 1926-1981*, 255.
53 Ernst Rudolf Huber, '"Positionen und Begriffe": Eine Auseinandersetzung mit Carl Schmitt', *Zeitschrift für die gesamte Staatswissenschaft* 101, no. 1 (1941): 30.
54 Ibid., 39.
55 Ibid.
56 Ibid., 41.
57 Huber, *Bau und Gefüge des Reiches*, 52.
58 Ernst Rudolf Huber, 'Großraum und völkerrechtliche Neuordnung', *Straßburger Monatshefte* 5 (November 1941): 748; 'Das neue Völkerrecht', *Pariser Zeitung*, 17 December 1943.
59 Huber, 'Positionen und Begriffe', 42.
60 Ernst Rudolf Huber, 'Reichsidee und Völkerrecht (Vortrag gehalten in Metz und Saarbrücken 1943)', 20. Nachlass Ernst Rudolf Huber, BArch N 1505, Nr. 202. In a self-exculpatory autobiographical sketch written after the war, Huber cited this passage as evidence of his critical stance towards 'German power expansion'. See Ernst Rudolf Huber, 'Exposé, 1946/47', in *Briefwechsel 1926-1981*, 551-2.
61 Ernst Rudolf Huber, 'Volks- und Staatslehre (zweites Exemplar)', 5-6. Nachlass Ernst Rudolf Huber, BArch N 1505, Nr. 756. The lecture manuscript refers to the fall of Aachen, Metz and Straßburg, which indicates that it was composed after November 1944 and intended for the University of Heidelberg, where Huber taught in the final months of the war.
62 On Huber's politics, see Ewald Grothe, 'Über den Umgang mit Zeitenwenden: Der Verfassungshistoriker Ernst Rudolf Huber und seine Auseinandersetzung mit

Geschichte und Gegenwart 1933 und 1945', *Zeitschrift für Geschichtswissenschaft* 53 (2005): 216–35; and Ewald Grothe, '"Strengste Züruckhaltung und unbedingter Takt." Der Verfassungshistoriker Ernst Rudolf Huber und die NS-Vergangenheit', in *Kontinuitäten und Zäsuren: Rechtswissenschaft und Justiz im 'Dritten Reich' und in der Nachkriegszeit*, ed. Eva Schumann (Göttingen: Wallstein, 2008), 327–48.

63 Ernst Rudolf Huber to Carl Schmitt, 21 February 1940, in *Briefwechsel 1926–1981*, 259–60.

64 Schmitt, 'Die Rheinlande als Objekt internationaler Politik', 26.

65 The phrase 'anti-imperial imperialism' is taken from Dan Diner, 'Rassistisches Völkerrecht: Elemente einer nationalsozialistischen Weltordnung', in *Weltordnungen: Über Geschichte und Wirkung von Recht und Macht* (Frankfurt am Main: Fischer, 1993), 107.

Chapter 9

KNOWLEDGE AS POWER: INTERNATIONALISM, INFORMATION AND US GLOBAL AMBITIONS

David Ekbladh

There is an argument to be made that the Great Depression was the first true global event – in the sense that the majority of the people around the world could have imagined themselves as undergoing an experience that almost all other peoples were sharing in one form or another. There are limits to this view, of course, but there was a palpable sense for those living through a period of deep interconnection that profound global forces were playing out in their daily lives. However, this trend was Janus-faced. Thickening connections across the planet served to transmit the corrosion of global systems and had devastating impacts on the national and the local.

Information, particularly in the realm of economics, generated by new relationships, approaches and institutions helped underwrite such perceptions. New understandings of how trade, labour markets, currency flows and other staples of economic life worked became available. Indeed, new approaches with global import were laid down. New mechanisms to gauge national income were pioneered in the era, and this led directly to that influential and controversial concept of measuring and comparing national economies: gross national product.[1]

Grasping these worldwide trends and transformations was an important part of the agenda of liberal internationalists trying to assert control in an uncertain situation. Today, inundated with data, we can forget how limited the tools were for a variety of policymakers at the time and these tools gave them new mechanisms to engage the global problems that were washing over them. More than that, these concepts, which were tied to longer trends of internationalism and state and empire-building, gave mechanisms to particular actors to wage battles in an intensely ideological period. The means to understand how a crucial segment of the global community—the world economy—operated and how it could be reformed, distorted, or also turned to other purposes. Information can be deployed to many ends, ends that depend on the agendas of those individuals and institutions that create, control and wield it. Various actors within the United States were part of an international community of liberals who sought to create information to understand the globe; that information would become a tool, even a weapon, for the United States to engage and transform the world.

The cultivation of information had not just facilitated international interconnection; it had also been a fundamental part of internationalism itself. Indeed, the late nineteenth and early twentieth century saw a remarkable expansion of bodies that provided organization and order to global interaction (think of the International Postal Union and other entities).[2] Supranational bodies are rightfully thought of first in these endeavours, but there was also a concomitant growth in national services to measure and engage the economic, health, financial and other issues that was instrumental in the consolidation and maintenance of the power of central states.[3]

The United States was just one part of this worldwide trend. It was regularly a participant in these larger international initiatives. It also evolved its own national systems of information gathering and surveillance, a trend that intensified during the interwar period. One of the leading exponents of building this national capacity was the Republican Herbert Hoover, who as secretary of commerce focused on what has been called 'associationalism'.[4] As president, these ambitions only increased with Hoover sponsoring an attempt to map the whole of modern America. The final report, edited by Edward Eyre Hunt, *Recent Social Trends*, was the work of a host of academics employing new social science methods to describe the rapid changes engulfing the country.[5]

This interest in employing social science to understand the impact of modernity drew Americans (even Republicans) to the possibility of the League. What is crucial is that the United States, or more rightly groups and institutions within its civil society, were drawing from and feeding into international institutions that were helping to generate information and methods that they themselves would draw on for their own ends. This was particularly true for a (if not *the*) central institution within the liberal internationalist ecumene, the League of Nations.[6] Contrary to the standard narrative, Americans did not fail to join the organization, the US government did. The League was host to, and indeed often dependent on, US input multiple critical areas. It is hard to extricate American experts and funds from the accomplishments of some of the League's most influential technical bodies. Crucially, what became the largest and most respected organ of the League, its Economic and Financial Section, was supported not only by just the funds of a leading American foundation – the Rockefeller Foundation – it drew on and drew in numerous US academics to draft its studies and staff its committees.[7]

A sign that Americans were interested in what the League could do in regard to understanding the unprecedented and rapidly expanding global crisis of the Depression was that Hunt was sent to Geneva in 1931 to a conference on the dimensions of what was then a relatively new issue. Hunt was impressed that the League was able to draw together a set of esteemed national delegates. He noted that the narration each provided for the impact of the Depression on their countries showed a 'geographical progression' of the crisis that collectively revealed its global scope. From this, an astute participant was able to see the Depression as the transnational force it was, its waves of instability breaking in different places at different times and in different manners but hitting all with considerable force. He was also flattered the US's that European counterparts had been influenced by work by Americans and were familiar with the data and conclusions of *Recent Social Trends*.[8]

Hunt made a concerted effort to inform a wide selection of Americans of the proceedings in Geneva – and his role in them. Empire was often not explicitly discussed at the meetings but significant segments of the general analysis of international political economy were generated by representatives of or institutions within imperial systems. How enmeshed Hunt was in a world structured by a specific type of imperial relationship comes into focus in his extracurricular travels during his European sojourn in those early years of the Depression.

Travelling the continent after the Geneva meeting, Hunt dutifully transmitted back to peers at home perspectives from British colleagues about public works and other responses to the Depression. He took time from chatting about economic catastrophe to take in the 1931 Paris Colonial Exhibition. The exhibition was one of a set of international fairs that dotted the era. These dramatic displays were themselves a part of growing global interconnection even as they offered a tactile representation of it. Fairs made varied parts of the world visible to audiences even as they focused that vision through specific lenses. Even for fairs not specifically focused on colonialism, one of the most intense of these lenses was imperial power.[9] Hunt, like many, willingly had his vision altered. Viewing the Paris Exhibition he would 'defy anyone' not to let out 'gasps of astonishment' at the spectacle of accomplishment the French constructed in regard to consolidating their empire. He was impressed by how the exhibition amounted to a broad 'dramatization of the power of France' when 'we are sick of the Philippines'. It also drove home 'the place of the colonies in the French economic and social and military scheme'. Still breathless after the exhibition, Hunt reckoned that the experience of suppressing and administering its colonial peoples had served metropolitan France as much as colonial resources. The French Empire, or rather particular *representations* of the French Empire, reveal how imperial elements were enmeshed in internationalist discussions often only coded by nation states. Even as they often obscured or evaded questions of colonialism in formal discussions, many internationalists were well aware of the images and implications of colonialism in their calculations of national and international relations.[10]

Like so many who had served in the Great War, Hunt was extraordinarily sensitive to tensions in Europe. During his visit he could not shake fears that the economic crisis had knocked the world order out of kilter, intensifying latent conflicts and simmering grudges. Sailing back to the United States in 1931, he wrote ominously to one of his constellation of contacts in the United States, Wesley Clair Mitchell (a policy entrepreneur instrumental in the establishment of the National Bureau of Economic Research and moving force in the *Recent Social Trends* project):

> It is surely a most dangerous situation, the economic depression deepening as political conflicts accentuate, with Europe taking the high road to Armageddon. …
> The League sits impotently by. … History is not prophetic but it holds the germs

of prophesy. We fear what may be because of what has been. ... Surely there would be no Second World War if there had not been a First. ...

I think that I can see more. I think that I can see the flashes of European guns and hear the drumfire again; can feel the shock of airbombs raining down on little villages far behind the lines, and scores of miles away, from a distant world called America a nightmare of patchwork-painted transports crazily zigzagging across three thousand miles of sea.[11]

The meeting in Geneva was a part of an overture by the League's economic organs to greater focus on the question of Depression and depressions in general. Much of this work would be supported by grants from the Rockefeller Foundation. Hunt's reports from the proceedings underline the interest in the League's evolving work in important quarters of American liberal internationalism. While the Rockefeller Foundation had given considerable resources to the League and related bodies, the interest in economic research on the Depression was a new tack. It points to the engagement of American organizations with the League because they found what it did useful, particularly in a period of chronic crisis. International organizations could provide vital input and analysis that could aid in both understanding and confronting the problems loose in the world. More to the point these American groups, which were almost universally liberal and internationalist in their orientation, were creating capacities in the League, shaping it to their needs as well. So there was a critical feedback loop in the creation of these capacities that supported the use of such information by various constituencies within the United States.

Recently, Rockefeller has been described as a 'silent ... partner' to the League's wide-ranging economic work on the Depression.[12] This understates the foundation's role with the League and the wider import of what it was attempting. Rockefeller was supportive of activities by the League to define global economic relations but its increased attention to its activities was linked to an understanding of what happens when the global economy breaks down, as in the Depression. Particularly during the worst of the crisis the foundation turned to international institutions in an anxious attempt to find the necessary information and insight to tackle the issue – albeit within a liberal framework.[13]

This sort of grounded, social-science-based analysis of how the rush of modern life transformed societies became even more important as it became apparent that the Depression was a lingering condition. There was a broad and explicit understanding that the economic crisis was intimately connected to the possibility of political and social instability. The key to this was information that could be loaned to interpretation and policymaking. The League cultivated a broad array of sources of information that became increasingly important as the problems wrought by an economic Depression spilt into social, political, cultural and diplomatic spheres. The economic views that the League supported have been called 'liberal fundamentalist' and the foundation patrons and experts it drew in from outside were of a liberal internationalist ilk themselves.[14] But then faith was required in a body that was supporting what was then a flagging liberal order.

The eagerness to exploit the potential of the League was not simply something limited to big philanthropies. Reformers, policy experts, academics and government officials all saw the role it could play as an international information hub. But this is not solely about a US relationship with the League. It reveals trends within international affairs generally. Data had come to play a critical role in international and American economics. Again, this was just to single out economics in what was an era of codification, measurement and information gathering.

The Depression added velocity to ongoing efforts to refine measures of economic life. In the early years of the Depression, Simon Kuznets came up with his trailblazing approach to national income. Kuznets was among those who looked at the generation of the raw material of statistics and other data as the lifeblood of good social science.[15] In turn, such analysis became a foundation for the measure (and the later much criticized) 'gross domestic product' that itself became a vital tool in post-war conversations about growth and economic development globally.[16] Such tools could be a revelation for those who were contending with wide-ranging economic questions. Indeed, the head of Rockefeller's Social Science programme, Joseph Willits, himself a former professor at the Wharton School, was extolling these new measures by 1940 as the 'perfect tool' for scholars and policymakers to understand crucial economic issues.[17]

Looking beyond the famous names to those who employed these evolving concepts in policy gives a broader sense of their impact. One such figure is the neglected Winfield Riefler, an economist and statistician who was FDR's 'interpreting economist' (as the press dubbed him) in the first phases of the New Deal.[18] In 1934 it was Riefler who proposed federally backed mortgages as a means to resuscitate and promote 'modernization' of a critical part of the domestic economy, the ailing housing market.[19] His talents and connections earned him a spot among the early classes of scholars at the Institute of Advanced Study (IAS) in Princeton and later he became the director of the National Bureau of Economic Research and a director of the Foreign Policy Association. Once at the IAS, he immediately proposed that the organization develop a programme to understand financial matters, an agenda naturally influenced by the Depression and the 'public problems with which the world is wrestling and will in all probability continue to wrestle during the next generation at least'. His hope was not just for first class research for US use, but also a means to stitch together a worldwide network of scholarship on the issue.[20]

His understanding of the importance of numbers was not academic. They were a means to diagnose economic problems and the social and political crises they could inspire. More than that they could facilitate the policy prescriptions to cure these illnesses. It also explained his internationalism. National governments had to contend with the problems emerging from modern life, but the problems themselves were often issues that reached beyond the boundaries and, therefore, the capacities of any single state. Riefler (long before it became academic fashion) grasped and sought to highlight what he termed the 'trans-national' import of such information.[21]

Like so many of his peers, he was drawn to the potential of the League as a means to collect economic data and provide analysis on the world economy.

He was one name in the long list of American members in League committees, serving on its Finance Committee from 1937 to 1946. Because of this work and his predisposition to see economic issues in an international context, Riefler understood what the League could still accomplish. During a 1938 visit to Geneva to discuss the Depression, Riefler saw that 'the fact the League has lost political influence seems to have thrown it back on the one asset left namely its ability to serve as an intellectual center'. That technical work was of a high order in his mind, reaching the level of an international 'super-university' making it a vital font of research and analysis.[22]

Riefler was among those liberal internationalists shocked into greater action by one of the great geopolitical disasters of the twentieth century, the fall of France.[23] In spring 1940 he was among a cohort of the internationally minded that called for direct intervention, even to the point of a declaration of war, to contain Germany.[24] But more than this he actively aided a plot that summer to move the League of Nations' economic section to the IAS, as he, like numerous others, saw its accomplished staff and peerless data as indispensable and something that should not fall into fascist hands.[25]

As the United States readied for war, Riefler was called back to service in Washington. Henry Wallace, at the apex of his career serving as vice president and head of the Economic Defense Board, drew on Riefler's expertise on economic questions, particularly the vexing ones about the shape of the post-war world.[26] In this capacity, Riefler grappled with a larger question besetting liberals concerned with the legacy of the global impacts of the fragmentation of the world. It led him to a worldwide vision of development, one where an 'International Development Authority' (IDA) that would oversee investment in poorer areas of the globe. Riefler realized he was not just discussing moving capital but the creation of new capacities in poorer nations. It was in part a reaction to the fragmentation of the Depression, but it was also a means to articulate post-war plans. These centred on an effort to stabilize the liberal capitalist world order by firmly linking poorer areas of the globe and their raw materials to the capitalist industrial centres in the West. Like Hunt, Riefler was conscious he was in a world where empires remained arbiters. However, the IDA proposal skirted the issue. Yet two imperial states, the United States and Great Britain, were to be the drivers of an authority that by its very nature would have to contend with the realities of colonialism.[27] The proposal was never implemented as such, but it became ingrained in high-level post-war planning. Riefler would join other influential economists in the War and Peace Studies held by the Council on Foreign Relations. The need for an economic development body infused their thinking, even to the point of helping them imagine a joint Anglo-American declaration for an international economic development board to fulfil the promises of the Atlantic Charter. This was fantasy but it led to reality. The enduring concept would influence figures inside and outside the government and inform the creation of an international lender of last resort: a 'World Bank' at Bretton Woods.[28]

As the United States entered the war, Riefler turned economics directly into a weapon, carrying his talents with him as one of the first Americans sent to London to wage economic war as part of the Board of Economic Warfare. Here Riefler's career segues broadly into another point about knowledge emerging from the social sciences – how so many seeking answers to the economics of crisis were driven to questions of economic development and thence to war (and sometimes back again). Although not involved in the blockade, other young, economically minded social scientists – a crowd that included names like Walt Rostow, Charles Kindleberger and Robert MacNamara – were drawn into the Army Air Force. There they waged economic war from the skies, guiding the unravelling of societies through air bombardment (MacNamara was not formally an economist but a former professor of management from Harvard yet still someone versed in the spirit of numbers – systems analysis).[29]

Economic warfare is a numbers game, it involves figuring out what the enemy has and needs and then how to deny them those materials. In this it was hardly new to history – peoples had long sought to cut off an enemy's resources long before there was a clear category of economics. But all these figures found their lessons—about how economies worked and could impact societies—enhanced by new information and approaches born in response to the Depression.

Another figure illustrating these professional trajectories is Henry Grady. Like Hunt and Riefler, he worked at the level of implementation, making ideas and assumptions into active policy. For Grady, economics was the hub of international relations. This is not surprising as he had and would have a long career that connected with the imperatives of international economics in various forms. Giving up the call of the Catholic priesthood, Grady embraced another faith, one centred on liberal capitalism. A PhD in economics eventually led to a professorship at the University of California, Berkeley. Remaining a committed Catholic, Grady perceived threats to the extended liberal society he also deeply valued. In this he was like many internationalist liberals believing that there were revolutionary forces radically expanding and pushing human relationships and that these things tore the social and political fabric.

Grady's interest in the international import of economics answers why he was a committed partisan for the League. Even at its lowest ebb at the end of the 1930s, Geneva retained its utility as a site from which to divine and measure how economics intersected with the realities of politics and ideology and also to state clearly how it was part of an emergent conflict. As official US representative to the League's Economic Committee, Grady primed the 30 March, 1939 meeting of the committee with opening statements that were frank, combative and revealing about how economics was already part of an ideological struggle.

He 'expressed the opinion that recent developments in Europe had made totally useless any consideration of an economic *rapprochement* with the "totalitarian" states whose trade methods are so inextricably tied up with their political ideas that the result is tantamount to economic warfare' (emphasis original). Although he did not suggest active pressures be applied to Germany he was 'emphatic' that the League body should consider condemning the use of trade for what he decided was 'aggressive purposes'. Grady summed up by stating an ideological view that 'he had been unable to find any evidence that the control systems could succeed in the long run'. It all led to the daunting conclusion that 'two diametrically opposed economic systems could not be maintained in the same world over any extended period'.

To be sure, other members of the committee were less inclined to be so confrontational. As the official US record of the meeting noted, Grady's 'more forceful' statements 'aroused the general interest of the Committee as well as a certain uneasiness'. The British representative, for example, was reluctant to add to the inflammatory rhetoric. This was, of course, reflective of national interests and European realities, something the uncommitted United States and its tough-talking representative did not have to face. Nevertheless, while Grady's commentary could hardly be called a clarion call to arms, it demonstrates how many who were involved in international affairs at a day-to-day, operational level had come to see the world economy fractured on ideological lines.[30]

Part of the stridency of the statements was undoubtedly a product of what he was able to divine as the impacts of German trade policy. Grady's Geneva visit also provided a window to view southeastern Europe in 1939 and gather further data and impressions. This led to a confidential report that measured the dynamics of the trade relationships between the Nazi regime and Greece, Yugoslavia, Bulgaria, Rumania, Hungary, Turkey and Italy. Economic data allowed Grady to draw a sharp picture of how trade policies were enhancing Germany's position in the region. These policies assured that countries in southeastern Europe that traded with the Reich were paid in Reichmarks. These were held in Germany in clearing accounts that were blocked – meaning they could only be spent by the holder on purchases in Germany itself. This created dependency on the part of Germany's trade partners and provided considerable economic, political and diplomatic leverage to Berlin. Aspects were leaked to the press to show how Germany's measurable gains were political as well as economic and were shutting other 'free systems' out of important sectors of the European economy, skewing general economic activity and even the internal development of states.[31] But the State Department, which had requested the report, was less interested in this than in how German policies could detach states from other regional arrangements and even the world economy. It was a way of reading how the impacts of a German imperial project in eastern and central Europe was working counter to those efforts of liberal states to shore up relationships seen as important to the health of a working liberal-capitalist system. Understanding such tactics took on more menacing characteristics as Americans realized that the Germans might attempt something similar in Latin America.

It should be emphasized that Grady was not a fringe figure but an appointed representative of the US government (in 1939 he was a member of the US Tariff Commission). After his jaunt to Geneva he returned home to become Assistant Secretary of State for Economic Affairs. Over the next two decades he was a first-string player in American diplomacy, being the first American ambassador to independent India, the ambassador to Greece as Marshall Plan and military aid began to flood in, and then the ambassador to Iran in the years before the CIA-sponsored coup against Mossadeq. In this litany of service there was one digression back into the private sector in 1941 but even then he took the lessons of economic warfare with him. He left the State Department to become president of the American President lines. This might seem a simple case of a government official taking advantage of an opportunity to parlay service into a profitable position, and perhaps it was. But it was also a tool in the economic war that Grady and others were committing themselves to. Under Grady's leadership the company would assist in snatching up strategic materials in Pacific Asia just before the US-Japanese war.[32]

But he appreciated what he had articulated in Geneva in 1939, something that held true in a new struggle with some similar characteristics. For Grady, as for so many of his peers, economic data and its analysis was a starting point to understand the scope of a potential threat and contain it, as well as a means to put it into an ideological context. Later, Grady would see his actions as part of a larger trend of international politics towards economic warfare that would become the default setting between ideological encampments. In fact, by 1940 the vision that economics had become a means to ideological combat was openly stated in the liberal camp. Grady's League colleague John Bell Condliffe, (who later taught economics at Berkeley and counted Albert O. Hirschman among his close colleagues) articulated the belief that the United States had to take a lead in guiding a 'reconstruction' of global trade. If the United States did not take bold moves on the international front, 'autarkic' blocs would carve out spheres of influence in lesser-developed areas of the world and choke off export markets and sources of raw materials.[33] In this increasingly clear struggle, information was just one more arrow in the quiver against enemies like Nazi Germany who were engaged in empire-building of their own. Grady was later explicit that his activities were one part of a 'cold war' against Germany in the late 1930s that presaged the later struggle against the Soviet Union.[34]

All of these questions must be linked to the maintenance and extension of liberal capitalist global hegemony. 'Empire' can be too historically and geographically constrained and might not effectively describe what the United States was seeking: a broader form of hegemony built on a particular type of global equilibrium. Nevertheless, the liberal world system the Americans increasingly came to dominate maintained and even depended upon empires as crucial moving parts to keep the whole system working. Grady, like many of his peers, was turning the tools of internationalism away from the maintenance of an international liberal order. He was forging them into weapons against those 'insurgents' who actively sought to replace a liberal order comfortable with empire with their own ideologically driven imperium.[35]

The shift of all of these personalities to war and then back to peace of course suggests the extensive nature of mobilization in this era of crisis. Such mobilization is not new to warfare. War, particularly modern war, drives wide swaths of individuals into military service. But the tools they brought to that struggle were qualitatively different and allowed them to do different things for particular ends. This should remind us that internationalist efforts to generate information as well as the knowledge, the justifications and legitimacy it creates and supports are not airy things. Such efforts allowed powerful, coercive and sometimes destructive actions to be taken. What is more, it forces an understanding that the elements deployed by the United States were the product of a transnational dialogue that shaped ideas and concepts in the United States and were actively shaped by the participation and inputs of American institutions. These elements then could be actively turned into tools and even weapons to fight for the liberal international order the United States sought to establish in a tumultuous period.

Notes

1. Diane Coyle, *GDP: A Brief but Affectionate History* (Princeton: Princeton University Press, 2014), 11–23.
2. Akira Iriye, *Global Community: The Role of International Organizations in the Making of the Contemporary World* (Berkeley: University of California Press, 2002); *Cultural Internationalism and World Order* (Baltimore: Johns Hopkins University Press, 1997).
3. See J. Adam Tooze, *Statistics and the German State, 1900–1945: The Making of Modern Economic Knowledge* (New York: Cambridge University Press, 2001).
4. Ellis W. Hawley, 'Herbert Hoover, the Commerce Secretariat, and the Vision of an "Associative State", 1921–1928', *Journal of American History* 61, no. 1 (1974): 116–40.
5. *Recent Social Trends in the United States: Report of the President's Research Committee on Social Trends* (New York: McGraw-Hill, 1933); David M. Kennedy, *Freedom from Fear: The American People in Depression and War, 1929–1945* (New York: Oxford University Press, 1999), 10–13, 41–2.
6. For a discussion of liberal international activities and the place of the League, see Daniel Gorman, *The Emergence of International Society in the 1920s* (Cambridge: Cambridge University Press, 2012).
7. Martin Hill, *Economic and Financial Organization of the League of Nations* (Washington DC: Carnegie Endowment for International Peace, 1946), 3–4.
8. Edward Eyre Hunt, 'The Business Depression: Memo of Meeting in Geneva, March 2–4, 1931', box 18, series 100, Rockefeller Foundation Archives, Rockefeller Archive Center (hereafter RAC).
9. Emily Rosenberg, ed., *A World Connecting, 1870–1945* (Cambridge: Belknap Press of Harvard University Press, 2012), 898–904.
10. Hunt to Mitchell, 21 July 1931, and Hunt to Mitchell, 31 July 1931, box 17, Edward Eyre Hunt Papers, Hoover Institution on War, Revolution and Peace Archives (hereafter HIA).
11. Hunt to Mitchell, 1 August 1931, box 17, Hunt Papers, HIA.
12. Patricia Clavin, *Securing the World Economy: The Reinvention of the League of Nations, 1920–1946* (New York: Oxford University Press, 2013), 74.
13. Raymond B. Fosdick, *The Story of the Rockefeller Foundation* (New York: Harper & Brothers, 1952), 203–4.
14. Craig Murphy, *International Organization and Industrial Change: Global Governance Since 1850* (New York: Oxford University Press, 1994), 157–8.
15. Simon Kuznets, 'Data for the Science of Economics', n.d. [1939], HUG FP-88, box 1, Simon Kuznets Papers, Harvard University Archives, Pusey Library, Cambridge, Massachusetts.
16. Coyle, *GDP*, 41–57.

17 Willits Memo, 25 October, 1940, RG 3, series 910, box 10, Rockefeller Foundation Archives, RAC.
18 'F.D.'s Expert is Identified', *Washington Daily News*, 2 November 1933.
19 Winfield Riefler, 'A National Program for Modernized Housing', 19 March 1934, box 2, RG 200 National Archives Gift Collection: Winfield Riefler Papers, National Archives and Records Administration, College Park, MD (hereafter NAMD).
20 Riefler to Flexner, 'Shall the Institute Concentrate its Work in Economics in the Field of Finance?', 13 March 1936; Riefler to Flexner, 'Program of Work in Economics for the School of Economics and Politics of the Institute of Advanced Study', n.d. (August 1936), box 27, Faculty File, Winfield Riefler Papers, Shelby White and Leon Levy Archives Center, Institute for Advanced Study, Princeton, New Jersey.
21 Winfield Riefler, 'Government and the Statistician', *Journal of the American Statistical Association* 37, no. 217 (1942): 1–11.
22 Riefler to Flexner, 14 July 1938, box 1, RG 200, NAMD.
23 David Reynolds, '1940: Fulcrum of the Twentieth Century?', *International Affairs* 66, no. 2 (1990): 325–50.
24 Miller to Riefler, 5 June 1940, box 2, RG 200, NAMD.
25 Letter to Woolley, 25 June 1940, PPF 537, President's Personal File, Franklin Delano Roosevelt Library, Hyde Park, New York [hereafter FDRL]; Memorandum of Conversation with E. J. Phelan, 23 October 1940, vol. 46, Jay Pierrepont Moffat Papers, Houghton Library, Harvard University.
26 Wallace to Rielfer, 9 April 1941, box 2, RG 200, NAMD.
27 Riefler to Wallace, 2 October 1941; Winfield Riefler, 'A Program to Stimulate International Investment', 4 October, 1941, reel 40, Henry Wallace Papers, FDRL.
28 Economic and Financial Group, 'Tentative Draft of a Joint Economic Declaration by the Governments of the United States and the United Kingdom', 3 January 1942; Alvin Hanson, 'Problems of Monetary Reconstruction', 1 April 1942 in Council on Foreign Relations, *Studies of American Interests in the War and the Peace: Economic and Financial Series* (New York: Council on Foreign Relations, 1946); Eric Helleiner, *Forgotten Foundations of Bretton Woods: International Development and the Making of the Postwar Order* (Ithaca: Cornell University Press, 2014), 124–7.
29 Deborah Shapley, *Promise and Power: The Life and Times of Robert McNamara* (Boston: Little, Brown, 1993), 20–38.
30 Bucknell to Secretary of State, 'Report on the Forty-Ninth Session of the Economic Committee', 9 April 1939, RG 59, Decimal File 500.C119/378, box 2535, NAMD.
31 Henry Grady, 'Summary of Material Obtained by Commissioner Grady Regarding German Trade Relations with Certain Balkan Countries', July 1939, box 4, Henry Grady Papers, Harry S. Truman Library, Independence Missouri (hereafter HTL). See also John T. McNay, ed., *The Memoirs of Ambassador Henry F. Grady: From the Great War to the Cold War* (Columbia: University of Missouri Press, 2009).
32 Profile: Henry Grady, July 1950, box 1, Grady Papers, HTL.
33 J. B. Condliffe, *The Reconstruction of World Trade: A Survey of International Economic Relations* (New York: W.W. Norton, 1940), 392–4.
34 Henry Grady, 'Adventures in Diplomacy', draft manuscript, n.d. [1963], box 1, Grady Papers, HTL, 115.
35 J. Adam Tooze, *The Deluge: The Great War and the Remaking of Global Order, 1916–1931* (New York: Penguin, 2014), 3–30; see also Mark Mazower, *Hitler's Empire: How the Nazis Ruled Europe* (New York: Penguin Press, 2008).

Chapter 10

KNOWLEDGE FOR EMPIRE: AMERICAN HEGEMONY, THE ROCKEFELLER FOUNDATION AND THE RISE OF ACADEMIC INTERNATIONAL RELATIONS IN THE UNITED STATES

Inderjeet Parmar

The risks we face are of a new order of magnitude, commensurate with the total struggle in which we are engaged. For a free society there is never total victory, since freedom and democracy are never wholly attained, are always in the process of being attained. But defeat at the hands of the totalitarian is total defeat. These risks crowd in on us, in a shrinking world of polarized power, so as to give us no choice, ultimately, between meeting them effectively or being overcome by them.

The whole success of the proposed program hangs ultimately on recognition by this Government, the American people, and all free peoples, that the cold war is in fact a real war in which the survival of the free world is at stake. Essential prerequisites to success are consultations with Congressional leaders designed to make the program the object of non-partisan legislative support, and a presentation to the public of a full explanation of the facts and implications of the present international situation.[1]

Intellectuals, journalists and state policymakers were in close conference at the Rockefeller Foundation amid alleged existential world crises in the (original) 'year of maximum danger': 1954. 'It is estimated that, within the next four years [i.e., by 1954, later revised to 1952], the USSR will attain the capability of seriously damaging vital centers of the United States, provided it strikes a surprise blow and provided further that the blow is opposed by no more effective opposition than we now have programmed.'[2]

It was claimed by many observers that world conditions, rather than America's will to global power, demanded nothing less than complete national mobilization of resources against the Soviet foe; the future of mankind depended upon the course of US national security and foreign policies. The 'novel' character of the 'Red threat', its existential challenge to the free world, and its characterization as necessitating a fight to the finish through a long, possibly permanent, war[3] all echo the threat-construction discourses about political Islam deployed by the

George W. Bush administration after 9/11.[4] Then as now, every section of society was to play its part in thwarting the enemy – at home and abroad, in churches, schools, workplaces, libraries and universities. Intellectuals, journalists and academics had a special role to play, particularly in ensuring that no subversive thinking infected the minds of the young. On the contrary, their role was to ensure the production of young minds ready to wage the struggle for freedom in all aspects of life, especially through graduate programmes suited to training in the foreign service and foreign policymaking apparatus. In addition, academics themselves were to supply to policymakers usable knowledge and understanding of the world and its strategic countries, regions and underlying transformative social, political and ideological forces.[5] Even more than that, academics were to strive to produce theoretical models and frameworks to make sense of the sheer volume of facts about the world that were becoming available to America's national security managers from its official and unofficial representatives across the world.

The foreign and national security policies that were going to save the world from the march of 'communist slavery' or, as is argued here, to promote American global hegemony,[6] were based, at least in part, on assessments and analyses of the vast amounts of information that poured into the State Department. But how was the department to assess the information? How was it to use knowledge to make better decisions that would, with the deployment of appropriate means and vigorous mass media campaigns, command the support of the American people? What could 'ivory tower' academics, whose very trade is knowledge, contribute to this? Could academic theories help make better policies and, thereby, secure peace and security under American world leadership?

In my view, the confluence of intellect and power, the meeting of ideas and action, of private actors and former, serving and future officials of the American state constitute the core compelling interest in the 1954 Rockefeller conference. In principle, it suggests that ideas were seen to matter, that intellectuals' voices were worth hearing, their expertise valued, and recognized at high levels of national power in the United States, and that intellectuals and their institutions made a difference. The composition of the meetings also suggests that in developing a better sense of America's national purpose, the conference might result in practical suggestions for improving the promotion to the general public of US foreign and national security policies. The year 1954 was, then, a moment for reflection, an attempt to explore, and for some an attempt to overcome, the boundaries of knowledge and power. This has normally been an unhappy experience for both intellectuals and public officials, as this chapter suggests.

Validation for (some) students of power came in the form of Dean Rusk, former public official and future secretary of state, and the then president of the Rockefeller Foundation. Paul Nitze, the main author of NSC-68 and former head of Policy Planning at the State Department, was an active participant. The dean of US foreign policy journalism, Walter Lippmann, was in attendance, as was the elder statesman of Christianity and foreign policy politics, Reinhold Niebuhr. Dorothy Thompson, the first senior woman in the State Department and later advisor and aide to US senator Henry 'Scoop' Jackson, also attended.[7] They wanted to know what international relations (IR) as an emerging academic discipline could do for them, whether IR theory possessed the 'key' to analysis and action. They interrogated elite university professors – Hans Morgenthau (Chicago), Arnold Wolfers (Yale) and William T. R. Fox (Columbia) – for days. The meeting was direct, the immediate outcome disappointing though instructive about the differing functions of academic theorizing and the needs of hard-pressed, and hard-nosed, national security managers. Yet, there was much more going on here than meets the eye. The road to and from the 1954 Conference is a story of the gradual – *albeit not unilinear and totally mapped out in advance, but with an inner logic nevertheless* – conscious development by elements of an emerging east coast US foreign policy. An important part of this story was the establishment of an academic discipline (international relations),[8] armed with a specific dominant theory – realism, and its several variants or, more accurately, *the development of a sense of the need to deploy 'hard power' as a basic factor in foreign relations* – at the core of which was a belief in the inevitability of interstate conflict, the role of force in world affairs, the necessity of wise statesmanship, total national mobilization and the need for US global leadership or hegemony.[9] The year 1954 seemed to be, at least in part, about giving a veneer of philosophical depth to American national interest-driven US foreign policy, differentiating the United States from its supposedly uncultured and uncivilized communist enemy.[10] It was also about reconciling values and interests, pointing up the value-based origins of national interests themselves. This was, then, an attempt to continue the development, under new conditions, of a myriad of programmes that had begun several decades earlier by elites that looked forward to 'the American Century'. The development of IR is viewed here as part of an elite 'project', however 'messy' in practice, for US global hegemony.[11]

Why did the Rockefeller Foundation arrange the 1954 Conference?

It is clear that the Rockefeller Foundation (RF), and other such philanthropies (such as Carnegie) had a long-standing interest in four matters in regard to US foreign affairs: first, and most broadly, Rockefeller wanted to strengthen US power in the world; secondly, and as a result, RF was dedicated to fostering and consolidating intellectual networks that would produce better empirical knowledge, conceptual understanding and practical decisions in regard to US foreign policy, the unity of analysis and action; thirdly, Rockefeller sought to improve the State Department's ability to assess threats, opportunities and the sheer volume of facts upon which such assessments were based; and, finally, RF wanted to assist in the determination of US national interests and the role therein of core values.[12]

RF was, I argue, a state-oriented and imperialistic institution from its very early-twentieth-century Progressive-era beginnings. It was dedicated to state-building and constructing a civil society that was supportive of federal executive power, especially in foreign affairs, where foundation elites looked forward to America's taking the political and moral leadership of the world. This mirrored the foundation's serious interest in domestic social reform and state-building to that end. RF's principle of 'private action for the public good' frequently led the way in later extensions of state power and institutional capacities, thereby building the American state.[13]

The Progressive-era roots of Rockefeller and other philanthropies are fundamental to their sense of historic mission.[14] Progressivism was characterized by elite attempts to come to grips with and to manage massive social, economic and cultural transformations within the United States; and to promote American power in a global context featuring intra-European military and imperial rivalries, rising nationalist and anti-colonialist movements, as well as socialism. Order through reform at home and increased influence abroad were intimately connected in the minds and activities of Progressive-era philanthropies.[15]

In a very profound sense, RF was a 'state-spirited' organization sitting at the heart of the emerging east coast US foreign policy establishment. As Antonio Gramsci observed, state-spirited leaders are the core elements of any thoroughgoing historically transformative movement: they see themselves as the state, as embodying the interests and values of the state, and as duty-bound to solve the state's problems as if they were their own. In the terms of Eldon Eisenach, foundations may be seen as 'para-state' organizations that, despite their private, voluntarist character, were motivated to their core by state interests.[16]

Given their historical, east coast elite origins at a critical time in American history, the foundations marked the emergence of a global consciousness within which the United States was historically best suited to a world-leadership role. Spreading the benefits of the American dream to the world was critical.[17] As the twentieth century progressed, the relationship between state foreign policymakers and philanthropic intellectual networks deepened and broadened, blurring the increasingly vague distinctions between state and society, public policy and private actors. By the end of 1945, philanthropic foundations were thoroughly integrated into the foreign policy establishment; they assisted America's rise to globalism by, inter alia, establishing university foreign affairs institutes, funding the work of key foreign policy think tanks, sponsoring international relations and area studies programmes and graduate training courses for foreign service officers and developing the research and analysis capacities of the State Department. Such efforts coalesced with the expansionist objectives of the American state with which foundation networks were intimately connected, both ideologically and personally.

RF sits well in Godfrey Hodgson's definition of the US foreign policy establishment: the establishment, Hodgson argues, is composed of groups of men who know one another, 'who share assumptions so deep that they do not need to be articulated; and who contrive to wield power outside the constitutional or political forms: the power to put a stop to things they disapprove of, to promote the men they regard as reliable, and to block the unreliable.' Hodgson further notes that 'the true establishment man prided himself on his bipartisanship, his ability to get on with and work with right-minded fellows of either party'.[18] The core elements of the establishment include Wall Street lawyers and bankers, Ivy League academics and the heads of the major philanthropic foundations.[19] Nelson

Polsby supports elements of that definition by arguing that the establishment tends to be centrist, pragmatic and executive-branch focused, as well as being educated in the east coast Ivy League schools.[20] Though recruiting principally from Ivy League universities and elite private schools, the traditional establishment was also open to talented people 'with the wrong family pedigree', part of the 'genius of the American Establishment', according to Max Holland.[21]

Hodgson argues that the post-Pearl Harbor foreign policy establishment was defined by a *history*, a *policy*, an *aspiration*, an *instinct* and a *technique*. It was forged historically in organizations like the OSS during the Second World War and the Cold War, in the building of the Marshall Plan, United Nations, IMF, World Bank and NATO; its *policy* was broadly anti-isolationist and liberal internationalist, advocating restraint but admiring the use of hi-tech military force; its *aspiration* was to the moral and political leadership of the world: heading 'a single Western coalition holding the world in balance against the infidel is fundamental to this establishment'. The establishment's *instinct* was for the 'non-ideological', pragmatic centre ground; its *technique* was to work through the executive branch – the National Security Council, Central Intelligence Agency, State Department and the White House rather than Congress, electoral politics or public opinion. To sum up, the post-1941 establishment was characterized by its pragmatism, centrism, elitism, multilateralism and more or less exclusive focus on the executive branch. This sums up the place and position not only of RF but also of most of the invited members of the 1954 Rockefeller Conference.

As a strategic organization of the establishment, Rockefeller viewed the academy and academics as a critical resource, as noted above. Broadly, RF *effectively* took a Gramscian approach to intellectuals' roles, though from a very different perspective: to promote the power of a capitalist state, rather than to undermine it. The Gramscian view, along with orthodox Marxism, is founded on an economistic analysis of power in capitalist societies. Capitalist corporations form the bedrock of economic power and, thereby, the basis of social, cultural and ideological power in civil society. Unlike orthodox Marxists, however, Gramsci made a radical departure from this view in order to explain Western capitalism's relative immunity to revolution. Gramsci noted the fact that there existed important protective layers of pro-bourgeois culture, ideology, values and institutions that had played a powerful role in shaping the minds of the masses in favour of the status quo and against violent revolution. In short, Gramsci made more explicit, and more specifically developed, what Marx himself had argued when he wrote that 'the ideas of the ruling class are in every epoch the ruling ideas'.[22] Gramsci, however, located ideological, political and cultural struggle more centrally into Marxist thought, thereby creating space in the theory for those who are the principal sources and disseminators of new ideas and theories: the intellectuals.

In effect, Gramsci's argument is that there is no simple way to define capitalist, or national, interests – in economic or political terms – and that interests are a matter of intellectual debate and competing interpretations. It is the role of 'organic intellectuals' – thinkers who are connected with the dominant class, for example within the universities, or the church, mass media, political parties – to develop, elaborate, refine, disseminate and teach the dominant ideas, values and norms, to make 'natural' and 'commonsense', what are, in reality, ideas that principally support the ruling class.

Similarly, politics and the state are not mere reflections of unequal economic relations: they are also sites of struggle and competition between rival ideas, values, policies, programmes and regimes. Through struggle, bargaining and compromise, and the building of enduring coalitions that cut across class, ethnic and racial cleavages, is formed the prevailing idea of 'reality', the dominant concept that underlies a particular set of political, institutional and economic arrangements: a regime. As political regimes – or hegemonic projects and alliances – are made up of cross-class coalitions, they require for their formation and sustenance public opinion mobilizations to convince the masses – or at least a critical proportion of them – that they have a stake in current arrangements, something to gain – such as a steady well-paid job and improved living standards – from supporting the regime. In short, the coalition – or historic bloc, in Gramscian terms – is generated and sustained by leadership based on the 'consent of the governed', under the hegemonic leadership of politicians and intellectuals of the capitalist class.

As the 'consent of the governed' is so vital to political and social arrangements, it is not left to chance. It is engineered[23] by intellectual, political and cultural elites not only through numerous channels that involve the state – through, for example, political speeches and the schools and political parties – but also through the sort of organizations that Hodgson's Establishment and Eisenach's parastates would recognize: the major private and public universities, the Council on Foreign Relations, and the great east coast philanthropic foundations – Ford, Carnegie and Rockefeller.[24]

In Gramscian terms, hegemony is constructed by an alliance of state elites and private ruling class organizations, including those led by intellectuals. Elite and popular authority are constructed by an alliance of state and private agencies in order to undermine the old order and to usher in the new. As noted above, central to the motivation of private elites is Gramsci's concept of 'state spirit' which, although a fairly 'conservative' sounding concept, infuses every successful social movement. State-spirited leaders contextualize themselves in the broad sweep of national and global historical development: their outlook 'presupposes "continuity", either with the past, or with tradition, or with the future; that is, it presupposes that every act is a moment in a complex process, which has already begun and which will continue'.[25] According to Gramsci, such leaders and intellectuals may even come to believe 'that they *are* the State'.[26] It is to one such specific initiative intimately related to the 1954 Conference – relating to Arnold Wolfers and William T. R. Fox – that this chapter now turns.[27]

Yale Institute of International Studies

From the 1930s, RF played a leading role in financing university programmes of research in international affairs and in 'non-Western' studies. It is important to emphasize that the two developments occurred together because they were part of a broader programme of work that aimed at the same outcome: expanding American power. Foundation officials were early to recognize the changing position of the United States in world affairs. This required, they believed, a new foreign policy. This in turn required trained experts and officers who spoke foreign languages and knew the history, politics and culture of societies that would enter the orbit of America's 'national interest'. University courses in international relations were important for educating these and other future leaders of community opinion – lawyers, bankers and teachers – who could be expected to secure general acceptance of the United States in world affairs. According to Olson and Groom, without the intervention of Rockefeller and Carnegie, 'the field of [international relations] could hardly have progressed as it did' in its formative years. The foundations, they suggest, alongside the Council on Foreign Relations, constituted a 'critical institutional base affecting the way in which IR developed'.[28] The foundations were simultaneously a powerful institutional base for the development of area studies.[29]

The Yale Institute of International Studies (YIIS) represents an excellent example of early foundation intervention. The Yale Institute was created in 1935 with a five-year Rockefeller grant of $100,000.[30] The year 1935, which saw the first of a series of four Neutrality Acts – forbidding US entanglements in foreign wars – was a critical year in the history of US foreign relations and a daring year to begin, consciously or otherwise, an overtly globalist programme.[31] From its inception, the institute aimed to clarify American foreign policy by focusing upon 'the subject of power in international relations' – an area neglected by American scholars.[32] The institute aimed to take a 'realistic' view of world affairs, to be useful to foreign policymakers, to produce scholarly but accessible publications and to train academics for governmental service.[33] That it was later nicknamed 'The Power School' by IR-insiders is adequate testimony to Yale's successful institutionalization of realpolitik.[34] What decided the question within the foundation was the fact that Yale had such senior academics as Frederick Dunn, Arnold Wolfers and Samuel F. Bemis.[35] In addition to the initial $100,000 in 1935, the foundation provided a further $51,500 in 1941 (to run over three years) and $125,000 in 1944 (to run over the following five years), a total of $276,500.[36]

The realpolitik approaches of those who directed the YIIS (Nicholas Spykman 1935–40; and Frederick Dunn, from 1940 until after the war) were a source of obvious satisfaction to Rockefeller officials.[37] Consequently, the drafting of 'abstract schemes of a new world order' and 'ivory tower speculation' – the YIIS's annual report for 1942 stressed – were *not* on the agenda. Instead, the institute focused upon 'basic research' to fill conceptual gaps in current thinking and knowledge of international relations.[38] By 1944, the institute was focusing even more upon 'those questions which are likely to cause the *most trouble*, such as Anglo-American and Western-Soviet relations, for American foreign-policy'.[39]

The memoranda and records of the Yale Institute bear out its effective realism. One document, for example, reports that the United States could no longer 'take a free ride' in the conduct of European affairs.[40] While Britain's international hegemony had effectively ended, Britain still constituted a key 'bridgehead' to Western Europe.

Consequently, Britain's continued survival was in America's national interest, to the point of war if necessary. Europe, the report noted, had to be kept 'in balance', and a new Napoleon or Hitler prevented. America had to engage in the 'dirty game of power politics', if she were not to be dragged into another foreign war. Interestingly, the report recognized the dangers of Soviet expansionism, while acknowledging the Soviet Union's legitimate security concerns.[41] While the Soviets ought to be decisively checked territorially, it would be a mistake, the memorandum warned, to oppose them by countering every movement for social reform. That would only convince Western liberals and radicals of the 'reactionary' character of Anglo-American policy, and 'drive [them] ... into the arms of the doctrinaire Bolsheviks'. Finally, the memorandum argued that the American economy had become the major factor in global prosperity. Not only must future US economic policies assist the regeneration of Europe (and so keep Britain and France 'going concerns'), but also run the American economy 'responsibly'. American domestic prosperity would create a stable market for the world's products and thereby add to global security. This imperialistic posture was endorsed by an internal foundation review of key books from the YIIS during the war.[42]

Both Arnold Wolfers and William Fox were deeply significant in developing YIIS but were also influenced by the institute. Fox, for example, later claimed that it was only after joining YIIS in 1943 that he 'realize[d] how ill-equipped I was to think about the responsible use of power by the United States'.[43] Wolfers, on the other hand, found Yale a ready platform for making influential contacts in the worlds of intelligence and policymaking. During the war, Wolfers was a consultant with the OSS, National War College, the Institute of Defense Analysis, the Army department and State Department.[44] In addition, Wolfers and other YIIS colleagues lectured on geopolitics at the School of Military Government, Virginia.[45] After the war, Wolfers was a recruiter at Yale for the CIA.[46] Kenneth W. Thompson, another of the 1954 conferees, argues that Wolfers was the most policy-oriented of the Yale group and 'had an insatiable yearning for the corridors of power'. Indeed, Thompson felt that Wolfers might have compromised his scholarly independence as a result of that yearning.[47]

However much the Yale Institute cherished its 'independence', usefulness to government was its first priority. In August 1944, Dunn told Joseph Willits of RF that the YIIS had set up a committee (with State Department representation) to consider how universities might 'produce good decision-makers'.[48] Two years earlier, the YIIS's annual report noted the first of several meetings with US War Department officials concerning Near Eastern policy. 'It was intended', the report stressed, 'as a test of the possibility of quick mobilization of academic knowledge and its application to practical questions of policy'. The 1941–2 report further noted that numerous 'foreign area courses' had been established at Yale to increase the awareness of foreign societies; that the institute was sending information to the US government 'on demand'; and that YIIS graduates were performing valuable roles within several government departments, notably the State and War departments, the Board of Economic Warfare and the Office of the Co-ordinator of Inter-American Affairs led by Nelson Rockefeller.[49]

The War Department asked the Yale Institute to establish a School of Asiatic Studies for army staff officers, which it duly did in the summer of 1945. Meanwhile, the State Department and YIIS established a joint committee, with Dunn as chairman, to improve the training of foreign service officers. The impact of such government connections was accepted within the broader political science community by the formation of a 'politico-military relations' panel by the American Political Science Association, under the chairmanship of Bernard Brodie (a YIIS member).[50] The institute approached foreign policy problems from a perspective not dissimilar to that of the State Department. One of the most telling examples appeared in its 1943 Annual Report, in a discussion of the importance of the Middle East to the United States. Security, the report noted, was not merely a military question: it also required a watchful eye on the peoples and resources that bordered strategic sea routes and military bases. The Yale Institute proposed an investigation of industrial development, the 'rise of nationalism', and 'race and population pressures as they affect the stability of these regions', with a view to early remedial action by the United States.[51] This was not only an early indication of the importance of national security-oriented area studies programmes that developed within and alongside the development of IR, but also symptomatic of the close interconnections between foundation-funded research initiatives.[52] IR's development cannot profitably be seen in isolation from those other developments.

The institute produced many books on the Far East, Anglo-American relations and the place of Africa in American security policy. Over a half-century later, two stand out: William T. R. Fox's, *The Superpowers: The United States, Britain, and the Soviet Union – Their Responsibility for Peace* (1944), which introduced the term 'superpower' into the language;[53] and Nicholas J. Spykman's, *America's Strategy in World Politics: The United States and the Balance of Power* (1942). Gabriel Almond argues that Fox's book 'defined the structure of the postwar system of international relations'.[54] According to historian John Thompson, Spykman's study was the 'most thorough analysis of America's strategic position made in these [war] years', the thrust of which was 'that American interests demanded intervention in the war to restore the balance of power in Eurasia'. (It was written before the Japanese attack on Pearl Harbor).[55] Spykman argued that total war characterized twentieth-century warfare. The United States, therefore, had to be prepared for a global strategy that combined and integrated the key factors of power: military preparedness, economic vitality, political efficiency and mobilization, and ideological clarity. Spykman also abolished the distinctions between peacetime and war as 'total war is permanent war'. Finally, and most profoundly, he argued that there is '*no region of the globe [that] is too distant to be without strategic significance, too remote to be neglected in the calculations of power politics*' (italics mine). Total, permanent war on a global scale: Yale's contribution to US grand strategy.[56] Interestingly, the universalistic views of US national interests and security expressed by Spykman, a hard-core realist, seem quite close to the 'containment thesis' as developed by Paul Nitze in NSC-68 and applied in the disastrous war of aggression against Vietnam with the full support of Dean Rusk as secretary of state to presidents Kennedy and Johnson.

Both books received considerable praise and sold well. According to its publisher, Harcourt, Spykman's book sold almost 10,000 copies within three months. In a letter to RF, the publisher argued that even these figures failed to give 'an adequate idea' of the books' importance. The letters he received suggested an 'influence quite disproportionate to the numbers sold'. Indeed, Spykman's book, the publisher argued, 'may be considered one of the really influential books of our decade'.[57]

Isaiah Bowman, a respected foundation advisor and political geographer commented that Spykman's book ought to be read in a million American homes and at least annually by official foreign policymakers. A foundation reviewer suggested that it sold well in Washington, DC,[58] while the foundation's social sciences director wrote that it was a 'great' book that deserved 'prayerful study'. Olson and Groom argue that Spykman's book continued to be influential because it 'held great appeal for Pentagon post-war planners'.[59]

The influence of the YIIS was built also through the teaching of international relations at undergraduate and postgraduate levels, mainly through the establishment of a major in International Relations in the BA degree in 1935. YIIS researchers were expected to carry out teaching as part of their core functions. The IR major was built principally around the theme of national security and war. As the course-guide summarized it:

> War as an instrument of national policy. Preparation for war in peacetime: mobilization of national resources. The conduct of war and its problems of social control. Military, economic, political, and propaganda instruments of war.[60]

During the 1940s, the US Navy ran courses at Yale on war strategy and the 'Foundations of National Power', coordinated by Princeton's Edward Mead Earle. This particular course was also offered at five other universities, including UCLA, Northwestern, Princeton and Pennsylvania, indicating the further dissemination of this line of thought and enquiry across the United States. Inevitably, there was some student resistance to the attachment to 'power', 'force' and 'war' in these programmes at Yale, especially from students who saw IR as preparation for Christian missionary and peace-building work. As Spykman wrote in his report to RF in 1939, 'The rather realistic approach to the subject at Yale sometimes shocked their [Christians'] youthful idealism but this only occurred after their arrival, and it did not deter them from recommending the treatment to others.' As Paulo Ramos argues, 'The conversion to realism was taking place.'[61]

Student numbers in IR at Yale were modest before the war (17 in 1937–8 rising to 52 in 1939–40) but increased to 88 in 1942–3, stabilizing at about 80 after 1945. In total, Ramos estimates around 600 students in total took the major in IR at Yale from 1935 to 1951.[62] Between 1935 and 45, Yale graduated twenty-seven MA and doctoral candidates. Well-known IR alumni include Bernard C. Cohen, Lucian Pye and William C. Olson.[63] Other alumni went on to join important US foreign policy-related institutions such as the Council on Foreign Relations, the Foreign Policy Association, US Tariff Commission, the Foreign Service and the State Department.[64]

The role of the US State Department in more closely orienting the teaching of IR at Yale to the State Department's concerns is interesting. In 1944, a committee was set up to investigate 'what the educational process can do to produce good decision-makers in the field of international relations', mainly to improve the calibre of graduate students entering government service and to provide in-service training to practising diplomats.[65]

That the influence of YIIS reached much farther than the academic world was important to its foundation sponsors. Its work was respected by other foreign policy 'influentials' and by policymakers. The State Department showed by their regular liaisons how important they believed its work to be. External advisers, such as Jacob Viner and Isaiah Bowman, continued to enthuse about the institute whenever the foundation asked for an assessment. Its research centre and seminars attracted well-known academics, such as the political scientist Harold Lasswell; journalists such as Hanson Baldwin of *The New York Times*; and State Department-connected men, such as Grayson Kirk, a member of the Council on Foreign Relations' War-Peace Studies Project. By 1945, the institute was broadcasting on radio (American Broadcasting System's Blue Network) on the 'problems of peace' prior to the San Francisco Conference, with the former under-secretary of state, Summer Welles, presiding.[66] YIIS members were also engaged as consultants by the State Department at the San Francisco Conference on International Organization in 1945.[67] The YIIS contributed significantly to the diffusion of the realist paradigm in America and Europe, and helped to generate what Olson and Groom call a new 'consensus of power' in the discipline of international relations.[68]

The institute's 'independent' status also helped legitimize its views. Specifically, there was little public acknowledgement of its continuous connections with either the foundation or with the state. The institute trained hundreds of undergraduates and dozens of graduate students for state service or academia – furthering the influence of its realist approach. By 1948, YIIS began a journal, *World Politics*, and ran one of the most prestigious programmes of postgraduate research and training in America.[69] The experience of the Yale Institute demonstrates the valued place of utilitarian knowledge-production – knowledge as technology – in Rockefeller's institutional and funding culture. It explains why the 1954 Conference was organized and funded by the foundation even if its aims were to rein in somewhat the excessive realism of YIIS, which by 1951 had moved to Princeton.[70]

The 1954 Conferees' biographies

The list of 1954 Conference participants is instructive: it is a mixture of leading academics, journalists and past, serving and future public officials, representing the increasingly incestuous worlds of knowledge-construction, news and policymaking. They were, in the main, keenly interested in America's struggle against the Soviet Union and the necessity of US global leadership. This emerges as a key subtext of the entire set of conference documents available in the Rockefeller archives. Yet, the lines between the three categories of conferee ought not to be drawn too starkly: there was a 'revolving door' between the three worlds depicted above sufficient to conclude that all conferees had policymaking or at least policy-related experience. The analysis below of the conferees' biographies demonstrates this and thereby puts flesh on the Gramscian concept of state-spirited organic intellectuals. It also shows the high degree to which the conferees were interconnected or operated in elite networks.

State links: the eleven conferees were, had been or would be very well connected with US state agencies ranging from the State Department to Defense to the Central Intelligence Agency. Put slightly differently, this group comprised the sort of people who operated within the boundaries of 'thinkable thought' in American foreign and national security circles and were destined to be a part of the debate in those policy areas for decades to come, even if they opposed the Vietnam War, for example, as 'flawed', as Morgenthau did.[71] They were part of an elite (not necessarily by birth but by personal achievement) whose significance rested not just with holding public office but with their continuous proximity (in numerous institutions) to public officials and other policy influentials. Nine members of the group had over twenty-five long-term connections with various agencies of the American state related to its foreign affairs or national security. The least connected of the group to the state was journalist James Reston (*New York Times*), who had served with the Office of War Information during the Second World War. Even Reston, however, was very close to several administrations and also to Henry Kissinger, Nixon's secretary of state. His fellow journalist Walter Lippmann (*New York Herald Tribune*) had served in the Department of War during the First World War, as a member of President Wilson's Inquiry in 1917–9, and as a delegate to the Paris Peace Conference in 1919. He is considered by many to have been the most respected foreign affairs commentator of the twentieth century.[72]

Conversely, other conferees, such as Paul Nitze and Dean Rusk, had long periods of service in the state and should be regarded, therefore, as 'men of the state' in career terms. Dean Rusk, who served two terms as secretary of state, 1961–9, served four presidents. Rusk was a hawkish proponent of the Vietnam War.[73] Nitze served presidents Roosevelt, Truman and Eisenhower in the 1940s and 1950s, Kennedy and Johnson in the 1960s, Nixon and Ford in the 1970s, and President Reagan in the 1980s. He was truly a servant of the American state. As head of policy planning in Secretary Acheson's State Department, Nitze was the principal author of NSC-68, the report that called for a massive US rearmament programme – trebling the federal military budget. Nitze was also instrumental in the public promotion of NSC-68 through the formation of the Committee on the Present Danger (CPD) – a group of hawkish liberal internationalists that included James Bryant Conant, president of Harvard, and Robert Bowie, another 1954 Conference participant. The CPD masterminded among the public what NSC-68 had been used to do in the Truman administration: bludgeoned the 'mass mind' of top government, as Dean Acheson had wanted. Nitze recognized the fundamental significance of public opinion mobilization decisively to shift US national security policy.[74]

It is remarkable that six members of the group had served or were otherwise associated as advisers with the Policy Planning Staff of the State Department:

Paul Nitze (director, 1950-3), Robert Bowie (director, 1953-7), Dorothy Fosdick (1948-52), Reinhold Niebuhr (1949), Arnold Wolfers (1949) and Hans Morgenthau (1949). While out of favour after Truman, Nitze directed the Foreign Service Educational Institute, which is often referred to as the 'PPS in exile'.

> PPS serves as a source of independent policy analysis and advice for the Secretary of State. The Policy Planning Staff's mission is to take a longer term, strategic view of global trends and frame recommendations for the Secretary of State to advance U.S. interests and American values. ... In his memoirs *Present at the Creation*, former Secretary of State Dean Acheson characterized the role of Policy Planning: 'To anticipate the emerging form of things to come, to reappraise policies which had acquired their own momentum and went on after the reasons for them had ceased, and to stimulate and, when necessary, to devise basic policies crucial to the conduct of our foreign affairs.'[75]

Dorothy Fosdick, the first senior woman in a policy position in the State Department, was appointed to serve in PPS in 1948. She had previously served in the State Department's Division of Special Research, the department's first attempt at long-term planning during the Second World War. PPS was, then, an internal think tank, composed of state intellectuals with access to external advisers as required. Of the 1954 conferees, Niebuhr, Wolfers and Morgenthau had acted as advisers to PPS.

In addition to enduring and, therefore, qualitatively significant connections with agencies of the state, several conferees were also linked with other institutions closely affiliated with the foreign policy elements of the state. For example, there were at least eight members of the bipartisan Council on Foreign Relations, the establishment's core liberal internationalist think tank (Fox, Wolfers, Nitze, Reston, Niebuhr, Thompson, Rusk and Bowie). Lippmann had been a member during the 1930s. Fosdick would have worked with CFR members during her years at the Division of Special Research as that was where the CFR's War and Peace Studies were conducted.[76] Niebuhr had been a leading figure in two key CFR-organized and led pro-war ad hoc single-issue organizations in the 1940-1 period: the Committee to Defend America by Aiding the Allies (CDAAA) and the even more hawkish Fight For Freedom (FFF).[77]

Philanthropic foundation connections were also strong. Of course, RF organized and hosted the conference. Dorothy Fosdick was closely associated with the Rockefeller family which supported her father's Riverside Church in New York; her uncle, Raymond B. Fosdick, was president of RF from 1936 to 1948. Fosdick's work in the wartime State Department was closely connected with RF-backed foreign policy-planning initiatives by the Council on Foreign Relations from 1940 to 1945.[78] The Ford Foundation was represented at the conference by its vice president, Don Price, while Chicago University's Morgenthau was a long-time adviser to what is now known as the Carnegie Council on Ethics in International Affairs, but was originally known as the Church Peace Union and later the Council on Religion and International Affairs. Price went on to become the founding dean of the Kennedy School of Government at Harvard.

Most of the conferees may be characterized, or characterized themselves, as one or other form of 'realist'. Nine conferees may be so categorized: realists (Morgenthau, Lippmann, Bowie, Wolfers); realist hawks (Rusk, Nitze); liberal realists (Fox, Fosdick); Christian realist (Niebuhr). Although such a categorization is open to challenge,[79] what further bound the conferees was their underlying assumption of the importance of military force in world affairs and, particularly, in post-war US foreign policy. Most of the conferees had been, of course, early-twentieth-century Progressives – state-builders armed with a sense of the importance of state regulation, rational policymaking and even a degree of planning. Their attitude in general towards the state and their 'realistic' view of the world, therefore, both combined to focus on *state power*, helping cement their ties with the American state as the principal vehicle for global leadership.

Finally, the enduring significance of the group of 1954 conferees is *underlined* by the fact that they still had a future in their chosen field: most of them were to continue in active service for many decades, indicating the enduring character of the foreign policy elite. Paul Nitze was again instrumental in resurrecting the second incarnation of the Committee on the Present Danger in 1976 and the third in 2002/3. Nitze also served as special adviser to the president and secretary of state in the Reagan administration. Dorothy Fosdick's long association – as aide and adviser – to Henry 'Scoop' Jackson continued until his death in 1983. Upon her death in 1997, Richard Perle paid a tribute to her. The names of Reinhold Niebuhr and Hans Morgenthau, both of whom opposed the Vietnam War, were invoked on opposite sides of the bitter debates over the American war of aggression against Iraq in 2003.[80]

The 1954 Conference

The content of the Conference proceedings receives appropriate attention in the rest of this volume. My own attitude to the proceedings stems from the core concern of this chapter: to suggest that the development of academic IR (along with many other older disciplines) was part of a broader, long-term foreign policy establishment project to promote American globalism, to expand the American imperium, to usher in 'the American century'. The funding over decades of academic IR, as well as other social sciences and university area studies programs, the sponsorship of relevant think tanks and so on, as exemplified but not exhausted by YIIS above, constituted the construction of the intellectual infrastructure for globalism. Wedded as this development was to the conception of the American century, it would ultimately, but not exclusively, be evaluated according to its outcomes, its impacts on producing the kinds of knowledge American globalism was thought to 'require'. Of course, professional academics are neither pawns on a chessboard nor the playthings of elites; that is not the argument here.[81] However, when intellectual institutions and programmes are financed, when the objective structures are established at the cost of hundreds of millions of dollars, there is a high degree of 'hard-wiring' into their very being the assumptions underlying their formation as well as 'policing' through the annual report to philanthropic foundations. That is, external factors are not entirely determining in the evolution of an academic discipline, but they are very important to the kinds of scholars recruited and financed, the theories and methodologies favoured, the lines of empirical research fostered and conducted, the networks within which prestige is sought and, very significantly, the lines of enquiry that become marginal or marginalized.[82] The 1954 Conference, viewed as a small step along the road to American globalism, was in its *broadest* sense, consistent with past RF efforts. The fact that it was not especially successful or productive is beside the point: it was not the only foundation initiative, as other US philanthropies – Ford, Carnegie and even Rockefeller – were funding a whole series of initiatives at the same time (a kind of 'basket' of investments by 'venture capitalists').[83] Nevertheless, the central question of the relevance of academic theory to the practitioner was a very tough test for Morgenthau, Wolfers and Fox.

Kenneth W. Thompson, a Conference organizer and, later, a vice president of RF, reported that policymakers want 'an applicable body of theory in foreign policy'. 'Practical men with first-hand diplomatic experience point to the need for rational generalizations and intellectual structures to extract meaning from the jet stream of contemporary events', he noted.[84] In particular, Paul Nitze asked some tough questions and raised serious concerns. In his view, 'the immediate object of our foreign policy must be the fostering and elaboration of an international environment in which nations organized as we are can prosper and survive. The means to this end must be the development of the influence and power of ourselves and our friends and the reduction of the power of our enemies.'[85] (This was precisely what Nitze had argued in NSC-68: that US policy was motivated by a desire 'to foster a world environment in which the American system can flourish', arguing that that would be achieved through containment of the Soviet Union but also, 'a policy we would probably pursue even if there were no Soviet threat ... [a] policy of attempting to develop a healthy international community' of US-dominated organizations, such as the IMF, World Bank, NATO, the Marshall Plan, the Inter-American system and so on.) The policymaker, however, in trying to do this, must deal with concrete cases while the theoretician deals in generalizations and abstractions. Nitze argued that 'a wrong theory, an oversimplified theory, or a theory applied out of context can produce disastrous results'.[86]

Conversely, William Fox and Hans Morgenthau argued that while theory could not provide a blueprint for action in most concrete circumstances, it could achieve a great deal by ordering evidence: theory 'gives order and meaning to a mass of phenomena which without it would remain disconnected and unintelligible. ... [Theory] helps us to understand and distinguish the relatively fixed, the changing but controllable, and the manipulatable aspects of world politics.'[87] Theory as the basis of policy technology, in other words.

Rusk pointed out that when the Truman administration, of which he was part as Assistant Secretary of State for Far Eastern Affairs, among other posts, considered the US response to the outbreak of the Korean War, the predominant 'theory', analogy or mental image, was derived from the 1930s – that is Manchuria 1931, Abyssinia 1935 and Munich 1938 – and the consequences of appeasing aggressors.[88] Thompson's conclusion to this was to suggest that practitioners' 'judgement and wisdom' often results from 'a pragmatic conception of theory' which, he argues, augurs well for continued and 'wider contacts between theorists and practitioners'. Both theorists and practitioners, he argues, each in their own language, accept that ideas and theories must be 'tested' against experience. They just needed to be more creative in their interactions.[89]

Conclusion

The immediate benefits of the 1954 Conference probably disappointed the participants. Certainly, Paul Nitze stated that he and his colleagues in Policy Planning felt 'that much of the contemporary academic work in the theory of international politics fell between two stools. It did not have sufficient depth in philosophic insight to give much light on the question of the long-range content of our national purpose and on the other hand much of it failed to meet the test of being relevant to the realm of possible action.'[90] Yet, benefits there were, including making practitioners and academics more aware of each others' roles and problems, dissecting theory-production and possible usages, introducing the complexity and difficulties inherent in crisis decision-making into academic theorizing, and suggesting ways forward to more fruitful future dialogue. Of course, one of the by-products of the Conference on its academic participants was a greater understanding of practitioners' dilemmas – in a nuclear world – and the filtering down of that understanding to colleagues, graduate students and so on. Nitze also – understandably from his experience of selling NSC-68 through the Committee on the Present Danger – called for greater academic attention to 'public opinion and [specifically] in reducing the area of conflict between public understanding on the one hand and rational consideration of the national interest on the other'.[91]

More concretely, participants suggested a number of initiatives to RF to try to improve work in the theory/practice nexus: more seminars, subsidies to retired professors to write theoretical work in IR as doctoral candidates usually wrote empirical theses; subsidies to university presses to encourage them to publish more theoretical work despite low demand; and the possibility of month-long summer meetings between academics and foreign policy practitioners in Washington, DC, to continue the 1954 dialogue.[92]

In the longer term, the 1954 Conference may be seen as an attempt at initiating a major boost for organized discussion of IR theory in the United States and Britain. For example, Rockefeller followed up 1954 by funding a symposium on IR theorizing in 1957, the book from which published the papers of several 1954 Conference participants – Nitze, Morgenthau, Fox, Wolfers, Niebuhr – and also Kenneth N. Waltz (Swarthmore College) and Charles P. Kindleberger (MIT). In addition, participants in 1957 included Bernard Barber, Arno J. Mayer, Warner Schilling, Kenneth W. Thompson, Robert W. Tucker and Martin Wight.[93] In 1959, a Rockefeller grant, prompted by its vice president Kenneth Thompson, supported the formation of the British Committee on the Theory of International Politics, while in 1961 Fox, Morgenthau, Thompson and Quincy Wright participated in a conference at the University of Maryland entitled 'The Role of Theory in International Relations'.[94] Interestingly, Tim Dunne suggests – citing Thompson – that the American IR theory group largely failed to achieve much beyond a couple of meetings due to 'deep divisions' between foreign policymakers and academics.[95]

Ultimately, the discussions between scholarly *theorists* and policymakers are likely to be frustrating due to the differing ends of each. Nitze expressed an essential belief among 'practical men' about the limitations of theory.[96] As Lewis Coser argues,

> The relationship between power and intellect usually proved to be unstable. The general tension between the intellectuals' preoccupation with general and abstract values and the routine institutions of society asserted itself. Intellectuals tended to turn in disdain from the practical concerns of decision-makers immersed in day-to-day compromise and adjustments, and men of power were wary of what they called the impracticality and the lack of realism of intellectuals. Power holders and intellectuals have ... [enjoyed] ... short periods of honeymoon, but no stable union has ever been achieved.[97]

It is unsurprising, then, that RF's IR theory initiative – proposed by Rusk – faded away with the escalation of the Vietnam War, which was famously opposed by the realist Hans Morgenthau. For the foundation, however, the 1930s and 1940s development of IR may have achieved at least a key part of its original purpose: to place at the very centre of scholarly thinking the importance of power and violence in world affairs,[98] the centrality of the state and, specifically, of US state leadership – a hegemonic power to replace Britain – and the need, therefore, for the political class and people of the United States to accept those basic facts. Thereafter, the most pressing need may have been for scholars engaged in empirical IR and, particularly, foreign area studies, who furnished voluminous empirical studies and developed powerful knowledge networks between the United States and the world's strategic nations and regions.[99] As Morgenthau noted in 1952,

> Practical needs ... still provide one of the major arguments in favour of area studies; they are also apparent in the selection of the areas most frequently studied. Russia and the Far East vie with Latin America ... with those areas that American foreign policy is primarily concerned ... . Aside from the training of prospective government officials, area studies are frequently motivated by the recognition of America's predominant place in world affairs, which ... entails the desire to learn all the facts about all regions of the world.[100]

In addition, there was great demand for *economists* in the bid for US hegemony to work with 'developing' the economies of newly independent Third World countries such as Indonesia, India and Pakistan in the heat of Cold War ideological competition.[101] Olson and Groom note that the post-war period witnessed the emergence of 'a "paper triangle" between academic entrepreneurs, the great foundations, and the national security establishment. The principal effect ... was to stress regional [country and area] and strategic studies.'[102] As ever, where the major foundations had made the initial investment, the federal government followed: the 1958 National Defense Education Act poured millions of dollars into area studies over the next twenty years, generating impressive advances in university foreign language teaching, new professional associations and conferences, and so on. As a Social Science Research Council survey showed in 1973, 'The centers and their faculties provide a repository of expertise on which government can and does draw for research, consultants, or temporary employment .... The government also uses these centers for the training of current employees.'[103] The Cold War university, then, served as a vehicle for the promotion of US hegemony.[104]

The 1954 Conference brought together some of the most significant elites in IR, the policy world and foreign affairs journalism. This was no random group but a subset of the confluence of elite forces identified by Olson and Groom. As individuals, they had already made a mark in American life: most of them continued for several decades to do so. The role of the major American philanthropic foundations was to foster a fairly narrow spectrum of intellectual developments in academic empirical research, theory and methodology with the ultimate underlying aim of promoting American hegemony. That the IR theory programme was not particularly successful shows that foundation and other elites do not always get what they want. But what the programme does show are the underlying principles for funding specific IR and other similar initiatives. Foundations provide the 'seed corn' for new initiatives and finance the seminars and conferences between leading scholars, policymakers and other elites. They finance knowledge networks – the intellectual infrastructure – that might generate new and useful ideas, new information or new perspectives that would practically benefit policymakers, as well as useful knowledge. Sometimes they fail, sometimes they produce unintended consequences. Much of the time, they succeed in generating large university programmes dedicated to research, teaching and training, with scholars fully networked with state elites, that directly and indirectly benefit American hegemony.

Notes

1 Extracts from NSC-68, 'United States Objectives and Programs for National Security', the April 1950 seminal Cold War blueprint, the main author of which was Paul Nitze.
2 Ibid.
3 Seymour Melman, *A Permanent War Economy* (New York: Simon & Schuster, 1985).
4 Richard Jackson, *Writing the War on Terrorism* (Manchester: Manchester University Press, 2005). For analysis of the Cold War equivalent, see David Campbell, *Writing Security* (Manchester: Manchester University Press, 1998). This is not to suggest that there was no such thing as a 'Soviet threat' or that there is no 'terrorist threat' today; it

is merely to argue that the threats were/are much exaggerated for political purposes, providing profound legitimacy for America's global expansionism. For analysis of the US' wartime planning for global expansion, *before* there was any 'Soviet threat', see Laurence H. Shoup and William Minter, *Imperial Brain Trust* (New York: Monthly Review Press, 1977), and Inderjeet Parmar, *Think Tanks and Power in Foreign Policy* (Basingstoke: Palgrave Macmillan, 2004).

5 Gabriel A. Almond, 'Area Studies and the Objectivity of the Social Sciences', in *Ventures in Political Science* (Boulder: Lynne Rienner, 2002), 109–30.

6 Indeed, the overall stated aim of NSC-68 recognizes a desire 'to foster a world environment in which the American system can flourish', arguing that that would be achieved through containment of the Soviet Union but also 'a policy we would probably pursue even if there were no Soviet threat … [a] policy of attempting to develop a healthy international community' of US-dominated organizations, such as the IMF, World Bank, NATO, the Marshall Plan, the Inter-American system and so on; NSC-68. As Thomas G. Paterson argues, the Truman administration exaggerated the Soviet threat to justify 'its own expansionism' and desire to 'practice global interventionism' for decades; Paterson, *Major Problems in American Foreign Policy Volume II: Since 1914* (Lexington: D.C. Heath & Co., 1989), 352.

7 Henry 'Scoop' Jackson was Democratic congressman and senator for Washington, 1941–1983 and mentor to the likes of Richard Perle, Douglas Feith and Paul Wolfowitz.

8 IR was not alone, however, as a discipline in part designed to serve elite interests: there were similar factors at work in other social sciences such as political science, area studies and economics; see, for example, Ido Orren, *Our Enemies and US: America's Rivalries and the Making of Political Science* (Ithaca: Cornell University Press, 2003).

9 For works on the history, politics and culture of the American foreign policy establishment, see Richard J. Barnett, *Roots of War* (Baltimore: Penguin, 1973); Priscilla Roberts, '"All the Right People": The Historiography of the American Foreign Policy Establishment', *Journal of American Studies* 26, no. 3 (1992): 409–34; Parmar, *Think Tanks and Power*; Shoup and Minter, *Imperial Brain Trust*. Of course, not all realists believed in US global hegemony – and Morgenthau is an example – but a very large proportion of realism's founders did.

10 That this was part of a broader concern among American east coast elites is evidenced by Henry Kissinger's Harvard International Seminar, designed to convince foreign elites of the depth of US national culture and, thereby, the credibility of US power; see Inderjeet Parmar, 'Challenging Elite Anti-Americanism in the Cold War: American Foundations, Kissinger's Harvard Seminar and the Salzburg Seminar in American Studies', *Traverse* 1 (2006): 116–29.

11 Antonio Gramsci, *Selections from the Prison Notebooks of Antonio Gramsci*, eds and trans. Quentin Hoare and Geoffrey Nowell-Smith (London: Lawrence & Wishart, 1971); Enrico Augelli and Craig Murphy, *America's Quest for Supremacy and the Third World: A Gramscian Analysis* (London: Pinter Publishers, 1988); Inderjeet Parmar, '"To Relate Knowledge and Action": The Impact of the Rockefeller Foundation on Foreign Policy Thinking during America's Rise to Globalism', *Minerva* 40, no. 3 (2002): 235–63; Inderjeet Parmar, *Foundations of the American Century: The Ford, Carnegie, and Rockefeller Foundations in the Rise of American Power* (New York: Columbia University Press, 2012).

12 An excellent example of this is the RF's funding of the Council on Foreign Relations' War and Peace Studies Project, 1940–45, which helped not only increase state planning capacity but also develop a sense of America's post-war ambitions for global hegemony (which included international institution-building, particularly the United Nations). What this shows is that foundation funds were used to construct a sense of national interests that would, in part, be realized through international organizations, mistakenly often seen as the preserve of 'idealist' Wilsonians; see Shoup and Minter, *Imperial Brain Trust*.

13 Robert F. Arnove, ed., *Philanthropy and Cultural Imperialism* (Boston: GK Hall, 1980); Inderjeet Parmar, 'Foundation Networks and American Hegemony', *European Journal of American Studies* 7, no. 1 (2012) (online).

14 Inderjeet Parmar, 'The Carnegie Corporation and the Mobilisation of Opinion in the United States' Rise to Globalism', *Minerva* 37, no. 4 (1999): 355–78.

15 William E. Leuchtenberg, 'Progressivism and Imperialism', *Mississippi Valley Historical Review* 39, no. 3 (1952): 483–504; Robert H. Wiebe, *The Search for Order, 1877–1920* (Westport: Greenwood Press, 1980).

16 Eldon J. Eisenach, *The Lost Promise of Progressivism* (Lawrence: University Press of Kansas, 1994).

17 Emily S. Rosenberg, *Spreading the American Dream* (New York: Hill & Wang, 1982).

18 Godfrey Hodgson, 'The Establishment', *Foreign Policy* 9 (1972–1973): 3–40.

19 Lewis Coser, *Men of Ideas* (New York: Free Press, 1965), 339. Coser names Dean Rusk, Dean Acheson and John Foster Dulles as examples of the interconnections of foundation heads and the American state; ibid., 339.

20 Nelson W. Polsby, 'Foreign Policy Establishment Moves to Middle', *Public Affairs Report* 34, no. 1 (1993).

21 Max Holland, 'The American Establishment', *The Wilson Quarterly* 15 (1991): 26.

22 Karl Marx, quoted by Ralph Miliband, *The State in Capitalist Society* (London: Quartet Books, 1984), 162–3. Marx further noted that 'the class which is the ruling material force of society, is at the same time its ruling intellectual force'.

23 Inderjeet Parmar, 'Engineering Consent: The Carnegie Endowment for International Peace and the Mobilisation of American Public Opinion, 1939–1945', *Review of International Studies* 26, no. 1 (2000): 35–48. The consent of the governed is 'organized … . The State does have and request consent, but it also "educates" this consent, by means of the political and syndical associations; these, however', Gramsci concludes, 'are private organisms, left to … private initiative', quoted in Inderjeet Parmar, *Think Tanks and Power*.

24 Clyde W. Barrow, *Universities and the Capitalist State: Corporate Liberalism and the Reconstruction of American Higher Education, 1894–1928* (Madison: University of Wisconsin Press, 1990).

25 Gramsci, *Prison Notebooks*, 146–7. The eighteenth-century conservative political theorist, Edmund Burke, noted that a key part of the state's stability was derived from a partnership 'not only between those who are living, but between those who are living, those who are dead, and those who are to be born'; see his *Reflections on the Revolution in France* (London: Penguin Books, 1986 [1790]), 194–5.

26 Gramsci, *Prison Notebooks*, 16.

27 It is clear, however, that YIIS was not the only IR initiative sponsored by the Rockefeller and Carnegie foundations: see Inderjeet Parmar, *Edward Meade Earle and the Rise of Realism in the United States Academy*, Manchester Papers in Politics, paper 3/01 (2001), Department of Government, University of Manchester.

28 William C. Olson and A. J. R. Groom, *International Relations Then and Now* (London: Routledge, 1991), 75–6.
29 David C. Engermann, 'New Society, New Scholarship: Soviet Studies Programmes in Interwar America', *Minerva* 37, no. 1 (1999): 25–43.
30 RFA, RG1.1 series 200 200S Yale University – International Relations, box 416, folder 4941; funding notes, 17 May 1935 and 16 May 1941.
31 Neutrality Acts were passed in 1935, 1936, 1937 and 1939. At the same time, movements to revise those laws also began; see Mark L. Chadwin, *The Hawks of World War II* (Chapel Hill: UNC Press, 1968); Parmar, 'Engineering Consent'.
32 See Yale Institute Annual Report, 1942 in RFA, RG1.1 series 200 200S Yale University – International Relations, box 417, folder 4957.
33 RFA; see Inter-Office memo by J.H. Willits, 29 February 1940; letter, Frederick S. Dunn (director of YIIS) to Willits, 2 June 1941; letter, Dunn to Willits, 11 August 1944; and YIIS annual report, 1938–1939, 3; all in boxes 416 and 417, folders 4944, 4947 and 4955. See also, William T. R. Fox, *The American Study of International Relations* (Columbia: University of South Carolina Press, 1966) for the policy-oriented character of YIIS, of which Fox was a member.
34 Olson and Groom, *International Relations*, 99.
35 RFA, box 416, folder 4944, memo, 'Yale University – Research in International Relations', 6 March 1940.
36 Figures compiled from annual reports and other internal RF sources.
37 RFA, box 416, folder 4944, memo, 29 February 1940. According to Fox, Dunn's motive, to advance practical knowledge to enhance US national security, was what ensured foundation support. The RF's director of the Division of Social Sciences, Joseph H. Willits, wrote that Spykman's ideas showed wisdom, maturity, 'hard-headedness, realism and scholarly standards'; quoted in Olson and Groom, *International Relations*, 50–1.
38 YIIS annual report, 1942, 3–4.
39 Ibid., 1–4; emphasis mine.
40 Inderjeet Parmar, 'Chatham House and the Anglo-American Alliance, 1939–1945', *Diplomacy and Statecraft* 3, no. 1 (2007): 23–47; Inderjeet Parmar, *Special Interests, the State, and the Anglo-American Alliance, 1939–1945* (London: Taylor & Francis, 1995).
41 RFA, memo, 'A Security Policy for Postwar America', 8 March 1945, in box 417, folder 4948.
42 See review, 'The Gyroscope of Pan-Americanism', November 1943, in box 416, folder 4946. Written by the historian Samuel Flagg Bemis, it was entitled *The Latin American Policy of the United States* and was published in 1943. The book, as described by a foundation reviewer, was 'readable and provocative'. Bemis claimed that US policy towards Latin America was a benevolent, or 'protective imperialism, designed to protect, first the security of the Continental Republic, … and the security of the entire New World, against intervention by the imperialistic powers of the Old World'. It was, he continued, 'an imperialism against imperialism. It did not last long and it was not really bad'.
43 Quoted by Paulo Ramos, 'The Role of the YIIS in the Construction of United States National Security Ideology, 1935–1951' (PhD diss., University of Manchester, 2003), 169.
44 Kenneth W. Thompson, *Masters of International Thought* (Baton Rouge: Louisiana State University Press, 1980), 98.
45 Ramos, 'Role of the YIIS', 165.
46 Ibid., 166.

47 Quoted by Ramos, 'Role of the YIIS', 167.
48 RFA, box 417, folder 4947.
49 RFA, YIIS annual report, 1941–1942, 18–19, 25.
50 RFA, YIIS annual report, 1945–1946.
51 RFA, YIIS annual report, 1943, 14–15.
52 Louis Morton, 'National Security and Area Studies. The Intellectual Response to the Cold War', *Journal of Higher Education*, 34, no. 2 (1963): 142–7.
53 See David Reynolds, *Britannia Overruled: British Policy and World Power in the Twentieth Century* (London: Longman, 1991), 173; also Olson and Groom, *International Relations*, 100.
54 Almond, 'Area Studies', 2. Almond was a member of YIIS.
55 John A. Thompson, 'Another Look at the Downfall of "Fortress America"', *Journal of American Studies* 26, no. 3, (1992): 401.
56 See Ramos, 'Role of the YIIS', 267.
57 RFA, box 416, folder 4945; Lambert Davis (Harcourt, Brace) to George W. Gray (RF). (So influential that it was also produced in Braille).
58 RFA, box 416, folder 4945.
59 Olson and Groom, *International Relations*, 99, fn. 49.
60 Ramos, 'Role of the YIIS', 240.
61 Spykman, quoted in Ramos, 'Role of the YIIS', 242.
62 Ramos, 'Role of the YIIS', 243.
63 Appendix C, in ibid., 372.
64 Ibid., 243.
65 Ibid., 245.
66 RFA, box 417, folder 4948; 'Radio Program Notice', 6 April 1945.
67 That YIIS members were so engaged with the UN's formation correctly suggests that the fledgling international organization was seen, at least in part, as a potential instrument of American power; see Shoup and Minter, *Imperial Brain Trust*; Robert Hilderbrand, *Dumbarton Oaks: The Origins of the UN and the Search for Postwar Security* (Chapel Hill: University of North Carolina Press, 1990).
68 Olson and Groom, *International Relations*, 106–11.
69 Olson and Groom claim that the publication of this journal was 'one of the most significant events in the history of the field [of international relations]'; ibid., 118.
70 The move to Princeton followed the inauguration in 1950 of A. Whitney Griswold as president of Yale. Griswold was opposed to YIIS' policy-oriented work and, especially its advocacy of globalism. Griswold also had a number of personal differences with Frederick Dunn; see Ramos, 'The Role of the YIIS'.
71 It is important here to recall that Morgenthau supported the view that the Soviet 'threat' drove US national security policy, that it was an authentic threat requiring 'containment', but felt that it was inappropriately, and badly, applied in Asia; see his 'We are deluding ourselves in Vietnam', *New York Times Magazine*, 18 April 1965, and 'Another "Great Debate": The National Interest of the United States', *American Political Science Review* 46, no. 4 (1952): 961–88. To be sure, such sentiments placed Morgenthau close to the boundaries of 'thinkable thought' but still within them; see Noam Chomsky, *Towards a New Cold War* (New York: Pantheon Books, 1982), 74.
72 Thompson, *Masters of International Thought*.
73 Warren I. Cohen, *Dean Rusk* (Totowa: Cooper Square, 1980).
74 Jerry W. Sanders, *Peddlers of Crisis: The Committee on the Present Danger and the Politics of Containment* (London: Pluto Press, 1983).

75 See www.state.gov/s/p/ (accessed 2 November 2007).
76 Shoup and Minter, *Imperial Brain Trust*.
77 Chadwin, *The Hawks of World War II*.
78 Inderjeet Parmar, *Think Tanks and Power*.
79 'Realism' is not an uncontested term or categorization: there are political realists, liberal realists, defensive realists, offensive realists, neo-realists, democratic realists, structural realists, among others. The core of realism, though, is the recognition that power is central to international affairs and that whatever our ethical position or values may be, without understanding the structure and dynamics of power in the world, a realist foreign policy or a realistic understanding of the world is impossible. On those grounds, men like Rusk and Nitze are 'offensive realists' in practice, maximizers of American power attempting to ensure its global hegemony. For the most developed version of offensive realism, see John J. Mearsheimer, *The Tragedy of Great Power Politics* (New York: W.W. Norton, 2001), and Robert Jervis, *American Foreign Policy in a New Era* (New York and London: Routledge, 2004). For an interesting history of the misrepresentation of protagonists in the great debates of IR, see Miles Kahler, 'Inventing International Relations: International Relations Theory After 1945', in *New Thinking in International Relations Theory*, eds M. W. Doyle and G. John Ikenberry (Boulder: Westview, 1997), 20–53.
80 John J. Mearsheimer, 'Hans Morgenthau and the Iraq War: Realism versus Neo-Conservatism', *Open Democracy*, 19 May 2005, https://www.opendemocracy.net/democracy-americanpower/morgenthau_2522.jsp (last accessed 17 October 2018); Joseph Loconte, 'The War Party's Theologian', *Wall Street Journal*, 31 May 2002, https://www.wsj.com/articles/SB1022803059822162800 (last accessed 17 October 2018).
81 For an argument that challenges this interpretation, Brian C. Schmidt, 'International Relations and the Search for the Authority of Knowledge', unpublished presentation notes for paper at *The Rise of International Relations Theory 1945–1955* International Workshop, Rockefeller Archive Center, Tarrytown, NY, 24–5 September 2007.
82 Coser argues that foundations are 'important gatekeepers of ideas. With the power of the purse, they are in positions to foster certain ideas or lines of inquiry while neglecting or de-emphasizing others'; *Men of Ideas*, 339; Kahler, 'Inventing International Relations'.
83 Warren Weaver, ed., *US Philanthropic Foundations* (New York: Harper & Row, 1967).
84 Kenneth W. Thompson, 'Toward a Theory of International Politics', *American Political Science Review* 49, no. 3 (1955): 733. This is a direct quotation from Dean Rusk's opening remarks at the 1954 conference: Conference on International Politics, Washington DC, 7–8 May 1954, in RF, RG 3, series 910, box 8, folder 70.
85 Quoted by Thompson, 'Toward a Theory of International Politics', 744, fn. 22.
86 Ibid., 738.
87 Ibid., 735.
88 Rusk stated that 'in the State Department with regard to the Korea situation, their general policy was based a good deal on what they had learned about aggression in the last 25 years'; Conference on International Politics, 7–8 May 1954, in RF, RG 3, series 910, box 8, folder 70, 24.
89 Thompson, 'Toward a Theory of International Politics', 739.
90 Paul Nitze, 'The Implications of Theory for Practice in the Conduct of Foreign Affairs', paper presented at the Conference on International Politics, 7–8 May 1954, in RF, RG 3, series 910, box 8, folder 69.

91 Ibid., 5.
92 Conference on International Politics, 7–8 May 1954, in RF, RG 3, series 910, box 8, folder 70, 42–4; Arnold Wolfers, 'Theory of International Politics: Its Merits and Advancement', RF, RG 3, series 910, box 8, folder 69, 7.
93 William T. R. Fox, ed., *Theoretical Aspects of International Relations* (Notre Dame: University of Notre Dame Press, 1959), x.
94 Schmidt, 'International Relations'; see also Horace V. Harrison, ed., *The Role of Theory in International Relations* (Princeton: Van Nostrand, 1964), the book of the 1961 conference.
95 Tim Dunne, *Inventing International Society: A History of the English School* (Basingstoke: Macmillan, 1998), 90.
96 The same appears to be the case today. As Stanley A. Renshon argues, 'There is [a] substantial gap between the contributions of professional international theory and research and the necessity of actual judgements under uncertainty'; see his 'Premature Obituary: The Future of the Bush Doctrine', in *Understanding the Bush Doctrine*, eds Stanley A. Renshon and Peter Suedfeld (New York: Routledge, 2007), 293.
97 Coser, *Men of Ideas*, 135–6. The sociologist Robert Merton put it more strongly when he suggested that 'the union of policy-makers and intellectuals tends to be nasty, brutish and short'; quoted by ibid., 140.
98 Olson and Groom argue that 'power' constituted the mainstream IR consensus by the 1950s, even if the self-same scholars backed the UN Charter; see their *International Relations*, ch. 6 (104–34).
99 Inderjeet Parmar, 'American Foundations and the Development of International Knowledge Networks', *Global Networks* 2, no. 1 (2002): 13–30.
100 Morgenthau, quoted by Immanuel Wallerstein, 'The Unintended Consequences of Cold War Area Studies', in *The Cold War and the University*, eds N. Chomsky, L. Nader, I. Wallerstein, R. C. Lewontin and R. Ohmann (New York: The New Press, 1997), 207–8.
101 George Rosen, *Western Economists and Eastern Societies* (Baltimore: Johns Hopkins University Press, 1985).
102 Olson and Groom, *International Relations*, 106.
103 SSRC survey, quoted in Wallerstein, 'The Unintended Consequences of Cold War Area Studies', 209–10.
104 This development was hardly new; see Carol S. Gruber, *Mars and Minerva: World War I and the Uses of Higher Learning in America* (Baton Rouge: Louisiana State University Press, 1975).

Chapter 11

CIRCUMVENTING IMPERIALISM: THE GLOBAL ECONOMY IN LATIN AMERICAN SOCIAL SCIENCES

Margarita Fajardo

Despite the absence of formal empires, Latin American social scientists produced ideas that were, nonetheless, particularly evocative of imperialism. After the end of the Second World War, the rise of United States as a hegemonic power swiftly transformed matters of economic and political hemispheric cooperation into problems of partaking in a global order. The tension between internationalism and national autonomy that marked the economic debates of the post-war era catalysed a novel intellectual endeavour in Latin America. Closer than any other region to the emerging hegemon, regional social scientists struggled to establish the subtle yet significant distinctions between imperial and global orders. The result of these efforts was 'dependency theory', Latin America's major conceptual contribution to the global social sciences.

The enterprise of development, the quintessential post-war project for the global South, became a fertile ground for regional intellectuals to conceptualize global capitalism from the vantage point of Latin America. In the aftermath of the Great Depression, Latin America's large economies embarked on a process of industrialization via import substitution that, by the end of the war, was imagined as the new path to economic development. Unlike the United States or Europe, Latin America recovered rapidly from the global crisis.[1] While the relative importance of its traditional primary product export sector declined, the new industrial sector became the engine of economic growth. Thus, regional social scientists began to explore the possibilities and limits of industrial capitalism in the context of regional and global market re-integration after the war, leading to new formulations about the intersection of capitalism and imperialism.

Rather than a stage in the process of capital accumulation, Latin American social scientists defined underdevelopment as a functional relation between the region and the global economy. They produced and mobilized concepts such as centre-periphery, external vulnerability and dependency to characterize an asymmetrical relation that shaped the region's development process. These concepts gained traction among government officials, policymakers and intellectuals creating a particular lexicon to imagine Latin America as region, intervene on its path to development and transform its position in the global order. Grouped under the term *structuralism*, ideas and theories using the lexicon of imbalances, heterogeneity and bottlenecks became pervasive in the economic debate during the first quarter-century of the post-war period.[2] The United Nations Economic Commission for Latin America (ECLA in English and CEPAL in Spanish and Portuguese) was the institutional fulcrum of this intellectual project.

Since this moment of social scientific effervescence in the region coincided with the emergence of the United States as the dominant world power, the political implications of the lexicon seemed plain. As the region south of the US border, Latin America was for all intents and purposes under the aegis of the new hegemon, either as its 'area of influence' or as an 'informal empire'.[3] In the transition from Great Britain to the United States, Latin American countries were just switching direction from one centre of power to the next. The mushrooming of anti-colonization and nationalist movements worldwide further coloured the aforementioned concepts with anti-imperial and even anti-capitalist undertones. Yet, Latin American social scientists were profoundly aware of Robinson and Gallagher's proverbial sentence: they, just like imperial historians, were 'very much at the mercy of [their] own particular concept of empire'.[4]

While they advanced notions to capture the phenomenon of global domination, *cepalinos* and the social scientists of their network circumvented imperialism. By focusing on the national sway of foreign aid and expertise, scholars have squared development initiatives worldwide with imperialism. The modernization endeavour of the global North – from river valley infrastructure projects to the green revolution initiatives, from multilateral loans to economic missions – were the continuation of older forms of domination.[5] Even when looking at initiatives stemming from the global South, scholars have placed national development projects and their advocates as local agents in the expansion of Western civilization and capitalism. In the wake of the Cuban Revolution, *cepalinos* and development experts were accused of complicity with imperial projects in reproducing underdevelopment. Neither compliant with, nor oblivious to, imperial pursuits, *cepalinos* provide a story about development from the global South.[6] With a global institution as their fulcrum and economic development as their goal, *cepalinos* catalysed an intellectual endeavour to reclaim development as a project *from* and *for* Latin America while exploring the contradictions of capitalism in the periphery. In the process, they fostered a regional social science and created a new notion of Latin America.

Latin American social scientists undertook the inescapable, though often overlooked, process of thinking globally while defining a regional economic unit. The 'region' and the 'world' were an inseparable pair in the post-war moment at both the intellectual and the policy levels. In the process of knowledge production, regional economic problems came to be identified as the product of an economic structure that was in turn the result of the region's functional relation to the global economy. As a guideline for action, social scientists and policymakers advocated guiding foreign capital and deepening global integration – with all its costs and contradictions – as a means to further industrialization and development. As they dealt with development and stability, regional and global dimensions, they advanced notions to capture the phenomenon of domination while circumventing the problem of empire.

This chapter is a first step to unravel why the most influential Latin American social scientists of the post-war period were so evocative of imperialism yet so reluctant to adopt such framework altogether. Therefore, it turns to the analysis of the context and process of production of two concepts that shaped Latin American social sciences in the post-war period: centre-periphery and dependency. I show here the theoretical questions, policy endeavours and global institutional framework driving the formulation of centre-periphery concept in the early post-war period, first, and of dependency in the mid-1960s, later. I demonstrate how in the transition from centre-periphery to dependency, Latin American social scientists confronted, both in practice and in theory, the limits and contradictions of national development projects within a hegemonic yet multilateral and institutionalized American global order. Therefore, they were forced to reconsider their own ability to grasp the entangled aspects of development and imperialism.

Centre-Periphery and the American global order

When Argentine economist Raúl Prebisch used the notion of centre and peripheries to characterize the position of Latin America in the global economy during CEPAL's second session in 1949, he launched a new intellectual project in the region. Professor, economic advisor and Argentina's former Central Bank manager, Prebisch used the notion to denounce the unequal gains from trade between industrialized centres and the producers of primary products and raw materials in the periphery. Based on this denunciation, he advocated for the industrialization of the periphery and the financial and economic cooperation of the world economic centre.

During the 1930s, Prebisch was forced to deal with the detrimental effects on growth due to restricted trade and declining export prices. If previous booms in commodity prices had fostered accumulation of capital for decades of what came to be known as 'outward looking development', the bust proved devastating, giving rise to what *cepalino* economists called 'inward-looking development'. For Argentina, like other countries with a pre-existing industrial base such as Mexico, Chile and Brazil, the restriction on imports encouraged the internal production of manufactured products to supply the internal market. Such process and period came to be known as import-substitution industrialization (ISI).[7]

Besides experimenting with innovative countercyclical policies during his Central Bank years, Prebisch accumulated experiences that would shape his interpretation of the relation between economic development and the position of Latin America in the world economy. Monetary and exchange controls served as a countercyclical policy to offset the effects of downwards turns. The need to deal with the cyclical nature of capitalist expansion through international cooperation measures such as price stabilization agreements, market quota distributions or development aid would drive Prebisch's entire career.[8] As a result, Prebisch conceptualized an interpretation of the region's development trajectory based on the unequal effect of business cycles on the centre and at the periphery of global capitalism.

This conceptualization of Latin America and its economic development in terms of centre-periphery relations was not unique. Like Prebisch, many economists and policymakers of his generation confronted first-hand the effects of declining prices, scarcity of foreign reserves, and the absence of internal savings to counteract the absence of foreign capital flows. The policymaking experience of the Depression and the war years made their mark on the region's social scientists.[9] When the British and American plans for what became the Bretton Woods institutions were introduced in 1943, Latin Americans voiced their concerns about the prospects of development within the new global order along the lines Prebisch would years later immortalize.

Both at the actual conference in Bretton Woods and in regional journals and conferences, Latin American economists highlighted the dependence of the region's development on external economic conditions. 'Our economic prosperity depends on the level of economic activity of the industrialized countries', said Víctor Urquidi, the technical advisor to the Mexican delegation.[10] Eugênio Gudin, prominent Brazilian economist and member of the Brazilian delegation argued, 'These economies, whose principal and perhaps sole export products were agricultural and mineral goods, are precisely characterized by being "reflexive economies" whose path follows that of the leading ones.' Thus, 'depression in the leading economies have direct effects over *reflexive* economies whereas disturbances in the latter have hardly no effect in the former', said Gudin.[11] In the same vein, Jorge Chávez, Peruvian delegate to Bretton Woods conference, claimed that specialization in a 'few export commodities', made the 'effects of world depressions deeper' and 'of a different character' than those experienced by 'large industrialized nations'.[12] The subordinate position in the international political economy was registered as a result of the structure of production. The 'derivative' nature of the region's growth, as the Mexican delegate claimed, was to be ultimately altered by industrialization.

Much like their counterparts of the global North, the interwar years had shaped the perceptions and aspirations of the region's policymakers regarding the postwar order. What regional economists and policymakers wanted was to avoid another depression. Nonetheless, within Latin America, avoiding depression was not a matter of domestic policy. Rather it rested on what Gudin called the leading economies and Prebisch would call the principal cyclical centre. Economic growth required regular export proceeds to finance the machinery and parts required by ISI. Given the restrictions on demand for their products during the Depression and of supply of capital goods and intermediary products for industrialization during the war years, Latin Americans were increasingly concerned about the prospect of economic development in the new American global order.

In fact, most were concerned about the ability of the United States to adequately replace Britain in such a role. The Peruvian delegate argued that the prosperity of 'small, primary producing countries' relied on the ability of the large countries to import as Britain had done in the past.[13] Prebisch later echoed this concern. Despite becoming the world's financial centre, the United States had not increased imports from the rest of the world nor had it expanded its capital exports, jeopardizing not only monetary stability but world economic growth.[14] What the rest of the world needed from the United States as global hegemon was larger and more stable markets and more financial investments abroad. By the end of the war, Latin Americans were sceptical about the abilities of the rising hegemonic power more than about the prospects of global domination per se.

The early post-war years confirmed the fears of Latin American economists and policymakers. Although the United States lifted price controls, international trade on industrial goods occurred mainly among developed economies. Since the United States maintained the wartime price of regional export products that were militarily strategic, countries like Chile continued to receive lower revenues. With the acquisition of machinery and equipment, the region's foreign exchange reserves, accumulated during the war, depleted rapidly. The need for more export proceeds to finance the industrialization process became even more pressing, making the global dollar shortage the crux of the problem.

The institutional framework of the United Nations put in place after the war offered a forum to voice the regional concerns with and within the global economic order. In early 1947, two regional commissions, one for Europe and one for Asia – the two areas physically devastated by the war – were created within the United Nations organization. For the Chilean delegate to the UN, Hernán Santa Cruz, as for many of the regional policymakers, Latin America had also endured the war toll. It had been devastated by the economic effects of the war and had contributed to the war effort via controlled, subsidized prices of its export products. Thus, the Chilean delegate proposed the establishment of an economic commission for Latin America to deal with economic development in the context of post-war reconstruction. Through the proposal, the Chilean delegate hoped to get down to some of the problems that the new global order aspired but had so far failed to redress.

To prove the need for the regional body within the global institution, Santa Cruz and the Latin American representatives and advisers defended a new view of Latin America and its economic problems. The 'region', said the Cuban delegate, was precisely defined by its 'colonial' relationship to the world economy. The scarcity of foreign exchange, especially of dollars, stemmed from their specialization as producers of raw materials and importers of manufactured products. That such specialization defined Latin American economies was reinforced by an economic report produced by the UN Secretariat and its Department of Economic Affairs. It was at the 'international trade level', the report stated, that 'Latin America's most typical characteristics reveal themselves'. Such characteristics make 'these economies particularly vulnerable to global shocks and present circumstances dependent on conditions and policies outside their control'.[15] It was Latin America's position in the global economy and its relations with the rest of the world that created obstacles to industrialization and development and therefore required global intervention.

The pursuit of industrialization and 'inward-looking development' did not foreclose Latin America's search for larger and more stable markets. From a very pragmatic point of view, to continue and expand the industrialization that had acquired momentum with the Depression and the war, Latin America required access to capital goods and certain raw materials, all of which had to be imported. The importance of the US economy as a market for regional products and a supplier of manufactured goods had increased dramatically with the war and the retrenching of European markets. Thus, from the eyes of Latin American economists and policymakers, development was embedded in the reconstruction of the global, yet American-led economic order.

The centre-periphery framework encapsulated the understanding of the region's relation to the world economy prevailing within the Latin American policymaking community. What had been loosely defined as a colonial or semi-colonial relation was replaced by the *centre-periphery* concept. Prebisch presented the framework to government delegates in the second session of the UN Economic Commission for Latin America at Havana in 1949. 'The specific task that fell to Latin America, as part of the periphery of the world economic system, was that of producing food and raw materials for the great industrial centers', Prebisch claimed. That systemic relation was the main obstacle to welfare and development in the region.[16] Yet, given Latin America's ongoing industrialization process, 'reality [wa]s undermining the out-dated schema of the international division of labor', Prebisch added. The rallying cry in support for industrialization and the calling for a new era in the relations between centre and peripheries made Prebisch's text a landmark in Latin America's political and intellectual fields. Encapsulating the region's development model, it came to be known as the CEPAL manifesto.

The manifesto was, however, a peculiar combination of protest and consent. While it denounced the global inequality in the gains of trade and the consequent obstacle for the development of the periphery, it advocated for larger economic integration and closer financial and economic cooperation with the global economic centre. Prebisch, like many Latin American economists and policymakers, believed that the industrialization of the periphery and the internationalism underpinning the new global order and its institutions were the keys to transform the relations between centres and peripheries.

They bid on the possibility of reconciling autonomous national development with global integration. Achieving this balance required the United States to embrace its role as the principal cyclical centre expanding its imports from the rest of the world and exporting capital. The existence of a hegemonic power within the international political economy was consistent with the possibility of capital accumulation in the periphery in so far as the centre played by the rules. The promise of autonomy hinged on the expansion of trade and on the earnings of foreign proceeds to sustain an ongoing process of ISI that for the short term demanded increasing needs of imported goods and capital. Embedded in the manifesto, this tension between autonomy and integration shaped the project of *cepalinos*, straddling regional aspirations and global norms while circumventing imperialism in the decades to come.

Having captured the ideas and concerns already in circulation, the notion of centre and periphery advanced in the 1949 manifesto quickly gained traction. It provided a sound response at the right time. Under Prebisch's leadership, *cepalinos* undertook national and regional annual economic surveys, promoted planning techniques, administered training courses for public functionaries and organized conferences to discuss policy initiatives such as access to international capital and regional integration. Through the production of economic knowledge about the region, imbued by the centre-periphery perspective, the influence of CEPAL became pervasive at both the policy and the intellectual level. The commission gained prominence as the major source of information and analysis about industrial and agricultural production, foreign trade and investment, and balance of payments and inflation. Through their research and advisory missions, training courses and advisory and decision-making positions in government, *cepalinos* created a network of expertise and defined the terms of the economic debate in Latin America. As the systemic problems imposed by growing US global and regional domination increased, the promise of autonomy through industrialization and internationalism faded and *cepalinos* began to re-examine the notion of centre and periphery.

Crisis of development and dependency

By the early 1960s, a growing feeling that something had gone wrong with the ISI model troubled *cepalinos*. Though the industrialization process in the large Latin American countries had advanced considerably, a profound malaise haunted them. Population was increasing rapidly and the growth in income barely caught up to make for real per capita increases. The modern, industrial sector was not expanding fast enough to absorb the growing labour force; instead, it was creating a 'marginal population' in the outskirts of the large industrial cities.[17] There were no real signs of the transformation in the relation between centres and peripheries that *cepalinos* and Latin American policymakers had anticipated in the early post-war years. The external vulnerability had not subsided; instead, Latin American economies, even the large, industrialized ones, were even more dependent on global markets, with rising demand for imported foodstuffs, energy and capital goods. Their project of development was in crisis.

The malaise was opening spaces for new approaches. Within the institution, a thrust for an analysis of development that surpassed the economic domain was intensifying. For the first time, *cepalinos* were putting the project of industrialization under scrutiny. While economists revisited the post-war trajectory, a group of sociologists and their project on the social aspects and agents of development gained momentum.[18] They began by looking at the national bourgeoisie, the very agents of industry to understand the limits of industrialization. To carry out such studies, the commission hired social scientists in Argentina, Brazil, Chile and Colombia as consultants. The most salient and consequential of these studies was the one undertaken by young Brazilian sociologist Fernando Henrique Cardoso.

Out of this conjuncture emerged an idea that post-war economists could not have imagined as it entailed a contradiction in terms.

A lecturer at the Universidade de São Paulo, Cardoso was part of the emerging *paulista* school of sociology. Under the leadership of Florestan Fernandes, a group of young sociologists moved away from ethnographic methods and the study of racial relations towards dialectics and the study of capitalism and industrial society in Brazil. While other members of the group worked on labour and the state, Cardoso was in charge of the study of entrepreneurs and the role of the national bourgeoisie in development. Cardoso and his colleagues were part of a new generation of social scientists for whom academia was a full-time profession and a career.[19] Though involved in academic politics and university reform, he remained distant from what was considered Rio de Janeiro's close connection between social sciences and the state, one which fellow countryman, friend and former CEPAL member Celso Furtado was, instead, very familiar with. Furtado, ten years older than Cardoso, had devoted his career to international civil service at CEPAL and to economic policymaking in Brazil while continuously publishing on the economic history and obstacles to development in Brazil. In mid-1964, Cardoso and Furtado would find themselves together in Santiago, triggering a debate that resulted in the production of the concept of dependency.

Whereas *cepalinos* were puzzled by the crisis of development, Cardoso and other sociologists in the region were more concerned about the problem of social change. By looking at the origins, actions and motivations of the entrepreneurs, Cardoso's early work sought to explain the emergence of the capitalist–industrialist order in Brazil. For *cepalinos* like Furtado, the thrust towards industrialization came from a reactive response to the global economic crisis of the 1930s, which, in shutting down external markets, had stimulated production for the internal market. That industrialization was the result of indirect economic forces, of stimuli and reaction, did not satisfy Cardoso. Interested in the interplay of social groups, Cardoso wondered where and how the motivations and actions to transform the traditional society emerged within an underdeveloped society based on the agricultural production of colonial export products. In direct confrontation to Furtado, Cardoso pushed farther: How can autonomy rise from dependent societies?[20] Cardoso was pushing the *cepalino* and the prevailing ideas about development in Latin America to the test.

In answering the question of the origins of development in Brazil, Cardoso pointed towards the national intelligentsia. Despite the long-term process of industrialization, the results of his research suggested that the modern entrepreneur in Brazil was a contemporary phenomenon. Only the young generation of industrialists was characterized by the willingness to rationally organize labour, the interest in technical innovation and the pursuit of long-term profits.[21] It was only very recently, Cardoso argued, that the industrialists had begun to organize themselves as a class and seek to impose their needs and interests for industrial capitalism and development to the rest of the nation. Instead, the push for development emerged from the state and its rising expert bureaucracy, he explained. During the Second World War, and especially thereafter, the state channelled national resources towards infrastructure in energy and transportation as well as to the building of basic steel and iron industries.[22] Those efforts were, according to Cardoso, the product of a rising, middle-class intelligentsia who embraced a national development ideology. They had come to occupy positions in power and made crucial decisions about the nation's path to development.

While Cardoso pointed to the power of ideas, Furtado came to terms with the limits of expertise, especially as the promise of autonomy through the industrialization of the periphery faltered. In an institutional meeting in early 1964, Furtado had questioned CEPAL's role and work. An intellectual pillar of the commission for its first decade, Furtado's words carried enormous weight. After his Plano Trienal, a three-year development plan, collapsed in the midst of rapidly polarizing environment in Brazil, Furtado had grown increasingly disappointed about economic policies designed to guide industrialization and development. 'Those who have responsibilities in government and are in direct contact with reality realize that those instruments do not by themselves change the structures', Furtado argued. Facing opposition from industrialists and unions, landowners and peasant leagues, the right and the left, Furtado felt besieged by the social forces contending for the reorientation of the path to development. 'Given a specific socio-economic structure, that is reflected in a particular equilibrium of power, economic planning is fruitless', Furtado added. To confront the limits of economic expertise, Furtado advocated for the 'study of the conditions on which power rests, that is, the conditions that uphold those structures'.[23] Rather than renouncing his conviction on the transformative potential of social scientific knowledge, Furtado urged *cepalinos* and development experts to broaden their perspective and explain the different national power structures. Furtado had become an ally in the push for the social aspects of development that had initially brought Cardoso into the *cepalino* fold.

The question of power loomed large over these Brazilian social scientists. The tensions that had marked the ascent of President João Goulart to power in Brazil in August 1961 had become more dramatic and severe by early 1964. Striving for conciliation and compromise, Goulart had opted for a gradual implementation of his plan of 'structural reforms'. To foster development and propound for social justice, Goulart sought to transform the unequal land tenure structure, impose limits on the repatriation of profits, make taxation more progressive, increase housing options in the cities and obtain the right to vote for the illiterate population. Land invasions and labour agitation attested to the impatience with the pace of social reform; rallies of women allied with the right wing of the Catholic Church and military uprisings and conspiracies illustrated the exasperation with left-wing reformism.[24] When a large majority of the press and public opinion rallied behind the conservative forces that opposed Goulart, the military intervened, deposing the elected government. After the military authorities revoked his political rights, Furtado returned to Santiago. Fearing for his future in the University of São Paulo, Cardoso also found refuge among *cepalinos*.

With the encounter between Cardoso and Furtado, a new intellectual project emerged in Santiago. Driven by the crisis of development, *cepalinos* had already begun to revisit the post-war industrialization trajectory. In a seminar gathering old and new *cepalinos*, economists and sociologists, Furtado urged the group to go back to the 1949 manifesto and the notion of centre and peripheries in order to find out why ISI had failed to bring about autonomous development. Cardoso took Furtado's call for a re-examination of *cepalino* tenets and ideas seriously, giving an answer to the conundrum about development and autonomy.

The development project that *cepalino* ideas helped cement was based on what Cardoso, alongside Chilean sociologist Enzo Faletto, called a developmentalist alliance. Since industrialists needed export proceeds to finance imported capital and intermediary goods, agro-exporting elites were incorporated into the project. Since development hinged on the expansion of the internal market, the growing urban popular sectors were incorporated both as labourers and consumers. The state not only mediated between industrialists, labour, and exporters but, through its entrepreneurial and regulating enterprises, also became an agent of development in its own right. At a crucial moment of the industrialization process, when export proceeds were falling and international cooperation faltering, the national bourgeoisies, with support of the state, turned to partnerships with foreign capitalists. As American corporations sought new markets abroad, the partners of the developmentalist alliance demanded new sources of capital to transition to the production of durable consumer and capital goods, deepening the industrialization process.[25] The result was what Cardoso called the 'internationalization of the internal market' and the advent of a new form of dependency in Latin America.

The new form of dependency presented a paradox for *cepalino* economists. Argentina, Brazil and Mexico had undergone dramatic changes in their structures of production, expanding both their industrial sector and the internal market. With the transfer of foreign capital, techniques and organization to the modernizing industrial sector in Latin America, production and consumption decisions became the product of a market that was at once local and global. Despite limits imposed to remittance of profits of foreign corporations, and the industrial growth and expansion of internal markets, consumption and exchange decisions were beyond the scope of the nation; they were the product of global market forces. The new structure of production, in turn, resulted in extreme vulnerability to changes at the global level in consumption and production. Heretofore considered sources of autonomy, industrialization and the expansion of the internal market had become the site and expression of dependency.[26] The external dependence that had characterized Latin America's relation to the global economy was transformed but did not subside. In other words, the failure of the model observed by *cepalinos* was the result of the limits of industrialization in dependent economies and of the ideology that buttressed industrialization. Industrialized yet dependent economies emerged in Latin America, which was a theoretical impossibility for *cepalinos* given that industrialization was the road to autonomy.

The notion of dependency was initially a blow to *cepalinos* and their ideas about development. Through dependency, Cardoso had put into question the fundamental premise of their project: that industrialization rendered autonomy. Through dependency, Cardoso also situated *cepalinos* and 'developmentalist ideology' as part and parcel of the dependent development trajectory adopted in Latin America. 'Developmentalism', Cardoso argued, 'was neutral regarding the foreign or national control of companies'.[27] While intellectuals and national bureaucracies had been crucial in outlining economic development as a project for the nation, they had also failed to include questions of control, ownership and decision-making, prioritizing the thrust for industrialization. Yet, despite the profound criticism of the *cepalino* project, Cardoso capitalized on their ideas.

While vindicating *cepalinos* as intellectuals, Cardoso advanced dependency as new approach to development. Unlike the modernization theory prevailing in the global North, Latin American economists had rightly characterized underdevelopment as a function of the international division of labour rather than an early stage in a process of capital accumulation.[28] Embedded in the notion of centre and peripheries was the fundamental premise of any analysis of economic development and capitalism. Although *cepalinos* had incorporated the global economic structures of power into their analysis, they had failed to account for the interplay of social forces in their struggle to define the specific path to development. Instead, dependency called attention to 'the specific and distinct forms of relation among the social groups in each country and between them and the external groups' that such integration presupposed.

Unlike theories of imperialism, dependency used the global structures as the point of departure rather than the endpoint of an analysis of capitalism in the periphery. The new interpretation highlighted the structural connections between the periphery and the hegemonic centres 'without making the latter the ultimate answer for the cause and direction of the development process in the former'.[29] Moving beyond *cepalino* economicism, Cardoso focused on the internal social and political forces that turned global 'economic forces' into policies and projects and presented a typology of Latin America's political economy of development. With dependency, Cardoso aspired to account for structural conditions and historical conjunctures, global and national power dynamics, economic and social forces, and thus inaugurate an agenda for an integrated approach to development. Vindicating and condemning their ideas and its political effects, Cardoso and Faletto's dependency was the beginning of a long process to come to terms with the ambiguous legacy of *cepalinos*.

Conclusion

In the late 1960s, at the peak of global mobilization against imperialism and capitalism, dependency circulated widely. As the concept inspired the struggles of writers, students, activists and insurgents, dependency became a shorthand for imperialism. A popular book of the era entrenched the dictum that Latin America's history had been 'repeatedly determined from the outside ... always for the benefit of the foreign metropolis of the moment in an endless chain of dependency'.[30] The reaction of *cepalinos* to the whirlwind of dependency varied. While Furtado claimed that a theory of imperialism was always embedded in the notion of centre and peripheries, Prebisch condemned the pervasiveness of 'ideologies that advocated for transforming the system root and branch'.[31] Though *cepalinos* and their network of social scientists made unequal global relations of power the subject of their intellectual project, they resisted the label of imperialism. Contesting and drawing from the *cepalino* ideas, dependency was the culmination of the *cepalino* project. Cardoso took upon himself to defend the *cepalino* vision of dependency and contest the one that, in their eyes, had come to prevail.

For Cardoso, characterizing the position of Latin America in the post-war global sphere required moving beyond inherited concepts of imperialism. The classical theories of imperialism, from Hobson to Lenin, assumed the perspective of the imperial centres. The trajectory of the regions at the other end of the relationship was only an extension of imperial power, denying them a history of their own and opening the possibility of intervention. Instead, dependency drew attention to the dynamics of capitalism within and from the periphery. More important than the constraints of the external structures and determined paths were the historical options of social classes and political forces to transform those structures.

While imperialism implied five centuries of colonial historical limbo, the new concept was meant, at least, to suggest change and the paradox of development and dependency. While imperialism implied an old international division of labour between industrial centres and producers of primary products in the periphery, Cardoso's dependency suggested the advent of a new era. While an industrializing periphery was far from creating interdependence between nations, it did signal a change in global dynamics, evident in what we vaguely call globalization, for which old categories such as imperialism lacked explanatory power. While imperialism implied revolution for social transformation, that option was historically unviable in the ambiguous context of dependency and development. If dependency were a regurgitation of ideas about imperialism, the thrust behind the project had been lost. Marked by the memories of revolution and counterrevolution, Latin American intellectuals engaged in enduring battles about the meaning and scope of dependency for decades.

Notes

1 See Rosemary Thorp, 'Latin American Economies in the 1940s', in *Latin America in the 1940s: War and Postwar Transitions*, ed. David Rock (Berkeley: University of California Press, 1994), 42–4.
2 On efforts at synthesis Latin American structuralism, see Ricardo Bielschowsky, ed., *Cincuenta años del pensamiento de la CEPAL* (Santiago: Fondo de Cultura Económica, 1998); Octavio Rodriguez, *La teoria del subdesarrollo de la CEPAL* (México: Siglo XXI, 1980); Cristobal Kay, *Latin American Theories of Development and Underdevelopment* (London: Routledge, 1989).
3 On Latin America as a US empire, see Greg Grandin, *Empire's Workshop: Latin America, the United States and the Rise of the New Imperialism* (New York: Metropolitan Books, 2007) and Michael Latham, *Modernization as Ideology: American*

Social Science and Nation-Building in the Kennedy Era (Chapel Hill: University of North Carolina Press, 2000). On hemispheric cooperation: David Sheinin, ed., *Beyond the Ideal: Pan Americanism in Inter-American Affairs* (Westport: Greenwood Press, 2000). Most recently, Atul Kohli, 'Nationalist versus Dependent Capitalist Development: Alternate Pathways of Asia and Latin America in a Globalized World', *Studies in Comparative International Development* 44, no. 4 (2009): 386–410.

4 A classical reference in the study of imperialism is John Gallagher and Ronald Robinson, 'The Imperialism of Free Trade', *Economic History Review* 6, no. 1 (1953): 1–15.

5 For literature on the history of development, see Arturo Escobar, *Encountering Development: The Making and Unmaking of the Third World* (Princeton: Princeton University Press, 1995); Gilbert Rist, *The History of Development: From Western Origins to Global Faith*, 2nd edn (New York: Zed Books, 2002); David Engerman, Nils Gilman, Mark Haefele and Michael Latham, eds, *Staging Growth: Modernization, Development, and the Global Cold War* (Amherst: University of Massachusetts Press, 2003); Nils Gilman, *Mandarins of the Future: Modernization Theory in Cold War America* (Baltimore: Johns Hopkins University Press, 2004); David Eckbladh, *The Great American Mission: Modernization and the Construction of the American World Order* (Princeton: Princeton University Press, 2010); Nick Cullather, *The Hungry World: America's Cold War Battle against Poverty in Asia* (Cambridge: Harvard University Press, 2010).

6 For the literature on development and CEPAL, see for instance, Celso Furtado, *La fantasia organizada* (Bogota: Editorial Universitaria de Buenos Aires, 1989); Edgar Dosman, *The Life and Times of Raúl Prebisch, 1901–1986* (Montreal: McGill-Queen's University Press, 2008); E. V. K. Fitzgerald, 'ECLA and the Formation of Latin American Doctrines', in *Latin America in the 1940s: War and Postwar Transitions*, ed. David Rock (Berkeley and Los Angeles: University of California Press, 1994), 89–108; Joseph Love, 'Economic Ideas and Ideologies in Latin America since 1930', in *The Cambridge History of Latin America*, ed. Leslie Bethell (Cambridge: Cambridge University Press, 1995), vol. 6, 393–462.

7 For classic interpretations of this period, see Carlos Díaz Alejandro, 'Latin America in the 1930s', in *Latin America in the 1930s: The Role of the Periphery in World Crisis*, ed. Rosemary Thorp (Basingstoke: Macmillan, 1984), 17–49 and Rosemary Thorp, 'A Reappraisal of the Origin of Import-Substituting Industrialisation, 1930–50', *Journal of Latin American Studies* 24, quincentenary supplement (1992): 181–95.

8 See Dosman, *The Life and Times of Raúl Prebisch, 1901–1986*. Prebisch was the head of the United Nations Economic Commission for Latin America from 1950 to 1963. Then, he led the first and second United Nations Commerce, Trade, and Development Conference in 1964 and 1968, in which the stabilization of prices of primary products was perhaps the main issue on the agenda.

9 On the Latin American participation in the Bretton Woods pact, see Eric Helleiner, *Forgotten Foundations of Bretton Woods: International Development and the Making of the Postwar Order* (Ithaca: Cornell University Press, 2014).

10 Víctor Urquidi, 'El significado de Bretton Woods', *Revista de Economía* 7, no. 7–8 (1944): 19–21.

11 Eugênio Gudin, 'Economía de producción primaria y su aspecto internacional', *Revista de Ciencias Económicas* 32, no. 272 (1944): 319.

12 *Proceeding and Documents of the United Nations Monetary and Financial Conference: Bretton Woods, New Hampshire, July 1–22, 1944* (Washington DC: US Government Printing Office, 1948), 743.

13 Speech by Jorge Chávez, the Peruvian delegate to the conference, ibid., 739–46.
14 Raúl Prebisch, *The Economic Development of Latin America and Its Principal Problems* (New York: United Nations, 1950).
15 *Review of Economic Conditions throughout Latin America: Report Prepared by the Secretariat* (New York: United Nations, 1948), E/AC.21/W.4, 48.
16 Prebisch, *Economic Development of Latin America*, 1.
17 *Exposición del señor Raúl Prebisch, Director Principal de la Secretaría Ejecutiva de la Comisión Económica para América Latina, en la primera sesión plenaria, el dia 5 de mayo de 1961* (Santiago: ILPES, 1961), E/CN.12/616; Benjamin Hopenhayn to Raúl Prebisch, Santiago, 5 June 1964, Archivo Raúl Prebisch, Biblioteca CEPAL.
18 CEPAL, *External Financing in the Economic Development of Latin America* (Santiago: ILPES, 1963), E/CN.12/649; María Conceição Tavares, 'Auge y declinio del proceso de sustitución de importaciones el Brasil', *Boletín Económico de América Latina* 9, no. 1 (1964): 1–62; Carlos Lessa, 'Quince años de política económica en el Brasil', *Boletín Económico de América Latina* 9, no. 2 (1964): 153–213.
19 Sergio Miceli, 'O cénario institucional das Ciencias Sociais no Brasil', in *História das Ciências Sociais no Brasil*, ed. Sergio Miceli (São Paulo: FAPESP, 1995), vol. 2, 7–24; Manuel Antonio Garreton, Miguel Murmis, Geronimo Sierra and Hélgio Trindade, 'Social Sciences in Latin America: A Comparative Perspective – Argentina, Brazil, Chile, Mexico, and Uruguay', *Social Science Information* 4, no. 2–3 (2005): 557–93; and Luis Carlos Jackson, 'Generaciones pioneras de las ciencias sociales brasileñas', in *Historia de los intelectuales en América Latina: Los avatares de la 'ciudad letrada' en el siglo XX*, ed. Carlos Altamirano (Buenos Aires: Katz, 2010), vol. 2 of 2, 630–51.
20 Fernando Henrique Cardoso, *Empresariado industrial e desenvolvimento no Brasil* (São Paulo: Difusão Europeia do Livro, 1964), 72, 76.
21 Fernando Henrique Cardoso, *El empresario industrial en América Latina: Brasil*, Décimo periodo de sesiones (Santiago: ILPES, 1963), E/CN.12/646/Add.2.
22 On the industrialization in Brazil, see Warren Dean, *The Industrialization of São Paulo, 1880–1945* (Austin: University of Texas Press, 1969), Olivier Dinius, *Brazil's Steel City: Developmentalism, Strategic Power, and Industrial Relations in Volta Redonda, 1941–1964* (Stanford: Stanford University Press, 2011).
23 *Actas Resumidas de la Cuarta Reunión del Consejo Directivo, 13 y 14 de Enero de 1964* (Santiago: ILPES, 1964), INST/32/Rev.1.
24 Jorge Ferreira, 'A estratégia do confrontação Frente de Mobilização Popular', *Revista Brasileira de História* 24, no. 47 (2004): 181–212.
25 Fernando Henrique Cardoso and Enzo Faletto, *Dependencia y desarrollo en América Latina: una interpretación sociológica* (Santiago: ILPES, 1967), 148–52.
26 Fernando Henrique Cardoso, *El proceso de desarrollo en América Latina: Hipótesis para una interpretación sociológica* (Santiago: ILPES, 1965), 29–32.
27 Ibid., 36.
28 For Cardoso's critique on modernization theory, see Cardoso, *Empresariado industrial e desenvolvimento*, ch. 2.
29 Ibid., 16.
30 Eduardo Galeano, *The Open Veins of Latin America: Five Centuries of the Pillage of the Continent* (New York: Monthly Review Press, 1997 [1971]).
31 Raúl Prebisch, *Change and Development: Latin America's Greatest Task* (Washington DC: IBRD, 1970), 9–20; Celso Furtado, *Os Ares do Mundo* (Rio de Janeiro: Paz e Terra, 1991), 33.

Chapter 12

WESTERN INTERNATIONAL THEORY, 1492–2010: PERFORMING WESTERN SUPREMACY AND WESTERN IMPERIALISM

John M. Hobson

Despite its claims, international theory in the last quarter-millennium has not been premised on a value-free positivism seeking to make sense of a world that exists as an object of study 'out there'. Rather, it has been intimately involved in shaping and constructing world politics through various Eurocentric discourses.[1] The overwhelming discursive form that this has taken is that of 'performing Western supremacy', of which the justification and nurturing of empire has been one, albeit not exclusive, key aspect. But while some international theories have advanced the cause of anti-imperialism, these have mostly been situated within various Eurocentric and scientific racist discourses and that, as such, it is important to underline international theory's propensity to perform *Western supremacy* rather than simply that of performing *empire*. However, despite the existence of numerous anti-imperialist strands of Eurocentric and scientific racist theory, my discussion here will focus exclusively on imperialist international theory in part because the imperialist thrust has taken precedence over its anti-imperialist cousin. Accordingly, I chart the manifold ways in which Western international theory has performed – that is, informed, justified and given rise to – both Western supremacy and Western imperialism in the practice of world politics.

The prime mandate of this chapter is to consider the ways in which external factors shaped the construction of imperialist international theory and vice versa. That is, I take it as axiomatic that the theory and practice of world politics are mutually co-constitutive. I trace the different discursive forms that imperialist Western-centrism has taken within much of international theory while also linking these to external developments that occur in the 'real' world. However, it is also important to appreciate that many of these external events do not simply speak for themselves as objective criteria but are perceived differently depending on which Western-centric discourse we are examining. Thus relating the performative nature of Western international theory is no simple or linear task. Accordingly, this means that a purely externalist account or purely contextualist account can produce only partial understandings of the development of international theory.[2]

To this end I shall examine some of the key turning points, beginning with a discussion of the 'invention of America' after 1492 given that this was the originary or formative moment in the rise of Western imperialist-international theory and international law. Having sketched some of the developments that occurred in the long period between 1492 and the mid-nineteenth century, the second section then considers the imperialist Eurocentric and scientific racist discourses, particularly the 'Hobson-Wilson moment' that unfolded between 1898 and 1945. The third section then considers the post-1945 development of 'subliminal' imperialist Eurocentrism within which neo-imperialist IR theory was embedded. The final section concludes by considering the post-1989 manifest Eurocentric imperialist moment that in many ways projects us back to the future of nineteenth-century manifest/explicit imperialist Eurocentrism. These sections relate external events with the development of international theory and vice versa.

Before proceeding, it is worth distinguishing between 'Eurocentric institutionalism' and scientific racism. The former locates difference between East and West according to cultural and institutional factors whereas the latter focuses on genes as well as climate and environment.[3] As specific forms of Western-centrism there are many differences but also numerous overlaps between them. But scientific racism, which emerged in the eighteenth century, more or less died in 1945 for reasons that I explain later. Eurocentric institutionalism has a longer history since its tentative origins emerged after 1492 (as the next section reveals) even though it matured after 1750. After 1945 it becomes the sole metanarratival base upon which IR was based, taking on a subliminal form down to 1989 and then returning back to a more explicit or 'manifest' modus operandi thereafter. But specifics aside, all of these metanarratives place Europe and the West at the pinnacle of world politics while simultaneously advancing provincial (Westernized) conceptions of the world that masquerade as the universal. This is as true of the anti-imperialist conceptions as it is for the imperialist visions. Equally, the whole issue of empire and the West's place in the world constitutes the normative political pivot around which they operate.

Inventing and colonizing America through the construction of imperialist international theory, 1492–ca.1900

The emergence of what might be called mature Eurocentrism in the post-1750 era can only be understood properly in the context of the prior invention of America after 1492. The deep paradox of what Edmundo O'Gorman called the 'invention of America',[4] was that it began with the imposing of Catholic ideas but ended up by launching medieval Christendom onto a secularized *European* identity-formation trajectory that would culminate in a mature Eurocentrism after about 1750.[5] Indeed, the only way that the principal interpreter, Francisco de Vitoria,[6] found to resolve the contradictions that America posed for the Christian *weltanschauung* and its tradition of just war theory was to construct new discourses that could be used to interpret the Amerindians.[7] Nevertheless, before I outline the five basic imperialist ideas that Vitoria expressed, it is worth noting a few points concerning the events-context within which he was writing.

In 1539 Vitoria was writing specifically in the context of an emerging colonial administration in America, with the first Spanish viceroyalty of New Spain having been established in 1535. This, then, was very much the formative period of Spanish imperialism in the Americas and the discursive or legitimating grounds upon which it was to be based had not yet been settled. Vitoria was one among three key thinkers debating Spain's role in the Americas. Bartolomé de Las Casas appeared to be the Indians' most vociferous defender, Juan Ginés de Sepúlveda their most hostile critic. The debate between these two men revolved around the stand-off between two conceptions of the Indians – the 'noble savage' (Las Casas) and the 'ignoble savage' (de Sepúlveda). The former conceived of the natives as innocent children of nature who would be fitting receptacles for Christianity, while the latter saw them as unable and unwilling to accept conversion and should therefore be subdued either by force or slavery or extermination. This was the backdrop to the famous Valladolid controversy of 1550. It is true that Las Casas won out because the Catholic Church supported him on the grounds that to admit that the natives could not be Christianized would be to go against the theory of monogenesis outlined in the Bible. But despite the ideological victory of Las Casas over Sepúlveda it would, however, be entirely wrong to assume that the church's conception of the inherent equality of all men precluded the unequal treatment of some of them. Indeed the two views of the Indian Natives gave rise to various conceptions of the imperial discourse that would come to fruition in the nineteenth century. The 'benign' view of Las Casas gave rise to a paternalist imperial mission in which the natives would be culturally converted along Western Christian lines so that they could come to enjoy the good (European) life: a conception that many though not all 'progressive' liberals would later come to support. Indeed, Las Casas never challenged the right of the Spanish to rule over the natives nor did he believe that they should be granted self-determination. The malign view of de Sepúlveda would be later developed in some, though by no means all, of the racist-realist conceptions of imperialism. Thus, at all times the debate presupposed the inferiority of the natives and was based on an ideology of enslavement versus a colonialist/assimilationist ideology.[8] In this way these apparently opposing ideological views of the natives sat logically, albeit awkwardly, together.

It was in this context that Vitoria was writing his text, *On the American Indians*, articulating not just an imperialist vision that later informed international law but one that set up a nascent Eurocentric discourse. It advanced five core imperialist ideas. First, Vitoria constructed a nascent 'standard of civilization'. Unlike de Sepúlveda, Vitoria believed that the Indians were humans who possessed the capacity for reason but that this was at that time deemed to be only latent as was evidenced by their 'inferior' institutions (economic, political and cultural). By comparison Europe's institutions were deemed to be founded upon reason. The second and third key ideas, which found their place in almost all subsequent Eurocentric and racist-imperialist tracts, were that of 'social efficiency' and 'terra nullius'. These worked in tandem, such that native countries were deemed to be vacant or waste-space given that the inhabitants had failed to develop their lands to productive ends so that it was a right or duty of the Europeans to take up residence among them in order to put their lands to productive use. And should the natives resist this 'social efficiency imperative', Vitoria constituted this as an act of war thereby justifying Spanish military retaliation. This conception was later advanced by the likes of Alberico Gentili, Hugo Grotius, John Locke and Emerich de Vattel (though *not* Kant). Fourth, the Amerindians were read to be living in a 'state of nature'; an idea that found its place within the thought of subsequent political/political-economic theorists such as Locke, Hobbes, Kant and Smith. Finally, this all culminated in the bipolar/schizophrenic construction of the international which stipulated that because European states were civilized so they were awarded the trappings of sovereignty, whereas non-European savage societies were deemed unworthy of sovereignty. Thus, while European states would be protected from imperial intervention, savage societies by contrast were constructed as 'ripe for imperialist intervention'. All in all, the twofold upshot of this discussion is that the emergence of European international theory and international law was forged in the imperialist crucible of a nascent Eurocentric discourse: something that would permeate much of subsequent international theory. And, moreover, international theory, based on a nascent Eurocentric discourse, informed in a proactive manner the development of imperialism in the Americas.

The American encounter was seminal in a further sense, given that for the first time since the fall of the Roman Empire the 'Europeans' came to feel superior to another people, having felt inferior (in a materialist sense) to their principal rival – Middle Eastern Islam – throughout the medieval era. Moreover, by the end of the sixteenth century, the medieval iconographic *Orbis Terrarum* maps (which shaped a circle of the Earth – the 'O' – inside of which is a T-formation wherein the waters of the Mediterranean separate the three continents, Africa, Asia and Europe), or 'Mappa Mundi' (which placed Asia above Europe), were superseded by a series of iconographic maps that depicted Europe as a queen standing above the so-called inferior continents of Asia and Africa. And while many Enlightenment thinkers – including Montaigne, Malebranche, Leibniz, Voltaire and Quesnay – still viewed Egypt and especially China as higher civilizations and drew in particular on Chinese ideas of rationality in their own theories, nevertheless the 1770s witnessed a key turning point, with the image of China as akin to a noble and wise Confucius being reconstructed all of a sudden into the image of a sinister and barbaric Fu Manchu. More specifically, having frequently cast China as the most advanced civilization in the world down to the 1770s, after 1780 the country was suddenly reimagined as a barbarous realm that was crushed by Oriental despotism such that it had apparently been languishing in stagnation for many centuries. This conception had fully fructified by the mid-nineteenth century when such denunciations were commonplace; to wit John Stuart Mill's proclamation that the Chinese 'have become stationary – have remained so for thousands of years; and if they are ever to be farther improved, it must be by foreigners';[9] much as Hegel and Marx concluded. Note that Mill, like his father James, had been employed for much of his life by the English East India Company (EIC).

All in all, the key upshot is that from about 1780 onwards the Europeans came to believe that Europe was the supreme civilization in the world. And to this end they constructed what I call a 'Civilizational League Table', which placed Europe in division one, the barbaric yellow societies in division two and the savage black societies in division three.[10] All Eurocentric institutionalists and scientific racists embraced this idiom, though some used it as a basis for advocating Western imperialism while others advanced an anti-imperialist politics.

By the mid-nineteenth century, proclamations of Western superiority were in full flow and nurtured the idea of imperialism within Western international theory.[11] This triumphalism was nowhere better symbolized than by the 1851 Great Exhibition, which was held in the Crystal Palace in Hyde Park (London) and which glorified British civilization in contrast to the barbarism and savagery of the non-Western world. And, of course, this mirrored the triumphalism associated with the Manchester School with its claim that Western liberal-civilization had delivered prosperity and peace to mankind. But much of Manchesterean liberalism, which is conventionally associated with anti-imperialism, turned out to embrace many imperialist sensibilities, found in the work of John Stuart Mill and Walter Bagehot and, most surprisingly, in the work of Richard Cobden and John Bright.[12] Equally, while various scientific racist anti-imperialist theories existed, nevertheless, these too reflected an endemic sense of Western supremacy (as in the writings of Robert Knox, Herbert Spencer, William Graham Sumner, David Starr Jordan, James Blair, Charles Henry Pearson and, later still, Lothrop Stoddard and Madison Grant).[13]

Critically, many of these thinkers were concerned not simply with an abstract problem of order but with the fundamental issue of imperialism (either for or against). Both Kant and Smith were disturbed by European imperialism, viewing it as an obstacle to the causes of progressive world order based on cosmopolitan human rights and economic development within Europe and in the non-European world. Smith's critique of mercantilism was very much framed within this problematique. Moreover, it is notable that the theory of the balance of trade upon which eighteenth-century European mercantilism rested was in part the result of the urgings of the various East Indian Companies who had lobbied their governments to allow the export of bullion to Asia (which was a principal trading activity of the companies).[14] In England, Thomas Mun was one who had been employed by the EIC to argue for the necessity of silver bullion export, the result of which was the publication of his *A Discourse of Trade from England to the East Indies* (1621). Moreover, the EIC's importation of cotton from India, which had been challenged by the rise of British domestic protectionism, was responded to by the company's push for free trading policies. To this end the company employed various thinkers to promote the cause of free trade resulting, for example, in Sir Josiah Child's *New Discourse of Trade* (1690) and Charles Davenant's *Essay on the East India Trade* (1696), which thereby set in train a new drive towards free trade: something which would be advanced most famously by Adam Smith, ironically, as a means of critiquing the EIC in particular and imperialism in general.[15]

Perhaps the key irony here, though, is that by the mid-nineteenth century many thinkers embraced the spread of free trade by Britain as a principal means by which the civilizing mission could be best advanced, thereby reiterating the point that economic policy was not simply the result of an abstract economic theory but one that itself was heavily implicated in the political economy of empire. And so it was in this context that much of Manchesterean liberalism operated, of which Britain's unilateral shift to free trade in 1846 was a symptom. And, of course, it was this imperial moment, alongside Britain's place at the top of the world, that the Great Exhibition signified and celebrated. Thus, many international thinkers reflected this triumphalist moment in their writings as much as they worked to enhance Britain's imperial glory within them.

However, at the turn of the twentieth century, a more complex situation emerged, wherein international theorists perceived new and changing world events in radically different terms and which led to radically different prognostications.

The bifurcation of Western-centric international theory, ca. 1889–1945

Near the end of the nineteenth century the Western sensibility of superiority and predestination split into various streams. The first carried on the triumphalist sensibility that reached a peak in the mid-nineteenth century. Thus, the scientific-racist-imperialist argument advanced by John Robert Seeley and Charles Dilke, which believed that white racial civilization would expand effortlessly across the globe to sweep aside the savage and barbaric non-Western world, was reinforced by the likes of John Fiske, Josiah Strong, Franklin Giddings, Harry Powers, Karl Pearson, Benjamin Kidd, Lester Ward, Theodore Roosevelt and Henry Cabot Lodge. But this was increasingly counterposed after about 1889 with the emergence of a pronounced stream of white racial anxiety which was concerned, if not terrified, by what such thinkers perceived as the rise of the Eastern peril – to an extent Islam but mostly Japan and China. I call this the 'Pearson-Mahan moment'. The seminal racist writer here was Charles Henry Pearson, whose 1893 book suggested that the era of white racial supremacy was already over and that the yellow races would take over the world in the near future.[16] Whether such thinkers advocated an anti-imperialist politics (as in Pearson and Stoddard) or, more commonly, an imperialist political response, all agreed that the white race was under threat. Alfred Mahan is particularly interesting because in the received IR historiographical imagination he is perceived to be a realist thinker, who argued that sea-power is the source of great power in the world, rather than being a key scientific racist who was concerned principally to defend white racial-civilizational supremacy. What, then, had brought about this general shift?

There were various domestic and international developments that loomed large in the white racial anxiety literature. By 1884, with the whole of the British male working class having been enfranchised, the cause of the aristocratic whites was now vulnerable to political attack. Moreover, the rise of the welfare state was singled out on the grounds that it promoted the white working class through state-dependency regulation. State support of the 'unfit' white working class would undermine the 'struggle for existence': something which is best adapted to not by the white races in general but by the white elites in particular. For what is not generally recognized is that for eugenicists 'white racial supremacy' could only be secured by the aristocratic elites.[17] The white working-class male – who was referred to as the 'under-man' (Stoddard) or 'sub-man' (Freeman) – was deemed to be a fetter or a drag on white racial supremacy. This belief fed into the late-nineteenth-century hysteria about relative demographics as the reproduction of the working class was thought to be expanding at the expense of the elites and thereby contributing towards that which Edward Ross originally called 'white racial suicide'.[18]

In the international arena, while the rise of the savage and barbaric threat began to loom large, it is important to appreciate the point that 'the crisis of whiteness predates the receding tide of empire'.[19] Accordingly, subsequent challenges to empire tended to feed into this threat-perception as much as they nourished it. A number of external events played a role in this rising tide of white racial crisis though these were very much filtered through various racist lenses. First, by 1890, the military war on the Indians in the United States was over, thereby opening up in the minds of many scientific racists the fear that without a new Other to marshal against the reproduction of American identity would have no anchor: an idea which nourished the turn to empire and the war on the external Other by the United States in 1898 (though equally the American turn to empire nourished future imperialist- and anti-imperialist-international theorizing). Second, particularly in the United States, non-white racial immigration during the 1870s and 1880s nourished a growing fear of the degeneration of the white race principally through miscegenation. This set off a clamour for strong immigration controls against the Eastern races, leading to a series of Exclusion Acts that culminated in the extreme and racially motivated 1924 Immigration Act (which remained in place until the mid-1960s). Interestingly, this was emphasized most by the scientific racist *anti-imperialists* who believed that American imperialism would open the floodgates to non-white racial immigration (as in the likes of William Graham Sumner, David Starr Jordan (pre-1919), Camp Clark and, most famously, Lothrop Stoddard and Madison Grant). Third, particularly with the colonization of Africa having been completed in 1885 European racists became worried that the four-hundred-year-old Columbian Epoch was now coming to an end as the 'empty spaces' of the world had pretty much now been taken: an idea that was made famous by Halford Mackinder (1904).[20] Fourth, the demographic and industrial rise of China as well as of Japan was a particular concern.

The fifth threat, that of the 'rising (anti-imperialist) tide of colour' (Stoddard), fed into this growing crisis of white supremacy. The first key event to shake Western self-confidence was the defeat of the Italians by the Ethiopians at the Battle of Adowa in 1896, something that was described as a 'disaster of the first magnitude'.[21] Then the most cataclysmic shock that marked one of the key turning points came in 1905 with the Japanese military defeat of Russia, which was later described by the arch-eugenicist, Lothrop Stoddard, as 'an omen of evil import for [our white] race-future' such that 'the legend of white invincibility lay, a fallen idol, in the dust'. For not only was 'the veil of white invincibility … shattered [but] the white world's manifold ills were laid bare for candid examination'.[22] This was a widespread omen that struck imperialist Eurocentrics such as Alfred Zimmern as much as it did scientific racists such as Stoddard. And equally it acted as a psychological spur for Asian solidarity, linking up pan-Islamic and pan-Asian movements into one broad transnational movement, something that took off during and after the First World War.[23]

But such fears also found their expression within scientific racist-*imperialist* thought. Alfred Mahan was particularly important, being one of the first racists to articulate the fear of the coming barbaric (Chinese and Japanese) threat (which was dubbed the 'Yellow Peril' by Hungarian General Turr in June 1895). Mahan's response was to call for a white racial alliance between the English and the Americans which should go on the imperialist offensive in order to contain this rising barbaric threat. He was echoed in Britain by Halford Mackinder in his famous 1904 article. In Germany similar fears exercised the minds of the anti-Semitic imperialists, of whom Adolf Hitler was the most well known. His concern with the Jewish Peril, a conception which had its antecedents in the likes of Heinrich von Treitschke and Houston Stewart Chamberlain, led him to call for the extermination of the Jewish race and the imperial expansion of Greater Germany. This side of the equation, of course, played a key part in the events that gripped Europe and later the world between 1919 and 1945. However, while this was one, albeit extremely important, side of the world politics ledger, the other side of which was the politics of the League of Nations which was embedded not within a pacifist liberal political agenda as we are conventionally told but one that advanced the cause of Western liberal-imperialism in the world. I call this side of the ledger the 'Hobson-Wilson moment'.[24]

1898–1945 – The 'Hobson-Wilson Moment': Maintaining and defending Western supremacy through 'sane imperialism'

One important liberal international thrust that came to play a key role in shaping the interwar international order was that which might be called the 'Hobson-Wilson' moment. Several points are noteworthy. First, while Woodrow Wilson is largely credited with the politics of liberal internationalism and the principle of self-determination that formed the key pillar of the League of Nations, this obscures the points that under the League Western imperialism continued unabated and was indeed given moral sanction through the Mandate System and that Wilson's liberalism was founded on a scientific racist-imperial politics which fundamentally denied the sovereign self-determination of non-Western polities. Second, the Mandate System was forged not in a moment of Western triumphalist sensibility but as a rearguard action to restore and maintain Western imperialism in the face of a rising Eastern challenge to empire. Indeed, this challenge was probably the foremost concern that exercised on the minds of many of the interwar liberal international theorists. And third, while Wilson played a key proactive role in creating the League, his racist imperial writings notwithstanding, probably the key thinker responsible for creating the intellectual architecture of the Mandate System and its mode of international imperialism was my great-grandfather, John Atkinson Hobson.

The 'Hobson-Wilson moment' was influenced by various external events, some of which differed from, and some of which complemented, those that informed the 'Pearson-Mahan moment'. Certainly fears concerning the challenge to empire were important. Also, on the racist side of this ledger (Hobson was a Eurocentric-institutionalist thinker, Wilson a Lamarckian-racist), Wilson's racism fed off the concern of non-white immigration into the United States as much as it reflected an antipathy towards concerns over Reconstruction and the northern desire for the south to give political and social rights to southern blacks. Simultaneously the US–Spanish War of 1898 also fed in with Wilson making a strong case for backing the new imperialist thrust, (as did the thinkers mentioned at the end of the previous section). By contrast, Hobson was absorbed by the Boer War, which for him was a prime example of imperialism-gone-wrong (or what he called 'insane' imperialism). Others, principally in the Fabian Society in England, viewed the Boer War as an imperial necessity since the British empire was deemed to be the vital means by which progressive civilization would be spread across the world.[25] Indeed, it was the Boer War that concentrated the Fabian mind on the whole issue of the importance and value of imperialism in the first place as it did for many others on the left including various New Liberals and British idealists. What then were the key aspects of Hobson's and Wilson's writings on international politics and how did these simultaneously feed into shaping world politics?

While many liberal Eurocentric imperialist thinkers envisaged Western imperialism as a civilizing mission that would enable the inferior peoples to become civilized for their own benefit, the most empathic conception of imperialism was advanced by J. A. Hobson. This is something of an irony given that Hobson is generally reported as one of the principal anti-imperialist thinkers in the West. But it turns out that Hobson was not against imperialism per se but a particular brand of it – what he called insane imperialism.[26] By this he was referring to the unalloyed exploitation of non-Western lands and peoples mainly by private Western interests operating under the banner of the various national imperialisms. Many assume that his posited antidote to the problem of imperialism was domestic reform via the raising of aggregate demand through redistribution and the welfare state – at least this is the stuff of standard reportage. And certainly this is the thrust of Part 1 of his famous text, *Imperialism: A Study*.[27] However, in Part 2 of the book, which covers a full 70 per cent of the text, he produces a very different argument. There he developed a paternalist-liberal Eurocentric analysis which advocated the need to undertake what he called a sane imperialism, the objective of which was to raise the backward peoples up to the levels of political freedom and economic prosperity that were enjoyed by Western civilization.

Hobson's conception of sane imperialism began with two initial paternalist-Eurocentric claims:

> First, that all interference on the part of civilized white nations with 'lower races' is not prima facie illegitimate. Second, that such interference cannot safely be left to private enterprise of individual whites [as in insane imperialism]. If these principles be admitted, it follows that civilized Governments *may* undertake the

political and economic control of lower races – in a word, that the characteristic form of modern Imperialism is not under all conditions illegitimate.[28]

And from this starting point he outlines his approach to sane imperialism in the long chapter in Part 2 of *Imperialism* entitled 'Imperialism and the lower races'. Hobson takes issue with those who argue that the native peoples should be left alone in sovereign isolation to develop the resources of their lands precisely because, he insists, they will *not* do so. Indeed, he reasons:

> Assuming that the arts of 'progress', or some of them, are communicable, a fact which is hardly disputable, there can be no inherent natural right in a people to refuse that measure of compulsory education which shall raise it from childhood to manhood in the order of nationalities. The analogy furnished by the education of a child is *prima facie* a sound one.[29]

Such a metaphor was applied directly to the 'races of Africa [whom] it has been possible to regard as savages or children, 'backward' in their progress along the same general road of civilization in which Anglo-Saxondom represents the vanguard, and requiring the help of the more forward races'.[30] Moreover, in terms of civilizational attributes he states that 'if Western civilization is richer in these essentials, it seems reasonable to suppose that the West can benefit the East by imparting them, and that her governments may be justified as a means of doing so'.[31] Indeed, he reasons that in the context of global interdependence the West must not 'abandon the backward races to [the] perils of private exploitation', as in insane imperialism, for this would constitute a 'barbarous dereliction of a public duty on behalf of humanity and the civilization of the world'.[32]

The most intriguing aspect of his proposal for a sane imperialism is that it is ideologically schizophrenic, invoking many sympathetic, even 'postcolonial', ideas but ultimately deferring to a paternalist-Eurocentric institutionalism. Thus, while the advanced nations must educate the backward races through transplanting various rational Western institutions and practices, albeit on a gradualist basis, this can only be achieved with a *strong degree of empathy* for the natives. This requires understanding native cultures, languages and environment. And he insists that the Eastern peoples should be approached carefully and should be legitimately persuaded of friendly motives while simultaneously discouraging any private imperial attempts to exploit their economies: an argument that is reminiscent of Kant's insistence that Western incursion into non-European lands must be undertaken in a non-exploitative and genuinely consensual manner.[33] Indeed the natives 'should be gainers, not losers' and 'the direct gains of development should pass on equal terms to all the world and not to the capitalist exploiters of a single nation'.[34]

Still, in contrast to many of those who were associated with the Pearson-Mahan moment, for those on the Hobson-Wilson side of the ledger none of this could be achieved in the absence of international institutional reform. To this end Hobson argued seminally that sane imperialism could only be guaranteed by an independent international government, which would ensure that the development of native lands would be conducted in their own interests, as well as those of global humanity's, over and against the exploitative private interests of individual imperialist capitalists. This he advanced in Part 2 of *Imperialism* as well as in various other texts.[35] Critically, Hobson's conception of sane imperialism became the blueprint for the Mandate System on the one hand, and for many of the interwar liberal/radical liberal international theorists on the other. For the moment, however, it is worth dwelling on Woodrow Wilson given the prevailing belief that he was the liberal international anti-imperialist par excellence.

Woodrow Wilson's writings on imperialism were advanced around the turn of the twentieth century. He embraced a scientific racist approach, based on Lamarckianism, which stipulated that the savage and barbaric races *could* become civilized but only on condition that the requisite rational institutions be delivered courtesy of Western imperialism. And while Wilson is considered to be the grandfather of twentieth-century liberal internationalism and the prime advocate of the principle of self-determination for all states on the basis of his famous 14-point speech that was delivered in January 1918, it turns out that within this speech self-determination applied only to the Eastern European states. Outside of the Western world Wilson was unequivocal that imperialism was the correct political solution such that it would supply the means by which the backward races could be brought into the bright light of liberal civilization.

In a 1902 article in the *Atlantic Monthly*,[36] Wilson insisted that the colonization of the Philippines constituted a critical means by which the Filipinos could be uplifted into civilization. There he concludes that the Filipinos 'must first take the discipline of law, must first love order and instinctively yield to it. We [the Americans] are old in this learning and must be their tutors'. Specifically, he argues that if the Americans can teach the Filipinos the noble ways of discipline and self-government – including justice and fairness in administration – so this 'will infinitely shorten their painful tutelage. ... We must govern as those who are in tutelage. They are children and we are men'. Above all, self-government cannot be simply 'given' but must be earned and graduated into from the hard school of life.

The key idea – that of *graduating* into self-government through imperial tutelage – means that self-determination for the colonized peoples would have to be postponed. This reflects his argument that constitutional political development is something that occurs over a very long period of time, as he argued in the case of Teutonic/Aryan constitutional state-formation in *The State*,[37] as much as it reflected his neo-Lamarckianism in which race progress can be achieved but only very gradually. And it was precisely this gradualist idea that underpinned his understanding of the League of Nations Mandate System. For Wilson's paternalist racism (as much as Hobson's paternalist Eurocentrism) was stamped all over Article 22, which spoke of 'peoples not yet able to stand by themselves'; 'that well-being and development of such peoples form a sacred trust of civilisation'; and that 'tutelage should be exercised by [the colonial powers] as Mandatories on behalf of the League'.

While the Mandate System was thought to provide a much more empathic *internationalized* form of imperialism it was, nevertheless, premised on the same principle of the old national form of the liberal civilizing mission – specifically paternalism and the 'sacred trust of civilization'. And significantly, even at the Paris Peace Conference Wilson maintained his stance that self-determination should be extended only to the East and East-Central European peoples, whereas with respect to the non-European peoples, as 'in the Philippines earlier, he applied the principle of national self-determination with great caution. He did not undermine British rule in Ireland, Egypt, and India, or French rule in Indochina'.[38] Moreover, the German colonial spoils were simply carved up and thrown to various Western powers (as well as Japan). In short, Wilson expected the Western great powers 'to fulfil the same [civilizing] mission in their League Mandates that the United States had assigned itself in the Philippines'.[39] Indeed Wilson viewed the Mandate System as an altruistic, paternalist contribution to the Eastern societies on the part of the Western colonial powers: 'It is practical … and yet it is intended to purify, to rectify, to elevate.'[40] Thus far from 'making the world safe for democracy', Wilson stood rather for imposing democracy in the world and making Western supremacy safe through imperialism.

While the imperialist ideas of Hobson and Wilson played a key role in performing the League of Nations, particularly the Mandate System, nevertheless, as was alluded to earlier, there were important external international events that Western liberal international theorists were responding to. In part the League was of course established to prevent a future world war from happening again. But also important was the rising Eastern resistance to empire, which had begun back in the nineteenth century and which took off in 1919. Indeed the year 1919 and its immediate aftermath witnessed the emergence of a string of movements and revolts aimed at dethroning Western empire, which included the May Fourth movement in China and the March First movement in Korea, the Khilafat movement in India, the Destour Party in Tunisia and, last but not the least, the Indonesian Nationalist movement. Added to this was a string of rebellions against empire and racism, perhaps the most famous of which were the 1919 Amritsar (Indian) massacre and the waves of violence that washed through various cities across the United States as blacks fought for equality and were confronted by the Ku Klux Klan, which had been revitalized during the war following the film 'The Birth of a Nation' in 1915.

Testimony to this general moment of European white/civilizational crisis was found in the timely publication of a string of well-known books such as Oswald Spengler's Eurocentric-institutionalist text, *The Decline of the West*, as well as in various scientific racist treatises.[41] The essence of this pessimistic message was aptly epitomized by Paul Valéry in 1919: 'As for us and our civilization, we now know that we are mortal. … And we now see that the abyss of history is large enough for everyone', leading him to ask rhetorically: 'Will Europe keep its pre-eminence in all things? Will Europe become what in fact it is … a small [promontory] of the Asian continent?'[42]

Not surprisingly, this episteme of Western anxiety fed through into Western liberal international theory, one prime voice of which was Alfred Zimmern.

Indeed, far from espousing an optimistic and rosy scenario for the future, the immediate context of Zimmern's argument lay in the massive dent to Western self-confidence that the First World War and the Eastern revolt against the West imparted (as it did for many other interwar writers). Jeanne Morefield's eloquent summary here is noteworthy:

> Murray's and Zimmern's writing in the wake of the Great War suggest that they experienced [a] loss of racial identity acutely. Their prose were redolent with anxiety, heavy with the sense that Western culture was under attack. The hum of fear – of the encroaching 'Oriental mind', that the 'immense number of different breeds of men' were becoming less differentiated, that the war had shifted world power away from Europe and toward the 'politically immature peoples' of the world – played like a constant low drone throughout their work.[43]

And for Gilbert Murray the racial threat was akin to a kind of 'Satanism', where 'satanic forces included all phenomena that threatened the imperial order, the movement of free trade and the idea of Western civilization'.[44] Indeed the coming race war was a theme that exercised, if not terrorized, the minds of many interwar liberal international theorists.

The common assumption held in IR is that interwar liberalism comprised a cultural-pluralist liberal internationalism that stood for self-determination and peace but that in contrast to classical liberalism advocated international institutional intervention via the League of Nations to achieve this vision. In the conventional historiographical IR imagination that was bequeathed by E. H. Carr's seminal realist text, *The Twenty Years' Crisis*, interwar liberalism is deemed to be utopian or idealist insofar as it believed that the 'harmony of interests' could be legislated for and guaranteed by the League, thereby failing to recognize the fundamental reality of state power and interests that are founded on self-help and conflict rather than other-help and peace.[45] Indeed, as we are usually told, it was precisely the problem of imperialism – German, Japanese and Italian – that realists pointed to when emphasizing the unavoidable reality of power, the absurdity of liberal utopianism and its inability to recognize the importance of imperialism, all of which fuelled the realist claim that the League was doomed to fail. This informed the turn to realism in IR, on the one hand, and the desire to create an objective science of international politics in the immediate aftermath of the Second World War, on the other, as was advanced most famously in Hans Morgenthau's *Politics Among Nations*.[46]

Here it is important to correct these common misconceptions, the first being that many of the seminal interwar liberals (and left-liberals) did not reject imperialism but positively embraced it. Wilson was adamant that white imperialism be continued and most interwar liberals echoed Hobson's 1902 argument by advocating the League as the vital international institution that could convert insane Western imperialism into a sane imperialist project (such as the Fabian Eurocentric writer Leonard Woolf and the scientific racist thinker Raymond Leslie Buell). Second, other liberals such as Norman Angell and Alfred

Zimmern argued that the League was a necessary but insufficient factor, given that peace, prosperity and civilization could only be secured if the British empire worked alongside the League. Third, these thinkers were not bright optimists who placed all their chips on the anti-imperialist roulette wheel of the League but were haunted by the rising tide of Third World anti-imperial resistance and were concerned fundamentally with finding ways to maintain Western imperialism – both in its British and international guises – as a means to defend Western hegemonic supremacy.[47] Critically, much of the debate was characterized not by a conflict between realist imperialism and liberal anti-imperialist idealism but rather by a particular brand of imperialism – that of the liberal paternal civilizing mission conception versus the racist-realist conception advanced by the likes of Nicholas Spykman, Karl Haushofer and, at the extreme, Adolf Hitler. And fourth, these 'liberal international' visions were often informed by a paternalist Eurocentrism or racism that reflected their patrician backgrounds. Typical here was Alfred Zimmern who asserted that

> the English gentleman represents a specific and clearly marked type of civilized humanity. ... For courage, for honour and loyalty, for tolerance, for wisdom and calm judgment, for self-control in emergencies, I doubt whether the world has ever seen his equal. ... The English gentleman has been, in fact, an unrivalled primary teacher of peoples.[48]

The Western colonial-racist guilt syndrome and the rise of 'Subliminal' imperialist Eurocentrism, 1945–1989

It is generally assumed that since 1945 Western theory underwent a public divorce from its West-centric, especially racist, pre-1945 tendencies and has been marked by positivist and cultural-pluralist sensibilities. But while this assumption presupposes a binary construction, where the alternative to racism is racial tolerance, this elides the presence of a third discourse, that of 'subliminal Eurocentric' intolerance which marked IR theory between 1945 and 1989. Subliminal Eurocentrism, as it played out in IR theory and across the social sciences, is far more hidden than its manifest/explicit predecessor, making it much harder to detect. In essence, subliminal Eurocentrism inverts the modus operandi of manifest Eurocentric institutionalism in the pre-1945 era, thereby sublimating rather than exorcising its many biases. Indeed, in subliminal Eurocentrism all the monikers of manifest Eurocentrism are present but reappear in terms that dare not speak their name. Thus, the trope of civilization versus barbarism transmogrified into those of 'tradition versus modernity' or 'core versus periphery', while imperialism morphed into that of 'hegemony' or 'international financial institution intervention'. Why then did this epistemic shift in the modality of Eurocentrism occur?

The principal factor in the rise of subliminal Eurocentrism was the emergence of the Western 'colonial-racist guilt syndrome' that was due in part to a series of intra-Western developments, which comprised the internalist critique of scientific racism within the academy, advanced most famously by the anthropologist, Franz Boas, as well as the revulsion that the Nazi atrocities invoked in the Western mind. But it also emerged as a response to the successful strategy of rhetorical entrapment that was deployed by the anti-colonialist nationalist movements, as they managed to discredit the ideas of scientific racism and formal empire and thereby win the case for decolonization.[49] Here it is noteworthy that characterizing the 1947–89 era as that of the Cold War, which was essentially an intra-Western civil war, deflects attention or focus away from the battle for decolonization between East and West. For it was this battle in particular that comprised an important milieu or backdrop in the development of subliminal Eurocentric international theory. In general, the upshot of the emergent Western racist-imperial guilt complex was not so much a turn away from imperialism in practice, given that both the Western superpowers continued it in a variety of ways between 1945 and 1989 – even if it reined in Europe's imperialist politics – but a desire to hide or obscure normative imperialism from view in the body of international theory.

An excellent example of the elision of imperialism lies in Hans Morgenthau's principal work, *Politics Among Nations*,[50] in which imperialism is reimagined not as a policy that the West had long deployed vis-à-vis the East but as a *normal* universal strategy of aspiring great powers in relation to each other. In this way, the specifics of Western imperialism are effectively expunged from the historical record. Indeed, many Western theorists sought to 'whitewash imperialism',[51] thereby (re)presenting it in a positive light. Typical is Hedley Bull's pluralist English School theory in which we encounter a retrospective justification of pre-1945 imperialism as a benign process that diffused civilization across the world to enable hitherto backward Eastern societies to enter the fold of civilized (i.e. European) international society. Moreover, as alluded to already, a (benign) conception of the civilizing mission emerged within neorealist hegemonic stability's conception of (Anglo-Saxon) *hegemony*, while neoliberal institutionalism did much the same with respect to the role played by Western international institutions, especially the IFIs. In both visions, the prime rationale of Western hegemons and their international institutions is to culturally convert Third World states along Western civilizational lines: the very essence of the paternalist-liberal civilizing mission.[52]

These two prominent IR theories, neoliberal institutionalism and realist hegemonic stability theory (HST), though traditionally understood as anti-imperialist, nevertheless in effect served to legitimize and restore America's neo-imperial role in the world in the face of decolonization and the rise of Asian economic power, even if their calls for it were voiced in terms that dare not speak its name. For it is notable that HST and liberal interdependence theory (from which neoliberal institutionalism was derived) emerged at the very time when American anxiety concerning its hegemonic supremacy was rising. By the early 1970s the East was challenging economically the hegemony of the West, whether it be through OPEC and the oil shocks, the calls for a New International Economic Order that sought greater weighting to the Third World in the global economy, the rise of Japanese economic power (as the latest Yellow Peril), or the emergence of global interdependence. This Western and American anxiety informed these theories, even if it was more obvious in the case of HST. Also noteworthy here is that in Bull's writings it is clear that decolonization and the Eastern challenge to the West is an issue that was very close to his heart. His writings are permeated by his contempt for such Third World challenges, typical of which is his description of the 'revolt against the West' as governed by 'tawdry rhetoric' behind which lay

> envy and self-pity ... false and shallow charges levelled against the historical role of the West, the vast gap between aspiration and achievement in the Third World, the bitter ironies of decay in the place of development, tyranny in the place of liberty, [and] the cases of reversion to superstition and barbarism.[53]

Another generic focus of subliminal Eurocentric IR theory was to shift the pre-1945 focus of scientific racism and manifest Eurocentrism away from its obsession with East/West relations in favour of a near-exclusive focus on intra-Western relations. In this vision the West is once again granted hyper-agency while Eastern agency is downgraded, if not erased altogether. That is, all developments within world politics are explained through Western hyper-agency, with the West being presented as the universal. This is a typical feature of classical realism (that is most closely associated with Carr and Morgenthau) as well as Waltzian neorealism and is to an important extent reproduced in neorealist HST. Indeed HST effectively instructs the student that she can learn all she needs to know about world politics/economics simply by focusing all her attention on the actions of the Anglo-Saxon hegemons. Significantly, one of the theory's prominent advocates replied to a question posed by an audience member (presumably a Luxembourg national) at the 1990 APSA conference: 'Sure people in Luxembourg have good ideas. But who gives a damn? Luxembourg ain't hegemonic.'[54] Such a narrow focus necessarily precludes the actions of small Western states (i.e. American ethnocentrism) and Third World states (paternalist Eurocentrism). Analogous to World Series Baseball that involves only North American teams, so for HST America is the world.

The foremost neorealist IR scholar, Kenneth Waltz, in his seminal 1979 text, *Theory of International Politics*, essentially advanced an approach which denied agency to non-Western actors and states and served to shore up American power in the world at the very time that it appeared under threat. This worked more at the subliminal level and was expressed through a series of arguments that appear in neutral and universal clothing. Three key conceptual claims are pertinent here. First, Waltz denies the existence of *international hierarchies* in world politics and that, in so doing, he elides the imperial formations that existed up to the era of decolonization. Second, Waltz's claim that bipolarity during the Cold War created the most peaceful and stable era that the world has ever known can hold only if we confine our attention to intra-Western relations and, moreover, intra-Western peace was only possible because violence between the two superpowers was displaced onto the terrain of the non-Western world.[55] Thus, from a Third World point of view, Cold War politics would have appeared not only as unstable and violent but also as 'a continuation of colonialism through slightly different means. ... For the Third World, the continuum of which the Cold War forms a part did not start in 1945, or even 1917, but in 1878 – with the Conference of Berlin that divided Africa between European imperialist powers.'[56] Third, Waltz's insistence that only the great powers are consequential in world politics obscures the manifold relations and interactions between the West and 'the rest' on the one hand, while ignoring the many ways in which small non-Western actors have impacted the superpowers, on the other (such as the Mujahideen defeating the Soviet Union or the Vietnamese defeating the United States, with both defeats having massive ramifications for both the superpowers). It is also noteworthy that at the end of the book Waltz gives the game away when he provides explicit support for US leadership in the world.

While it is certainly the case that liberal modernization theory and dependency/world-systems theory focus *explicitly* on North/South or East/West relations, nevertheless, they turn out to be the exceptions that prove the subliminal Eurocentric rule. The Eurocentric cues are found either in the guise of the reification of Western agency and the erasure of Eastern agency or in the point that the East is awarded a mere derivative or emulative agency insofar as it should replicate the Western development path, the five stages of which weave a linear line that begin with replicating British industrialization only to culminate with the age of high-mass consumption, US-style (as in modernization theory).[57] Walter Rostow was particularly important and found his place in the Johnson administration, providing strong support for the Vietnam War. But it was his modernization theory that he is most well known for. In *The Stages of Economic Growth* Rostow viewed non-Western economies as in effect barbaric and savage (though he cloaked this by referring to them as founded on 'tradition') and that salvation lay with following the Western modernization path. In this respect his theory performed Truman's neo-imperial doctrine, part of which asserted that 'we [the United States] must embark on a bold new program for making the benefits of our scientific advances and industrial progress [i.e. American civilization] available for the improvement [i.e. neo-imperial uplift] and growth of underdeveloped areas'.[58]

Post-1989 international theory: Back to the future

The end of the Cold War signalled on 9 November 1989 (with the fall of the Berlin Wall) and the collapse of the Soviet Union in 1991 ushered in a seemingly new phase of IR theory. Much as it is assumed that the post-1945 era of international theory reflected a new epistemic phase that was based on positivism and cultural pluralism, so it is largely assumed that the end of the Cold War ushered in a new cosmopolitan phase where the triumphant elevation of the norms of human rights, tolerance and democracy to the centre of world politics marked a yet more progressive thrust. The post-1989 era has, in fact, projected us back to the future of nineteenth-century (manifest) Eurocentrism. What then were the external processes that promoted this shift?

Two principal events are conventionally emphasized here – globalization and the end of the Cold War. It was not an accident that the 1990s saw the rise of a new buzz-word – 'globalization' – for the end of the Soviet Union, the exit of the Soviet Bloc from the world stage and the end of the divide between the two Cold War blocs were linked in the minds of many with the rise of cross-national and regional integration, given that the whole world was now opened up to unchallenged and unalloyed liberal capitalism. However, two key qualifications are noteworthy here.

First, both globalization and the end of the Cold War were interpreted very differently by the key mainstream Eurocentric international theories. 'Western-realists' (who range from US neo-Conservatives to realists of various persuasions) view these twin events as ushering in the 'new barbaric threat and the coming anarchy' that necessitates a neo-imperial containment strategy to maintain civilization and world order. Conversely, the 'Western-idealists' (liberal constructivists, liberal humanitarians and cosmopolitans) view these twin events as furnishing a golden opportunity to universalize Western civilization for the 'betterment' of global humanity. The second key qualification is that both globalization and the end of the Soviet Union constituted *intervening* variables that acted as catalytic factors in the development of post-1989 international theory. For the principal variable that is obscured within conventional historiography is a third identity-based factor: specifically the ending of the 'Western imperial guilt syndrome'.

In many ways the 1945–89 era was marked not simply by a focus on the intra-Western Cold War but by the sublimated or 'Silent (racial) War' between East and West.[59] Between 1914 and 1989, the West underwent three near-consecutive debilitating civil wars – the First and Second World War and the Cold War – the crucial upshot of which was the denting of Western supremacy in Eastern eyes that in turn served to present the West as both divided and fallible. Moreover, as already noted, during the era of decolonization/postcolonial independence, when the battle against empire and international scientific racism had been won, the West – especially Western Europe – found itself semi-paralysed by its own imperial identity crisis. Most confronting of all was the presence of an East that enjoyed the newly gained status of sovereign-equal: something which, of course, had been consistently denied it by the West throughout the colonial era. Not surprisingly, then, even the all-too-brief postcolonial era was viewed with distrust and sometimes seething resentment by international theorists in the West. Ultimately, this giant postcolonial criticism challenged the central supposition of Western Eurocentric superiority: namely the subject status of the West as the imperial-metropolitan agent of global politics and the passive status of the East. Stripped of its imperial status, Europe, in particular, was largely unable to intervene in its old colonial haunting ground, leading to a rising tide of frustration.

Crucially, it was against this background of imperial semi-paralysis and rising frustration that the dissolution of the Soviet Union and the end of the third Western civil war of the twentieth century furnished the West, especially the United States, with the golden opportunity to reunite and reassert itself as the prime neo-imperial actor of global politics. This was partly fed or nourished and partly reflected by the First Iraq War in 1991, though the incomplete nature of this victory was something that would prove a running sore that festered in the minds of those who were involved in the post-1997 *Project for a New American Century* (particularly Richard Perle, Robert Kagan and Paul Wolfowitz). And this movement, of course, would later influence President George W. Bush in his decision to go back to war with Iraq in 2003 in order to complete the unfinished task. Critically, much of Western international theory since 1989 has proffered the solution of rolling forward Western-sovereignty so as to restore its neo-imperial *hyper-sovereign* status alongside the rolling back of Eastern sovereignty into the neo-imperial conception of *conditional sovereignty*. The key upshot of which is that the West could in triumphant fashion happily relegate the 'postcolonial interlude' to an unfortunate footnote in the long normal Eurocentric history of Western supremacy.[60] Thus, in finally putting to rest its identity-crisis/imperial guilt syndrome that had constrained it during the wilderness years of decolonization, the West went back on the imperial offensive. In essence, to paraphrase Niall Ferguson,[61] it's back – the E-phrase – 'Eurocentric empire'.

To summarize what I identify as the two wings of post-Cold-War mainstream international theory mentioned earlier, both Western-idealism and Western-realism conceptualize the world through pre-1945 manifest Eurocentric lenses.[62] In essence, four key moves underpin this. First, these theories rehabilitate the tripartite hierarchical idiom of the standard of civilization. This was typified by Robert Cooper's delineation of three worlds with civilized Europe occupying the first world of 'postmodern states', autocratic Eastern states residing in the second world of 'modern states' (termed Oriental despotisms in nineteenth-century Eurocentric parlance) and 'pre-modern polities' residing at the bottom and living in a domestic state of nature (termed savage societies in nineteenth-century Eurocentric parlance).[63] Or in John Rawls's terminology we confront civilized liberal states which are contrasted with (barbaric) 'outlaw states' in the second world and 'burdened societies' languishing in the Third World.[64] Second, both sets of theories place importance on globalization but articulate it through the tropes of either 'globalization-as-Eastern barbaric threat' (Western-realism) or 'globalization-as-Western opportunity' (Western-idealism). Third, as noted already, both sets of theories demote Eastern states to the status of conditional sovereignty and promote or restore the status of the West to the hyper-sovereign neo-imperial subject of world politics. Fourth, both sides advocate the neo-imperial intervention of the West in the East either explicitly, as in the likes of Robert Kagan, Max Boot, Robert Cooper, Michael Ignatieff and Niall Ferguson, or implicitly, as in the cosmopolitan literature on humanitarian intervention. Western-realists view the East as a direct threat to civilization (i.e. the West) and hence to world order and seek to contain it through imperialism; by contrast, Western-idealists seek intervention designed ostensibly to heal the Third World though this is enacted by effectively eradicating the East by imposing cultural conversion to the Western liberal standard of civilization.

The reason why I refer to the post-1989 era as one that is marked by the return of manifest Eurocentrism is that explicit calls for imperialism have returned to the centre of IR. For example, taking on President George W. Bush's public pronouncement made in November 2003, that the United States does not seek to be an empire, Michael Ignatieff responds by asserting:

> Yet what word but 'empire' describes the awesome thing that America is becoming? ... America's empire is not like empire of times past, built on colonies, conquest and the white man's burden. The twenty-first century is a new invention in the annals of political science, an empire lite, a global hegemony whose grace notes are free markets, human rights and democracy, enforced by the most awesome military power the world has ever known.[65]

Echoing Ignatieff's argument about 'empire-lite', this imperialism is portrayed by Robert Cooper in terms that are reminiscent of the nineteenth-century concept of the civilizing mission – 'one [that must be] acceptable to a world of human rights and cosmopolitan values ... an imperialism which, like all imperialism, aims to bring order and organisation but which rests today as the voluntary principle ... [based on] the lightest of touches from the centre'.[66] And to this can be added a string of Western-realist writers such as Max Boot, echoing the central theme of Niall Ferguson's *Collosus*,[67] who argues that 9/11 was not in fact 'payback' for American imperialism, for such a view

> is exactly backward: The September 11 attack was a result of insufficient American involvement and ambition; the solution is to be more expansive in our goals and more assertive in their implementation. ... Afghanistan and other troubled lands today cry out for the sort of enlightened foreign administration once provided by self-confident Englishmen in jodhpurs and pith helmets.[68]

Then again, William Pfaff, in his Western-realist book *The Wrath of Nations* asserted that

> the immediate future of Africa ... is bleak, and it would be better if the international community would reimpose some form of paternalist neo-colonialism in most of Africa, unpalatable as that may seem. The mechanism of the international mandate, employed by the League of Nations ... might be revived.[69]

And numerous other quotes could be presented from the writings of Paul Johnson, Robert Kaplan and many others.

It is certainly true that many Western liberals do not articulate their Western interventionist visions in terms of imperialism, but their paternalist desire to culturally convert non-Western states along Western civilizational lines is precisely reminiscent of the rationale that underpinned the discourse of the civilizing mission that was advanced by many liberal-imperialists in the nineteenth century. Only rarely is it conceded that this constitutes imperialism, though Ignatieff is one who has explicitly rehabilitated the E-Word in the context of humanitarian intervention: 'What is exceptional about American [humanitarian] messianism is that it is the last imperial ideology left standing in the world, the sole survivor of imperial claims to universal significance.'[70] And so it is that the theory and practice of Western imperialism is as important to contemporary IR theory as it was to its nineteenth- and twentieth-century forebears.

Notes

1. John M. Hobson, *The Eurocentric Conception of World Politics: Western International Theory 1760-2010* (Cambridge: Cambridge University Press, 2012).
2. A prime example of externalism in IR is Stanley Hoffmann, 'An American Social Science: International Relations', *Daedalus* 106, no. 3 (1977); 41–59. For an application of 'contextualism' to IR, see Duncan Bell, 'International Relations: The Dawn of a Historiographical Turn?' *British Journal of Politics & International Relations* 3, no. 1 (2001): 115-26.
3. See Hobson, *Eurocentric Conception*, chs. 1 and 13.
4. Edmundo O'Gorman, *The Invention of America* (Bloomington: Indiana University Press, 1961).
5. Beate Jahn, *The Cultural Construction of International Relations* (Houndmills: Palgrave, 2000); Naeem Inayatullah and David Blaney, *International Relations and the Problem of Difference* (London: Routledge, 2004).
6. Francisco de Vitoria, 'On the American Indians', in *Vitoria: Political Writings*, eds Anthony Pagden and Jeremy Lawrance (Cambridge: Cambridge University Press, 1991 [1539]), 231-92.
7. Cf. Ronald L. Meek, *Social Science and the Ignoble Savage* (Cambridge: Cambridge University Press, 1976); Jahn, *Cultural Construction*; Inayatullah and Blaney, *International Relations*.
8. Tzvetan Todorov, *The Conquest of America* (New York: Harper & Row, 1982), 46-7.
9. John Stuart Mill, 'On Liberty', in *On Liberty and Other Essays*, ed. John Gray (Oxford: Oxford University Press, 1991 [1849]), 80.
10. Hobson, *Eastern Origins*, ch. 10.
11. Jennifer Pitts, *A Turn to Empire: The Rise of Imperial Liberalism in Britain and France* (Princeton: Princeton University Press, 2005).
12. Hobson, *Eurocentric Conception*, ch. 2.
13. Ibid., chs. 4 and 6.
14. Emily Erikson and Yingyao Wang, 'Global Trade and the Development of Economic Theory', in *Global Historical Sociology*, eds Julian Go and George Lawson (Cambridge: Cambridge University Press, 2017), 182-99.
15. Ibid.
16. Ibid., 187-90.
17. Alistair Bonnett, *The Idea of the West: Culture, Politics and History* (London: Palgrave Macmillan, 2004), ch. 2.
18. Michael S. Teitelbaum and Jay M. Winter, *The Fear of Population Decline* (London: Academic Press, 1985), ch. 2.
19. Bonnett, *Idea of the West*, 16.
20. Halford J. Mackinder, 'The Geographical Pivot of History', *Geographical Journal* 23, no. 4 (1904): 421-37.

21 The *Times*, 5 March 1896, quoted in Paul Gordon Lauren, *Power and Prejudice: The Politics and Diplomacy of Racial Discrimination* (Boulder: Westview Press, 1996), 71.
22 L. T. Stoddard, *The Rising Tide of Color against White World Supremacy* (New York: Charles Scribner's Sons, 1920), 12, 154.
23 Cemil Aydin, *The Politics of Anti-Westernism in Asia* (New York: Columbia University Press, 2007).
24 I am grateful to Jeremy Adelman for suggesting this term to me.
25 The key Fabian proponents of empire were Sidney Webb and George Bernard Shaw. For the final formulation of the Fabian Society, which was published in 1900, see Shaw, ed., *Fabianism and the Empire: A Manifesto by the Fabian Society* (London: Grant Richards, 1900).
26 See also David Long, 'Paternalism and the Internationalization of Imperialism: J.A. Hobson on the International Government of the "Lower Races"', in *Imperialism and Internationalism in the Discipline of International Relations*, eds David Long and Brian C. Schmidt (Albany: SUNY Press, 2005), 71–91.
27 J. A. Hobson, *Imperialism: A Study* (London: George Allen & Unwin, 1938/1968 [1902]). Note that this book was first published in 1902.
28 Ibid., 232.
29 Ibid., 229.
30 Ibid., 285.
31 Ibid., 286.
32 Ibid., 231.
33 Immanuel Kant, *Kant's Political Writings*, ed. Hans Reiss (Cambridge: Cambridge University Press, 1970), esp. 172–3.
34 J. A. Hobson, *The Recording Angel* (London: George Allen & Unwin, 1932), 78.
35 For example J. A. Hobson, *Towards International Government* (London: George Allen & Unwin, 1915); J. A. Hobson, *A League of Nations* (London: Union of Democratic Control, 1915).
36 Woodrow Wilson, 'The Ideals of America', *Atlantic Monthly* 90, no. 6 (1902): 721–34, http://www.theatlantic.com/issues/02dec/wilson.htm
37 Woodrow Wilson, *The State* (New York: D.C. Heath & Co., 1918).
38 Lloyd E. Ambrosius, *Wilsonianism: Woodrow Wilson and His Legacy in American Foreign Relations* (Basingstoke: Palgrave Macmillan, 2002), 130.
39 Ibid., 130–1.
40 Wilson, quoted in Lloyd E. Ambrosius, *Woodrow Wilson and the American Diplomatic Tradition* (Cambridge: Cambridge University Press, 1987), 78.
41 Oswald Spengler, *The Decline of the West* (London: Allen & Unwin, 1919/1932); Madison Grant, *The Passing of the Great Race or The Racial Basis of European History* (New York: Charles Scribner's Sons, 1918); Stoddard, *Rising Tide*.
42 Paul Valéry, quoted in David Abernethy, *The Dynamics of Global Dominance* (New Haven: Yale University Press, 2000), 119.
43 Jeanne Morefield, *Covenants without Swords: Idealist Liberalism and the Spirit of Empire* (Princeton: Princeton University Press, 2005), 108.
44 Ibid., 113.
45 E. H. Carr, *The Twenty Years' Crisis, 1919–1939* (London: Macmillan, 1981 [1946]).
46 Hans J. Morgenthau, *Politics among Nations* (New York: Alfred Knopf, 1948).
47 Hobson, *Eurocentric Conception*, ch. 7.
48 Alfred Zimmern, *The Third British Empire* (Oxford: Oxford University Press), 102–3.
49 Frank Füredi, *The Silent War* (London: Pluto, 1998); Lauren, *Power and Prejudice*.

50 Morgenthau, *Politics among Nations*, ch. 5.
51 Frank Füredi, *The New Ideology of Imperialism* (London: Pluto, 1994), ch. 5.
52 Hobson, *Eurocentric Conception*, chs. 8 and 9.
53 Hedley Bull, 'Justice in International Relations: The 1983 Hagey Lectures' (1984), in *Hedley Bull on International Society*, eds Kai Alderson and Andrew Hurrell (London: Palgrave Macmillan, 2000), 244. Note that this essay was first published in 1984.
54 Stephen Krasner, quoted in Hobson, *Eurocentric Conception*, 195.
55 Kenneth N. Waltz, *Theory of International Politics* (New York: McGraw Hill, 1979), chs. 8–9.
56 Odd Arne Westad, *The Global Cold War: Third World Interventions and the Making of Our Times* (Cambridge: Cambridge University Press, 2005), 396; it was the 1884–85 Conference of Berlin that divided Africa.
57 Walter W. Rostow, *The Stages of Economic Growth: A Non-Communist Manifesto* (Cambridge: Cambridge University Press).
58 President Truman, quoted in Thomas McCarthy, *Race, Empire and the Idea of Human Development* (Cambridge: Cambridge University Press, 2009), 194.
59 Füredi, *Silent War*.
60 Füredi, *New Ideology of Imperialism*, 103.
61 Niall Ferguson, 'Hegemony or Empire?', *Foreign Affairs*, September/October 2003.
62 For a full discussion, see Hobson, *Eurocentric Conception*, chs. 11–12.
63 Robert Cooper, *The Breaking of Nations: Order and Chaos in the Twenty-first Century* (London: Atlantic Books, 2004).
64 John Rawls, *The Law of Peoples: With 'The Idea of Public Reason Revisited'* (Cambridge: Harvard University Press, 1999).
65 Michael Ignatieff, 'The Burden', *New York Times Magazine*, 5 January 2003, http://query.nytimes.com/gst/fullpage.html?res=9B03E6DA143FF936A35752C0A9659C8B63
66 Robert Cooper, 'The New Liberal Imperialism', *The Observer*, 7 April 2002, http.www/observer.guardian.co.uk/print/0,38584388912-102273,00.htm
67 Niall Ferguson, *Colossus: The Rise and Fall of the American Empire* (Harmondsworth: Penguin, 2004).
68 Max Boot, 'The Case for American Empire', *The Weekly Standard*, 15 October 2001, http://www.drake.edu/artsci/PolSci/pols75/boot.pdf
69 Wiliam Pfaff, *The Wrath of Nations: Civilization and the Furies of Nationalism* (New York: Simon & Schuster, 1993), 158.
70 Michael Ignatieff, 'Introduction: American Exceptionalism and Human Rights', in *American Exceptionalism and Human Rights*, ed. Michael Ignatieff (Princeton: Princeton University Press, 2005), 16.

EPILOGUE: EMPIRE AND THE GLOBAL KNOWLEDGE REGIME

Jeremy Adelman

The history of ideas has joined social and economic history to track the ways in which its subjects crossed borders and integrated societies. Like migrants, commodities and capital, ideas and intellectuals have been world-makers. They have transported ideals from one site to another, spread practices – like taking censuses, categorizing, making ministries and translating – so that increasingly, the modes of organizing societies and managing economic life in Asia, Africa, Europe and the Americas looked more and more alike. As the late Christopher Bayly has noted, global integration created more likeness across societies while creating more complexity and heterogeneity within them.[1] What is coming into view is the role intellectuals and their ideas played in this process.

But there is one difference that marks out global intellectual history from other dimensions of the transnational turn: while social scientists helped make the world, they did so by observing and analysing it, crafting the categories which made sense of integration and diversification. The concepts, frameworks and institutions they built helped structure the flows of other integrative factors. So, it is not just the diffusion and adaptation of ideas that drives the burgeoning field of global intellectual history: it is the ways in which the intellectual, and one might say the social scientist above all, was a world-maker by making it visible, intelligible, mouldable and even resistable.

Among the many ways and directions in which the social scientist has been a world-maker, the authors in this volume have asked how social scientists serviced one form of institution that braced worlds into one: empires. For centuries, empires contoured the basic structures of trade, migration, investment and political dominion. Part of our objective here is to provide a deeper history of social scientific engagement in world-making that predates, runs through, and follows the age of nations. One may ask in the continued habits of meddling in other countries, grabbing and bullying, how much has changed? Have new political structures, like international organizations, companies and agencies – from the Gates Foundation to the International Monetary Fund, two actors on the global stage teeming with PhD's in the social sciences – really transcended the ways in which empires got subject peoples to conform to rules and models designed elsewhere?

In this sense, political economists, demographers, ethnographers and strategy thinkers were not neutral players. Therein lay two sources of tension which we see playing out across places and times.

On the one hand, the social scientist aimed to produce knowledge about the world that stood above the particular demands of political forces – often with dreams of a value-free, disinterested, stance. Increasingly, professional rituals of their disciplines asked them to conform to objective norms to create universal laws. For centuries before the late 1800s, before the rise of the modern research university, before the urge to create professional associations and their self-referential inclinations, this need for detachment was not so pressing; social scientists didn't imagine themselves so strongly as outside observers on the world. It was, after all, empires that summoned them, gave them status, put their ideas to work – or rejected them. There is a paradox: as the demands for objectivity and professionalization grew over the course of the twentieth century, so did governments' (and later private and civic actors too) appeal for the services of the social scientist, because the complexity of global arrangements required the analytical insights from knowledge producers, many of whom pandered to the needy policymaker, sometimes in utterly shameless ways. But there was a basic conflict, nonetheless, buried deep in the making and remaking of the social sciences.

If there was a tension between engagement and detachment, there was another dividing line over what kind of power or normative order social scientists imagined. For some social scientists, working for and within imperial states was part and parcel of an effort to uplift and improve through global hierarchies. By the time of the Cold War, we see this played out explicitly in humanitarian and development policy. For others, uplift and improvement could only happen in defiance of hierarchies committed to keeping some sectors or regions in place at the expense of others. Social scientists were neither necessarily pro- nor anti-empire. Very often, economists and demographers could find themselves squaring off against each other, one economist feuding with another, one anthropologist at odds with their cousin over the legitimacy of their political (pay)masters. The debate over imperial norms and justifications very often involved a struggle among social scientists themselves. Either way, empire was the crucible that forged global knowledge producers.

The result was a complex global knowledge regime. John L. Campbell and Ove K. Pedersen have coined the term 'knowledge regimes' to describe the ways in which models of national societies produced by the latticework of universities, think tanks and civil agencies shaped policy choices and preferences when it came to national welfare systems.[2] Regime, as a coinage, has two advantages that suggest pathways for a future agenda for the global social sciences. First, it points to the multiplicity of interdependent actors in the business of producing knowledge, from states to foundations, universities and outfits like 'councils' of advisers, all of them laced together into a system of interlocking parts. These parts did not always work like the elements of a well-functioning machine. Within the regime, there was competition for resources, status and voice. But the competition unfolded within an underlying structural interdependence, often with the research university at its core. The knowledge regime operated at a global scale too. Indeed, it operates ever more with global, and not national, horizons.

Second, regime denotes the political features of the knowledge arrangement and allows analysts to view the non-neutral dimensions of knowledge production, its connection to the reproduction of hierarchies and fundamentally the ties between the social scientist and the wider political economy – and the ability of the social scientist to validate basic preferences and policies, from mercantilism to free trade, from colonization to democracy, from the definition of group identities and rights to economic development. The introduction to this book refers to a durable tension between empire and the social scientists, of mutual regard, recognition and dependency as well as of distance, aversion and scepticism, all of which get stirred into a political economy of knowledge production at – and for – a global scale.

How do imperial framings help us to rethink global intellectual history? First, they draw attention to the partial, engaged and functional properties of the knowledge produced by social scientists – to think of knowledge flowing across borders in the service of building hierarchies of societies divided by borders. If Bayly is right and global integration produces similarity across societies, similarity does not mean equality. Often, it means the obverse. In this fashion, ideas, like capital and commodities, operated as integrator and separator at the same time. As we consider how globalization also created new asymmetries and inequalities in our day, we should be mindful of the ways in which previous rounds and moments of global convergence forged by empires also yielded to new divides, and the ways in which social scientists enabled, explained and challenged this dynamic.

Second, this global intellectual history, by thinking through empires, will have to be ever more polycentric. This is especially challenging in the history of the social sciences, which of all the strands of intellectual history stands to be accused of Eurocentrism. This is for good reason. The self-conscious social scientist was very much a European creation and very much got mobilized to work towards the making of a Eurocentric world. And so many social scientists – from Japan to Brazil, the United States to China – moulded themselves in the image of European styles of observation and European theories of modernization. But this did not make the globalization of the social sciences a history of replication. There was always adaptation, transformation and inversion. Capturing the shifts and mutations that occur when ideas cross borders – and cross levels of global strata created by empires – is going to be vital for a more global history of knowledge.

Notes

1 Christopher Bayly, *The Birth of the Modern World, 1780–1914* (Oxford: Blackwell, 2004).
2 John L. Campbell and Ove K. Pedersen, *The National Origins of Policy Ideas: Knowledge Regimes in the United States, France, Germany, and Denmark* (Princeton: Princeton University Press, 2014).

INDEX

abolitionist movement   51, 57–8
Academia Sinica   70
Acheson, Dean   164–5
Adelman, Jeremy   42 n.1, 83, 103 n.1, 136
affective histories   79
Africa   3, 96, 194, 200
agricultural development school   113
Akira Iriye   5
All-India Opium Act I (1878)   88
Almond, Gabriel   161
America. *See* United States
American Civil War   114
American Political Science Association   161
America's Strategy in World Politics: The United States and the Balance of Power (Spykman)   161
Amerindians   192–4
Amritsar massacre (1919)   202
Anderson, Benedict   103
Angell, Norman   203
Anglo American universities   8
'The Anhui Constitutional Government Survey Bureau Edited and Submitted Civil Affairs Customs Answers, 1908–1911'   101
annexed states   57
annihilation   68, 71
anthropology   66, 95, 96–7, 99, 102, 106 n.33
anti-bullionism   23
anti-imperialism   136, 195, 197, 199
anti-opium movement   81–2
anti-slavery   55, 57
apprenticeship system   59–60
Arendt, Hannah   7
Argumossa Gándara, Theodoro Ventura de   23
Aristotle   40
army department   160

Asia   3, 67–9, 96, 113, 119, 181, 194–5
Asiento   24
associationalism   142
Association of Catholic Academics   126
Atlantic Monthly   201
autonomy   58, 132, 177, 182, 185, 186
Auxilios para bien gobernar una monarquía católica (Macanaz)   21

Bagehot, Walter   195
Baldwin, Hanson   163
Bandit Suppression Campaign   71
Bank of England   22
Barber, Bernard   169
Bayly, Christopher   215, 217
beinsa crimes   84–5, 87
Beiyang Gongbao   69
Beiyang government   102
Bemis, Samuel Flagg   159, 173 n.42
Benda, Julien   2
Bengal Council   88
Bentham, Jeremy   52–5
Bentham, Samuel   51–9
Benton, Lauren   96
Biblioteca del Palacio Real (BPR)   18, 20
Biblioteca Nacional de España (BNE)   18, 20
Bickers, Robert   3
The Birth of a Nation (1915)   202
Blair, James   195
Bloch, Marc   66
Board of Economic Warfare   147, 160
Boas, Franz   205
Boer War   9, 199
Bohannan, Paul   96, 99
bondage   51, 52, 57, 59
Book of History, The (Shang Shu)   65
Boot, Max   209–10
Botero, Giovanni   32
Bouguer, Pierre   20

Bourbon Reforms   17, 19
Bourbon Spain   4, 17
Bourgon, Jérôme   97, 99, 107 n.40
Bowie, Robert   164, 165
Bowman, Isaiah   162, 163
Boxer Rebellion   93
Brent, Charles Henry   81
Bretton Woods   8, 146, 180
Bright, John   195
Britain   21, 56, 132, 146, 159–60, 169, 195–6
   alliance with Russia   52
   conquering Spanish American markets   24
   criminal law   56
   Egyptian independence   126
   labour institutions   54
   rule in India   55, 57
   skilled workers from   53
   structural-functionalism   96
   values and institutions to India   56
British Burma   79–89
   moral wreckage   83–9
   opium and empire   80–3, 90 n.16
British Committee on the Theory of International Politics   169
British India   83, 88–9, 102
British India Society   58
Brodie, Bernard   161
Buell, Raymond Leslie   203
Bull, Hedley   205–6
bullion   21–2
Burbank, Jane   118
bureaucracy   16, 113–14, 184, 187
Bureau for the Revision of the Laws   98, 107 n.46
Burke, Edmund   56–7, 172 n.25
Bush, George W.   123, 154, 209, 210
Bushido: The Soul of Japan (Nitobe Inazo)   112

cameralism   33, 43 n.11
Campbell, John L.   216
Campillo y Cossío, José del   18–20, 26 n.3
capital accumulation   177
capitalism   38–9, 178, 187–8. *See also* global capitalism; industrial capitalism; liberal capitalism; Western capitalism

capitalist economy   127
capitalist modernity   64
Capron, Horace   114
Cardoso, Fernando Henrique   183–8
Carnegie Corporation of New York   6
Carnegie Council on Ethics in International Affairs   165
Carnegie Endowment for International Peace   111–12
Carnegie Foundation   158–9, 167
Carpani, Francesco Maria   31–2, 34–6, 40–1
Carpenter, Kenneth E.   42 n.1, 43 n.13
Carr, E. H.   203
Carrera de Indias   24, 25
Cary, John   44 n.15
Catholic Church   193
Central Intelligence Agency   157
cepalinos   178–9, 182–8
Chakrabarty, Dipesh   64, 79, 119
Chamberlain, Houston Stewart   198
Charles V (King)   23
Chávez, Jorge   180
Chiagaku Zashi (The Journal of Geography)   72
Chiappelli, Alessandro   40
Chicago University   165
Child, Sir Josiah   195
China   3, 38, 194, 197
   customary law in   9
   customs   94–6, 99
   ethnicities in   63, 69
   extraterritorial rights in   108 n.59
   legal system   93–4
   multi-ethnic diversity   95
   political philosophy   97
   sovereignty   69
   tradition and Western law   100
China National Geological Survey   70–1
Chinese Academy of Sciences (CAS)   70
Chinese Communist Party   103
Chinese universities   70
Christianity   193
Church Peace Union. *See* Carnegie Council on Ethics in International Affairs
civil affairs customs   98

civilization   68, 69, 193
  culture and   94
  human   66
  theory of   66–7
'Civilizational League Table'   195
civil law   93, 97, 99, 103
civil law codes   93–4, 102
Civil Procedure Law Draft (1910)   101
civil war   64, 208
Clark, Camp   197
Clark, William S.   115
'Clash of Civilizations' (Huntington)   66
Cobden, Richard   195
Code of Civil Procedure (1890)   106 n.37
coercion   9, 51, 60
Cohen, Bernard C.   162
Cold War   3, 7, 11, 157, 205–8
Cold War university   170
Collosus (Ferguson)   210
Colonial Development Bureau   113–14
colonial elites   51–2, 57, 59
colonial enterprise   112
colonialism   3, 7, 56, 143, 146
colonial policy studies   111–12, 117
colonial slavery   51
colonization   111–14, 116–17, 128
comercio libre (free internal trade)   18, 25–6
commerce
  illicit   25
  improvement   25
  and power   24
commercial affairs customs   98
commercial fairs   24
commercial liberty   25
commercial statecraft   17
Committee on the Present Danger (CPD)   164, 166, 168
Committee to Defend America by Aiding the Allies (CDAAA)   165
Communist Manifesto, The (Marx and Engels)   39
Communist Party   71
'communist slavery'   154
Conant, James Bryant   164
conditional sovereignty   209
Condliffe, John Bell   149
Conference of Berlin (1878)   207
Confucianism   94

Confucius   194
'consent of the governed'   158
continental civil law   95, 97
Cooper, Fred   118
Cooper, Robert   209–10
corporal punishments   101
Coser, Lewis   169, 175 n.82
Council on Foreign Relations (CFR)   6, 146, 158, 159, 162, 163, 165, 172 n.12
Council on Religion and International Affairs. *See* Carnegie Council on Ethics in International Affairs
Court of Colonial Affairs *(Lifanyuan)*   96
Crime and Custom in Savage Society (Malinowski)   96
Criminal and Civil Affairs Procedural Law (1906)   101
criminal law   54, 56, 106 n.39
cross-border systems   4
Cruz, Hernán Santa   181
Cuban Revolution   178
Cultural Revolution   39, 74
Current Criminal Law (1909)   101
customary law   94, 96, 97–9, 101, 102

Dalzell, P. W.   85
Davenant, Charles   195
Declaration of the Rights of Man and of the Citizen   33
Decline of the West, The (Spengler)   202
decolonization   205–6, 209
De l'esprit des lois (Montesquieu)   23
democracy   1, 5, 153, 202, 207, 210, 217
Deng Xiaoping   40
Department of Economic Affairs   181
Derman, Joshua   12
Destour Party   202
developmentalist alliance   186
dialecticism   39
Dili Xuebao (Journal of Geographical Sciences)   70
Dilke, Charles   196
Ding Shan   72–3
direct rule   51, 57
Discourse of Trade from England to the East Indies, A (Mun)   195
Discurso sobre la America española (Macanaz)   19–20, 22

Division of Special Research   165
Doeff-Haruma Japanese-Dutch Glossary   117
Draft Penal Code (1837)   58
Dreyfus, Alfred   1
Dreyfus Affair   9
drug trade   81
Dryden, John   34
Duara, Prasenjit   64–5
Dudden, Alexis   9, 11
Dunn, Frederick   159–61, 173 n.37
Dunne, Tim   169
Durkheim, Émile   32

Earle, Edward Mead   162
East India Company (EIC)   56–8, 194–5
École des langues orientales vivantes   5
Economic and Financial Section   142
Economic Bestsellers Before 1850, The (Carpenter)   43 n.13
Economic Commission for Latin America (ECLA)   178–9, 182–5
Economic Committee   147
economic crisis   34, 143–4, 184
economic data and analysis   149
Economic Defense Board   146
economic development   178–81, 195
economic imperialism   126
economic knowledge   183
economic problems   145
economic rationality   59
economic theories and policies   35
'The Economic Turn'   34
economic war   146–7, 149
Edward VI (King)   34, 44 n.17
Egypt   126, 194
Eight-Nation Alliance   93
Eisenach, Eldon   156, 158
Ekbladh, David   10–11
Elements of International Law (Wheaton)   64
'el espíritu guerrero' (the warring spirit)   23–4
Elliott, John H.   16
empire and knowledge   32–3
empire building   52, 95, 96, 141, 149
Empire (Hardt and Negri)   119

'Empire of Humanity'   41
Empires in World History (Burbank and Cooper)   118
Engels, Friedrich   39
England   22, 56, 59, 195
English Financial Revolution   21–2
English-Japanese Dictionary (Hori Tatsunosuke)   117
English Muscovy Company   33
English School theory   205
Enlightenment   17, 36, 38, 40, 41, 59
Ensenada, Marqués de la   20
Erie, Matthew   9, 11
Erudicción política (Argumossa Gándara)   23
'Escape from Asia' (Fukuzawa Yukichi)   67
Essai politique sur le commerce (Melon)   22–3
Essay on the East India Trade (Davenant)   195
ethnography   94–7, 96, 102
Eurocentric discourse   193, 194
Eurocentric institutionalism   192, 195, 202
Europe   160, 181, 192, 209
  civilization   194
  conceptions of territoriality   64
  early modern   35, 36, 40
  expansion of empires   10, 68
  imperialism   33, 126, 195, 205
  imperial semi-paralysis   208
  international theory   194
  modern American   127
  social sciences in   64
  trade methods   147
exchange   5, 11, 22, 97, 101, 128, 179, 181, 186
expansion   56
  American power   159
  dangers of Soviet Union   160
  of European empires   68
  of higher education   5
  of internal market   186
  Japan's overseas   112
  Spain's military   19
  Western civilization and capitalism   178
  white racial civilization   196

Fabian Society 199, 212 n.25
Fairgrieve, James 71, 73
Fajardo, Margarita 10–11
Faletto, Enzo 186
Falü xuetang 101
'Father Abraham's Speech' 36
Febvre, Lucien 66
Federated Shan States 81–2
Ferguson, Niall 209, 210
Fernandes, Florestan 184
Fight For Freedom (FFF) 165
Filipinos 201
Finance Committee 146
First Iraq War (1991) 209
First World War 6, 124–5, 127, 128, 138 n.40, 164, 198, 203, 208
Fiske, John 196
'folk system' 99
forced labour 53–4, 55, 60
Ford Foundation 158, 165, 167
Foreign Affairs 66
foreign contraband trade 20
foreign laws 93, 98, 106 n.39
foreign policy 66, 114, 123–4, 128, 130–1, 134, 136, 154–7, 159, 161, 165–9
Foreign Policy Association 145, 162
Foreign Service Educational Institute 162, 165
Fosdick, Dorothy 165–6
Fosdick, Raymond B. 165
Foster, Anne 81
Foucault, Michel 53, 55
Fox, William T. R. 155, 158, 160, 161, 167–9, 173 n.37
France 22, 24, 125, 143
Franklin, Benjamin 32–3, 35–9, 40–1, 42 n.1, 43 n.8
Fredona, Robert 42 n.1
freedom 25, 51–4, 58–60, 59, 60, 153–4
free labour 51, 53–5, 59–60
free trade 9, 195
French National Bank 22
French Revolution 33, 37, 59
Fukuzawa Yukichi 67, 69
funding 11, 156, 163, 166–8, 172 n.12
Furtado, Celso 184–7

Galdi, Matteo Angelo 36, 40
Gallagher, John 178

Geertz, Clifford 55
'The General Theory of the *Volk* and State' 135
Geneva 142–4, 146–9
Gentili, Alberico 194
Geographical Institute (Chongqing) 70
geography of modern Chinese empire. *See* modern Chinese empire
Geography and the Rise and Fall of Chinese Civilization (Dili yu zhonghua minzu zhi shengshuai) 72
Geography and World Power (Fairgrieve) 73
George, Henry 115, 116
Germany 125, 134, 147, 198
  civil law tradition 99
  trade policy 148
Giddings, Franklin 196
Gilbert's Act 54
Gladstone, William 83
global capitalism 177, 180
global economy 144, 181, 205. *See also* Latin America, global economy in
global hegemony 154–5, 172 n.12, 175 n.79, 181
global integration 2–3, 5, 8, 12, 178, 182, 215, 217
globalism 7, 119, 156
globalization 4–5, 41, 123, 188, 208, 209, 217
global knowledge regime 6, 8, 11, 216–17
'global war on terror' 123
Glorious Revolution 59
Gluckman, Max 96, 99
gobierno polisinodial 21
Godin, Louis 20
Goulart, João 185
Government of India 88
Grady, Henry 147–9
Gramsci, Antonio 156–8
'Grand Shen' and modern law 100–3, 108 nn.59, 63
Grant, Madison 195, 197
Great Britain. *See* Britain
Great Depression 7, 141–7, 177, 180
Great Exhibition (1851) 195–6
Great Qing Civil Law Draft 99, 102
Great Qing Criminal Procedural Law Draft (1910) 101

Great Qing Law Code   93, 95–6, 97, 101
Great Qing New Criminal Law
    (1907)   101
Great War   143
Griswold, A. Whitney   174
Groom, A. J. R.   159, 162–3, 170
gross domestic product   145
gross national product   141
Großräume ('great spaces')   123, 133–6
Grotius, Hugo   194
Gudin, Eugênio   180
The Guiding Measures for the Revision of the Laws by the High Officials for Legal Revision (1907)   106 n.39
Gu Jiegang   72
Gu Yanwu   65, 66

Habsburg Milan   31–2
Han Chinese   63, 69, 102
Han dynasty   73
Hanway, Jonas   55
Han Wudi   73
Hanzu xiguan (Han customs)   109 n.71
Hanzu xisu (Han conventions)   109 n.71
Harcourt (publisher)   162
Hardt, Michael   118
Harrington, James   34
Hartlib, Samuel   22
Hartlibian Circle   22
Hastings, Warren   56–7
Haushofer, Karl   204
hegemonic stability theory (HST)   205
hegemony   123–4, 127, 134, 149, 158
Hemment, Michael   42 n.1
Hindenburg   133
Hindu law   57
Hirschman, Albert O.   149
historicism   64
historiography   32, 64, 119, 208
History of Change in China's Frontier Regions, A (Gu Jiegang)   72
Hitler, Adolf   123, 198, 204
Hobson, John Atkinson   9, 10, 198–9, 199–203
Hobson, John M.   12
'Hobson-Wilson moment'   192, 198–204
Hodgson, Godfrey   156
Hodgson's Establishment   158
Hokkaido   113–15, 116

Hokkaido Development Office   114
Holland, Max   157
Holy See   34
Hoover, Herbert   142
Hori Tatsunosuke   117
Hostetler, Laura   65
Huang Guozhang   70–1, 74
Hubei Xuebao   68
Hubei Xuesheng Jie   69
Huber, Ernst Rudolf   10, 124, 133–6
Hu Huanyong   74
humanitarian intervention   123, 209–11
humanity   5, 8, 35, 36–7, 41, 46 n.28, 201, 208
human peace and progress   36
human rights   35, 36–7, 51, 129, 210
human welfare and happiness   36–7
Hunt, Edward Eyre   142–3
Huntington, Ellsworth   66
Huntington, Samuel   66
Huxley, Thomas Henry   66
Hu Xusheng   107 nn.42, 46

'The Idea of the *Reich* and International Law' (Huber)   135
'Ideas of World Peace' (Schmitt)   126
Ignatieff, Michael   209, 210
Imam of Muscat   58
Immigration Act (1924)   197
Imperial Agricultural College   115
imperial classification   102–3
imperial government system   15–29, 115. *See also* political economy; Spain; Spanish America
imperialism   32–4, 64–5, 67, 68, 69, 74, 81, 118, 126–7, 177, 178–9, 182, 187–8, 202–3, 209–10
    British   45 n.22
    Huber on   133–6
    as universalism   129–33
    in Weimar and Nazi Germany   123–5
Imperialism: A Study (Hobson)   199–201
'Imperialism and the lower races' (Hobson)   200
import-substitution industrialization (ISI)   179–80, 182–3
India
    British control   51
    cotton importation India   195

export trade 80
  labour in 51
  opium industry and trade 80, 83
  utilitarianism in 52, 55–9
indirect rule 58–9, 96
Indonesian Nationalist movement 202
industrial capitalism 177, 184
industrialization 177, 178, 180–7
information 141–2, 144–5, 149
Inquiry into the Nature and Causes of the Wealth of Nations (Smith) 35
insane imperialism 199–200
Institute of Advanced Study (IAS) 145–6
Institute of Defense Analysis 160
Institute of Geography 70–1, 74
Instituto Valencia de Don Juan (IVDJ) 19–20
Inter-Allied Rhineland High Commission 127
Inter-American system 167, 171 n.6
interdependence 11
  global 3–4, 7, 200, 205
  liberal 7
  models 6
International Development Authority (IDA) 146
international economics 147
international imperialism 198
internationalism 6, 7, 10, 141–2, 145, 149, 177, 182–3
'internationalization of the internal market' 186
International Labor Organization 6, 81
international law 8, 64, 123, 128, 130–1, 133–6, 192, 193, 194
international legal order 124–5, 132–3, 136
International Legal Order of Great Spaces, The (Schmitt) 123, 132
international liberal order 149–50
International Monetary Fund (IMF) 4, 157, 167, 171 n.6, 215
International Postal Union 142
international relations (IR) 155, 159, 162, 168–70, 171 n.8, 203–5, 207, 211
Interpreter's College (Tongwenguan) 64
'intervention treaties' *(Interventionsverträge)* 126–7, 129

interwar liberalism 203
intra-Western Cold War 208
'inward-looking development' 179
Islamic law 58, 96
Ivy League schools and universities 157

Jackson, Henry 'Scoop' 155, 166
Japan 106 n.33, 197. *See also* Meiji Japan
  civil law system 93
  colonial policy studies 111–12, 117
  construction of empire 113
  economic power 205
  history of empire 65, 112–13, 118–19
  imperial expansion 113, 115–18
  invasion of China 69–71, 73
  law models 101
  modernization 98, 217
  modern legal system 106 n.37
  overseas expansion 112
  'planting people' 118
  universities 11
  writings on geography 68
Japanese Government 114–15
Jewish race 198
Johnson, Paul 210
Johnson, Lyndon B. 161
Jones, William 56
Jordan, David Starr 195, 197
Journal of Geography, The (Dili) 70–1
Juan, Jorge 20

Kagan, Robert 209
Kaitakushi 114
kanshuhou('customary law') 98
Kant, Immanuel 194–5, 200
Kaplan, Robert 210
Kaplan, Steven L. 34
Karl, Rebecca 68
Kellogg Pact (1928) 129
Kennedy, John F. 115, 161
Kennedy School of Government 166
Keynes, John Maynard 8
Khilafat movement 202
Kidd, Benjamin 196
'kidnapped language' 55
Kim, Diana 9–10
Kindleberger, Charles P. 147, 168
Kirk, Grayson 163
Kissinger, Henry 164, 171 n.10

Knox, Robert 195
Kramer, Paul 94
Ku Klux Klan 202
Kuznets, Simon 145

labour 56, 112, 187
  control 52
  criminal-law control and 54
  institutions 54, 60
  markets 141
  surveillance 53–4, 59
La Condamine, Charles Marie de 20
Lamarckianism 201
land banks 22
language 55
Las Casas, Bartolomé de 193
Lasswell, Harold 163
late Qing reforms 93, 95, 98, 100–1
Latin America 3, 128, 129, 132, 148
Latin America, global economy in 177–88
  centre-periphery and American global order 179–83
  crisis of development and dependency 183–7
Lauterpacht, Hersch 8
Law, John 22, 28 n.44
law and custom 97
League of Nations 6, 81, 112, 125, 128–9, 132, 142, 144–7, 198, 201–2, 203–4
legal modernization 93, 97, 101, 102–3, 107 n.40, 108 n.63
legal pluralism 96
legal science 94–5, 100, 103
legal system department (*fazhike*) 98
Lei Haizong 72
Lenin, Vladimir 102
L'Historien 35
Liang Qichao 66–7, 69
Liang Zhiping 97
liberal capitalism 147–9
'liberal fundamentalist' 144
liberal internationalism 10, 144, 146, 157, 198, 201, 203, 204
liberal modernization theory 207
Lin Tongji 72, 75
Lin Zexu 66
Lippmann, Walter 154, 164–5
Li Xudan 74
Locke, John 22–3, 194

Lodge, Henry Cabot 196
Lo que hay de más y menos en España (Campillo y Cossío) 18
Luca, Placido de 37
Lyall, James 84–5, 87–8

Mabie, Hamilton Wright 111
Macanaz, Melchor Rafael de 15–17, 19–26, 26 n.3
MacKenzie, Alexander 88
Mackinder, Halford 71, 73, 197–8
MacNamara, Robert 147
Magdalen Hospital 55
Mahan, Alfred 196, 198
Malinowski, Bronislaw 96, 97
Manchesterean liberalism 195, 196
Manchester Guardian 9
Manchester School 195
Manchukuo 65
Mandate System 198, 201–2
Mao Tse-Tung 38–41
'Mappa Mundi' 194
March First movement 202
Marshall Plan 157, 167, 171 n.6
Martin, W. A. P. 64
Marx, Karl 39, 40–1, 102, 157, 194
Masters and Servants Acts 56
Maule, Robert 81
Mayer, Arno J. 169
May Fourth movement 202
Meiji (emperor) 113–14
Meiji Japan 67–8, 97, 106 n.37, 107 n.40
Meiji Restoration 38
Melon, Jean-François 22–4, 26, 28 nn.44–5
mercantilism 195
Mexican-American War 114
Middle East 7, 161
Mill, James 56, 57
Mill, John Stuart 58, 194–5
'*ministro di Economia*' 31
Ministry of Agriculture and Forestry 71
Ministry of Defense 71
Ministry of Foreign Affairs 5
Ministry of Justice 102
Minshi Xiguan Diaochao Baogaolu (Abstracts of the Report on Civil Affairs Customs) 107 n.46
Mitchell, Timothy 116

Mitchell, Wesley Clair   143
modern Chinese empire   63–75
  civilization history   73
  genre of *wangguo* literature   68
  geographical tradition   65
  geography and issue of foreign policy   66
  GMD and land reclamation plans   71–2
  historical geography   65, 72, 74
  Japanese invasion   69–71, 73
  Liang's geography   67, 69
  mapping and ethnographical studies   65
  nationalism   63–4, 67
  political geography   65–6
  process of state-making   64
  spatial reconceptualization   70
  threat of imperialism   68–9
  transition from Qing to Republican China   66–7
modern Chinese law   93–103
  assessing custom as imperial classification   102–3
  civil law codes   93–4
  custom and customary law   94–5, 97–100, 102
  ethnography and empire   95–7
  'Grand Shen' and   100–2
modern geography   67, 70
modern imperialism   16, 123–4, 126, 200
  global arbitration and   127–9
  Rhineland and   125–7
modernity   36, 40, 142
modernization   6, 103, 145, 178, 187
modern war   149
Mohammedan Law   58
Monarquía de España   16
Monroe, James   128
Monroe Doctrine (1823)   123, 128–9, 131, 132
Montesquieu   23
morality and politics   35
Morefield, Jeanne   203
Morgan, Lewis Henry   102
Morgenthau, Hans   155, 165–6, 167, 168–9, 174 n.74, 203, 205
Mughal feudal law   57
Mullaney, Thomas   94

multilateral free trade order   7
Mun, Thomas   195
Murray, Gilbert   203
Muslim law   57

Nanjing government   102
Napoleonic Wars   57
National Bureau of Economic Research   143, 145
National Defense Education Act (1958)   170
national governments   2–3, 145
national income   141, 145
nationalism   4, 8, 63–5, 67, 69, 125, 161
Nationalist (GMD) army   70–2, 74
national knowledge regimes   6
National Security Council   157
National Socialism   123, 135
National Socialist legislation   130–1
'National Socialist Legislation and the Reservation of "Ordre Public"' (Schmitt)   130
National War College   160
nation-building   3–4
nation states   1–2, 64–5, 67, 95, 143
North Atlantic Treaty Organization (NATO)   157, 167, 171 n.6
Naumann, Friedrich   138 n.40
Navio de Permiso   24
Nazi Germany   123–5, 130, 131–2, 135, 149
Nazi New Order   123, 125, 133, 135
Negri, Antonio   119
neo-Aristotelians   22
neo-imperialist IR theory   192
neo-Lamarckianism   201
neoliberal institutionalism   205
New Deal   145
New Discourse of Trade (Child)   195
New England institutional model   116
New International Economic Order   205
New Policies reforms (1898–1912)   93, 96, 98
'New Qing History'   96
New World   15–17, 23, 24, 26
The New York Times   163
Niebuhr, Reinhold   154, 165–6, 168
9/11 attack   210
Nitobe Inazo   9, 111–13, 115–18, 120 n.5

Nitze, Paul 154, 161, 164–6, 167–9, 175 n.79
Noda Yoshiyuki 106 n.38
Nomos of the Earth in the International Law of the Jus Publicum Europaeum, The (Schmitt) 123
non-Chinese people 103
non-governmental organizations 5
non-Han people 94–5
non-metallic currency 22
non-Western taxonomies 99
non-white racial immigration 197, 199
Northwestern University 162
Note by the Financial Commissioner on the extent to which Opium is consumed in Burma and the effects of the Drug on the People (Smeaton) 84
Noticias secretas 20
NSC-68 154, 161, 164, 167–8, 171 n.6
Nueva Planta (1714) 21
Nuevo sistema de gobierno económico para la América (Campillo y Cossío) 15, 17–23, 26, 26 n.3, 27 n.13
Nuevo sixtema para el perfecto gobierno de la América (Macanaz) 19–20
Nuremberg Laws 130–1
Nüxue Jiangyi 69

Oeconomicus and *Poroi* (Xenophon) 35
Office of the Co-ordinator of Inter-American Affairs 160
Office of War Information 164
O'Gorman, Edmundo 192
oikonomia 35
Okada Asatarō 108 n.63
Olson, William C. 159, 162–3, 170
On the American Indians (Vitoria) 193
'On the Term "Colony"' (Nitobe Inazo) 116
opium
  and British India 83, 88
  consumption and crimes caused by 84–5, 87–8
  and empire 80–3
  prohibition laws 81
  significance 91 n.16
Opium War (1839–42) 9, 73, 108 n.59
Orbis Terrarum maps 194
oriental despotism 57, 194

orientalism 5, 51–2
orthodox Marxism 157
Office for Strategic Services (OSS) 157, 160
Ottoman Empire 52
The Outlook 111
'outward looking development' 179

Pan-Asianist imperialists 118
Panopticon in Russia 52–4
Papen, Franz von 133
paper currency 22
Paris Colonial Exhibition (1931) 143
Paris Peace Conference (1919) 125, 164, 202
Parmar, Inderjeet 10–11
particularist approach 51
paternalist Eurocentrism 199–200, 204
paternalist racism 201
Patiño, José 19
paulista school of sociology 184
Pearson, Charles Henry 195, 196
Pearson, Karl 196
'Pearson-Mahan moment' 196, 199–200
Pedersen, Ove K. 216
Peile, S. C. F. 84
Penn, William 115
Pennsylvania University 162
People's Republic of China (PRC) 63–4, 74
Perle, Richard 166, 209
Permanent Court of International Justice 6
Pfaff, William 210
philanthropic foundations 156, 165, 167, 170
Phillip II (King) 16
Phillip V (King) 20–1, 26 n.3
Plano Trienal 185
Platt Amendment 126
Polanyi, Karl 2
Policy Planning Staff 164–5, 168
Political-Economic Relationships Between Free Nations (Galdi) 36
political economy 9, 15–17, 26, 31, 52, 116, 182, 196, 217
  early modern 33
  in foreign markets 34
  and imperialism 32–6
  international 143
  Italian 36

and social science 35–8, 40–1
utilitarian 52
political Islam 153
Politics Among Nations
 (Morgenthau) 203, 205
Polsby, Nelson 156–7
Poor Law 54–5, 59
post-1989 international theory 207–11
post-Pearl Harbor foreign policy 157
post-Versailles international order 130
post-war planning 146
Potemkin (Prince) 52–3
power 8–9, 24, 32, 142
Powers, Harry 196
Prebisch, Raúl 179, 181–3, 188
premodern laws 99
President Wilson's Inquiry (1917–19) 164
Price, Don 165–6
Price, Rachel 103 n.1
Princeton University 162, 174 n.70
principal cyclical centre 180, 182
prison project 53–4
Progressive-era philanthropies 156
Project for a New American Century 209
Provincial Council of Patna 57
Proyecto económico (Ward) 18
Pye, Lucian 162

Qazi courts (appellate courts) 56
Qing Empire 11, 63–4, 65, 67, 73, 74, 94–5, 94–8, 95–6, 98, 102–3
Quotations from Chairman Mao Tse-tung 35

race 67, 69, 161, 200–1
racism 66, 74, 130, 193, 198, 199, 202, 203–4
Radcliffe-Brown, A. R. 96, 105 n.29
Ramos, Paulo 162
Ratzel, Friedrich 66, 69
Rawls, John 209
Real Academia de la Historia in Madrid (RAH) 19–20
realism 175 n.79
Recent Social Trends (report) 142–3
Reflections on the Revolution in France (Burke) 56

Regulations for the Commercial Customs of Every Province 107 n.46
'The Regulations on the Civil Customs Survey in Ten Articles' *(Diaocha minshi xiguan zhangcheng shitiao)* 98–9
Reich 123, 132–5
Reinert, Erik S. 43 n.13
Reinert, Fernanda 43 n.13
Reinert, Sophus A. 9–10, 42 n.1, 43 n.13
'The relationship between Geography and Civilization' 68
Renshon, Stanley A. 176 n.96
Republic government 102
research 5, 7, 65, 70–2, 74, 79, 144–6, 156, 158–9, 161, 163, 167, 170, 183–4
Reston, Even 164
Reston, James 164
Rhineland and modern imperialism 125–7
'The Rhineland as an Object of International Politics' (Schmitt) 123
Ribbentrop, Joachim von 123
Richard, Poor 37, 39
Richards, John 80
Richardson, J. 57
Riefler, Winfield 145–7
Robinson, Ronald 178
Rockefeller, Nelson 160
Rockefeller Conference (1954) 154, 157–8, 163, 166–70
Rockefeller Foundation (RF) 6, 142, 144–5, 153, 154, 155–60, 162, 167, 169, 172 n.12
'The Role of Theory in International Relations' 169
Roosevelt, Theodore 128, 132, 196
Ross, Edward 197
Rossi, Pellegrino 37
Rostow, Walter 147, 207
Royal Commission on Opium 80, 82–3, 88
Royal Institute of International Affairs in London 6
Royal Treasury 19
Ruhr industrial region 125
Rusk, Dean 154, 161, 164, 167, 169, 175 nn.79, 88
Russia 51, 59. *See also* USSR
 Panopticon in 52–4

Said, Edward   52, 55
San Francisco Conference on International Organization (1945)   163
sane imperialism   200–1
Sapporo Agricultural College   113, 116
savage and barbaric threat   197–8, 201, 208–9
Say, Jean-Baptiste   38
Schapera, Isaac   96
Schilling, Warner   169
Schmitt, Carl   10, 64, 123–36, 126, 138 n.37
School of Asiatic Studies   161
School of Military Government   160
School of Oriental and African Studies   5
Schumpeter, Joseph A.   35
science   68, 74
science of commerce. *See* political economy
scientific geography   67, 70
scientific racism   192, 195–7, 198, 201, 204–5, 206, 208
Scotland   22
Second World War   7, 123–4, 157, 164, 165, 177, 184, 203, 208
Secretarías de Estado y del Despacho Universal   21
Seeley, John Robert   196
self-determination   7, 10, 125, 193, 198, 201–2, 203
self-government   201
Self-Strengthening movement (1861–95)   93
Semple, Ellen Churchill   66
Sepúlveda, Juan Ginés de   193
serfdom   51–2, 55, 59, 60
Seven Years War   34, 36
Sha Xuejun   72, 75
Shaw, George Bernard   212 n.25
Shellen Wu   11
Shen Jiaben. *See* 'Grand Shen'
shu kan   107 n.40
Sieyès, Abbé Emmanuel   32
Siku Quanshu   65
'Silent (racial) War'   208
Sino-Japanese War   68
Sino-Soviet cooperation   74
slavery   52, 55–6, 57–9, 60

slave trade   51, 58
Smeaton, Donald   84–5, 87–8
Smith, Adam   23, 35, 37, 55, 194–5
Smoking Opium Exclusion Act (1909)   81
social science   1, 32, 95. *See also individual entries*
American models   11
of anthropology   96
approach for colonization   114
in Europe   64
global   6, 8
hermeneutic tradition in   79
history   2–3, 8
and Latin America   178–9
modern   36, 119
and political economy   35–8, 40–1
practices   120 n.6
Social Science program   145
Social Science Research Council   5, 170
social scientific approach   115
social scientists   2–3, 7, 9, 12, 36, 66, 79, 89, 94, 215–17
functioning as intermediators   6
history   4
Latin American   177–9
and nation states   1
PRC and   74–5
role as agent of national managing   5
and social institutions   8
from United States   10
sociology/sociologists   5, 10, 183–4, 186
Sonenscher, Michael   35
sovereignty   7, 51, 56, 59, 63, 72, 125, 127, 129, 131, 132, 134, 138 n.40, 194, 209
Soviet Union. *See* USSR
Spain. *See also* imperial government system
American markets   24–6
becoming commercial empire   16–17
bullionism   21–2, 26
commercial system   16–18, 21, 23, 25–6
destroying Amerindians   23
military expansion   19
as polycentric monarchy   16–17
pursuit of mines   23
theory of commercial empire.   18, 21
and trade   24

Spaniards 18, 23–5
Spanish America 19
   comercio libre (free internal trade) 18
   government 17
   provisioning of slaves 24
   territories 15–16
Spanish-American War 126
Spanish imperialism 193–4
Spanish metropole 15, 17–19, 25–6
Spanish War of Succession (1700) 24
Spencer, Herbert 195
Spengler, Oswald 66, 202
spirit of conquest 23–4
Spykman, Nicholas J. 161–2, 173 n.37, 204
Stages of Economic Growth, The
   (Rostow) 207
Stanziani, Alessandro 9, 11
State Department 148–9, 154–7, 160–4, 164–5
Stein, Barbara H. 19
Stein, Stanley 19
Stoddard, Lothrop 195, 197–8
Strong, Josiah 196
study abroad programs 8
'subliminal' imperialist Eurocentrism
   (1945–89) 192, 204–7
subsidiary system 57
Sui Hongmin 101
Sultan of Sharja 58
Sumner, William Graham 195, 197
Sun Yat-sen 7
Superpowers: The United States, Britain,
   and the Soviet Union - Their
   Responsibility for Peace, The
   (Fox) 161
supranational bodies 142
survey bureau *(diaochaju)* 98

Tan Qixiang 72
Tang Dynasty 93
Tavárez, Fidel 9–10
teaching 116, 162–3, 170
Theory of International Politics
   (Waltz) 206
Third World 10, 205–7, 209
Thompson, Dorothy 154
Thompson, John 161
Thompson, Kenneth W. 160, 167–8, 169
Tiananmen massacre (1989) 103

Tiffert, Glenn 103 n.1
Tilly, Charles 89
Tilly, H. L. 84
Tokugawa shogun 113
totalitarianism 125
total war 115, 161
trade 21, 24, 26, 34, 81, 112, 141, 182, 195
traditional Chinese law 97
transatlantic slave trade 57
transnational structures 5
Trans-Salween Shan States 81–2
Treaty of Utrecht (1713) 24
Treaty of Versailles 7, 127–9, 134
Treitschke, Heinrich von 198
'Tributes of Yu' *(Yugong)* 65
Trinchera, Francesco 37
Triplett, Kyle R. 42 n.1
triumphalist sensibility 196, 198
Trocki, Carl 80
True Constitutional Means for Putting an
   End to the Dispute Between Great-
   Britain and the American Colonies
   (Franklin) 32, 43 n.8
Truman, Harry S. 164, 167
Tucker, Robert W. 169
Turn to a Discriminating Concept of War,
   The (Schmitt) 131
Twenty Years' Crisis, The (Carr) 203

Uchimura Kanzo 116
University of California Los Angeles
   (UCLA) 162
Ulloa, Antonio de 19–20
'Unequal Treaties' 108 n.59
United Nations (UN) 8, 11, 157, 174 n.67, 181
United States 10, 146, 148
   colonization strategies to Japan 114
   economic policies 160
   economy as market 182
   encouragement of Japan's imperial
      expansion 113
   financing slave trade 58
   foreign policy 114, 123, 128–9, 133
   global expansionism 171 n.4
   globalism 166–7
   hegemony 10, 154–5, 169–70, 177, 181

imperialism 74, 128, 132, 134, 197
information gathering and
    surveillance 142
invasion of Iraq (2003) 4, 123, 166, 209
inventing and colonizing
    (1492–ca.1900) 192–6
liberal international order 149–50
method of intervention treaties 128
national security and foreign
    policies 153–6, 159, 161, 164, 166–7, 173 n.37
non-white racial immigration 197, 199
opium prohibition policies 81–2, 89
Panama and 126
philanthropic foundations and 156
as principal cyclical centre 182
reconstruction of global trade 149
relationship with League of
    Nations 144–5
response to Korean War 168
rise to global power 134
Spaniards travel to 25
transforming world 141
in world affairs 159
'The United States and the International
    Legal Forms of Modern
    Imperialism' (Schmitt) 128
United States Congress 108 n.60
universalism 7, 52
universalist approach 51–2
Universal Relations (Botero) 32
Universidade de São Paulo 184
universities 6, 8, 11, 111, 117, 158, 160
University of Bonn 125, 133
University of California 147
University of Chicago 66, 70
University of Königsberg 128
University of Maryland 169
University of São Paulo 185
University of Tokyo 111
university programmes 158
UN Secretariat 181
Urquidi, Víctor 180
'The USA and the International Legal
    Forms of Modern Imperialism'
    (Schmitt) 123
US Court for China 108 n.60

US federal narcotic laws 81
US Navy 162
US-Spanish War (1898) 199
USSR 153, 160, 167, 171 n.6, 174 n.71, 207–8. *See also* Russia
US Tariff Commission 162
utilitarianism in India 52, 55–9

Valéry, Paul 202
Valladolid controversy (1550) 193
Vattel, Emerich de 194
Vietnam War 164, 166, 169, 207
Viner, Jacob 163
Vitoria, Francisco de 192–4
vocational schools 117
Völker 134–5

wage labour 55, 60
waifan 69
Wallace, Henry 146
Waltz, Kenneth N. 168, 206–7
wangguo literature 68–9
War and Peace Studies 146, 163, 165, 172 n.12
Ward, Bernardo 18
Ward, Lester 196
War Department 160–1, 164
War of Resistance 71
War of Restoration Over 115
Warring States period (475 BC–221 BC) 65
Way to Wealth, The (Franklin) 35–8, 40, 42 n.1
Webb, Sidney 212 n.25
Weber, Max 32
Weimar Republic 123–5, 131, 134
Wei Yuan 66
Welles, Summer 163
Wennerlind, Carl 22
Wertz, Daniel 81–2
Western capitalism 64–5, 157
Western-centric international
    theory 196–8
Western-centrism 191–2
Western civilization 199, 200, 208
Western colonial-racist guilt
    syndrome 204–7
Western imperialism 95, 103, 128, 195, 198, 199, 201, 203–4, 211

Western imperialist-international
    theory   191–211
  bifurcation of Western-centric theory
    (ca. 1889–1945)   196–8
  colonial-racist guilt syndrome
    and 'subliminal' imperialist
    Eurocentrism (1945–89)   204–7
  'Hobson-Wilson moment'
    (1898–1945)   198–204
  inventing and colonizing America
    (1492–ca.1900)   192–6
  post-1989 international theory
    207–11
Westernization   67, 101
Western laws   99, 100–1
Western supremacy   191, 195, 202, 209
What is the Third Estate? (Sieyès)   32
Wheaton, Henry   64
white racial civilization   196
'white racial suicide'   197
white racial supremacy   196–7
Wight, Martin   169
Williams, William Appleman   113
Willits, Joseph H.   145, 160, 173 n.37
Willoughby, Sir Hugh   34
Wilson, Woodrow   115, 128–9, 132,
    198–9, 201–3
Wittfogel, Karl August   66
Wokler, Robert   36

Wolfers, Arnold   155, 158, 159, 160,
    165, 168
Wolfowitz, Paul   209
Woolf, Leonard   203
World Bank   146, 157, 167, 171 n.6
World Politics   163
Wrath of Nations, The (Pfaff)   210
Wright, Ashley   81–3, 88
Wright, Quincy   169

Xenophon   35
xiguanfa   98
Xinmin Congbao   68
Xu Jiyu   66

Yale Institute of International Studies
    (YIIS)   158–63, 174 n.67
Yanaihara Tadao   111
Yatsuka Hozumi   106 n.38
Yukiko Koshiro   113
Yunnan Province   74

Zhang Qian   73
*Zhan Guo Ce (Warring States
    Policies)*   72
Zhang Yintang   75
zhimindi ('colony')   98
Zhu Jiahua   71
Zimmern, Alfred   197, 202–4

www.ingramcontent.com/pod-product-compliance
Lightning Source LLC
Chambersburg PA
CBHW050327020526
44117CB00031B/1830